EUCLID
AVENUE

EUCLID AVENUE

OUR SCARS MEAN SOMETHING

R. K. RYTARAN

TATE PUBLISHING
AND ENTERPRISES, LLC

Published by Tate Publishing & Enterprises, LLC
127 E. Trade Center Terrace | Mustang, Oklahoma 73064 USA
1.888.361.9473 | www.tatepublishing.com

Tate Publishing is committed to excellence in the publishing industry. The company reflects the philosophy established by the founders, based on Psalm 68:11,
"The Lord gave the word and great was the company of those who published it."

Book design copyright © 2016 by Tate Publishing, LLC. All rights reserved.
Cover design by Norlan Balazo
Interior design by Jomar Ouano

Published in the United States of America

ISBN: 978-1-68270-533-9
1. Family & Relationships / Dysfunctional Families
2. Family & Relationships / Marriage & Long Term Relationships
16.02.03

Contents

Perspective

Perspective (per spek'tiv). *Webster's Dictionary* defines this special word in a variety of ways: (1) a technique of depicting volumes and spatial relationships on a flat surface; (2) a picture employing this technique especially one in which it is prominent; (3) a visible scene, especially one extending to a distance, vista; (4) the manner in which objects appear to the eye in respect to their relative positions and distance; (5) one's mental view of facts, ideas, etc., and their interrelationships; (6) the ability to see all the relevant data in a meaningful relationship; (7) a mental view or prospect; (8) of or pertaining to the art of perspective, or represented according to its laws.

This story is entirely about perspective from its very beginning unto the end. Although it could very well be told by a variety of different methods, by many different people, and with varying degrees of accuracy, it is, however, told strictly through the eyes of one young boy as he became a man and through his pain-filled eyes alone.

The reality of the matter, however, is that this novel is not necessarily one of judgment, although that task would be an incredibly simplistic task. Better yet, this is a story of a series of lessons, both of those who are in the story and as well as for those who read it. They are lessons depicted through the means of human treatment, of depravity, and of the most incredible of evils.

But, most importantly, they are lessons about decisions. This is intensely so because our decisions are the everlasting cornerstone of every human event.

With all of that said, the greatest lesson of all is how we deal with the emotions that all decisions ignite. The most dangerous and volatile of these emotions is that of anger. The means by which those emotions are delivered is of no real importance, but it is the purposeful decision of what to do with them is the greatest goal of all.

Message

Orphan, now isn't that a fascinating term? Doesn't it even roll off of your tongue just a little more differently than do most other words? It can be a name, a noun, or perhaps an insult. As *Webster's Dictionary* states, the definition could be that of a child without parents, a young animal without its mother, or a person or thing without protective affiliation or sponsorship or better yet, one who is bereft of parents.

Imagine to have your entire life under the constant control of someone else, someone totally unrelated to you, a paid employee of the local government. That person would be a stranger and someone not of your own choosing. So just how unreal and different would such a life be? Imagine if that person had the authority to construct your daily schedule, its very structure, and to devise some of the more personal details of your life. Then after all of those items had been accomplished, that person would then require your complete acceptance and obedience to all of those things. Just how strange would those events be? That person would also be there to oversee your every move and additionally to also record all of your comings and goings. How eerie would that be to feel eyes upon you at all times, to be closely, constantly, and carefully monitored?

However, that person would also be there to guide and direct you, to answer questions, and to listen to you. But even so, wouldn't it be as if they were ordering your every footstep? At first glance it almost sounds as if it were a jail or a prison.

But then again, I would know precisely what to expect from those adults. My life would not be full of bizarre twists, turns, and other surprises. Each day would not be yet another lesson in human manipulation and depravity. I would not be required to be a daily witness to one crime after another. I would also not have my silence not only expected, but to also have it demanded of me. I would not be told lies every day and stolen from every week. I would not be made to feel as and to be used as property just as you would a lowly and worthless slave. Also, I would not be forced to witness atrocities that no adult, much less a mere child, should ever see. Finally, I would not then be purposely and cruelly abandoned once my usefulness was gone. Oh, to be an orphan.

However, there are many other details within such a life that would have an incredible appeal to me. I would sleep in a clean bed every night, never having to check the sheets for roaches and other bugs. Every meal would be cooked in clean pans, in a clean kitchen, served on clean plates, and with clean spoons and forks. The food would also be good, tasty, and abundant. I would never again have to fight with and then wait while first the parents and then the screaming little kids made sure that they filled their plates with all they wanted. I wouldn't then choose hunger over eating after trying to brush away flies, roaches, and other vermin that always wanted their fair share. But there would be more.

I also know that even though my wardrobe would be small, it would certainly be sufficient. It would also be clean and pressed, never torn, ragged, or off sized. My clothes would never be something for the kids at school to make fun of either. Therefore, I wouldn't ever have to be ashamed of my appearance ever again. But the best thing of all is that I would be alone with no one to call family. However, it would be a very good thing for dozens of both personal and private reasons.

But the saddest reality of all is that I am the eldest of twelve children, but I am also an only child, as perplexing as that may sound. Orphan, just to be an orphan. I simply wish that I were one.

My Town

At that early time, which was my favorite time of the day, I watched it all in the early-morning hours. I envisioned it all from a great height as the pinkish hues of the dawn of a new day touched its gentle fingers upon the wispy clouds above and then, after some moments later, to the landscape farther below. From such a perfect vantage point a mile or so above the scene, it was easy to see that my town was actually more than just a town. Although it technically qualified as a city, it was actually a fairly small one, with a population of only fifty thousand people.

From those heights of observation, the city lights showed themselves to be a crazy, misshapen grid. A single snapshot would have covered it in its entirety, and I believed that it would have been a very nice one. Some in our society stated that it was the perfect-sized city in which to grow up. However, if that were the case, then I shouldn't have blamed anything at all on the city itself, despite its lack of innocence. Perhaps I shouldn't have blamed anything in my life on anyone but myself. That would have been the responsible thing to do. But I had, after all, acted as only humans tend to do. Therefore, such an act was exactly what I had chosen, and therefore, I battled with that debilitating mind-set for a prolonged period of time.

If only I possessed eagle's wings and could have taken in everything from that particular vantage point in the sky. How completely fascinating and thrilling it would have been. Oh, to be so far above everything and yet be completely untouched by anyone. What a very perfect dream to experience. After all, it would truly be the best of all places to see everything and yet not be affected by anything as well. However, such a view below, in its picturesque splendor, told a very incomplete story. But all in all, it would have been a fascinating view indeed.

There in the midst of the corn and soybean fields, far beyond the city's eastern edge, lay the county's greater area airport. In actuality, it was just a few unimpressive acres carved out of the surrounding farmland. It carried quite a proud name but in reality it only existed for area crop dusters and hobbyists. Nearby, running north and south as a ribbon of red and white lights at that early hour was the interstate highway. More than anything else, that highway defined the eastern edge of the city. Clusters of large dark blocks revealed themselves to be factories along the highway on the city's north and south sides, which provided the majority of the employment for the area. As one traveled in a clockwise fashion to the south and then banked west, the outskirts of the city proper could be seen. Here were the golf courses, large mansion-sized homes, and high-rise condominiums. As a youth, I had only ridden in a car through that area. It was impossible for me to comprehend such a neighborhood. I certainly never knew anyone who lived there.

Farther north on the west side was a large section of the city that was known to all as *the boulevards*. Located here were huge, massive older houses with fences that surrounded every lawn and where every street had a manicured strip of grass and trees that ran down the middle. Every lawn was ringed about with brick walls or wrought-iron fences. These were the houses that were lavishly decorated during the holidays with incredible displays that looked like something out of a magazine or a movie. No matter how many times that I had seen them and no matter how often I stared at them, they simply didn't seem real. Even when I stood there beside my bicycle at the curb, they still appeared distant. These were the homes of doctors, lawyers, politicians, and the majority of the prominent businessmen within the city. Along with my family, early in my youth, we had driven through those neighborhoods to look at the colored lights and decorations at Christmastime. I was always in open-mouthed amazement and awe.

Additionally, for families such as ours, it was only a neighborhood to drive through. It was an area only to marvel at, and it was only safe for people as us to only travel through at night. If we ever had the audacity to drive through those neighborhoods during the day, it would have certainly brought about an unscheduled stop by a watchful police cruiser. I also knew better from my earliest days than to ever personally show my face in those neighborhoods during the day. I intimately knew and had personally seen how the adults reacted to people like me. The prevailing thought that always terrified me was if any of the neighborhood boys had ever caught me as I foolishly rode my bicycle on their streets. I attempted it on a few rare occasions and had been run off with shouts, curses, and thrown rocks. I knew full well just where I was not wanted, those neighborhoods that I should avoid, and precisely where I actually belonged. But even after such experiences and with those memories forever lodged within my mind, I still found it to be a very incredible and irresistible place. Perhaps it was merely my youthful imagination, but I believed that even the air smelled cleaner there.

On the northwest side of the city was the obligatory indoor shopping mall surrounded by smaller stores, new- and used-car lots, and wonderful-smelling restaurants. It was an incredible place of bright lights, color, and activity. Money was the name of the game there, the mandatory requirement for admission, which automatically ruled me out. I had ridden my bicycle there on occasion and had been chased out of that area as well. It was literally and painfully obvious that I just didn't belong. However, it still held an indescribable attraction to me.

Heading east from the mall could be found the curving grids of the newer subdivisions comprised of perfectly kept ranch-style and split-level homes. There in abundance were chain-link fences, pristine sidewalks, brand-new metal swing sets, and dogs on leashes. Everything here was neat, tidy, and in nearly perfect order. Everything about the area completely amazed me nearly as much as the boulevards had.

These neighborhoods were so completely foreign to me and, therefore, never failed to captivate my attention. However, I always visited them in October for candy on beggar's night. There was usually much loot to be gained here and generally it was quite a good haul. However, I had to constantly remind myself of my own limits and to be carefully aware of all of the unspoken rules that were so fully set into place. My friends and I were only permitted to be there for a specified period of time. After which, we were bluntly informed when it was time to leave by all concerned. Even the police cruisers took their turn in reminding us of our social status. Even a few extra spent minutes caused us to be chased out of there. It was the same familiar tune. We were informed that we didn't belong there, weren't wanted, and sternly told to never come back. Naturally, we always returned every Halloween, and since we were in costume, they never really caught on. Secretly I harbored the unreachable dream that perhaps I could even live there someday. I wanted such a life so badly that at times, I could barely stand it.

Heading due south from the subdivisions were dozens of blocks of older two-story and Cape Cod homes. Everything in these neighborhoods was still very nice and properly kept up. I would have been more than happy to live there as well. But I still knew in my heart that such a dream was just as useless dream as any other fantasy. I was firmly trapped by my family, our heritage, and by our degrading lifestyle. I knew in my heart that some things could simply not be changed.

Just a few blocks farther south was one of the many railroads that ran through our city. A particular one traveled east and west and also defined the northernmost edge of the downtown business district. Just on the south side of the railroad was the dairy warehouse and a constant flow of trucks. Then, just across the street was the county courthouse, which appeared to me as a carved soldier, surrounded by plain-looking boxes of buildings. I always wondered in amazement at just how such a building was built and who accomplished such tasks. The amount of natural creativity and good schooling needed to accomplish such a creation must have been intense. I believed that someone had to possess a special ability in order to take something from within your mind, transform it onto paper, and then transform it into reality must have been incredibly fulfilling to someone. That would have to be a truly satisfying job to walk into every day. Again I knew full well that such dreams were foolishness for a person of my heritage. Therefore, I did what I always did and forced such a dream from my mind and forced myself back into reality.

At street level in the downtown business area, there was so much more to be observed. With such a vantage point people could be watched within their workplace scenarios as they unfolded. Crossing North Street from the courthouse complex, one then entered the downtown area proper. Here were city blocks where there was one storefront followed immediately after another. There were places to buy suits, shirts and ties; places to obtain loans, shoe stores, dress stores, jewelry stores, and so much more. In such places, I always knew exactly where I was welcome, where I was merely tolerated or where I was simply not wanted and was subsequently shown the door. At times it was an actual forced event committed by a clerk who deemed such an action necessary. At times I knew it before I opened the door, and the bell above it rang. My favorite scenario was the store clerk setting up displays in the front window. In more than one such place and on more than one occasion, such an event took place. It was almost amusing to watch as the hired clerk gave me the ever-so-slight negative move of the head as I reached for the door handle before I had even gotten inside. I really didn't understand it, and my mind certainly couldn't fully grasp the entirety of the situation.

I had done nothing wrong. I had never committed a crime, and unbeknown to the clerk, I even had the money to spend. However, I was judged before I acted or spoke a single word. I didn't even know these people, and they certainly didn't know me. In my mind, I figured that it was all about appearance and what people could see on the outside. I believed that for myself and for those within our city like me, it was simply the way that it always would be. Society would never change.

After just a few more blocks of stores, South Main Street began its slope downhill to the river. That river accurately characterized our little city. It wasn't very big, it certainly wasn't small, but it could have used some real cleaning up. In the summertime it really made itself known as it smelled to high heaven. Realistically, geographically, and most important of all, socially, it defined the southern edge of the downtown area. It also defined just exactly where I belonged. My neighborhood was across the bridge and on the south side of that river. Every day as I crossed that bridge, absolutely everything changed.

There were still retail shops along South Main Street, but they were all of the run-down or secondhand variety. There was also a franchised supermarket, but it was fully staffed by security as much as stock boys, and both groups manned the entrance doors. But then again, the same could also be said of the bowling alley as well as the drugstore on the corner. These were the neighborhoods where the really old houses were. This was an area where everyone was a renter and no one was an owner. No one there actually took care of their yards or anything else for that matter. It seemed as if hardly anyone even bothered to try. Every house, duplex, and apartment building was crammed right next to the one beside it, with only enough space to shove in an abandoned old car or other unwanted debris.

The entire neighborhood was rife with chaos, noise, and questionable activity. There was always a continuous and never-ending racket, with yelling, screaming, racing car engines, police sirens wailing, and people everywhere. All day long, every day of the week, it never ever seemed to stop, and sometimes it just drove me right up the wall. The only time of any real peace and quiet was that short window of time after the bars had closed and the city woke up in the morning. This was my favorite time of the day as it was the only restful time that I ever had to myself. It was why I always woke up early and was just one of the reasons why I enjoyed spending time alone.

On South Main Street was that same supermarket, a large rectangular building with parking lots on the north and on the south sides. Immediately next to the south lot one could see the bowling alley and its placarded and designated parking lot. What appeared as only an entrance to the south parking lot of the supermarket was actually my little one-block-long street. It was lined on the south side with a row of old and worn-out duplexes. Years of neglect and abuse had transformed them into merely large multicolored boxes surrounded by assorted piles of refuse and abandonment that only we humans are capable of leaving behind. That little alley of a street then opened up on the north side into a large gravel lot at the rear of the supermarket. That lot was used primarily for truck deliveries. Those delivery trucks ran in and out of that gravel parking lot eighteen out of twenty-four hours of every day. They churned up a cloud of choking dust that covered everything on our street that sat still for more than a few minutes. It existed throughout the course of the day, every day of the week, and we had simply learned to live with it.

Unfortunately, that gravel lot also happened to be our playground. As odd and dangerous as it seem, it was safer to play in the paths of those trucks than in our own postage-stamp-sized yards. Those so-called yards were full of waist-high weeds that hid broken glass, bits of metal scrap, nail-riddled boards, and old car parts. I had made more than one trip to the emergency ward at the hospital for stitches and had the scars to prove it. Therefore, the choice was incredibly simple as we took our chances with the trucks that we could see, rather than the rats and the other dangers that we could not. In some ways it was a bit frightening as we dodged those trucks, but it was so much fun to taunt and scare the truck drivers. They screamed, yelled, and swore at us, but it was really just part of the game.

We were children on the loose, completely unsupervised from the break of day until well after the sun had set. We were without rules, without structure or morals, and generally without remorse of any kind. Perhaps it was no small wonder that the adults ran us off from their businesses.

But truthfully, who could have really blamed them? If I were a businessman, would I want a bunch of dirty, tattered-clothed little monsters in my store? As a group, they walked through the doors and disrupted everything. They ran through the aisles, harassed customers, and shoplifted, generally wreaking havoc everywhere they went. Certainly those same customers didn't want those same kids running around their vehicles, climbing on hoods and trunks, and even attempting to get inside. Certainly good and decent law-abiding citizens and taxpayers should be protected from such human vermin. It was just those speeches that we heard from the store staff, security people, and police every time one of us were nailed for some offense, real or imagined. They always lumped all of us into a single category whether guilty or not. Why were we painted with the same brush? As for me, I kept to myself, chose not to run with the crowd, and thereby also chose the life of a loner as well. I believed within my heart that I was not one of them and attempted to convince myself of such a fallacy. But even so, we were not completely alone in our meager existence. Others were aware of our dilemma.

There were those who stated that it simply wasn't our fault, that it was the way we were and how we were raised. However, I never believed any such things and thought it all to be nonsense even though I had no real facts to back up my opinion. As far as I knew, we were all perfectly aware of what we were doing and whether it was right or if it was wrong. But then again, perhaps there were forces at play that forced our hand. Even though some families had both parents, many households in our neighborhood had but one parent in them. There were some whom I knew who desperately fought the odds that raged against us. But perhaps they were right after all, and we were products of our environment.

Perhaps it was true that we had grown up on our own, uninstructed, undisciplined, unguided, and most of all, unloved by nearly anyone. I certainly couldn't speak for anyone else, but I knew without a shred of any doubt that my parents could have cared less about my daily comings and goings and certainly far less about my future.

However, despite all of that and my few years, I had found in all of those things of life, that it was very important to truly become a detailed student of human behavior. If I were to become something better than my parents, then it was important that I sought out far better examples. I quickly decided that I had to start by carefully choosing those persons to emulate and then spent time observing them. With that, I began to study how people acted throughout every aspect of their daily lives. I listened carefully to how they spoke, the words that they used as well as those that they didn't. I observed how they walked, their posture, and how they carried themselves. I watched how they conducted themselves around others as well as noting what they did not do. All of those habits and mannerisms I determined in my heart to learn so that I would be just as the gentlemen and the businessmen that I came into contact with on my paper route.

They were for the most part well-spoken, kind, courteous, and appeared to be quite intelligent. They exhibited modest demeanors, but also conducted themselves with a curious air of authority. They appeared to be actually in charge of their own lives, which had an incredible appeal to me. Such things I found easy to understand, but there was something else that escaped me. There was something else that I just could not quite grasp.

I noticed that my schoolmates, whom I never permitted any closer to my home than the tree house, were not forced to live as I did. Although we lived in the same general neighborhood and our households had basically the same incomes, their lives were very, very different from mine. Although they weren't by any means wealthy or possessed an overabundance, their school clothes were always neat, cleaned, and pressed. I could easily detect that they used real shampoo on their hair, not cheap, pink dishwashing soap. Those items and a number of other personal health habits were quite obvious as well. Additionally, there were the rare occasions when someone invited me to their home for dinner. However, it was far more than just a meal. For me it was an incredible event, an amazing spectacle for dozen of reasons or more. I always watched the entire ordeal in quiet and unspoken awe.

The entire affair was vastly different than my household from the very beginning. For not only did the children and parents eat the same meals together, but they also did so at the same dinner table. It was the exact opposite of how things operated in my house. Not only did they eat their meals together, but everything was also spotless and in a particular order. As I followed along with them, I did my very best as to not embarrass myself. I tried very hard to follow their example as I used forks, spoons, and napkins. It was so unfamiliar to me. We never used napkins in our house, and our tableware was in very poor condition and always in short supply. I took great pains to eat quietly, taking small bites and always with my mouth closed. It was all so very different. I felt so out of place, but so envious inside because I wanted that sort of lifestyle so very badly. However, throughout it all, I enjoyed it very much.

But in addition to the meal, what truly shocked me were their parents. These adults actually talked *to* them, had conversations *with* them, listened *to* them, and seemed to actually care *about* them. They were told, unrehearsed and within my hearing, that they were important and someone to be proud of. Then the incredible and heart-wrenching statement was added *that they were loved.* Someone actually spoke those incredible words to them! My heart ached within my chest not with animosity but with great unresolved and unfulfilled envy. How I wanted all of that for myself. How I knew very much that I desperately needed it. But I also knew within my heart that there was no possible way that it could ever be for me. The odds for attaining such success were so remote that I might as well have been on another planet.

Therefore, after returning, I always went to my little tree house. There, far away from everyone and alone, I found meager comfort with my back against the tree, softened by an old sofa cushion and with my body wrapped in an even older quilt. There was frequently a bit of swaying as the gentle wind slowly rocked me back and forth. Small traces of that wind found its way through the gaps in the boards. It was somehow strangely comforting. It was always so quiet up there, with just a few refreshments and a good novel that kept me company throughout the afternoons and evenings. It was my favorite method of relaxation.

But most importantly of all, I was far too high above the ground to be bothered by anyone. It was as close to real contentment as I could ever achieve. As my gaze returned through the gaps in the boards to the duplex across the backyard, my calm introspective always changed. There I could see through the windows of the house and the permanently open back door all of the activity that a dozen people were capable of making. Nearly worse than all of that was the deafening chaos that came from within a home where no one spoke softly, but everyone yelled or screamed in a weird sort of bizarre contest. All communication within that house was loud, demanding, and hostile. Once again, the decision about where to sleep that night became stupidly easy. Yet another evening spent alone in the tree house.

Would it be cold out that night? Would any one bother to check on me? Did that really matter? Did I really matter? Was that all that we were about? I really didn't know, and I certainly didn't have any answers. So perhaps we actually were all about living for the day, what would happen, what we would do, where we would go, what we would eat or even if. In reality, we weren't actually living; we were merely existing. Unfortunately it was my life, it was my neighborhood, it was my family, and in depressing truthful finality, it was me.

The Event: Euclid Avenue

It was a defining time in my life. It was a time when I decidedly ended my dependence upon adults. Through an event inflicted upon me, I discovered that they simply could not be relied upon, believed, or trusted. The events that transpired during that portion of my sixth school year changed my perspective on every facet of life. There was nothing left untouched, and due to that singular event, I became cynical about everything that confronted me thereafter. Once that horrific event had reached its outrageous conclusion, I secretly declared my independence from my parents.

It was as cold as it possibly could be there on the front porch. It was early, just after four in the morning, but it was still my favorite time, as the neighborhood was quiet, and I was left alone. However, across our little street, the back dock area of the supermarket was alive with activity. The front of the store might have been dark, but at the rear of the place, the stockmen unknowingly kept me company even if it were from a distance. They went in and out of the big metal door as they laughed, yelled, and cursed. In between the deliveries, the men brought all of the unwanted garbage and other debris out from inside the store. No sooner had the heavy-metal door banged close when an army of mangy dogs, cats, and rats appeared from the night and began fighting over whatever bits of treasure they could find.

Whenever the fighting began, I moved back into the shadows of the porch canopy and stayed as quiet as possible. I was terrified that if I made any sort of noise, they would notice me there only a few yards away. But soon enough they found whatever it was that they wanted, and just as suddenly, they were gone. The cold of the night always drove them back to their own hiding places.

If only I had something warmer than an old quilt to have wrapped around me. There was barely enough roof over the cold concrete porch to keep the random flakes of snow from falling on my head. As I sat there I only wished that the newspaper delivery truck would simply arrive. In addition to having one paper route to operate in that weather, my father had used my sister's name to shoulder me with yet a second one. By observation and habit, he had always proven that it was always easier to break the rules than to follow them. Since he was in charge of that particular department at the newspaper, it was very easy for him to do so. It would have been a great deal easier to tolerate if I saw any of the money that I worked so hard for each week. But it did give me time away from the house, and I managed to work around some of those rules for my own personal gain.

So there in the early hours of Saturday morning, I waited for the newspapers to be dropped off. But that was nothing compared to the following morning as it would be seven or eight bundles for the huge Sunday paper. Once the truck had made its delivery, I spent the better part of an hour wrapping each newspaper with rubber bands. I then filled the double canvas bag full and put the rest in the corner for the second lap around the south end of the city.

As I headed south on Main Street, I dropped papers at each of the many storefronts. I then climbed the stairs above the drugstore for the apartments above it for deliveries there. I then crossed Kibby Street and went up four flights of stairs inside the big apartment building on the corner. My former fourth-grade teacher lived in that building, and she was one of my favorites.

She always had time to talk and never failed to provide a baked treat for me on collection day. I felt as if she actually cared about me. She was certainly one of the very few.

In those early-morning hours, I was always in a hurry. Once I left the apartment building, it was on to the funeral home, a few more store fronts, a couple of houses, then across Main Street to the east side as I headed back northward. On the east side of the street were a few more stores and three bars in just that one block. My last customer was a small used car lot. It was always neat to see everything that the owner had for sale. During the week he always took the time to talk to me, showed the cars, and occasionally added a bit of advice about life. He even let me borrow a cigarette or two and, in my mind, was certainly one of the good guys.

That part of my morning work generally took about an hour, but then I was only half-done, as there was the other route to do. Even though the route was in my sister's name, she never participated in the work. There was no one to fault as I doubted that she even knew that there was a route in her name. We never talked about it or anything else for that matter, and I never saw a reason to bother her about it. What would really have been the use?

However, once I had returned to the duplex, I did have a reason to smile. Having been assigned that second route gained me something of great importance, a bicycle. I knew that it was an old man's bicycle because it was a full-sized bike, and it had double-wire baskets over the back wheel made just for delivering things. At first I hated it, but it was perfect for newspaper hauling, and most important of all, it was mine. I thought it was great because I could load the baskets up, ride on the sidewalks in front of the houses, reach behind as I grabbed a newspaper, and make a good throw. Even though it was a larger route, I always finished with it in far shorter time than I ever had the first one. As an additional bonus, I didn't have a canvas bag digging into my skinny shoulders. It was almost as if I hadn't worked at all.

Once the routes were finished, I did whatever was necessary to avoid my family throughout the remainder of the day. Given my mind-set, I figured that was certainly a worthy accomplishment. With my chosen and solitary lifestyle, they were nothing more than a nuisance and a constant source of never-ending pain and irritation. They were to me a living, stifling thing that seemed to choke my very life. There were times that I simply couldn't stand it. I always felt like screaming.

But despite my parents' deliberate tactics after "the event," I did have a source of pride and enjoyment. Actually it was a place, and more specifically, it was my very own place. In those postage-stamp-sized backyards, the grass and weeds fought a desperate last stand as they competed for the right to exist in a never-ending battle with the trash and other garbage. A couple of dozen or so heathen kids that ran the neighborhood didn't help matters any either. But among all of that chaos was my very own little corner of the world. It was my sanctuary, my place of retreat, a small place that I called my own. There along the back edge of the duplex row of lots stood a few unkempt and overgrown mature elm trees. They barely had any bark or branches below six feet, the obvious scars from doing daily battle with hordes of kids. But above all of that was a wonderful network of branches that just begged for a young boy's particularly unique brand of construction.

My tree of choice had an old Chevy sitting below it, which provided an excellent ladder to my little roost. Its headlights had been broken out long before by rock-thrown target practice. The roof was nearly caved in by an endless column of young feet, and the remainder of the windows were either cracked or broken out. That heap of a car was completely rusted and barely kept itself off of the ground by three flat tires and a concrete block. But twelve feet above all of that and hidden from view by foliage was my little masterpiece, that tree house.

It was comprised mainly of wooden pallets liberated during the late night hours from behind the supermarket. It was true that the boards that I used to fill the gaps weren't cleanly sawed off and looked pretty ragged. It was also true that at times the roof leaked profusely, and there was just enough space inside to stretch out, but it was mine. I enjoyed my little abode as I ate my breakfast and read the newspaper or a novel. But by far the best part of all was that I was never bothered by underwear- or diaper-wearing beggars who screamed for what they thought belonged to them as I carried meals up into the tree. It was no small wonder that I hated kids.

As I sat on the cold front porch on yet another early weekend morning, waiting on a delivery truck, the mind games once again began their constant torture. Sitting there in the dark, I took a long draw on a cigarette as my mind began to wander once again. I purposely fought against it, but the more that I fought it, the harder the awful memories shoved through the self-constructed barrier within my mind. It was then that guilt pushed through as if it were on a divine mission. It happened the same way ever time. Once it began, it tore through my mind with a vicious intensity as the unsolvable questions followed immediately behind.

Why did I allow it to happen? Why did I permit her do those things to me? Why did I allow her to get away with her crimes? Just what was that sickening power that she held over people? Where did she get it and who gave it to her? How had she ever become such a good actress? Why had I listened to her? Why had I done exactly what she wanted? Why hadn't I stood my ground when she made her demands and then questioned her bizarre orders? But it was far too late; it was all done and over with. The deed had been done, and the task had been completed. There was no way for me to return and change what was now the past. However, I knew that I could do something about the future, but I was still so very confused.

Why didn't I just run away? Why didn't I just leave her house and not return? But where would I have gone? What would I have done? Could I have stayed in the tree house and avoided her? What would she have done with or to me then? But what was I going to do after the fact anyway? Why? Why? Why? My mind was in utter torment as my head felt as if it were about to explode.

CRACK! My right foot instantly screamed in pain. At that very moment in my anguish, as I once again waited for the delivery truck, I had kicked a slat or two out of the porch railing and out into the street just a couple of feet away. I was so angry and so completely sick of everyone and everything. As I wiped away the tears that streamed down my face, I knew just two things: First, I needed to control my anger somehow. But it was becoming harder to deal with every day. Second, somebody was going to be in trouble, and payment would have to be made for that broken railing. But then, I quickly put those matters out of my head as the physical torment once again took over. Instantly, I began to shake uncontrollably with a fervor that was akin to a seizure. There was nothing I could do to stop, and it certainly wasn't caused by the coldness of the night air. At times I felt as if there wasn't any way that I could possibly stand it anymore. Occasionally it felt as if I was about to lose my mind. Then, like an animal being chased as prey, the questions hunted me down once again.

Would I ever be calm, collected, and at peace again? Would there ever be a time when I wasn't angry all the day long? Would I ever find a way to be happy again? The questions just went on and on, with never ending repetition. I hated it whenever I got into those fits because my hands always shook so badly that I could barely light a cigarette. One long steady drag, exhale, then followed by another, and then another. That always seemed to help the shaking to go away. I just hoped I could finish my smoke in peace before the delivery truck arrived. The driver never finked on me, but he always had something to say about twelve-year-olds smoking. However, understanding was evident in his words as he knew my family very well.

But even if he had told my father, the very most that I would have gotten from it would have been a sixty-second lecture. Such a talk would have had more to do with wasting money than anything else. But then, in only a second, as I once again thought about my family and particularly her, my mother, as the pressure and the guilt returned, unwanted and unneeded. It seemed that my family always took what they wanted, they always had, and then like an unwanted thing, once again they distanced themselves from me. However, finality and reality were at hand as I counted down the days and the hours to the conclusion of "the event." But just then the lights of the delivery truck came around the corner, helping me to banish the angry thoughts, even if it were only a momentary reprieve.

It was nearly impossible to wrap newspapers with rubber bands with your gloves on. As I had finished nearly two hundred of them, my fingertips were almost numb from the cold. With my anger never really in check, that act itself set it off, and unfortunately, I allowed it. But then again, nearly everything in my life affected my ever-present anger at that time. I seemed to fight with everyone that I came into contact with. At times I just wanted to stand in the middle of the street and scream at the sky. It wasn't that I believed that there was anyone up there listening. But I just wanted to scream and to hope that someone heard the truth about my never-ending heartache. But yet at the same time, I didn't want to talk to anyone either. I just wanted to be left alone. There was nothing more to say. No one would have listened to me or would have believed me anyway. Certainly no one would believe me if I changed my story at that point. Most importantly, she was in charge, she was in control, and she had everyone completely fooled, just as she always did. But I knew who and what she really was. I knew the complete truth. But I was alone with the facts and had no one to back me.

However, it was just another normal morning as I shoved the newspapers into the double bag with all of the force that I could manage as I packed it completely full. As I crawled beneath it and struggled to stand, the weight of it pressed down upon my shoulders and caused me to stumble as I attempted to stand to my feet. As I stood there I just wanted the blasted morning over with. However, I was strengthened by the anger and, with it, was able to then stand with some stability. But as I headed across the grocery parking lot to Main Street, it came over me once more like a flood. There was really nothing that I could do about it, and nothing seemed to ever stop it. It just took off with me and ran like a large dog on a leash with a little boy in tow. I was powerless against it.

As the newspaper bag bit into my neck and shoulders, each step raised the anger to yet another frustrating level. My teeth were clenched so hard that my jaw ached, and my head began to throb. The questions just seemed to race through my head. *Why? Why? Why? Why?* If I could only turn back time, I would change it all, right down to the last detail. I would have changed everything about that night.

I arrived at my first house as the newspaper flew onto the porch with an angry toss. At the second house my next throw sent cats running in all directions. At the next place there was a streetlight shining just above a storefront window, and it caused me to stop. The glass was but two feet away, but in my mental state, I simply stood there dazed and completely bewildered. At first it was as if I looked at someone else. On that face I saw deep, raging hatred, killing and dying hatred as it radiated and glared from that face in the window. Curiously I knew who it was, but yet at the same time I couldn't fathom that the horribly contorted face so full of anger was mine. But then recognition and reality came fast and hard once again.

It was me. It was me! I quickly turned away from the sight of it and leaned up against the building wall. As I slid down the wall and dropped to my knees, the newspapers spilled out from the canvas bag. I sat there on the cold sidewalk and cried as I once again asked myself the familiar questions. Would the torment ever end? Would it ever stop? I didn't know if I could take it anymore. Sometimes I actually wished that I were dead. On occasions I truly wished for it. Everyone would have been better off, I thought, wouldn't they? Wouldn't I have been better off? After all, could it possibly have ever gotten any worse than what it was? I didn't believe that I could take any more of the torture. As I sat there sobbing in the dark, on the cold concrete and all alone, the event came back with an incredible degree of clarity. It had all been just a month before, the evening of my never-ending, wide-awake nightmare.

It was very early Saturday morning, and I had just finished both of the paper routes. I had dropped off the extra free newspaper at the donut shop and then headed over to the hamburger joint on the corner of Eureka and South Main Streets. The deal worked the same at both businesses, free newspapers for free food. It was a deal that was good for them and far better for me. Then the hardest part of the deal arrived as, no matter what time of the day it was, I always had to sneak around the grocery store building without any of the vulture brats in my family seeing me before I could get up into my tree. They always thought that they were entitled to anything that they saw. They were greedy and selfish little brats who acted just like animals. I wished that I didn't have to deal with them every day. I secretly wished that I wasn't part of the family. But I was stuck with them, and there wasn't anything that I could do about it. But none of it was important once I had gotten up into my private hideaway in the tree.

That evening I had gone into my hiding place where I kept my books, cigarettes, and other personal things. I always loved to read and enjoyed buying secondhand books as they were my only escape from the horrible reality around me. My favorites were *The Mouse That Roared* stories, John Steinbeck novels, and science-fiction adventures. As I read by candle and streetlamps, it was my only means of relaxation. Oftentimes I stayed there until well into the night, even on school nights or until the cold, damp air or the rain chased me inside. So it was on that horrible night, a night that began as any other night.

As was my habit, I had fallen asleep in the tree house and afterward had shivered myself awake. I was tired, cold, and had decided that it was best for my health to go inside the house. As I crept in the back door, all was quiet; nothing and no one stirred. Since it was a weekend evening, my father was at the newspaper at that hour, and everyone else was upstairs sleeping. I didn't know why I always tried to be so silent. Everyone in the family knew where I was, where I could be found, and it wasn't as if anyone ever bothered. But again, it wouldn't have mattered if they made an attempt. I simply would have done my best to ignore them, just as I always had done every day before that one.

The kitchen clock revealed that it was just after midnight. That meant that the delivery truck wouldn't be there for a few hours. But most importantly, it meant that I could get some warm rest after being outside in the damp and cold. As I entered the dark dining room, I looked for my favorite furnace register in the floor against the wall and shoved all of the junk out of the way for a place to lie down. I pulled the old quilt over the register and waited for that wonderful sound that meant that nice, hot air would soon be along. Usually, it only took a little of such comfort to put me to sleep. As the warm air began to move beneath the quilt, my eyes closed, and then just before sleep fully took me away, I heard it.

I sat up with a start. What was that? Was it a noise? I guessed that it was a noise as it obviously wasn't the furnace. It almost sounded as if it were the front door. But just then I thought that I heard another noise. That one was different than the others, it came from the living room, and it almost sounded like snoring. As I listened further, I realized that it was indeed snoring. The front door was just around the corner from where I lay in the darkness. I was not but a few feet away from it, and the front room was immediately next to that.

What was going on there? Had someone come in through that door? Who was it? It couldn't have been my father as he was at the newspaper. It was where he always was, where he could always be found, seven days a week. Just what in the world was going on in the house that night? My curiosity, as always, had gotten the best of me. I had to find out just what was up. Quietly, I pulled the quilt off me, stood to my tiptoes, and looked around the corner of the doorway. There at that second, even if it were only a questionable glance, I thought I saw a man's leg and shoe as it went up the steps. But then I wondered, had I actually seen something, or was it nothing? As I rubbed my eyes, I looked again, saw nothing, and wondered about everything that had happened in those few brief minutes. However, there was still that snoring noise going on, which caused me to wonder just who that could be. I decided that I had better investigate the living room and figure everything out. There wasn't any possibility of going back to sleep.

I walked as quietly as I could into the living room and moved to the end of the sofa. Sure enough, as I looked down, I could see who it was, and with that, I allowed myself to relax. It was one of my uncles, my favorite one, and there he was passed out drunk again. I could smell the beer, and even in the dim light that came in through the window, I could see his name printed on his shop jacket. He and my aunt must have had another one of their infamous fights again. It seemed that the nonsense between the two of them never ended as it happened every day, day in and day out. It was the same situation with my parents and nearly everyone else in our extended family. It seemed to me that all that adults ever did was fight with one another. But it was especially true in his case.

After I had heard the stories that he had told me about her, I knew that I would never ever get married. No matter what the alleged benefits may possibly be, it just wasn't worth the grief that I had observed in my family and especially in his life. I didn't want any part of that nonsense. But as I stood there contemplating his life and my future, I still didn't know what was going on in the house. But at the same time, I knew that I had to get at least a few hours of sleep before the delivery truck arrived. Therefore, with my curiosity partially satisfied, I hurried back into the dining room, crawled back under the quilt as the furnace was running, and with the warmth, sleep once again came very quickly.

Suddenly I awoke, bewildered, cold, and wondered for a few seconds just where I was. I quickly determined that I was still in the dining room and that the furnace had stopped. As I sat there and cleared the cobwebs from my head, I heard a noise once again. I couldn't define it, but I knew that I had heard it before. What was that noise? Where was it coming from? Voices? I thought that I had heard voices. After I had strained my hearing for a few minutes, I was then certain that I could hear voices. But just who, what, and where was it all happening? I shook the sleep out of my head and tried to decide just what to do next.

I figured that I had better check the situation out. I stuck my head into the living room and confirmed that my uncle was still there, just as noisy and smelly as he had been. As I looked out the front window, my father's company van was nowhere in sight, so it was obvious that he wasn't home. I didn't see any newspaper bundles on the front porch, so the delivery truck hadn't arrived. It was all very interesting, and my curiosity had gone beyond the norm. I didn't really know just how long I had been asleep, but I was willing to bet that it had been less than an hour.

As I stepped into the entranceway near the stairs, the voices, noises, or whatever they were became slightly louder. I checked the front door, found that it was locked, stood at the bottom of the steps, and just listened. I believed that there were two voices, one higher pitched and the other significantly deeper. It almost sounded as if it were a chant of some sort or another. It was all too weird, and since curiosity was always a tough master for me, I once again gave in to its call. So I dropped the quilt in a careless pile at the bottom of the steps and slowly crept up them as quietly as I possibly could. It was difficult, as I tried to avoid all of the familiar creaking spots and took it one slow step at a time.

Halfway up the stairs I stopped and listened. My doubt had been replaced with facts as I now knew that the noises were voices. Those voices were coming from behind the closed door at the top of the stairs, which was my parents' bedroom. What was it? What could it have been? But then I waited as new information came to me. Was it her voice? Yes, no, maybe?

Then suddenly I heard a man's voice. What was going on in there? My father was at the newspaper—I knew that much to be a fact! Whatever it was and whoever it was, at that moment I knew that it couldn't be any good. Was it some sort of trouble? What was going on in there? But at the same time, I could hear her stereo playing that boring old people music that she liked so much. There was something very confusing about the whole ordeal. But the more that I thought about it, the more I felt as if I wanted to run.

Then I heard a shout! It was a female's voice! It was her, my mother! She was in some kind of trouble! Something was terribly wrong! Was someone hurting her? Had someone broken in? What was going on in there? I then questioned myself. Should I do something? What should I do? I was now at the top of the steps and only a few feet from the door. The noises were continuing and had gotten much louder. I took the few steps remaining toward the door. I had one hand on the doorknob. What was I to do? Should I go in? But why would anyone have broken into our house? There wasn't anything there worth having. But then the noises became louder and more intense. I had to do something!

I turned the paint-chipped doorknob in my hand ever so slowly, first a click, then a pause, as the voices and noises could still be heard. Then I turned it another click and knew then that the door would easily open. But I still didn't know what to do. I really didn't know what to expect, but my curiosity demanded that I had to open that door! I couldn't just walk away from the door and go back to sleep until I knew what was going on! So I opened the door just a crack, as a glimmer of light from the room escaped into the dark hallway. I opened it a little further, not much more than any inch as the noises, voices, and music became much louder than ever before. With that the door was open just enough for a good look, no more than two to three inches. I pushed my face again the doorjamb, opened my eyes, and then looked into the room.

Shock! Pure shock! Just like a photograph, frozen forever and for all eternity etched into my brain. There before my eyes were two naked bodies, with my mother sitting upright in the bed. It was terrifying, frightening, and revealing all at once. I must have made a noise, screamed or something, because she turned instantly to see me there in the fully opened doorway. I had made a mistake, a very big mistake! Then just that quickly I heard an ear-piercing scream as a thrown blanket covered both the doorway and me. I stumbled back into the hallway, pulled the blanket from around me, and spun endlessly in circles. I wondered which way to run, what to do, what to think and why, why, why? I had to get out of there. I had to run! First, I ran down the hall toward the other bedrooms, then back to the stairs, then I stopped right where I had started in panic and terror. *I didn't know what to do!*

Then a thought sprinted through my mind. The tree house! I would be safe there! No one could get to me there! As I turned for the stairs with my back to the bedroom door, I suddenly found that I could go no farther. There was an iron grip on my wrist. She was there, my mother. She was wearing a house robe, and she held my arm so tightly that it hurt! I looked up into what had to be the most angry and evil face that I had ever seen in my life. I shook with a full-body chill right to my very bones, and it scared me to death. What was she going to do to me? Then with a vicious yank, she knocked me off my feet, pulled me into the bathroom, and slammed the door loud enough to have awakened the dead. Then just before she began speaking, I heard her bedroom door open, close, and then footsteps as they quietly went down the stairs. At least, that was what I believed that I had heard.

When I turned to look at her, she was staring upward at a corner of the ceiling with her back to me. Her fists were clenched at her side as she visibly shook. Then she suddenly calmed herself as she put her open hands to her face. I was confused and wondered just what she was doing. Then she turned around, and I saw her tear-stained face. It was weird, very weird, and in fact, it was all just too weird. She acted so completely different than she had just a short moment before. It completely freaked me out as fear rushed into my heart.

Then in a strange, sickening, and a truly unfamiliar sweet voice, she began asking a number of very strange questions. Had I seen a man in the room, and had I also seen his face? Had I really wondered if she was being hurt, and did I understand that just by my interrupting, I had actually prevented her from being seriously injured? But then she also asked a lot of other things that I really didn't understand as confusion set in. Then her nice voice began to go away as she seemed to become very frustrated. She pressed and pressed me to answer her questions. It seemed that she not only wanted me to understand her and everything that she was trying to say, but she also wanted my agreement with everything as she had stated it. She used a lot of words, spoke them quickly and all in that unfamiliar voice. But I believed that I knew what she meant. She claimed that I was a hero.

Then suddenly, she sat on the stool, put her hands on my arms, and brought her face just inches from mine. For a full minute or more, she just stared cold and hard into my eyes. Then the talking and the questions continued as she started in again. But I didn't feel like a hero, for how was I to have known that something terrible was happening? I was just a typically curious kid and had only wanted to know what the noises were all about. Why had she felt so lucky and where was all of that talk heading? The only thing that I knew for certain was that I quickly became very confused and even light-headed. Suddenly the room began spinning as I felt sick to my stomach and didn't know what to do next.

But what in the world was she talking about? How had I had saved her life? Was that what had happened? Was that what was going on in her bedroom? Had she really been in any kind of danger? Who was that man? How had he gotten into the house? What was he there for? I had never seen his face, and I didn't understand why that was so important to her. What was going on there? None of it made any sense. I didn't understand any of it. Every word that she spoke made my head hurt. Then suddenly, she became silent for whatever reason and appeared to be deep in thought as she stared at the floor. The only noise that I heard at that moment was my own heartbeat as it pounded loudly in my ears. More than ever, I desperately wanted to run for the tree house.

Then she tore at me with more questions that seemed completely bizarre as she suddenly referred to my uncle. What did he have to do with anything that night? I agree that I knew all about how much he drank and how crazy he always became when he did. I also agreed that he had a habit of getting a little out of hand on occasion. I agreed with her that it was true that he probably could use some kind of help and that he probably needed that help. I just figured that it was something for the adults to deal with. It really never concerned me much at all as I liked him just the way that he was.

I told her that it all sounded like adult things, and I really didn't understand or want to know anything about it. Then she went on to say more things that really didn't make much sense either. Who were the authorities, why should they be involved, and just what did she mean by saying how much help that could they give to my uncle? Of course I cared about him as everyone knew that he and I were best buddies and that I would do anything for him. Naturally I wanted the very best for him.

That was what friends did, didn't they? It was all so very odd and bewildering as she carried on as she did. I just couldn't get my head wrapped around anything that she said. She must have kept me in that bathroom for ten or fifteen minutes.

Then just that suddenly, she screamed and yelled something at the top of her lungs, which scared me right out of my skin. Then just that quickly, she became completely hysterical, and I was at a loss to understand her or anything that she said. However, I did understand a few words that were coherent. But in that exact moment, I had my chance, suddenly found my wits, and I told myself to run. Her screaming put my mind into a tailspin as I just didn't know which way to turn. But then in that instant, the panic that wanted to send me to the tree house snapped within my mind. For whatever strange and unknown reason, I surrendered to her words and to her orders.

She screamed the words loud enough for the entire neighborhood to hear.

"RUN! RUN! RUN!" Her orders were very clear. Down the steps I would go! I would run across the street to the back of the grocery store! There I would tell them to call the police! They would take care of all of that mess, and I wouldn't have to. They would find the man that tried to hurt her, and I wouldn't have to bother with any of it anymore. I would do what she demanded.

I stood there as my mind raced violently. She then screamed even louder as I responded by yelling in my head at myself, as my feet finally moved. Then and only then did she open the door to the bathroom. "NOW! NOW! NOW! GO! GO! GO!" I didn't know if the words were hers or the ones inside of my head. But I knew that it was what she wanted me to do. But for some reason, I couldn't seem to make my legs work. Suddenly she was silent.

I could only stare at her in complete and bewildered terror. My mind felt as if it had been in a milk shake blender, I couldn't think. I couldn't move. I was terrified. She had me scared to death. My head spun in a twisted and tormented fashion. I was lightheaded, my throat locked up, and I felt as if I couldn't breathe! Then just that suddenly, she shoved me out of the bathroom door with such force that I tumbled across the hallway into the railing, bounced off of it, and nearly fell down the steps. All of the while my mind screamed out just two words—*go!* and *police!*—over and over again, without ceasing. I had no choice. I had to run for help. I could do nothing else.

I tore down the steps two at a time and yanked open the front door. For a split second, I paused and realized that it was unlocked. As I did, I shoved the screen door so hard that it bounced off of the side of the house and then into the night air I went. It was cold out there in jeans, a short sleeve shirt, and no shoes! I went down the porch steps and then into the street. The gravel was really sharp there in the parking lot, and I hurried as best as I could. I quickly scooped up a handful of it to throw at the rats that scurried around the back door of the grocery. Once there, I then pounded with everything that I had on that steel door.

I backed away just in time as an angry employee threw the door open with a "whaddaya want" kind of attitude. Then as he saw my face, he softened a bit as I told him what had just happened and that we needed the police right away. Then he began yelling men's names, pulled me inside, and sat me on a chair. He had one employee stay with me while another was already on the phone. Curiously it seemed that yet another man was both looking at me but also intent on hiding his face from me. Or perhaps he was just busy? I couldn't tell for certain.

Had it all been my imagination? Everything was so confusing! My head was spinning, as I suddenly felt clammy, cold, and then sick to my stomach. I needed a drink of water or something. As I stood to my feet, my knees instantly buckled as I collapsed to the floor. The big guy who had met me at the door picked me up as if I weighed nothing and laid me out on a counter. He put a bag of rice beneath my head for a pillow, placed a cold rag on my forehead, and then yelled at someone to watch me. Feeling safe, I closed my eyes as the world around me just faded away.

I open my eyes to an official-sounding voice and saw a very serious man in a uniform, a police officer. There were actually two of them as they stood there next to me. Then one of them gently sat me up, informed me that they had already been to our house, and that everything was fine and everyone was safe. Then he began his interrogation. He asked if I had heard noises. Had I heard a man's loud voice? Was I certain that my uncle had been in the house, and had he been asleep? I agreed to all of that, but I had no idea whatsoever as to where the officer was going with his questioning. Then he proceeded to inform me of the situation.

They had already taken my mother's statement. As he related her story to me from his notepad, she had been asleep, had been awakened by someone on top of her with his hands on her neck. She had struggled and yelled for help as best as she could. That was when I must have heard the noises, opened the bedroom door, interrupted the crime, and had apparently saved the day. I was so confused. I had saved the day? Alarms suddenly went off inside of my head. But the other officer chimed in by stating that they had already taken the bad guy into custody and that the situation was completely under control. The first one then added that my uncle wouldn't be in jail for more than a few days, and it wasn't as if he hadn't been there before. My mind raced viciously and chased itself into dark and dead-end corners. Uncle? Uncle? What were they talking about? Just what was going on?

I physically broke away from the both of them. I went out the back door of the grocery store in a full run. I tore across the gravel parking lot, oblivious to the sharp stones cutting my feet, only to come to a sobbing halt at the fender of the police car. I could see my uncle's head in the backseat, and I could tell that he was still about half-gone, as his head was rolling from side to side. What was going on there? What were they doing to him?

Hadn't he still been in the living room when I had gone upstairs? Wasn't he in the living room when I gone across the street for help? He was, wasn't he? Wasn't he? Or was he? Had I really seen him there or not? He couldn't have done that to my mother! He couldn't have done something that terrible. He was the only friend that I ever really had. As the police cruiser pulled away, leaving me alone there in the street, I looked up to see her on the front porch. My aunts, her sisters, were all around her, comforting and hugging her. Even in that light I could see that her eyes were suddenly all red and that her face was tear stained. Was all of it for real? Had all of it really happened? Then it all began.

She called me up onto the porch as if it were a stage. I turned to see the two officers. Once on the porch, I felt as if everyone was talking to me at once and pounding the words into my head. It really wasn't his fault. He always became mean and angry when he had gotten drunk. He had a drinking problem, and it had put him into jail before. He and his wife just had a nasty fight earlier in the evening before he had arrived at the house. He had been drinking ever since he had gotten off work and had been at it for about four or five hours. Once all of those ingredients were mixed together, then something terrible was bound to happen. He already had a record of disorderly conduct, reckless operation, public intoxication, and numerous assaults. He needed help, we needed to help him, and with the authorities involved, we were going to help him. But it would take all of us working together to accomplish that.

With police officers and all of my family standing next to me, waiting on my every word, I surrendered and agreed. So fine, we needed to help him. But as the confusion set it, I wondered just what did they mean by *we*? What did they mean I had to help? What did I have to do? Why did I have to do it? The adults surrounded me like a wall and began talking all at the same time. No, I couldn't say for sure who was in the room. No, I couldn't say for sure where my uncle was at all times. Yes, I guess it could have been possible that he could have gotten around me somehow. I didn't know how it might have happened! I didn't want to do anything! But yes, I did want to help him!

With that, the officer stepped forward, took down my full name in his notebook, and asked a number of questions that seemed to me to be curiously worded. I was shaking, my head was spinning madly in circles, and I was so completely confused. I felt really sick then. I needed a cigarette right then and there and in the very worst way. But I wisely realized that it wasn't a good time to light one up, twelve-year-olds just don't do that, now did they? I was so confused and so angry that I just wanted to hit someone or something. I didn't know whether to scream, to laugh hysterically, or to break down and cry. I felt as if I were losing my mind! The one thing that I knew for certain was that I just wanted to get out of there.

I then realized that my father had come home, and he informed me he and two of my brothers were going to take care of the paper routes that morning. My responses were far less than respectful. I then asked questions to no one in particular. Did that mean that everyone was going to leave me alone? Was that it? Were there any more stupid questions? *Could I just leave!* I then informed them all of my intended actions and expectations. I was going to the tree house. I didn't even care how cold it was. I was sick of everyone. With each step up into the tree, as I dragged my quilt behind me, I felt a little better. Once inside, I wrapped the old quilt around me, broke out my secret old cigar box, and lit a cigarette up. My hands shook so badly that I was barely able to strike the match. That one cigarette had to be the best smoke of the day. All I could do after all that I had experienced in those early hours was to just lean against the wall of the tree house and hoped that I would pass out. But thinking was all that I could do, and therefore, sleep never arrived, but the dawn of the next day certainly did.

A week had passed as everyone in the family talked to one another, but no one talked to me. I would have thought that someone would have been concerned about my mental state. I had been thrown into the midst of the whole event and had certainly been important enough to be used by everyone that night. But once everything had been set into place, I found myself forgotten and abandoned once again. It was as if I didn't exist to anyone. Once more, so long as I was out of sight, I was out of their minds. It was the normal course of daily events.

I practically lived in the tree house day and night at that point. I only went into the house once a day for a bath and for clothes. I didn't want to be around anyone, and I certainly didn't want to talk to anyone. Since no one bothered or wanted to talk to me or include me, I then withdrew myself into seclusion. But that solitary lifestyle brought about its own dangers. Even as I tried to keep my mind on track, the questions ruthlessly raided my mind, unwanted and uninvited every minute of the day.

Had he really done it? Had he really done anything? Had it really happened just like she had said? Had I really missed something? Who had come in the front door that night? Wasn't my uncle still in the living room snoring away? Who was the man in my mother's room? Why couldn't I remember his face? What was my mother doing when I opened the door? She certainly wasn't being choked; that much I knew for certain. Was there so much that I didn't understand about adults, or was I thoroughly confused? Or could it have been true that I was the only one that knew the truth? Should I have trusted my memory and my feelings about that night? But there were other issues that were just as confusing. Why was I the key for him to get help? What did they really need me for? Why did I have to go in front of a judge and a bunch of strangers and say everything that they wanted to be said? Everyone kept trying to get me to stick to some speech and to practice it. I was so sick and tired of all of it. They all just made me want to throw up.

I guess the only good that came out of all of that mess was the new outfit. I had never had brand-new clothes before. Someone had purchased a new button-up shirt, really nice blue dress pants with cuffs at the bottom, and even new brown shoes. It was the first outfit that had ever been given to me that hadn't come from a garage sale. It wasn't from a secondhand store or was hand-me-down from someone in the family. Why did you always save the tags when you bought new clothes? Was there a reason that they had to be kept? At the time I believed that it wasn't all that important and had decided that it was a grown-up thing. I didn't understand, and truth be told, I really didn't care.

The court date finally arrived. It had been nearly two weeks since "the event." I just wanted to get the matter over with and to be left alone with my solitary life once again. I was sick of everyone and everything. For the most part, I was really tired of my mother and the way that her moods changed minute by minute. At one moment, as she talked to me about what to say in court, she was all sweetness and nice. At other times, I caught her as she stared at me in a way that chilled me to the bone. It almost looked predatory, the way that I had observed a cat just before it pounced on a mouse. It was the same exact look that she had given me outside of her bedroom door on that night.

I also knew deep within my innermost being that she hated me. While she had never said the words out loud, I felt them within every single moment of every single day. But at the same time I wondered about it all. What had I ever done to her? What was it about me that she so despised? Sometimes by the way that she acted, I felt that she believed that I had ruined her life somehow. But since I was her firstborn, didn't that mean something to her? Or did that fact mean everything to her? More than once I caught myself as I chased myself in mindless circles and had to forcibly bring it all to a halt. Then, just as I had accomplished that feat once more, I had to force all of that out of my head because it was time to get ready to go to the courthouse.

I concentrated on the matter at hand as I took the new clothes from their hangers. As I put them on my body, they just felt incredible! It was almost unbelievable just how good it felt to wear brand-new clothes. The feeling itself was so new, so unusual, and so unfamiliar. I felt like a million bucks. I really liked it more than I could find words to express.

As soon as I was ready, I tore myself away from the mirror as she ordered me out into the car. As we rode down the street with the radio on, I sat in the backseat alone as the adults sat in the front and talked quietly in near whispers. I really didn't care, because to me, sometimes it was nice to be ignored. But it was a very quick ride, only about five or six blocks and then we were in front of the courthouse.

It was a very big and impressive place even on the outside. As I walked in through the large doors, I found that it was even bigger with ceilings that were way up high and far out of reach. Wasn't it something? I looked at everything in the place, at all of the people and the fact that they were everywhere. What could they all be doing? Wouldn't that have been a neat place to go to and work in every day? Everyone there seemed nice, they all wore nice clothes, and everyone talked in normal voices. What an interesting and fascinating place. I was completely intrigued by it all.

Then a very nice man in a very nice suit and tie called our names, spoke quietly to my mother, and then pointed to a bench just outside of the courtroom. That was where I was to sit until someone called for me. As I sat there, my mother and my aunts paced back and forth as they smoked their cigarettes, one right after the other. Whatever was happening, they were certainly nervous about it all. But I agreed with them on one thing, I sure wished that I could have had one right then. Then a man stepped out from the open doorway and called all of them inside. But I was to stay there on the bench.

That, however, was not good for me. It allowed me too much time to sit and far too much time to think. As I sat there, it all started to get to me. What would I say once I was inside? What if I didn't say what she wanted me to say? What would happen when I said whatever I decided to say? But most of all, it seemed that she was getting to me more than anything. For the last two weeks she had been in my ear every chance that she could as she told me what to say and how to act. She always added all kinds of assorted threats and promises that she evidently thought were necessary. But curiously she hadn't said a word to me on that day other than ordering me into the car. Once again, I was totally ignored as if I didn't even exist. Then suddenly I was yanked out of my thoughts again.

That same man had appeared beside me as it was now my time to go inside the courtroom. He put a hand on my shoulder with a slight rub, and together we walked through the courtroom door. It seemed as if every eye in the place was on me as I walked all of the way toward the front. There was the judge who sat behind a big desk that was elevated above the floor. I was so nervous. I was so uncomfortable. If I turned around right then and ran, would they have chased me down and caught me? A quick glance behind me told me that it probably wouldn't have worked. As I walked closer, I was suddenly startled out of my self-absorbed thoughts. There on my left, as he sat at a long table with his head in his hands was my uncle. He wore a weird sideways striped uniform of some kind, and he didn't look up at anyone or anything. It almost appeared as if he were going to cry. In that moment, I never felt sadder about anything else before in my entire life. It was as if there was a huge, empty, and painful space in my chest. I instantly hated that place.

The officer gently led me to a chair next to the judge. He was a really old guy in a black robe, but something in his face told me that he was nice. He asked about my school, my hobbies, and my paper route. It sounded as if he knew everything about me! Then he told me that the only reason that we were all there was to help my uncle to get better. Wasn't that what I really wanted? Then another man in a suit stood up from the opposite table and walked toward me. He told me his name and said that he was the prosecutor. It was his job to enforce the law, it was my job to tell the truth, and it was the judge's job to take care of my uncle. Was all of that acceptable to me? Did I agree? Wasn't that important? Then he asked the questions that I knew that he was going to ask.

Where precisely had I been in the house when I had heard the noises? What exactly did I do when I heard them? What had I seen in detail? Had I seen my uncle inside of our house? I paused and didn't want to answer that question. It felt like a trap of some sort. As I looked over at him, I saw that his stare never left the surface of the table before him. I just couldn't stand it. I had seen him happy and goofy drunk, angry, and fighting mad drunk, but never before had I seen him like this. I had never seen him beaten, defeated, and totally lost. That just wasn't him. It wasn't the man that I knew so very well.

But the fault was mine, and I had allowed it to happen. At that instant, I thought that I should have done something or maybe anything. I thought that I should have told them that he was passed out on the sofa and had never moved. Perhaps I should have told them all about him and what he meant to me. I should have told them a hundred different things. But before I spoke another single word, the judge dismissed me. I stood to my feet, paused, thought for a moment, but before I could open my mouth, the officer gently took me by the arm and began to lead me out of the room. For just one second as I passed my uncle, I stopped, which caused the officer to stop as well. I needed to say something! I needed to say something as it was my last chance!

But at that very instant my eyes locked onto her, my mother, as she sat there in a seat behind the divider. They were the all too familiar cold and penetrating eyes from that horrible night. My throat locked up tightly, and my voice instantly disappeared as the emotions overwhelmed me like a flood as I burst into uncontrollable tears. The officer took me by the shoulders and quietly herded me down the aisle to the door, where we walked outside, and I sat on the bench once more. He then motioned to a nice lady who brought over a box of tissues, patted me on the head, and then they all went away. As I sat there and wiped my nose, I breathed a sigh of relief.

It was over, it was finished, it was done, and now my part of it was completed. However, the questions once again tormented me.

Would my uncle get the help that everyone said that he needed? He would be better for it, wouldn't he? Wouldn't the courtroom situation help him? Wouldn't it help his family? Wouldn't it make his life better? Would they put him in the hospital? Did doctors fix that kind of stuff? Wasn't that really the best thing to do? Hadn't I done the right thing? What if I was wrong about everything? What if I had been used?

Just then, I heard a loud noise from within the courtroom. For a moment it sounded as if it were my uncle's voice. Then it almost sounded as if someone were crying. I knew that it couldn't be him. There was no way in the world that it could be him. He was far too tough for that sort of thing. But it was then that I saw my opportunity. The officer who stood guard at the door was looking the other way for a moment. He seemed to be more than a little distracted by a younger, very dressed-up lady. The situation was perfect as I needed to know what was going on in that courtroom. I thought that if I took a chance while the officer was distracted, I would be able to peek inside the door. I had to see just what was going on.

As I cracked open the door, I could just barely see inside. I was able to see the judge's face, and it didn't appear to be a very good one. It certainly wasn't the face that he had worn when he talked to me. He looked at my uncle who was standing at the table where he had been previously sitting. Then I heard him say something about my uncle's past history—criminal record,... alcohol,...out of control, and then the word *jail*. Jail! No one had ever said anything to me about jail! They had only said that he needed help! How was jail going to help? It was nothing but trash; it was all lies! Ninety days in jail! No way! They couldn't do that to him! He was going to hate me forever! I had to say something. It was then the judge noticed me at the back of the room and angrily pointed in my direction. His finger drew a line from me and then to an officer as he motioned for me to get out of his courtroom. Then just that quickly, I was back on the bench with plenty of words to say and not a soul to say them to. It was all done, it was over with, and it was finished. I guess that I had already had my chance.

On the way home, as I sat in the backseat by myself, nothing about that day made any sense at all. My mother and her sisters were laughing and carrying on as they sang to the radio as if we had just left a party. Every time I even tried to ask a question, they simply ignored me, waved their hands, and turned the radio up louder. I just might as well have forgotten all of it. My uncle was in jail, and I knew that he would probably never speak to me again as long as he lived. He would never take me anywhere again. We would never talk about cars or girls or anything else ever again. He would never take me car shopping or scouting the junkyards for cars and parts ever again. It would never happen again. Therefore, I was totally alone and obviously no one cared.

Hours later I watched as the sun sank behind the trees to the west. It was strange just how pretty and relaxing it was there in the tree house. It was the exact opposite of my now-truly miserable life. What a beautiful end to a truly bizarre and ugly day. Already the night chill had set in as I wrapped the old quilt tightly around me. I was so sick to death of people, especially my family and especially her, my mother. She had proven just what she was made of as soon as we had gotten out of the car. We had been home from the courthouse less than a few minutes when she had ordered me to change out of my new outfit. Once I gotten back downstairs after having changed, I could see that the clothes were folded, tagged, and all ready to go back to the store where it had come from. It was so very typical of her. She wasn't even the person that had paid for it! But I knew that she was certainly going to pocket the money for it! I just couldn't stand to be around her. After everything that had happened, I wanted nothing more than to be alone.

My best and only real friend was now gone. I was certain that as he sat there in his jail cell, he hated me. Sarcastically, I really hoped that everyone in my family was happy. I knew that my mother certainly was. She certainly acted that way, at least, until someone stopped by the house. It was then that she sobbed and carried on as if she were some sort of pathetic victim or something. She made me sick, very sick, and even physically sick. She had become very, very easy to hate.

Every day I sat all alone in my tree house. No one ever bothered to come by. No one ever called my name. No one ever yelled at me to come in for dinner. No one ever called out the back door that it was bedtime and to come in for the night. No one ever did anything. Everything was just as it had always been. It had become the normal scheme of things. I had once again become unwanted and unneeded. I was there for a specific purpose, was used for that purpose, and apparently that was just the way that it was. I was miserable, unhappy, depressed, and no one cared. I remembered having been happy once. But that was a long, long time before when I was very young, and even then, it hadn't lasted for very long.

How could a young boy who was forced into the realm of the adult world and into the most horrible of adult situations have ever possibly understood just what had taken place within his life? How could he have possibly comprehended the depth, the breadth, and the depraved motives of a well-versed and talented manipulator? How could he have possibly known that the emotion of anger would prove to be a demanding, overwhelming, and all-consuming master? Soon he would find out.

Water

My grandparents were the best people in the world. I was the oldest kid in my family. My mom was the oldest in her family. My grandparents were her mom and dad. That made me the first grandchild. But I wasn't the only one. I had a sister, a brother, another brother, and a younger sister. They were all younger than me. I was four years old when all of the bad things happened.

My grandparents took me everywhere. They took me out for ice cream. They took me to all of the stores. The best place that they ever took me was to the zoo. There were animals and lots of good stuff to eat. It was the best day ever. I also really liked to ride in my grandpa's Buick. It had a big shiny grille on the front and a giant backseat. He always let me stretch out in the back window, and when he put on the brakes, I bounced onto the backseat. That was the most fun of all.

Their house was full of stuff, lots of stuff, but it was all neat and clean, and it always smelled good. It was nothing like our house at all. Our house wasn't any of those things. It wasn't ever clean. There usually wasn't any good food to eat either. It always smelled bad too. It was never quiet either, always loud and everything. I liked my grandparents' house much better. I always wanted to stay there. I liked it there a lot. I didn't like it at home. Why did I have to stay there? I had a hard time sleeping in my parents' house since that bad day. I always had bad dreams when I was at home. I always had bad dreams ever since that day.

I was at our house. It was a regular day. I tried to eat breakfast at the dinner table, but the other kids made too much noise and always threw food everywhere. So I did what I always did, took my cereal bowl and my book, and hid behind the back of the sofa on the floor under the window. That was my place. No one else was there. I brought one encyclopedia back there at a time. Mostly I looked at the pictures. Then I tried to sound out the small words. It got easier for me with each time. I liked it. I always liked books. That was when it was almost as good as at my grandparents. At their house, they always helped me to read, but at our house no one ever helped me to read. But it never stayed good at our house, and it sure wasn't good on the bad day.

My dad came home from work. When I heard the front door and his voice, I looked out over the top of the sofa. I watched as my mom came stomping down the stairs just as he dropped into his favorite chair. Right away they started fighting. All they ever did was fight and yell at each other. They always fought. I don't think they liked each other very much. Then my mom grabbed her purse, stomped out the door, and made it slam really loud. My dad just sat there in his chair and stared at the floor. Then he lit a cigarette, put it in the ashtray, and fell asleep right away. I never understood how he did that. My brothers and sisters were running all over the place, yelling and fighting, and all he ever did was sleep and snore real loud.

Then I noticed something that day. Something wasn't right. I waited a minute and looked around. Where was my youngest brother? I didn't see him. Then I tried to find him. Sometimes I tried to look out for him. My grandma always said that he had problems and that he was very special. I wondered where he might be. I looked in the dining room and then in the kitchen. He wasn't in either of those rooms. I just didn't see him anywhere. The back door was locked, so I knew that he didn't go outside. Where was he? Then I wondered if he had gone upstairs. So I went up the steps, but at the top I didn't see or hear anything.

Then I thought that he was in one of the bedrooms. I looked through each one, behind the doors, under the beds, and in the closets, but I still couldn't find him. So then I went back down the hallway to the stairs. From downstairs I could still hear the others kids yelling, screaming, and running around. But I was confused. Where was he? Where could he be? Then I thought about the bathroom. That had to be it! I never looked in the bathroom. But as I stood in the doorway, I didn't see any sign of him, but the room sure was a mess. There was stuff everywhere! Then I knew that he had been in there. There was bathroom paper all over the place. There was water all over the place. It looked like it had just happened. That told me he had to be in there somewhere. But there really wasn't any place to hide.

The evidence of his presence was obvious. There was a wet towel in the corner and another one in front of the old iron-clawed bathtub. Everywhere that I looked there was water; it was all over the place. Then suddenly I felt cold inside as if something was wrong, very wrong. It reminded me when someone had forgotten to shut the back door during the winter, and cold wind blew in. But most of all, I was scared. I was really scared and didn't even know why. At first glance, there was certainly nothing to be afraid of in that room. I was torn as I wanted to go into the room, but at the same time, I didn't want to go into the room. But I had been everywhere else. That meant that he had to be in there. With a great deal of caution, I took just one step inside the door. It didn't feel good at all. Then I took two more steps on the thoroughly soaked and wet floor. Just what had happened in there? My mother had come down from the second floor when my father had arrived home from work. I wondered it had looked like that then? Had my mother been in that room during that time? Had she seen all of this? It really looked bad.

But then I took three more steps. At that point, I could see that the bathtub was full of water. Another glance told me that a towel or something was floating in it. Then I took a few more steps and began to shake all over.

Was that a leg? Was that my little brother in the water! I grabbed the sides of the bathtub with both hands, but for some reason, I couldn't move. But it was my little brother, and he was floating face down in the water! I reached as far as I could, but I could barely touch him, and when I did, he just floated away! Then I smacked his leg, and he still didn't move! Then I yelled as loud as I could, and yet again, he still didn't move! Then I screamed for my dad over and over! Obviously, he was still sleeping. Couldn't he hear me? Why couldn't I pull my brother out? Where was my dad? Where was my dad? When I finally got a hold of his ankle, I pulled as hard as I could and still couldn't get him out. Where was my dad? Where was he? As big as he was, I knew he could get him out! Then I yelled at myself.

RUN! RUN! RUN! RUN! I turned around, slipped, and fell on the wet bathroom floor. I got up, ran down the stairs, tore across the living room, and stopped at my father's chair. I screamed his name until my voice almost went away. Only then did he open his eyes and even then, just barely. So I then began hitting him on the arm. "WAKE UP! WAKE UP! WAKE UP!" By that time, I was crying.

Finally my father opened his eyes. Then he saw me. Then he realized just how wet I was. As I was out of breath, terrified, and probably in shock, I could only say a solitary word. "Bathroom, bathroom," was all that I could say. It was then that his eyes became big, really big. He jumped out of his chair, knocked me completely out of the way and onto the floor as he pounded up the steps. I couldn't do anything but stand there in the middle of the room, dripping wet as the other kids continued to scream and run around all over the house, oblivious to the death that had just occurred.

Noise. I didn't know how else to say it. It was a yell that came from I didn't know where, but it caused me to run and hide in my secret place. I had never been so scared. Then I recognized it. My father was yelling and crying as he came down the stairs. I looked to see him with my little brother wrapped up in a big towel. I watched as he half-ran across the room, slammed the front door wide open with his big shoulder, and went out into the night. Where was he going? What was I supposed to do? Suddenly, even the other kids were quiet, as they were obviously scared too. But I didn't know what to do. I wasn't an adult, I wasn't a parent, so what was going on? Was he coming back? Was anyone going to be there with us? How long were we going to be left alone? It turned out to be only a couple of minutes.

Then lights. Lights everywhere. Flashing lights. People. Lots of people. Outside there was an ambulance, and there seemed to be people everywhere. There were loud voices and a lot of shouting. Then more people arrived, first outside the house and then inside. Noise, noise, noise. There was so much noise it made my head hurt.

My name. I heard someone called my name. Then I heard them shout it. In that moment, I didn't recognize the voice and wondered just who it was. Then suddenly strong arms grabbed me from behind and lifted me off the floor. It was my uncle, my favorite one, and he was crying too. Pain was clearly written on his face, which told me that something was very bad. With me in his arms, he turned, and out the front door we both went, through the crowd of people and then into the backseat of my grandpa's car. His face was saddened as well, and it was then that I knew for certain that my brother's condition had to be very bad. But before I could think another thought, the car took off, and just a few blocks later, we were at their house. Just the sight of their house brought a measure of peace to me even as my heart was in utter turmoil. My uncle still had his hold on me and carried me into the house. Once upstairs and into the bedroom that he shared with my other uncle and about a hundred model cars, he finally put me down. From a dresser drawer he tossed me a set of my pajamas kept there for me. Then I had a nice hot bath, was put under the covers, and the next thing I knew, I was ready to go to sleep. I was tired, so tired, it was dark outside, and my uncle kept asking if I was okay. I only wanted to close my eyes for just a minute.

Smells. Paint and glue. I opened my eyes to see sunlight there in the bedroom. It was my uncle's room, but I was the only one there. Where was everybody? As I sat on the edge of the bed, I could see that both of my uncles' beds were made. There was certainly no way they had slept in them that night as my grandma always had to yell at them to make their beds. Oddly enough, the bedroom door was shut, which was also unusual. I just had to see what was going on.

When I opened the door, I could hear voices coming from downstairs. As I walked down the hallway and ran my hand on the railing, the voices became louder, but I still couldn't understand them. I followed the railing around the curve and walked slowly down the steps. Once I reached the bottom, I could hear the voices well enough and sat on the very last step to listen. I believed that I knew most of the voices, but even though I heard the words, I couldn't understand what they were talking about.

Who was in the hospital? What about the doctors? What does saving someone mean? Who was watching the other kids? I could probably have answered that question. We watched ourselves a lot. But the curious conversations continued.

What was a coroner? What kind of house was a funeral home? Who lived there? I knew that there was one just down the street from my grandparents' as I had seen the sign. My uncle always told me that it was a very sad place. Who would want to live in a sad place? Who couldn't be helped? Who was so young? Who was so small? What were they talking about? I wondered if anyone was going to tell me anything about what was going on. But the conversation was not yet over.

What was a bar? What was a bar on a street? What kind of place was it? I heard a voice that stated that it was the place where they had found my mother. I still didn't understand. But then there was another curious statement. What? A boyfriend. According to the conversation my mother had a boyfriend, and she was found with him at the bar. Then the confusion really set in. None of it really made any sense to me. My uncle had always stated that he was somebody's boyfriend. He also said that he had lots of girlfriends. Was my mother's situation the sort of the same thing? Then I noticed that everyone had gotten quiet. Evidently someone must have heard me.

Then everyone came running out of the living room, picked me up, kissed me, and wiped my face. Both my uncles were there, my grandparents, aunts and other, but not my parents. But that was fine as I was happy and content with those who were there. My grandma quietly said something to my uncle, and he took me out to the kitchen and seated me at the table. Then he took my special cereal bowl from the cupboard and poured a bowl of his own his own cereal. My day was looking better already.

He then stated that we were going to run errands about town later. But something was still wrong, and his eyes looked peculiar to me. I wondered what it was. But I was anxious about the day's possibilities, finished eating my breakfast, dressed, and went out the door with one uncle on either side. I felt so special.

First we headed downtown as we walked past their high school on West North Street. They didn't care much for school, but they say that I probably would due to my liking for books. We walked past the post office and into the paint store on West High Street where their friends worked. So we spent a few moments there as they talked while I just watched and listened. We finally left which was good as I was beginning to get bored.

We then walked eastward on High Street to the lunch counter where one of their girlfriends worked. It was a great place. I had fries with ketchup and a cup of chocolate pudding with nuts on top. Could anything be any better? They talked to the girls until their supervisor told us we had better get going.

We crossed the street and went into the department store on North Main Street. There we spent the next half an hour chasing each other on the escalator until a manager ordered us out of his store. Then we crossed onto the other side of the street to the best store in town. In my opinion, it might have been the best place in the world. There they sold all kinds of nuts, candy, and other treats. They put everything into little white sacks so you could try as much as you wanted. It was a great place.

Then my uncles told me that we were going somewhere new. We walked south into the public square and turned right onto West Market Street. After we had gone five blocks, we stopped at the entrance to the hospital. The two of them informed me that this was the place where they fixed people. Then my questions began.

Was my little brother there? Was he okay? They told me not to worry, that he wasn't there, but that he was just fine, and they would explain it all later. Then I continued. Why were we there? We were there to visit somebody. My uncle then stopped me before I could ask the next question and asked one of his own. Would I like to play a game? Of course I would, but what game? So, then we sat down on a bench as they told me exactly what to do. They also promised me that I wouldn't get into any trouble and would get a new model car. I declared it a deal.

The three of us walked into the hospital, got into the elevator, rode a bit, and then got out. Then we went to the place where all of the nurses were and where they had benches for people to sit and wait. It was there where the game began. As we sat on the bench, the nurses walked back and forth past us doing their duties. My uncle picked one he liked and told me to get ready. I was nervous, but they both reminded me of the reward and that it would be fun.

Just then she walked toward us and when she was right in front of us, I reached up and pinched her quickly on her bottom. She screamed, spun around, looked at all three of us, and slapped my oldest uncle on the right side of his face. She was very angry and stomped away as both of my uncles cracked up laughing. I guess that was part of the fun.

Soon enough, I saw her glancing at us from her desk. My uncle walked over and talked to her for a little while. Then she wrote something on a piece of paper, looked around, and gave it to him. I didn't know what was on it, but it certainly made him smile. When he sat down, he grinned and stated that he was going to buy me two model cars because of the game.

Just as we were enjoying ourselves, a man in a white coat stopped in front of us and asked to speak with my uncles privately. They took me down to the nurses' station where they let me sit in a chair behind the desk with them. They walked away telling me that they wouldn't be long. It was just that they just had to see how someone was doing. Within a few short minutes, they were back, and we left the hospital.

That visit became the longest amount of time that I ever spent with my grandparents. In all, it lasted well over three weeks, maybe almost a month. It was my very favorite place, and I didn't want to ever leave. It had to be the best place in the entire world. My grandparents took me places, spent time with me, listened to me, and told me that they loved me. My uncles showed me how to build those cars as we sat on the front porch, where we counted and named real cars as they went by. Everything there was fun. But most of all, they told me that they loved me. I never heard any of those things at home, and I never ever wanted to go back.

But on that particular day as we sat on the front porch in the evening, my grandpa sat in his chair and was very serious with me. He usually wasn't like that at all. He sat me in his lap and told me that my family had a new house to live in that was out in the country. He told that it was a very nice place and that I would like it a lot. I wondered if that meant that I had to leave his house. What if I didn't want to go? But he said that I had to. Then he told me that the next morning was Saturday and that we would drive there in his car to see it. With that I was happy! A ride in the country! I always liked to go with them for car rides.

It was a bit of a ride, but not all that long. As we pulled off the county road and into the driveway, I could see that it was an old farmhouse. Immediately I wondered if it had a big kitchen in it with good things to eat just like my story books. As the car came to a stop, everyone came out of the house. I looked to see that everyone was there but my little brother. It was just as my grandpa had said.

He told me everything about it as we sat on the front porch. It was very sad. He said that my little brother was special, so he had gone to a special place. He said that when I was older, he would make sure that I understood it better. He thought that I would be better off not to think about it right then. He then said that everything was okay and that it would all work out, whatever that meant. Then, as always, my family interrupted.

My brothers and sisters ran out of the house yelling and screaming just as they always did. Even though I had only been with them for a few moments, I hated their noise already. It was so quiet at my grandparents' home. But then I was startled as my mother picked me up and asked if I missed her. I just said no. I squirmed in her arms, got down, got away from her, and ran inside the house just to look around. But it was just like the other house with boxes and stuff everywhere. It was a mess, and it didn't look like grandparents' house at all. With that, I decided I had seen all that I wanted of the place.

I walked outdoors, found my grandpa, grabbed his hand, tugged at it hard, and told him that I was ready to go. Then I let go of his hand, ran to his car, and got into the backseat where I always sat. Then everybody came to the car, including my mother. They looked in the window and jokingly asked why I was leaving already. I answered all of them by saying, "Well, at least I came and visited you, now good-bye."

The little boy knew just a little, but he certainly couldn't have known just what had actually happened to his littlest brother. He certainly had no knowledge of any of the events that had precipitated his awful discovery. Someday, one day many years into the future, he would stand next to an unmarked and lonely grave. Only there, in that silent place, would some of the answers come to his heart and mind.

Moving

I was so sick of their nonsense! Every time I turned around, my family did it again. It never failed. Just as soon as I began making new friends, it happened again. As soon as I finally started getting a new school figured out, it happened again. As soon as I finally began fitting in with everybody and had gotten used to everything in a new neighborhood, it all happened again. What had caused it to happen again? The list could probably go on forever.

Had the neighbors gotten roaches inside of their homes again? Had they gotten sick of seeing trash thrown and scattered all over the neighborhood? Had my brothers and sisters gotten into people's flower beds and into their garages and cars again? Or was it the old standby, the sheriff with one hand on his gun and an eviction notice in the other? At times I thought that they did it just to embarrass me. I knew for a fact that they never thought about me, the other kids, or anyone else. They only thought about themselves, just as they always had. I believed that I had the most selfish and irresponsible parents in the world. It happened on average at least once a year, sometimes even less, occasionally after just a few months. I had kept cardboard boxes longer than I had friends. And then it started all over again. So there we went, once more and for one more time. They always lied to me and said that it would be the last time. It was something that I should have been used to as they never ever kept their word about anything. We were moving again.

First Grade: North Cool Road

It had gone on like that forever, it seemed. Just before first grade began, we moved into yet another old farmhouse out in the country. It seemed to be a pretty decent place, but my parents fought about it from day 1. That house was within sight of my grandparents' house, my father's parents. Since their house was on the other side of the road, back a lane and up on a hill, allegedly, they could see just about see everything that ever happened at our place. As a kid, I could have cared less, but my mother really and truly hated it. She thought that they were all spying, checking up on her, and trying to control her life. But then again, she was never happy about anything. She walked around the house all day long as she growled, complained, and cursed about anything that crossed her mind or her path. At times I believed that she hated everything. But once in a great while, I noticed that she did find something to smile about.

From the first day while the other kids played outside, I listened in on her telephone conversations. I knew that it was wrong to eavesdrop, but it was sometimes funny and often interesting. I was never certain who it was that she talked to, but it must have been someone she trusted. She complained about my father and his job. She complained about his money, which was never enough, and about his weight, which was always too much, and practically everything else about him. If he was really all that bad, then why in the world had she married him? As she told the story, there wasn't a thing about him that she cared for. It all seemed more than a bit stupid to me.

But after a while, I was able to tell of differences when she spoke. After a while, it was obvious when she was speaking to one of her girlfriends, one of her sisters, or when it was somebody else. My belief was that whoever it was, it was a guy because she always became ridiculous, just like the high school girls on my bus. But even as a first grader, I knew that married people weren't supposed to act like that. Weren't married people supposed to only be interested in the one with whom they were married? Didn't they make promises about that kind of thing? Didn't promises mean anything? Weren't promises important? Sometimes she simply made me sick.

When it was time to begin my first year in school, my mother and I somehow came to an interesting arrangement. It all happened at the kitchen table. After a long, drawn-out speech about being the oldest, setting a standard for the others, and all of that kind of nonsense, she then announced an interesting grade-card incentive. Her speech went along the following lines: First grade can be tough, especially when you skip past kindergarten, so you have to work really hard and put a lot of time into your schoolwork. So for a reward, she decided that she would give me one dollar for every A that I managed to get on my grade card. How about that? Money, money, money. I figured that she just might regret this.

School was a little tougher than I thought it would be, but I did have something to drive me as well as something to look forward to. It was even more difficult that my parents were always too busy to help me with my schoolwork. Every time that I asked for help, they always said that they had to spend all of their time with the other kids because they were younger and smaller. But I managed to figure out ways to find the answers on my own just as I always had. I simply had to dig into my work and find it all for myself. I quickly discovered that my books always told me everything that I needed to know.

But then the day that I had waited for finally arrived. I had kept all of my school papers, every single one of them, for all of the nine weeks. I was certain of what I would see on my grade card. I could not wait to get home that afternoon. That had to be the longest bus ride of my life. I remembered getting off the bus and tearing up the gravel driveway at a full run. Then I stomped onto the back porch, flung open the wooden screen door with a bang, and went looking through the entire house until I finally found her. I was beaming and knew it. Had my grin gotten any bigger, my cheeks would probably have split. But the look on her face drove all of that away. It was not what I had expected from her. Looking back, I really don't think that she expected what I had shoved under her nose either.

Straight As. My grade card was full of them, in every single subject, all seven of them. Was she in shock? Why wasn't she smiling? Wasn't she happy that I had done well? Wasn't she at all pleased? Wasn't she proud that I had worked so hard and had gained that much? She turned her back on me and just left me standing there in the kitchen as she walked away holding my grade card in her hand. She wasn't gone but only a few minutes. When she returned, she was wearing the same frowning and scowling face. She looked at me as if she wanted to say something, decided against it, and then handed me seven one-dollar bills. She stood there for just a moment and then announced that we would never ever do that again. It proved to be the very last promise she would ever keep to me for the rest of my entire life.

My first year of school went by quickly. It seemed as if spring had arrived almost before I was ready for it. I had two sets of cousins that lived on the same road but just a quarter of a mile north of my grandparents' place. Together we spent our free time either swimming in a pond or playing in the barns. We rarely ever got into any kind of real trouble as it was all just good, innocent fun. We threw rocks into the creek and swung from ropes in the barns from one side of the hayloft to the other. It was great fun, and I never wanted it to end. But then school was out, and things were about to change long before I wanted them to.

At the time, my mother's habit was to meet my father at the door as soon as he walked in from work. From that point until the man finally went to sleep, she complained and argued about everything under the sun, but especially where we lived. She really did hate that place. She let my father know that every chance that she could. She wanted a change and demanded it. Who could possibly stand against a never-ending attack like that, day after day after day? So, after a while, he caved in to her, just as he always did and unfortunately for all of us, just as he always would.

So then we moved to a little town where my mother had lived when she was just a kid. Even though the town was only ten miles away, it might as well have been a hundred. I knew then that I had to get used to a whole new school, a new neighborhood, new people, all new kids, and all kinds of new crap. What a bunch of junk it was. The two of them always did whatever they wanted. They never talked to me, and they never asked how I felt about anything. I believed that what I wanted out of life never mattered to them. I always wondered if anyone ever thought about how I felt about such things of life.

Second Grade: South Pendleton Street, North Cool Road, Eversole Road

Our new house was in a town so small that I could walk from one end to the other in less than twenty minutes. But even in that tiny little town I could see what the big picture actually was. It really didn't take that long for me to figure out, probably less than two weeks. A two-lane state highway divided the town evenly in half. On the west side were the older, bigger, and fancy houses as well as the newer ranch houses with all of the neat yards and nice stuff. On the east side of the highway was a short three-block downtown area. There was a post office, a grocery store, and a few other shops. Then there were the original neighborhoods with regular-sized houses, and just beyond that, there was the railroad. That was where our street was, on the other side of that railroad, literally on the wrong side of the tracks.

Our little street began at the main street that went through town; then it traveled south two blocks, crossed the railroad, and ran about a block and a half before it dead ended into a farmer's field. All of the houses there were really small, and most of them were quite old and in very bad shape. The yards weren't any better as they were really small as well, and abandoned old cars sat in most of them. It was almost as if all of the junk in the town had been dropped off there. That was my new neighborhood. I didn't care what my mother said about it. It sure was a lot better at the farmhouse. I was much happier there.

But even at the new house my parents still fought every night, however my father seemed to be doing it this time around. As I understood it, the little house had belonged to my mother's family somehow and was bought for taxes, whatever that was supposed to mean. Also, my father had gotten a new job with the newspaper back in the city ten or twelve miles away. I didn't know if they fought more about his working hours or about living in her old hometown with her old high school friends. He especially seemed to have had a real problem with that. I just knew that I didn't understand any of it. I figured that it was best for me to just try and ignore both of them. That just seemed to work out for the best.

Then there was the first day of school. It was horrible, and I just hated it. I hated every minute of it. It was as if I was put on trial for some kind of crime. My new second-grade teacher was very nice, but for some reason she insisted on having me stand at the front of the class where she introduced me to everyone. I guess that she had her reasons, and I suppose that they might have been good ones. But that also gave me the chance to look into the faces of all of my new classmates. It wasn't very good. I saw very little kindness there, more than a little disgust and only one or two potentially friendly faces.

On my first day, I naturally wore the very best outfit that I owned. However, I knew that my shirt was sort of wrinkled, that my jeans almost had the knees worn through, and that my shoes were kind of messed up. But should all of that really matter? Why was my appearance always so all-important? Was that any reason for those kids to look at me with such disgust? None of those kids knew me at all, and yet they thought that they had me figured out in just five minutes. It simply wasn't fair! I already hated the school, the town, and my parents for having brought me there.

But things were a little better in our own neighborhood on the other side of the tracks. We were in our own little kind of place, cut off from the rest of the town, there on our little dead-end street. That railroad was always a very visible reminder of just where our neighborhood ended and the nicer part of town began. Even in a town that small, the kids at school never let me forget exactly where I belonged. Nearly every day a group of older boys and girls always made certain that we never stopped walking until we crossed those railroad tracks. I guess they believed that we needed to be reminded of just where we had to stay as well as where we weren't wanted or allowed.

But even so, with a dozen or more kids close to my own age, we managed to keep ourselves entertained. Our street was long and straight to the guardrail at the end, so it was perfect for bicycle races and fun stuff like that. When dusk arrived and the streetlamps came on, it also made for a good game of hide-and-seek. All around us were cornfields that also promised endless opportunities for fun.

At some point that harmless and innocent type of fun took on a very different turn. There was a girl in the neighborhood. I believed that she was in the fourth or fifth grade. I wasn't really certain. I just knew that she was much older than I was. But the difficulties began when she began asking curious questions about the type of things that I didn't even begin to have answers for. At first, they were simple questions about boys and girls and our differences. But then the questions and statements became very complicated. I simply didn't have any answers for any of those questions. It made me very uncomfortable but also very determined to find those answers. I decided that it was time to ask for serious expert advice, and there was only one place where that could be found.

My uncle came to visit on a Saturday morning. He had driven to our little town to see the place, and besides, it gave him somewhere to go as he had just gotten his driver's license back after some kind of traffic ticket sort of thing. After my mother had shown him around the house and everything had settled, he and I went for a walk through the neighborhood and to the end of the street. After a very brief period of time, I became impatient, told him that I had a problem and needed answers from him that I knew that he had.

As soon as we sat down on the guardrail, I just flooded him with questions. I told him everything about the girl and the questions that she had asked. I told him that she had talked about boys and girls holding hands, kissing, and lots of other things that embarrassed me. I took a deep breath and then told him about the magazines she said her dad had hidden away in his garage that her mom didn't know about. I told him what she had said about the naked people in them and that she had asked if I wanted to see them. Then I told him that she had asked if I wanted to see her naked? I was shocked that my uncle wasn't shocked about by anything that I said or by any questions that I asked. We then spent the next two hours or more together. We talked about girls and boys, all about body differences, about how babies come into the world, and just what everybody thought about all of that stuff.

I thought it all seemed very interesting as he informed me of the social graces between the sexes. I was amazed at how one thing led to another and how it was all about taking the right steps. It was really interesting as he talked about human nature and how he said that relationships were supposed to operate. It was so much simpler than I had ever thought that it could be.

According to him, you saw a girl, there was something about her, and she was interesting to you. You decided to spend some time with her, and when you knew that she liked you, then you kissed her. After a little more time went by and she really liked you, she would let you know, and that was when it was time for all of the clothes to come off. He was really detailed about how all of that worked as he took me through all of the different ways that those things could take place. I thought that it was all really very, very fascinating. I would never in all of my life have guessed any of that stuff on my own.

He continued by stating that after all of that had gone on for a while, but only after I had gotten older, I might have found out that I loved that person. Then he added that I might have to go through all of that stuff a number of times. But when the time was right, I would know it. Then he continued, and on each point, he was quite clear.

She might or might not have been the one, because that was a tough thing in life to try to figure out. But the most important thing of all was to make sure that your head was clear, be positive, and know for certain just exactly what was going on. Only when I had tried everything, was absolutely sure about everything and had enough experience under my belt, then and only then should I decide that it was the person that I should marry. It was an incredible amount of advice. I would never have gotten anything even close to something that good from my parents. They probably wouldn't have even wanted to talk to me about it. I was so lucky to have had someone like him to talk to. How had he ever gotten to be so smart?

He answered every one of my questions, even to the point of saying that girls were a lot like cars: you test drove every one of them and as many of them as you could until you found the one that you wanted to keep. He had to be the smartest person that I knew. He was also the very best friend that I ever had. He was the only one who ever took any time to listen to me.

Then he did something very special for me. It was as if I had turned a corner in life. With everything that we had discussed at that time, he then let me try one of his cigarettes. Now that was pretty cool. I thought that he was a bit shocked as I did it without choking, not even once. Naturally, I had seen my parents and everyone in my family smoke for as long as I could remember. Therefore it really wasn't a big deal. However, he was so impressed that he let me keep a partial pack, gave instructions as to where best to hide them, and sternly lectured me about the dangers of matches. Then of course, I had to swear on my life that he had not given them to me. He believed that although my mother may yell at him, my grandma would probably skin him alive for it. But that was all good as I could keep a secret. I was already keeping plenty of them. With that, I was informed, armed, and ready to take on the world. I could barely wait for my first chance.

Later that afternoon, after my uncle had gone home, the older girl stopped me as I rode my bike. She said that she had seen something very interesting in one of her dad's magazines. It was something that two people had done together. Did I want to see the magazine or did I just want her to show me herself? I decided to follow my uncle's lead and told her that the magazines didn't interest me in the least and that I would rather have the real thing. I think she was shocked as her eyes became really big and wide.

So with that said, I parked my bike, and we made our way through a yard. We made certain as we went that no one watched as we zigzagged our way deep into the cornfield. Since it was late September, the corn was well over our heads, and it made for a nice secluded place. We decided on a spot, stopped, and it was as we stood there facing each other that she fully made the dare. If we both took off our clothes at the same time, she would show me what she had seen in her dad's magazines. I agreed to it, but then stated that she would then have to do something that my uncle had told me about. She asked what it was, but I refused to say exactly what it was, only that it was something that adults did. Then I added that if she were too scared, then the entire dare was off. At first the fear could easily be seen on her face, but she attempted to be bold and then reluctantly agreed. After all, a dare was a dare.

So as we stood there in the cornfield, we each removed our own clothes and then just stood there a few feet apart as we looked at each other from head to toe and back again. She took a step or two toward me, wrapped her arms around me, and squeezed me tightly about a dozen times. With that accomplished, she stepped back and then announced that we had now done *it*. Wow! Wow what? What exactly had we done? It all seemed to be a bit boring to me. I decided that I must have missed something. According to the earlier conversation that I had with my uncle, what had just taken place was as far from doing *it* as possible. But as quickly as the clothes had come off, we both had them back on again. In her mind, her part of the dare had been completed. Therefore, it was my turn.

As we sat down in the dirt with the cornstalks towering above us, I took out something wrapped in an old towel. She watched, with curiosity written all over her face. I then unfolded the towel to reveal my prize and the cigarettes. She protested at first, but after all, a dare was a dare, and being who she was, she was not about to back down. After all, she was the older one in the contest and was not about to be outdone.

I then followed my uncle's instructions implicitly. I took the pack, turned it upside down, tapped the back of it with my hand, and then let one of the cigarettes fall out. I put it in my mouth, tore a match off, ignited it, and cupped the fire in my hand. I then lit the end of it and took a long steady drag. It worked so perfectly that I leaned back onto my elbows and then handed the cigarette pack to her. She said no, that she would just try the one that I had going already. That was fine with me, but it couldn't have been more perfect. She gingerly removed the cigarette from my hand, took just a slight draw on it, and then choked until her eyes nearly bugged out of her head. I thought for a minute that she was going to faint because she nearly turned green. I took it back from her and casually finished it while she coughed and hacked her way back to normal. I had won the dare and was the victor. There was no doubt about it.

However, just two days later, it seemed that the word about our actions had gotten out to the entire neighborhood. I never really did know exactly what was said or who had said it, but no matter, the damage was done. Right then, even in our own little neighborhood, I was suddenly off limits to all of my newfound friends. Was it a case of just growing up quicker than the others? Or was it something else that I didn't quite understand yet? Was it the beginnings of understanding just how society worked? Did I really want to be a little kid anymore? It was bad enough in my mind that the word had gotten out to everyone about getting naked and smoking cigarettes. However, those were easily denied especially when the older girl didn't want to embarrass herself, and I certainly never bragged.

That itself was also a profound observation. It was to be something that I would turn into a lifelong habit. I could do whatever I wanted, get away with what I wanted, and do it much more often than I ever thought possible if only I didn't boast. It was one of two very good lessons that I learned. The other was that neither of my parents, even though I knew that they knew about the whole thing, not a single word was ever said. I had heard them talking about it late at night, but they only talked between themselves and never confronted me about anything. I just found it all to be very interesting.

But after a short period of time, either the stories went away or were at least half-forgotten. But I could still tell that some parents were not too happy with my hanging out with their kids. It was bad enough when you lived in an old junkyard of a neighborhood and you were still labeled as some sort of low life trash. It also didn't help when the other kids looked in the windows of our house, saw the filth and trash inside, and then reported that news to their parents. It seemed we were forever stuck with the labels that other people believed we needed. But such things were nothing compared to the problems that I was about to face.

It was later in the school year when the real turmoil began. The entire situation was absolutely terrifying. I was too afraid to discuss it with anyone, but also had no idea of how to deal with it on my own. There was no one for me to turn to. I didn't think that even my uncle could have helped me with what was going on. I also didn't think that anyone would ever believe me. It was just too weird and otherworldly.

At first the problem began with an inability to sleep. The problem wasn't my parents and their fighting, although that went on just as it always had. But oftentimes when my father was at work in the evenings at the newspaper, I could hear my mother in the living room as she did her astrology and other mystical stuff. She would read it all out loud, but only after we kids had gone to bed. She also did some other really weird stuff like chants and things with words that I didn't understand. It never really made any sense to me. But in a much different fashion, it bothered me deep inside in a way that I couldn't quite figure out. Then it progressed to the point where I started to be afraid to go to sleep.

It was the noises. Actually they were more than noises. I wanted to call them voices even though I couldn't understand anything that they said. At first they were so quiet that I had to wonder if I actually heard something or if my mind was playing tricks on me. I had to strain to hear that I actually heard something. Then in no time at all they became louder. I really didn't understand any of it. Was it because they thought that I was interested? What were they? Who were they? I even tried to plug my ears but that really didn't help. It seemed that I heard them from inside my head. Was I going crazy? Was I losing my mind? It would've helped if I could understand them, I thought. If only I knew what was being said. But maybe I didn't want to know what they were saying.

But although I couldn't understand a single word, the emotions behind the voices were very obvious. Anger, it was very great, vicious anger, and there was plenty of it. There was no wondering about that at all. But why were they so angry with me? What had I ever done? What had I done to them? What had I ever done to anybody? Who were they? What were they? At times it went on for hours until I could barely keep my eyes open.

But even then I still couldn't sleep for all of the voices pounding inside of my head. Then just as suddenly as it had begun, it ceased. In that instant, I almost sensed a fading away as I would literally fall forward and cried into my mattress. Why couldn't they just leave me alone? Then I always collapsed into an exhausted sleep.

Night after night the torture was repeated. It became just one cruel, vicious, and ruthless assault after another. It was the worst kind of torment, but one night there came an unexpected release.

It seemed almost twice as bad that night. After two long hours of it, I decided that I simply couldn't take it anymore. The pain and the turmoil inside of my head were more than I possibly could stand. I got out of my bed, stumbled into the hallway, and ran my hands down the wall in the dark. I tripped over trash in the kitchen and went out the back door with my hands over my ears. The voices pounded so hard inside of my head that I couldn't take it anymore. My head screamed in pain like I had never felt before, and as I leaned up against the house, the voices just became louder and louder. Then, when I felt that I couldn't take it any longer, I screamed out loud, dropped my hands from my ears, and ran out into the street wearing nothing but my underwear. My feet pounded on the pavement as I ran as fast as I could until I reached the streetlamp at the guardrail at the dead end. There I stopped and struggled to catch my breath. It was then that I realized that all of the voices were gone. They were simply gone and I instantly felt better. However, it certainly was chilly out there at night with next to nothing on. Then the thought crossed my mind that since the turmoil was over, perhaps I could go back home and try to get some sleep.

But as my bare foot left the pavement and touched the grass in the yard, the voices returned in full force, as if I had hit an immoveable brick wall. Instantly it felt as if my head was going to explode. They hit me with such force that I fell into the grass, crying and totally confused. I picked myself up and ran back into the middle of the street, and then I suddenly realized it.

The voices had stopped, and the barrier was the property that my parents' house stood upon. Also I was wet from the grass, and the breeze that moved down the street made me very cold.

But what could I possibly do? I reasoned that there wasn't much to do. In actuality, there really wasn't any choice at all. So I walked back to the end of the street and climbed over the guardrail. There I got as close to a bush as I possibly could and shivered myself to sleep. I stayed there until dawn.

But then, just as my life was becoming perfectly horrible, things became even worse. On one particular evening my father had gone into the city to work at the newspaper for the weekend run. As soon as he left, my mother suddenly decided that everyone needed to go to bed right then and there. It wasn't even all that late and I also had my own motivations. I knew that I didn't want these awful nightmares to start any sooner than they had to. But she was loud, nasty, and forceful as was her character, and therefore, we all complied.

So we went to our rooms, and for some reason that I really couldn't figure out, all of the kids were quiet. They just laid there in their beds and before I knew it, they were all sleeping loudly. I reasoned that perhaps it was due to the fact that they were all just scared of her, especially the little ones. But even after an hour had passed, it was all very quiet, with no voices to be heard, neither outside of my head nor in. What a relief! I didn't really know what to think of it all. Maybe for one night, they were actually going to leave me alone. As I looked around the room once more, I could see that everyone was still asleep. I just couldn't believe that all of them had sacked out that early.

But then there was a noise. Was it a door? It sounded as if someone had just walked in through the back door. I could see that a light was on somewhere in the house through the gaps around our bedroom door. Then I heard them. Voices and they were real voices this time. I could hear the people talking, but I couldn't quite make out the words. Who was it? I wondered.

Was it her? It sounded like her, but it also seemed as if they were all trying to be very quiet. Who was with her? What were they talking about? Then there was that same noise once more. Once again, I thought that it was the back door. The more that I thought about it, there was no doubt about it and whoever it was they just went back outside again. Then there was silence, not a sound, not a single noise to be heard. There was nothing at all. It was weird, very weird.

Fifteen minutes passed by. Then there was another noise. But it was a different noise this time. It sounded like something crackling, as if someone were crunching up paper or something like it. Then I stood up from the bed and looked around the room more closely. From around the door I could see that the hallway lights were flickering. First, they were off, then they came back on again, and then they went off for good.

It then became completely dark in the house as I strained my ears with everything that I had. But then there was something else to alert the senses. What was that smell? Was something burning? Had she left something on the stove again? Maybe not, but yet it didn't smell anything like food burning, it smelled different. Something about it just didn't feel right to me.

What was that? Even in that dim light in the bedroom, it seemed as if something was crawling around the gaps of the bedroom door. I couldn't tell what it was, and it was then that I became scared. At first I thought that I was just seeing things. Then I wondered if it was just like hearing things, but whatever it was, this time it was for real. It was then that the smell became much worse. Whatever the other thing was it had now crawled up the wall and was moving across the ceiling. That really freaked me out. What was it? Then reality arrived within my mind.

Smoke! Smoke! It was smoke! Was the house on fire? The house was on fire! I began yelling and screaming and woke up all of my brothers. Then I shoved them out of the bedroom and down the hallway and pushed them toward the front door. All the while I screamed at them to get outside, just to get outside! I then returned back the hallway to my sister's bedroom and did the same thing to them.

"Wake up! Wake up! Wake them up! The house is on fire! I" shoved them all down the hallway, through the living room, and right out the front door into the night air. Then I went into my parents' room only to find it empty. I was shocked and just stood there as the smoke swirled all around me. Where were they? My father was at work, but where could she possibly have been? The hallway was now thick with choking smoke as I traced one hand down the hallway and covered my mouth with the other. My eyes stung so bad that I couldn't keep them open. It burned my nose and lungs and nearly made me sick to my stomach. I felt the corner that told me I was in the living room and bolted for the front door. Air! Fresh air! I fell to my knees coughing and choking until my head hurt. Then I looked around.

There she was. She stood in the middle of the street with all of the kids huddled around her. In that all important moment, all that she did was stare at me. She never held her hands out to me. She never offered me comfort in any way. She just stared at me as if I had done something wrong.

Soon the neighbors showed up, and the sirens could be heard. Then, from out of nowhere, there was a cry and a scream. It was one of my younger brothers. His toys, he wanted his stuffed toys. Suddenly he tore loose from everyone, and screaming for what was most important to him, he ran. Before I could even blink, he broke loose from the group and ran directly for the burning house, yelling all of the way. Without thinking, I broke into a run, caught up with him, and tackled him to the ground. He kicked, screamed, and yelled that he wanted his toys and was angrier than I had ever seen him. A neighbor lady ran to our side, picked him up, and returned him to my mother.

There was nothing that I could do except sit there in the yard and watch as the black smoke rolled from the windows as the fire trucks arrived. Once the crews were there, more and more people began showing up. I watched it all for only a few minutes, stood up, and then turned away. I looked at everyone gathered there, walked past them, and headed down the street to my favorite spot. Once I arrived at the streetlamp, I sat on the guardrail, watched all of the commotion, and just waited. Foolishly I actually believed that after a few minutes, someone would have wondered about me, would have found me, said or done something. But it never happened. Even after the fire trucks had finished their work and had left, still no one came. No one bothered to find me. No one bothered to see how I was, how I felt, or anything else. So after a while, I walked back to the scene alone.

It was a mess. The house still stood, but only as a nasty, smoldering shell. My mother made the decision to return the following day after the fire department had completed their investigation. Thus far, the theory presented was that it probably had been an electrical fire of some kind. The authorities were fairly certain that it had started at some point in the kitchen. The plan was that on the following day, my parents and the older kids would return and attempt to salvage whatever possible. But where would we stay, not only that night, but the next night and the ones to follow?

The answer brought to me more than a little shock as well as a fair share of curiosity and fear. The decision had been made for us to stay with my grandparents. That would be my father's parents, the ones who lived in the farmhouse back the lane and on the hill. We would be staying with the very people that my mother despised, cursed, and hated. That would certainly prove to be very interesting. I wondered just how it was all going to work out.

That particular grandfather, my father's father, was a farmer and a carpenter. He was a good man, and, in fact, I believed that he was a very good man. He was nice but also was very strict. He had rules and simply expected them to be followed. If you broke the rules, then all of the fun was taken away. It was simple, it was easy, and I actually liked it in a strange sort of way. It was very hard to actually describe, but it almost felt comforting.

However, my grandmother, my father's mother, she was another story altogether. Among the grandchildren, she most certainly had her very special favorites. That much was always very obvious to everyone, and even I understood it. They were the cousins who lived closest to them and were the ones that she saw all of the time. Also, even though I was her grandson, at the same time I always felt that I was her enemy. She was never nice to me, and at times, with the looks that she gave, just her eyes alone made me want to run and hide. But even so, I knew that I had to try to get along with her. We would all be living in the same house, and I had no idea just how long that would have to be. So, I had to figure out a plan to simply stay out of her way. What other choice did I have?

At their house, the day after the fire, we had a big family meeting. The adults did all of the talking as we kids sat there on the living room floor and quietly listened. Together they laid out the rules as well as my grandparents' expectations. The entire second floor was ours as they had no need of it. However, it would be inspected on a daily basis. It was to be kept clean, and nothing was allowed to be out of place. There was to be no yelling, screaming, or running through the house. According to the rules, a house was for eating, bathing, and sleeping, while the outdoors was for work and playing. Such were the rules, and there were absolutely no options. Then we kids were sent outside in order that the four adults could have more discussions among themselves. As I was walked out, it was obvious by the look on my mother's face that she was just barely containing her anger and wasn't enjoying any of it one bit. She looked as if she had been sentenced to prison. However, I thought that it was kind of funny. But I didn't think that it was funny for very long.

Every morning we dressed and did it very quietly. That always felt strange as we certainly never did that at home. Then we filed silently downstairs, sat at the kitchen table, and ate our breakfast in absolute quiet. No one was allowed to say a single word. This rule was enforced by my grandmother who never let us out of her sight for a minute while we were downstairs. Then we three oldest kids went off to school, returned in the afternoon, and then sat at the same table for at least one hour to do our schoolwork. Then and only then did my grandmother permit any playtime. It was how my father had excelled in school, and my grandmother believed that it would work just fine for all of us.

In the beginning I thought that I might enjoy our time on the farm. However, after two short weeks, a terrible habit began that nearly destroyed everything and me along with it. I did anything that I could and tried everything possible to avoid it. I tried anything and everything in order to keep it from happening again. But every Saturday morning, no matter what I did or how I tried to avoid it, it happened just the same.

It was horribly repetitive. We went downstairs, ate our breakfast, and then returned upstairs for teeth and face cleaning. Then all of the other kids hurried downstairs and went outside. Then my mother, believing that we were all gone, would drag herself outside to do the chores that my grandmother had assigned to her. I knew she hated having that woman tell her what to do. I always heard her mumbling, cursing, and calling her names under her breath. After she went downstairs, I watched out of the upstairs window and waited, wondering if I could have made it outside with the others that time. Whenever I had gone down with the rest of the kids, she always called my name and singled me out for questioning. So I avoided her whenever I possibly could.

I crept down the stairs as quietly as I could, avoiding all of the squeaky parts and holding my breath almost the entire way. The bottom of the stairs opened into the kitchen. Once I had gotten that far, I could see out the kitchen window above the sink. I could also see the back door, and it was so close, so very close. But it might as well have been a mile away. She and I were always in the house alone. The attack always came out of nowhere.

"AAAHH! MY HAIR, MY HAIR, MY HAIR!" My scalp felt as if it was on fire! It was her, my grandmother. With one hand she had my head by my hair with an iron grip and a fistful of shirt with the other hand. Through gritted teeth, her angry words flew with spitting force into my face. The words were always the same. It was my fault that her son's life had been ruined. My mother was useless, worthless, and according to her, she was a tramp and a whore, whatever those words meant. She had great plans set in place for her son's life. He was supposed to graduate from college and was supposed to become someone with a respectable career. Because of my mother and especially because of me, all of those plans had vanished. His life was ruined. Then with another nasty yank of my hair and a horrible scream from her, my feet completely left the floor. Bastard! Bastard! What in the world did that mean? I didn't understand the word and had not heard it before. I guessed that I needed to look that one up.

Then with her face less than an inch from my nose, she once again declared that she wished that I were dead. Better yet, she wished that I had never existed. If I wouldn't have happened, if I wouldn't have come along, then her son's life wouldn't be the total disaster that it was. With those condemning words slammed into my brain once more and with a barely stifled scream, she threw me by the hair across the kitchen. With incredible force, I slid along the tiled floor and slammed painfully against the cabinet doors below the sink. I just lay there in agony.

Pain, pain, pain! My head hurt so badly that I couldn't open my eyes, and my scalp felt as if it were on fire. It hurt to even touch it. My side hurt, my knee hurt, and I knew without looking that my body was already turning black and blue. It even hurt to breathe. As I lay there sobbing, I could barely open my eyes and was afraid to even try. I was terrified that she might still be there and that she wasn't finished with me yet. Maybe there was more that she wanted to do to me. But as I opened my eyes, I found that the kitchen was empty. I struggled against the pain and grabbed for anything that would help me to stand. Once again, I looked around for her, but she was nowhere to be seen. But I knew that she was still in that house somewhere.

Not being able to see her was almost as scary as having her shouting in my face. But I knew that it was my only chance to get outside. I knew that I had to do it right away! I ignored the pain and ran out of the back door with a slam, knowing that she would be angry about it. But I didn't even care.

Run, run, run, I told myself as I sprinted to the back edge of the field. I ran until my lungs burned, and I could barely see anything because of the tears. There, next to a fence, was a large oak tree, and up into its hiding leaves I climbed. There no one could find me, and no one would bother to look. I decided to I stay up there all day if it were necessary. Although I didn't understand her anger, there certainly weren't any answers to my questions. Why did she hate me so much? What had I ever done to her or anyone? Why was it my fault? Did everyone in the family hate me?

Despite the frequent abuse, the weeks passed quickly, and soon it was near the end of the school year. Fortunately we hadn't stayed at my grandparents for that long even though I felt as if it would never end. My parents rented a farmhouse just outside of the little town, which made it easy to finish the school year. It was very quiet and peaceful there, just as it was at my grandparents' farm, but no one bothered or did anything to me. There were even some interesting things to observe while we lived there. The biggest event happened during the spring on Palm Sunday. I never expected to witness anything like it in my life.

It was a typical Sunday morning and we did what we always had done around the house. We never went to church as my grandparents, and the rest of my father's family did. After all, what was the use? If going to church still let you abuse little kids, then what was the point in going? But then again, my mother always reminded us that she didn't like or agree with anything about church. She always reminded us that she had more than enough of that useless stuff when she was a kid.

It began as a normal and ordinary spring day. Then as we played outside in the yard, the sky suddenly became all weird yellowish looking with big dark-blue and black thunderstorms that towered off in the distance. From two miles away in the little town, I then heard a siren going off. Immediately I wondered if there was a fire in town. Then suddenly, it became very quiet as the birds stopped flying and even they became silent. Nothing moved, nothing at all, not even the slightest bit of breeze. It was really very strange. Then my mother came running out of the house all freaked out, wide-eyed, and yelling like a crazy person. She screamed for everyone to get inside the house and to go down into the basement. However, I stayed behind, sat on the front porch in an old metal chair, and watched as it all happen.

There it was, off in the distance, perhaps a mile or two away I guessed. It marched directly toward us from the south, a dark-gray and white funnel cloud that came down from out of the sky. It looked as if it were something alive. It was dark, angry, and powerful, but at the same time it was just so cool to watch. As I observed, it crossed the open fields and plucked trees out of the ground just as I would have pulled dandelions from our yard. It moved with an unbelievable speed. Soon it was less than a mile away from where I sat.

Across the field on the next road over I watched as it touched a barn and stood to my feet in amazement as it just exploded into toothpicks. It was absolutely the most unbelievable thing that I had ever seen in my life. I was in awe as I had never before seen anything like it. It was the most amazing thing in the world to sit and watch. As it was now closer, I could see swirls of dark color, black, gray and brown combined with ground pounding power. Then it suddenly just marched away toward the east until it was out of my sight. The next thing that I knew, the skies cleared and the siren in the little town sounded again. Within minutes, police cars and fire trucks could be heard wailing off in the distance somewhere. It was then that my family came out of the house. My mother had a completely bewildered look on her face as she stared at me in a way that I just couldn't comprehend. I could tell that she was really angry with me, but I simply didn't care. I had a ring-side seat for the most awesome show in the world.

But just as it was with everything else that I enjoyed, the show came and went, and so did the school year. Summer arrived, and that meant just one thing: we were moving again. I just hated it. That meant another house, another neighborhood, and another blasted school. I wondered what it would be like. I was certain that it would be another chance to stand in front of a bunch of kids and be judged by how I looked, by my clothes, by my hair, and naturally, by where I lived. They wouldn't even know me, and yet they would still believe that they had me all figured out. Ha! Not a chance. No one could do that. They didn't have a clue. They were just like all of the rest.

Third Grade: West Robb Avenue and East Market Street

Our new house was on the northwestern edge of the city. It was an older house, much older than the houses around it, but it had a big yard, which was most important to me. There was also room to play in a small wooded area nearby, which offered opportunities of exploration and escape from my family. After a short time, I actually began to believe that my parents' latest choice might not be a bad one after all.

The first day of school was exactly what I had expected. The teacher was nice enough, but she still forced me stand up in front of the class in order to introduce me. I knew that I was being sized up by some of the boys, while others just made faces. The girls were even worse, making nasty faces, gagging noises, whispered, pointed, and laughed. The ordeal seemed to last forever until the teacher finally finished. All eyes were on me as I took my seat, and I felt like I just wanted to die. I hated changing schools, and I hated meeting new kids. I hated new houses and neighborhoods. I just hated everything about it. Why did we always have to move? Why couldn't we ever stay in one place? Why couldn't I simply attend one school until I graduated? My cousins were allowed to do exactly that. It would have been so nice to actually live somewhere long enough to make friends and to know people outside of my family. I truly hated my life.

As kids, we played outside from the very first day and ran all over the place. We discovered, as we always did, that our neighbors did not want us in their yards. Were all neighborhoods the same? Were they all full of mean, nasty people who thought that their yards were museums or something that was in a magazine? Who wanted a yard that was so perfect, you were always afraid to mess it up? Was everyone like that, and why did they hate kids so much? Were we really all that bad?

One particular evening, after my parents had gotten tired of hearing us run all over the place, we were ordered all of us upstairs. But instead of camping out in a corner of the living room, hiding behind the sofa sleeping or reading a book, I was stuck in one of two small bedrooms with all of them. I just hated those little brats. They were always running, screaming, and fighting with one another. On that night I just couldn't take it any longer. So I started yelling at them. Then one of the little brats grabbed one of my model cars in his grimy little hands and threatened to break it. I cornered him and tried to get the car away from him. He instantly began yelling that it was his and quickly broke a wheel off it. It was then that I lost my temper. I threw a fist at him, missed his head, and drove my hand right into the wall.

In shock, I pulled my hand out of the wall as every kid in the room became instantly quiet. Then a voice from downstairs yelled a question. As if in response, all of them went tearing down the stairs yelling about what had just happened. Then I heard the real heavy footsteps and knew that both of them were on their way up. I just stood there, crossed my arms, and waited. Initially they were angry with me, but with one look at the wall, their anger quickly turned against our landlord.

Cardboard. The walls weren't built with drywall or plaster but were nothing more than painted cardboard. As we had just experienced a house fire earlier in the year, this discovery created quite a bit of drama. My mother was furious! She began yelling firetrap, firetrap, as if she was possessed or something. She screamed at my father first and soon thereafter at whomever was on the other end of the phone. Personally, I had enough for one day and just wanted to get some sleep. So I ignored them all, found a corner piled with boxes, and pulled a blanket over my head. However, my troubles were far from over.

The next day at school proved to be just as miserable as all of the rest. My classmates made fun of my jeans, my shoes, my shirt, and even what I had packed for lunch. What a bunch of nonsense. They teased and tormented me while informing me that I was nothing but trash and didn't belong in their fancy suburban school. I hated that school! I hated the rich, snooty kids, and I really hated my life. But something was about to happen that I would like even less.

As soon as I stepped off the bus, I was instantly angry. It was a familiar scene, and I knew exactly what it meant. There in our driveway was my grandfather's station wagon, and behind it, his homemade wooden trailer. I had seen this sad movie far too many times before. We were moving again.

Our short stay in suburbia had lasted less than two months. Therefore, half of our stuff was still packed away in boxes. But here we were once again, half a dozen cars filled with all of our junk as we headed to another house, another neighborhood, and another school. I was so angry that I could have spit in someone's face. I was furious, but no one listened, and no one apparently cared. Where were we moving to *this* time? I found out in short order that I really didn't like the answer that I would soon receive.

The caravan of cars stopped at the curb of one of the busiest streets in the city, and I just couldn't believe my eyes. I knew that the suburban school had been a pain and the kids were awful, but at least our house was on the edge of town, where we had room and a yard. The house standing there in front of me was something far different. It was an old paint peeling, ancient-looking, two-story dump of a place. It looked absolutely horrible. If that house had been a car, you wouldn't have been able to drive it, and if you could, you probably wouldn't have wanted to. The houses on either side were close enough that you could have spit on them from the bedroom window. There was also a nasty-smelling river a few doors down, and the railroad tracks were only three blocks away. Those two items made one thing clear as day. We were living in the slums again.

But even though I hated the place from the start, there was something very weird and oddly familiar about the neighborhood. It was a strange and quite curious feeling that I simply couldn't describe. It was as if I had an itch in my brain that I couldn't scratch. It was there from the very first moment that we arrived, always in the back of my mind and it never left me alone.

My first day at the new school was interesting in a number of ways. It was the first time that I had changed schools during the school year, which proved to be a less than wonderful experience. On my first day, as I put on my very best clothes, which weren't very good at all, I thought about the neighborhood. With that I wondered if just maybe these kids wouldn't care so much about my clothes. As I thought about those issues and everything else, I naturally wondered why my life had to be such a never-ending disaster. My cousins never had to deal with any of this sort of nonsense. They always had nice clothes, lots of other neat things, and they had lived in their houses forever. I really didn't think that I knew anyone else who was forced to live in this condition.

However, the school was only three blocks from the house, so the walk was very short. But when I arrived at the school, I couldn't believe what I saw. The school in the suburbs was new, neat, and clean, but the one in front of me was something else entirely. It reminded me of one of those big, old, and scary mansions on television. It was dark and nasty looking, and even the sign above the door said that it was almost seventy years old. I was certain that I was really going to love the place.

I walked up to the first adult that I spotted and asked him for directions. He looked me up and down and then sent me on my way. He certainly wasn't very nice, but his instructions were good enough, and I had no trouble finding my new classroom. My new teacher was there at the doorway. She was young, not old like all of my other teachers had been. She smiled at me and stooped down to my eye level. While she talked to me she reached over and buttoned my shirt collar as if she cared about me and how I looked. I really liked that. She seemed very nice, and with that, I began to believe that perhaps the new school wouldn't be so bad after all.

The bell then rang, and my teacher brought me to the front of the class, stood behind me, put her hands on my shoulders, and introduced me to everyone. I thought it was nice, and I appreciated it more than anyone could have known. Some of the kids looked a little mean, but none of them appeared to be snotty or snobbish. Actually the majority of them just looked bored. Most of them were dressed a little better than me, but not by very much. I thought to myself that maybe this new school would be just fine.

After the first month, I discovered that it actually wasn't too bad. Our house didn't have any yard to play in, and the school was just okay, but my teacher always had something nice to say every morning. That more than made up for any problems that I could have named. However, there were a couple of smart-mouthed boys who always had something to say at recess, but I ignored them and kept to myself. As I was the new kid, I figured that they believed that they had something to prove. It seemed to me that they were just trying to look tough and scary.

But one particular day those same boys tried to start a fight at recess. It began as they surrounded me in a circle and put me into the center of it. Naturally, the biggest of them was their leader. He made a point to say a lot of mean words and added a few nasty names for good measure. I believed that he was trying to make me cry, but after all, my own grandmother had said far worse than that. When he finally realized that his words weren't going to work, he shoved me. When he did, I lost my balance and fell down into the gravel. But before it went any further, the teacher on the playground ran up to us and stopped everything. He then sent me back inside the school building to clean myself up.

When we returned to the classroom from recess, at first everything seemed normal enough. But then I noticed the tough boy and his friends as they sat together whispering. When the bell rang at the end of the day, I followed my daily habits. I got my coat, walked out of the building, jumped down the steps, ran across the street, and then headed for the house.

Ow! What was that? My leg screamed in pain. As I looked across the street, I spotted them, all four of them armed with stones in their hands. One of them had gotten me in the leg but good. So I just stood there and quickly went over everything that my uncle had told me about situations just like this one. He had instructed me that there were certain things to watch for, to never panic, and to always wait for the right moment. So I just waited.

They yelled and called out more names, but mostly they repeated the same ones they had used on recess. I said nothing but silently motioned for them to cross the street and join me. They looked at me, looked at each other and then quietly asked questions of the tough boy. So I stood there with my arms crossed, stared at them, and never took my eyes off any of them just as I had been taught.

The four of them got close to the curb on the other side of the street while the tough boy talked. When their talk was finished, they sort of lined up on the other side of the street. Then they said a few things about my mother. I just shrugged my shoulders with enough exaggeration, which meant that I didn't care. After all, it wasn't anything that I hadn't heard before. As we looked at each other, it appeared that we had reached a stalemate. I then decided that it was time for the ultimate weapon.

That was when I used what my uncle had always called the fight starter. He had warned me not to ever use it unless I was prepared to fight because it always started a fight. According to him it never failed to do so. In his experience, it had worked every single time. It wasn't just a finger, it was *the* finger, and I presented it to each and every one of them from my spot across the street. All the while, I never took my eyes off the tough boy. Then sure enough, my uncle was proven to be right, as from across the street they came. It suddenly became a case of now or never. I either had to do what he had taught me or allow myself to become a coward and then permit everyone in the new school to push me around. I had to make the decision. He also had said to never change the look on your face. He said to never answer their challenges, but only react to them. That made the choice incredibly easy.

They stepped over the curb on my side of the street and surrounded me just as they had on the playground earlier that day. Then the tough boy stepped into the circle, got right in my face, and began yelling. Then all of them began yelling. Right on cue, everything happened just as my uncle had told me. As they yelled, I closely watched the tough boy's hands. As I remembered my uncle's words, he said to watch his right arm bend and then just before he made a fist, I had to quickly make the move. So, just at that moment, as he did what my uncle had predicted, I saw the opportunity, took my chance, and drove my fist right into the tough boy's nose.

It happened instantly, taking but a mere second, as he dropped screaming to the ground. His hands were over his face as the blood then began to run through his fingers. The other three boys were instantly silenced, and then two of them just ran off. The other one looked at me as if it were an all new experience. But the truth of the matter was that I had to admit that I actually enjoyed what had just happened.

As the remaining boy helped the tough boy to his feet, I turned on my heel and walked away. I never looked back, and I never heard another word from any of them. Within me, I felt a welling up of pride that I had never felt before. I couldn't wait to tell my uncle everything.

Upon arriving home, the house was the same as it always was when I walked through the front door. Kids were running and screaming throughout the place, and no one spoke in normal words or volume. The television blared loudly as my parents fought so much and with such intensity, it seemed as if they wanted to kill each other. I was still keyed up from the fight just a few moments before and really needed somewhere to relax and calm down. I only wished that I had a place to go, to hide, and to just be alone. However, in the new neighborhood, there was nothing to be found.

Weird, it was the only way that I could describe it. School on the following day was just weird. My teacher said never anything to me, not even the first word. She didn't look at me, talk to me, or anything of the sort. Had I done something to upset her? Had I done something wrong? Just what was going on there that day? Additionally, as I walked into the classroom, I felt the stares as everyone looked at me and then turned their heads when I glanced their way. Later, at recess, I saw those same boys huddled together at the fence, as they talked and looked my way. They were all there but one. I didn't see the tough boy anywhere in school throughout the day.

Recess had barely started when the teacher on the playground walked up to me with another man and stated that I had to go to the principal's office. What did I have to go there for? I had heard stories about what they did to kids inside that office. I didn't want to go there! I wondered if it was about what had happened with those boys. Within my heart I knew that was the issue.

Once inside, they showed me to a hard wooden chair in the hall and, with a finger in my face, sat me there and warned me not to move. Then they just left me there for well over an hour. At first I was bored, then I became frustrated, and then my nerves became set on a razor's edge. Unfortunately, there was a clock on the wall, so I knew exactly just how much time had passed. Also, even though they had the office door shut tight, I could still hear a lot. Actually, I heard just about everything that they had to say, even though I couldn't tell for certain just who had said what. It all came to me in bits and pieces.

From what I could gather, it seemed that those boys had been in trouble before. The biggest one was always bullying someone around the school. It wasn't the first time that he had been caught in the middle of something. But then I heard them state, over and over again, that they did have rules there, and punishment had to be carried out. Then I heard them say that my mother had been called. Evidently, she had been informed of the doctor's report and had thrown a nasty, foul-mouthed fit about the bill. They decided that the issue was ultimately between the parents since it had occurred off school property. Therefore the school didn't have anything in it. As for my mother's opinion about any punishment for me, she didn't care what they did. She also added that she wasn't coming to the school and that they could do whatever they had to do.

Then the door opened, and the two men brought me into the office and sat me in a chair across from a big desk. They both took turns as they went into a big speech about what was right and wrong. They talked about violence and how it supposedly never solved anything. Then they informed me of my punishment. I was going to get five whacks of the board, and as they spoke I could see that board. It had eight holes in it. The principal had it hanging on the wall behind his desk, just over his left shoulder. I had been looking at it throughout his entire speech. My uncle had told me about that too. Boy, was it ever going to hurt.

Then, just as my uncle had informed me, the instructions began. I had to walk to the end of the desk, put my palms flat on the surface of the desk, and then hang on for dear life. Then in just a split second, a strange whistle was immediately followed by incredible exploding pain. Oh man! How was I supposed to live through that? No sooner had the thought passed through my brain when another blistering swat arrived on my backside. Tears and more tears. How could I possibly take any more of this? I wasn't at all familiar with any of that sort of discipline. I certainly hadn't gotten any of that at home. It hurt worse than anything that I had ever felt before in my life. That guy was brutal. After the third swat, he stopped, forced me stand up straight, looked me right in the eye, and asked if I was ready to apologize to the boy whose nose I had broken. My uncle had informed me about that tactic too. So, I had a response for the man with the whistling board. Not a chance. Then I looked *him* in the eye without blinking and demanded that he give me the last two hits.

It appeared that he wasn't ready for that response because he laid the board down on the desk and walked directly out of his office. But as I stood there, I wondered just what was I supposed to do now. I wanted to sit down, but there wasn't any way I could physically do that. My butt was throbbing, burning, and screaming in pain. But I wondered just where the men had gone and what were they going to do to me. Then I became angry. Why was I being punished like that? After all, I hadn't done anything more than to defend myself. Did I really deserve that kind of punishment? So I just stood there in anger without any answers and waited.

He returned ten minutes later and stated that there was to be no more boarding that day. But I would receive failing grades for the day and then sent home. Great, that meant that I could go to the house and soak my stinging butt. Man, did it ever hurt. But I also knew what was in store for me when I got to the house. I was sure to receive a lecture from my mother about how much money I was going to cost her and, on top of that, nothing but mustard sandwiches for lunch. I could hardly wait. Whoopee.

But later that night, I received a phone call that made it all worthwhile. Together, my parents had lectured me together about my actions for ten minutes before they turned on each other. But at least my uncle was proud of me. He asked me for every detail and kept me to my word that I didn't puff it up. I also told him that my parents didn't say anything about the entire situation except for the money. Then I asked him for the truth. Had I done the right thing, or was I completely wrong? Should I have stuck up for myself, or shouldn't I? I didn't start the whole mess, but I believed that I had finished it. He agreed with me and told me that he was proud of me. I also believed that it had worked out for the best because I didn't have any trouble from anyone else for the remainder of the school year.

But there were other problems that just seemed to never go away. My parents still fought like cats and dogs every single night. However, she always said much more than he ever did. In a way it reminded me of those four boys, a lot of screaming, name-calling, and threats. She was far worse than he was and could she ever curse. She could peel paint off the wall. I really learned a lot of words from her. But in addition to all of those things, there was one other situation that was a life-changing event. It was frightening, bewildering, and incredible all at the same time.

That evening had been especially bad. It was in the spring, and it was almost warm outside. She started in on my father just as soon as he had walked in the door after work. She called him every name in the book and then some, changing his first name to everything but his given name. It was a very bad night of it. It was so bad that he finally got in his car and left with a lot of tire and racing engine noise. I knew that she had given him an ultimatum. I had heard it with my own ears. It was the standard or else, or else, or else. I knew what she had meant by that, and so had he. That was something else that my uncle had explained in detail to me. It was all about how and why women threaten, and what little there was that men could do about it. It really didn't matter. It was always her way, no way, or a full-out war. She was always the only one that ever won those things.

Ten minutes after he had left, she walked out onto the front porch with a slam of the front door that made me cringe. I had been sitting in the part of the yard that was a couple of feet above the sidewalk, next to some thick bushes. The street was always busy, and I liked to sit there and call out cars by the year, make, and model as they went by. It was a fun game, and I had done it for years, ever since I had been little. My grandpa and uncles had gotten me started doing it a long time before at their house. But in addition to the cars, it was also quiet there, with no fighting parents, no screaming kids, just a little alone time. Around our house and with my ridiculous family, I had to take what I could get.

Also from that vantage point I could see her, but she couldn't see me. Through the bushes I watched as she stood at the top of the steps, at the end of the porch, and stared directly ahead. What was she looking at? Her jaw was set hard, and she tightly clenched her teeth. Then abruptly, she sat down on the step, put her hands over her face, and began to cry. I had never seen her cry. It was all too weird. What in the world was going on here? The drama went on for fifteen or twenty minutes. Then suddenly she stopped and put her hands on her lap. As she did, I could see that her face was tear-stained. She wiped each cheek with her sleeves, but she continued to stare straight ahead. What in the world was she looking at? Then I drew a line from her face and eyes to a position somewhere across the busy street.

All that I could see was a house. It was just an ordinary house, a white house in fact. But it actually wasn't a house so much as it was a duplex, a two-family dwelling. I had never really paid much attention to it before or anything else on our busy street. But evidently that house was of some importance to her. But what was so special about that particular house? What did all of it mean? Whatever it was, it had to really be something important that it made someone like her cry. But as I thought about it, somehow the place seemed a little familiar to me as well. Then as

I realized it, I instantly felt strange, uneasy, and cold as my skin suddenly crawled and became full of goose bumps. What was it?

However, the more that I thought about it, the more that something strange stirred deep within me. It was as if something told me that I knew the place. What was it about that house across the street and my mother's angry and crying stare? The two of them were tied together, that much was obvious. I wondered if it had anything to do with why she hated living in this neighborhood. Was that one of the reasons she fought with my father so often? But the real unanswered question was still *why*. Why? Within my mind it then began coming to me bit by bit, as if they were tiny crumbs of understanding. Then suddenly it hit me with enough force that it literally rocked me back into the dirt.

Why did I know that house? Oh man! Oh man, oh man!! That was it! That was it!

As I sat there, I was completely blown away by the sudden awareness of the facts and fought to catch my breath. It was then that I fully knew why she hated that place. But my mind fought against it as I thought that it really couldn't be it, could it? Could that actually be the truth? But despite my questions, despite my wanting another answer, something inside of me kept saying yes. From somewhere a quiet, polite, and still voice just kept saying yes. Could that really be it? It was no wonder that she was so upset. Every day at this new address must have been pure torture for her. It must have reminded her of everything that happened on that most ugly of nights so very long before. I knew then that I would never look at the house on the other side of the street the same way ever again.

It was years in the past. My little brother had died in that house. That had been the very house where I had found him floating face down in the bathtub. In that instant, it all came back in crisp, vivid, and horrible detail. Recollection came bluntly to my mind as every word, sound, and even every smell marched through my brain.

I remembered my father's terrifying roar, the way that it shook the entire house and me along with it. I still remembered the awful way that he looked at me as he carried my brother out the front door. Even then, I still wondered, by that look of his, if he somehow believed that I had anything to do with what had happened to my brother. Did he still think so, even to this day?

I remembered that my uncle came for me and that I had stayed at my favorite grandparents' house for a long time. I remembered all of the questions that the adults had asked each other the next morning. I didn't have any of the answers at that time, but I had them now as I stared across that busy street. I knew what a drowning was. I knew exactly what a bar was. After my uncle's many talks, I knew enough about boys, girls, my mother, and her boyfriend at the bar. In that moment, I knew for certain why she hated that place and why she and my father fought every night. I also knew why she was always so sad. I also believed that she deserved to be sad. No matter what happened from that point on, one thing was certain. I knew the truth.

As I thought about those things and many others, my mother just sat there on the edge of the step. But just then in an instant, she changed before my eyes. Previously she had been broken and crying. Now she suddenly became very defiant. As I watched, her hands balled into fists as if she were ready to fight with someone. Then she stared angrily at the house across the street as if it were her sworn enemy. Then, I watched in amazement as she actually shook her fist at it. Then, she spun on her heel, marched onto the porch and back into the house, slamming the front door hard enough to break a hinge loose and announce her actions to the entire neighborhood.

That night, as I sat alone on the porch roof and just outside of my bedroom window, I could hear the two of them. It actually wasn't much of an argument at all. She merely gave him orders.

They were orders that were pure and simple, flat and final. It was her "or else" declaration, and it was very detailed, clearly defined, and to the point. She left absolutely no doubt in my mind about how she felt. She ordered him to march into work the next day, go directly to his boss's office, and demand a raise and a promotion as well. That was that, and there was no room in the conversation for any debate.

If it weren't for the girl talk that my uncle had discussed with me, I wouldn't have understood the rest of her ultimatum either. But I certainly understood it fully now. From thereon out his life wouldn't be worth living for a minute. He had no choice whatsoever but to give in to her. He was to go after the supervisor's job at the newspaper first thing the following day, and he would do whatever it took to get it. Then he would get her out of that dump, into a decent house, or she would find someone who would. He knew full well that not only could she do it, but that she would also do it. I knew that I had learned at least one very important lesson from that night: I would never marry a manipulating witch like my mother.

School was out soon after that, but we never stayed at the house. As soon as my father left each day for the newspaper, she packed a big lunch for us and loaded everyone into the car. From the house, she took us to the city park where we stayed for the entire day. We played on the swing sets and the other equipment and ran all over the wide-open spaces. But in my mind, I silently wondered about the sudden change.

Was it the house across the street? Was it because she didn't have to watch us at the park? Or was it because while we were occupied, she always walked away from the play area every day to sit with someone in a dark-blue sedan? I was certain that she never gave any thought as to whether any of us saw her or if we knew what she was doing. But I knew that I did. I had watched her do it almost every single day. When I talked to my uncle all about it, he had some answers. He filled me in on all of the details of just what might have been happening in that car. It was sickening. My father was such an idiot, and he probably always would be.

The park visits only lasted a few short weeks until the moving announcement came. A house had been found, and it was in a much better neighborhood than any that we had ever lived in. We were told that everything would have to be different. There would be rules, there would be structure, and they would be enforced. Although I knew what that meant for my father, I wondered just exactly what that meant for all of us.

Fourth Grade: South Nye Street

I quickly found out that everything at the new house was going to be far different than anything I had experienced before. Even before we moved in, I realized that both of my parents had gotten new jobs. My father had taken my mother's threats seriously and had been successfully promoted to the foreman's job at the newspaper. My mother had also gotten a job, working at the hospital just three blocks away.

But life took an even different turn as while they were both away at work, a babysitter was now hired to stay with us. I didn't care for that particular turn of events. It was all that I needed, just one more adult to watch my every move and to give me orders.

On the other hand, the new house was quite nice. The neighborhood itself was so unreal to me that at first I couldn't believe that we actually lived there. The place was so completely different than anywhere we had ever lived before. Every yard was mowed, and everything on the properties was neat and tidy. Absolutely everything was in its proper place. Every car was either in the driveway, in a garage, or parked along the curb. As I walked through the neighborhood, I never saw anything out of place. There were never any old cars to be seen sitting behind any house. There also wasn't a speck of trash or litter to be found anywhere. Just what kind of place was this? Had we finally arrived at last? Were we finally able to live in a place that I could actually be proud of? Were we finally going to live as normal people do? It almost felt as if I were dreaming.

The school itself also seemed to be different, even before my first day. One evening, two very nice ladies knocked on our door and introduced themselves to us. I watched from the dining room as my mother talked to them. One of them did make a bit of a face when she told them what school district we had come from, but that was the extent of it. As the conversation continued, they made the school sound so good that I actually looked forward to attending.

On the first day I discovered that the school was actually everything that the ladies had said that it was. Although it wasn't the newest school in town, it was nice, and everyone seemed to be very friendly. My class was great, my teacher was wonderful, and I made straight As in no time. My teacher seemed to like me a lot, and I got along fine with nearly everyone in my class. Had I finally arrived at last? Was this what life was intended to be?

That school year proved to be the best year of my life. My teacher was so good, she was so helpful, and she paid attention to me every day. I actually made a few friends and never developed any trouble with anyone. In fact, I never even encountered the first sign of a fight. But despite that fact, my two uncles decided that it was the appropriate time for me to learn proper self-defense. They believed that such a talent was an essential part of growing up. They took it upon themselves to instruct me in street fighting, something that stressed no rules and only surviving. I was intensely curious, as I certainly wanted to be a survivor and then some.

The younger uncle, who had just begun his military career, also began giving me first-level lessons in martial arts. However, his emphasis was always on defense and never offense. He continually stated that his instructions were only for self-protection and nothing more. I found that it was all very interesting.

At the new house, I had also gotten my very first job. The neighbors next door were a very nice couple, older than my parents, and with no children in their home. I soon learned they were all grown up and gone. The gentleman taught me how to use his lawn mower and was very detailed in his instructions. He was also very serious about safety, maintenance, and always cleaning the machine afterward. He showed me how to trim around sidewalks, bushes, and trees. Later, as winter arrived, he also taught me all of the little tricks to shoveling sidewalks and driveways, where to put the snow, and how to break up the ice. He and his wife were the nicest people, who gave me a little bit of money, home-baked snacks, and a fair amount of advice. It actually felt good to work hard and even better to be rewarded. But the very best of all was to be thanked and appreciated.

But there were other incredible things in the neighborhood that I found interesting. In the very back part of our yard was a large tree. One of the jobs that the neighbor next door had given me was to take apart an old and quite large doghouse. He instructed me on the proper use of a hammer in order to separate the boards and how to carefully remove the nails. He was never one to throw away anything of value, so he showed me how to straighten the nails with a hammer and a brick and to keep them in an old soup can. Then as he showed me where and how to stack the lumber, he stopped and declared that he had an idea. He asked if I wanted to build a tree house. I had never thought about it before, but I was delighted and honored with the idea. I believed that it would be perfect to have a place of my own and out of the reach of my brothers and sisters. I was overwhelmed that he wanted to do something like that for me. I hadn't felt that special for a very long time.

There really wasn't enough wood to construct a complete tree house, but with his help, I managed to accomplish quite a lot. As we began, the two of us sat in the grass beneath the tree with paper and pencil. As we talked, we finally came up with an idea. Therefore every day after school I worked on my new special project.

First, I nailed the supports into the tree. Then I used the boards from the sides of the doghouse for the floor. We nailed them across two branches that spread out from the tree. The other two sides of the doghouse were used for the roof by nailing them to some branches that were similar to the ones that we had used for the floor. An old fruit crate with a hinged lid was used as a seat and for storage, and it took up about a third of the floor space. Then when we were all done putting it together, we painted it all a light shade of green from a can that he had brought up from his basement.

So there it was my own little space away from everyone. It was high enough in the tree that I could almost see into the second-story window of our house. Even though it didn't have any sides for safety, it was still very comfortable to me. Since it was later in the spring, the leaves actually helped to make walls for the place. It felt so good to sit up there on the crate with a book to read and with my back against the tree. The wind would blow a little bit sometimes, and the tree would sway, but it almost felt as if I were being rocked in someone's arms. It made me miss my grandma. But even so, it was just too good.

After about six months of living there, something happened within our family. It must have been good news because suddenly my mother was very happy and smiled all of the time. I hoped that it wasn't because she was pregnant again as we certainly didn't need any more kids in the house. She was always pregnant it seemed, so I really hoped that it was something else. But what really seemed strange was that even my father was in a good mood, and as I thought about it, I couldn't remember the last time when I had heard them fighting. Was that how life was actually supposed to be? Was this how a normal family acted?

Then there was the announcement. My father was getting another promotion at the newspaper. It was a new and very important executive-level-position job. He would be making more than double the amount of money that he was currently earning.

That explained everything as to why my mother was so happy. She was always all about the money. It was her favorite thing to talk about and the only thing that seemed to motivate her. In the days that followed, I overheard many of their conversations. I gathered that my father's boss had secretly told him that he had the new job. But since it wouldn't be official for about a month or more, he had to keep very quiet about it. There were details of some sort that had to be worked out, whatever that meant. But that really didn't matter, for as long as those two were happy, it made it better for all of us.

The next thing that I knew, both of my parents began bringing all kinds of new stuff home nearly every night after work. One day it was new lamps, then it was video equipment, then a new stereo, and it just went on and on. I heard them talking in the living room every night about our new life and how great it was going to be. It was then that I heard the real news. The new job was out of town. I didn't understand as I had thought that the new job was at the newspaper? What was the deal there? When were they going to tell all of us? That meant that we would have to move again. I just didn't understand why we had to move again. I liked everything about our neighborhood. I didn't want to leave. Life had finally gotten to be just how I wanted it.

One Friday evening, once both of my parents had gotten home from work, they sat all of us at the table in the dining room. As was always the case, my mother did all of the talking as my father just stood there with his arms crossed and nodded his head. It was then that my mother began her speech.

As I understood it, my father had gotten the promotion and would be given the official word and date of when to start the new job in about two weeks. The new job would pay much, much better than the one he currently had. In fact, it paid so much better that my mother would be able to stay home. The worst part of the deal was that we would have to move as soon as school let out for the summer. For although my father's new job was still in the newspaper business, it was with another newspaper in the same chain of newspapers, but in another state and city. That got the kids all excited, and when my mother added that it was in a city near the ocean, they really got carried away. They began yelling and carrying on and were all happy and everything. But the questions raced through my mind: Would I ever see my uncles again? Where would we live? Would the house be as nice as that one? Would I be able to build a tree house there? What were the schools like? But the biggest question in my head was, did we really have to move again?

It was Saturday morning the very next day. My mother, moving very quietly and with coffee cup in hand, woke me up and whispered for me to go downstairs to the dining room. As I rubbed the sleep from my eyes, I stumbled down the steps to find that it was just barely six o'clock in the morning. The sun wasn't even over the trees yet. What in the world did she want at that time of the morning? As I walked into the room, she was sitting at the table and motioned for me to sit in a chair next to her. I stubbornly decided to sit in one across the table from her. With that, she just grinned and then began talking.

With one of her hands around her coffee cup and a cigarette in the other, she began to speak in a quiet and kind voice. That was completely out of character, and I was instantly on my guard. She spoke of how mature she believed that I was for my age. She then stated how for the second time in my life the authorities at school had offered to skip me a grade. Why would I want to do that? What was she talking about? Just what was she getting at? Where was she going with all of this chatter? What was she up to? Why all of a sudden was she acting so nice to me?

Then she began talking about my uncles, how the three of us were so close and just how important we were to each other. Then she added that she had already talked to both of them and that they had agreed with her decision. I was instantly confused. She had talked to them about what? They had agreed with her about what? I didn't think that they agreed with her about anything. To hear the two of them talk, they never even liked being around her. She should have heard some of the great names that they had for her! So, what was she talking about?

She continued running off the mouth about a lot of sweet and nice stuff until it was obvious to her that I couldn't stand it anymore. Then she stopped speaking, stood up, walked into the kitchen, and poured herself another cup of coffee. She returned, lit another cigarette, and began talking about our neighbors, those who lived next door. She talked about how good they were, just what they thought of me, and how much that I had learned from them.

I agreed that they were very good people. It was also true that I had learned a lot from them. They never shoved me away when I had a question, never silenced me when I tried to talk about something, and never ever ignored me. They always listened to every word that I said and always seemed to care. So what was she talking about? What was the point of this early-morning conversation?

She stared into her coffee for just a moment, took a long drag of her cigarette, and stated that the family would be moving within the month. We were headed south. Everyone had been talked to, and everyone had been consulted. The decision that she was about to reveal to me had been made, and there was nothing about it that could be changed. Then she looked me straight in the eye, paused for a few seconds, and then let the hammer drop. I don't remember the exact words as she spoke them as the shock was far too great, but I knew exactly what she meant. She informed me that I was staying behind.

WHAT? The family was moving, and I was being left behind? Everyone was going away out of state, and I would have to stay behind? But I was only ten years old! They couldn't just leave me behind! I knew that at my age I didn't have any say in anything, but this was ridiculous. But her response was a very angry negative. Inside of my head, I fought with myself about the whole ordeal. No, I didn't want to leave my uncles, and yes, our neighbors were great, and yeah, maybe my life would be better. But was that how things were supposed to be done? My heart was instantly filled with abandonment as it went cold and dark.

But then I stopped, quit thinking, and decided to just shut up. However, I wondered just why she now looked at me as she did? I wondered why, in the midst of my obvious inner turmoil, was there a smile on her face? How could she be happy about such a decision? Was the sight of seeing me upset pleasing to her in some way? Was that the result that she wanted? Did leaving me behind make her happy? Did it make everyone else in the family happy? Didn't they want me in the family anymore? Did they all hate me? In the middle of all of the turmoil that went on inside, she continued to look at me with that same stupid smile. Then she got up from the dining room table, refilled her coffee cup, and walked out of the room. She just left me sit there. It was just after six o'clock in the morning, and she just left me sit there at the table to deal with my broken world alone. Everyone else was still upstairs sleeping as I sat there alone in my turmoil. I was there by myself, and for all intents and purposes, I was abandoned already.

Then I got mad. I became very angry and totally upset. I really didn't know what to think other than I was completely confused. I just didn't know what to do. I stood up from the table, knocked the chair on the floor, and ran out of the dining room. I went through the kitchen and then out the back door. As I stood in the backyard, there was only one place to go, up into the tree, to my only place of safety and comfort.

Once I was there, the questions flooded through my mind. Why didn't they want me? Why didn't they want me to go with them? Didn't they want me in the family anymore? Didn't they care about me? Had they ever cared about me? Was that why they never spent time with me? Was that why they treated me so much differently than the others? As I sat on my crate and leaned against the tree, I felt the breeze as it swayed the branches, and I missed my grandparents more than ever. Despite the height from the ground, I curled up on the floor of the tree house and I just cried myself back to sleep.

I spent that entire day in my tree. I had no appetite and wanted nothing. I was simply angry. I was angry with them for what they had done, and I was angry with myself. But I was also sick of crying and acting like a little baby. It was then that I made a serious decision. Never again, they were not worth crying over, none of them, not a one of them. I was sick of all of them. They never cared about anyone but themselves.

My father was gutless as he would do whatever she wanted. He was always too afraid that she would run off and find someone else. Well, as I thought to myself, it was just a little too late for that. That time had come and gone already. He was a coward and a stupid fool. But what about her, how did I feel about her? I found within myself in that tree house that day that I hated her. I really hated her. She had told me that she was leaving me behind, and she did it with a smile on her face. With that, I was glad that they were leaving, all of them, but especially her. Although I thought that it was true, that I would be better off living with the neighbors, I still hated her. But I didn't care about any of them anymore, especially her.

The long-awaited day finally arrived as the big announcement at the newspaper was made. It had been ten days since my mother had made her grand announcement to me. Since that time she had been busy making her plans for the great move down South. She had boasted to everyone who would listen just how perfect and glorious everything was going to be. However, I had already put everything that I owned but my clothes into my crate in the tree house. I had even been eating all of my meals there. I found it quite interesting that no one ever bothered to stop me.

I happened to be at the neighbors mowing their yard that afternoon as I noticed my father arriving home much earlier than normal. It was early in the afternoon, and it was very odd as he never came home that early. As he got out of the car, I could see, even from that distance, that he wasn't feeling well. He looked sick—really, really sick. He was very pale, and he didn't seem to be able to hold his head up. I turned the mower off and watched as he walked up onto the front porch steps of our house. He moved very slowly, and as he reached for the door handle, I saw him pause. Then I watched as he took a deep breath, opened the door, and walked inside.

It wasn't but a few minutes later when I heard my mother's voice. She screamed, and it was loud, very loud. However, it wasn't a scream as in the movies; it was something completely different. It was a deep and angry scream, full of raging and boiling hatred. I couldn't hear the words, but I knew her voice. It was bad. It was very bad, and it didn't sound as if she was going to stop anytime soon. I would have bet anything that she was just peeling skin off my father's back side with her words. I really didn't know what it was about, but if she didn't like it, well then, that was just fine with me. With that, I simply smiled to myself, turned the mower back on, and finished my job. I cleaned the machine up and had supper with the neighbors as I always did on mowing day.

When I walked out of their back door, I was surprised to see all of my brothers and sisters sitting in a group in the backyard. The older two looked worried, but the younger ones just played and didn't seem to care. Then my sister gave me the shocking news.

Later that evening as I sat in my tree house eating an extra piece of desert from the neighbors, I thought it all over. Justice was so sweet. There was no promotion. In truth, it actually sounded as if there had never been one for him. As the story went, there evidently was some kind of betrayal at the newspaper. It seemed that a friend of his at the newspaper had somehow snatched the job away. It was all a little vague, but very interesting.

But somehow, I just couldn't seem to keep a smile from my face. However, I knew that I had better put on my best poker face before setting foot inside the house.

But all was not completely lost as my father still had the supervisor's position. But that didn't seem to help my mother's mood at all. She could still be heard screaming and cursing at him every evening and even hours after he had gotten home. I heard her stop every now and then, but only momentarily, for as soon as she caught her breath, she started all over again.

It was getting late, but as I looked down, I could see that the other kids didn't want to go inside. It was obvious that they were scared and terrified of her. But even so, just how cool was everything? I really couldn't help but laugh. If there really was a God of some kind out there somewhere, then maybe my mother was getting exactly what she deserved. I know that I was certainly enjoying it.

However, not getting that promotion changed everything in the household. First, they fired the babysitter. Then my sister and I were left in charge of the little kids. I didn't know what my parents would have done if school hadn't just gotten out. But then I didn't think that either one of them really cared about any of us. But really, what kind of a decision had my parents made? My sister was only nine years old, and I was but ten, and yet we had to watch those brats all day long. Wasn't that just great?

With every passing day, the condition of the house just became worse and worse. When my mother came home in the afternoon from the hospital, she did absolutely nothing. Her routine was to sit on the sofa, smoke her cigarettes, and watch television. My father, on the other hand, worked every hour that he could. Oftentimes that meant double shifts, and once he arrived home, he practically collapsed in a chair. It all seemed a bit ridiculous. But the worst was yet to come.

By the middle of the summer, people from businesses in town began showing up and taking things away. First, it was the television, then the stereo equipment, then all of the video stuff. Then it was the washer and dryer and even some of the furniture. The house would have probably looked bare if it weren't for all of the trash, clothes, boxes, and all of the other stuff that lay around everywhere. Nobody wanted to listen, nobody would listen, nobody cared, and I finally just gave up. Each day, as soon as my mother came home from work, I just went outside. I didn't want to be around her. She was the last person that I wanted to spend any time with.

By the end of summer, the house had literally turned into a garbage can. Nothing was picked up, and nothing was ever cleaned. We would have used a sweeper, but a man knocked on the door and took that away too. I knew that I could probably have done more, but I had tried, and I knew that my sister still tried, but I was done with it all. Besides, I had work to do next door and would rather be there anyway. After all, if my parents didn't care, then why should I have bothered?

The house and the kids themselves looked so bad that after a while other family members started asking questions and then tried to do things for us. There were offers to do the laundry, to clean the house, and even to fix some decent meals. My mother took all of those generous offers as personal insults and screamed at anyone who was ever brave enough to offer the second time. Did she like the house to look that way, didn't it matter to her, or did she just not care? So, with that in mind, just what were we, as mere children, supposed to do about the situation? Was that any way to live? Could it possibly get any worse?

One day as I mowed the yard at the neighbor's, a plain-looking brown sedan pulled up to the curb. Inside the car were two people, a man and a woman, and they were both dressed very nice. He looked like a banker or something. I wasn't sure exactly what they wanted because I didn't think that we had anything else that could be taken away. The lady was in the passenger seat, and she put an arm out of the window and motioned for me to come over to her. I turned the mower off and walked over to their car.

They asked about mowing the yard and other questions such as was I enjoying my summer vacation and did I like my neighborhood. Then she asked if I knew the family next door and pointed to my own family's house. To myself, I thought that was an interesting question. It was obvious that she believed that I lived at the neighbor's house, and so I naturally decided to play along. Sure I knew the family. As I talked to the lady and answered her questions, I noticed that the man wrote something on a tablet of paper. Then her questions continued.

Had I ever been inside the house? What did it look like? How clean was it? Where were the parents during the day? Was there an adult in the house during the day? Was there ever an adult there during the day? What did the kids do all day? What were the parents like? Did I know what happened there in the evenings? How did the parents treat the kids? The man wrote down every answer as I gave them to the lady. Then she told me that she didn't want to know my name, because it was always better that way. She then thanked me for my time and apologized for interrupting my yard work. Then she told me to have a good day as the two of them drove off.

As I continued mowing, I wondered just what that had all been about. Who were those people? Who did they work for? Why were they so interested in my family? Something inside of me told me that it wasn't good. But then I wondered if I should I have talked to them. Should I have told them all of that stuff? What were they going to do with all of that information that the man had written down? Should I have been honest and told them who I really was?

Two days later my mother suddenly came home at noon. She was upset, not angry upset as she usually was, but worried-sick upset. The look on her face was bad, really bad, something that I really had not seen before. Although I had seen her upset plenty of times before, on that day it was very different. Actually, it seemed that she was more than just upset. I believed that she was scared out of her wits. Something had really gotten to her. As soon as she hit the door, she gathered all of the kids in the front room and then sent my sister to find me. When I walked in, the younger kids were all upstairs supposedly cleaning their rooms. Then she gave me my orders.

We then spent hours and hours working as we filled bags and boxes with trash. One of my aunts stopped by, and my mother filled the trunk and the entire backseat of her car with dirty laundry. A few hours later my father arrived home with a big van from the newspaper. He backed it right up to the rear door of the house as we hurriedly filled it with bags and boxes of trash. Then he took it out to my grandparents in the country to be burned.

We were in a lot of trouble! Actually, the family was in trouble, and it was very, very serious. Listening in on my parents' conversations as I worked revealed that someone had called my mother in secret. Whoever it was informed her that the house was to be inspected the very first thing the following morning. A group of people from a place called Children Services was due to arrive at the house, and it would be very bad for us if they didn't like what they saw. If the house wasn't clean, they would take the kids away, probably split us up, and then we would never see anyone that we knew ever again. I would never see my uncles again. That was completely unacceptable.

Was it all because of me? Was it my fault? Was that the reason those two people had been there that day and asked those questions? But I had questions and concerns of my own. Would they really split us all up? But then again, the more pressing question in my mind was, wouldn't we all be better off? Wouldn't our lives be better? Wouldn't it help our lives to be normal? Living in that neighborhood and practically living next door most of the day had taught me a number of things. Most important of all, I had learned just how normal people lived, and that was certainly not how my family operated.

But that was the kind of life that I wanted. After all, wasn't it just a couple of weeks or so before that the whole family had been more than ready to leave me behind? Hadn't they made plans to do just that? So what difference would it have made if an agency had done it? Maybe I shouldn't have been so worried about it. What was the big deal?

It was after eleven o'clock that night, and I thought that everything had been done. Everything was clean enough I believed, and I was dead tired. All of the other kids were upstairs and asleep by that time. Therefore, I was more than ready to call it a night. Every bone in my body ached, and I was long overdue for a night of good sleep. As I headed for the stairs, *she* marched across the room and blocked my path. Then she grabbed me by the shoulders, spun me around, and shoved me toward the back of the house.

When we walked into the kitchen, she handed me a butter knife, a bucket of soapy water, and pointed me to the ground-in filth on the linoleum floor. So for the next four hours, I scraped black crud from the floor with that knife and water. By the time that I had finished, my hands were prunes, and my fingertips were red and raw. Why did I have to do that job? Why was she always so mad at me? Had she found out somehow that I had talked to those people in the car? But the bigger question to me was, who had told her that they were coming the next day?

Then, with the job finally done, I turned out the kitchen light, walked into the living room, and discovered her asleep on the sofa. Now wasn't that just great? As I slowly made my way up the stairs and around the corner into the bedroom that I shared with my three brothers, I stopped for a moment and made a serious decision. I just didn't want to live there anymore. I really had wished that they had moved out of state. But even if I was stuck with them, I decided at that moment that I would stay as far away from them as I could, whenever I could, even if I had to do with as little as possible. With that decision set in my mind, I grabbed my blanket, walked downstairs, and went right out the front door. In the crisp summer, very-early-morning air, with the moon and the stars shining, I curled up in a corner of the front porch. There with peace and quiet and some fresh air, I went fast asleep.

Sixth Grade: West North Street

We had moved from the house on South Nye Street when the sheriff came knocking on our door. My parents obviously hadn't been paying any of their bills for quite a while. They had been stashing all of their money somewhere. I had heard them talking about it late at night after my father had gotten home from work. But we were ready to go when the police showed up at the door to do their job. We had already loaded everything that we wanted to take into the newspaper van, our station wagon, and onto my grandfather's trailer.

When we moved into and then out of the slum duplexes on Euclid Avenue, we pretty much followed the same sorry process. But I really regretted leaving that tree house. I had put a lot of time and effort into creating my own little place. In many ways, it almost seemed that I grew up there to some degree. But there was far too much history at that address for me to ever possibly tolerate. I was tortured nearly every waking moment there after the event. Moving from that place was probably the best thing that happened to me.

The duplex on West North Street wasn't a much better place to live either. It was about the same size as the one on Euclid Avenue, but by that time we had grown to be a family of eight kids with one more on the way. That meant that we had eleven people living in a small three-bedroom house. It wasn't even on a miserable little street as before, but on a busy state highway that ran through town. It was interesting in that it was only two blocks from the hospital where my mother worked, just on the west side of it instead of on the south. However, I did have to give up my newspaper route since we were living on the other side of town. Although it was nice not having all of that responsibility, I really missed the work, the people, and the little bit of money that I was able to make. But one thing was for certain, I really didn't appreciate having to change schools again. On that occasion it occurred once again during the school year, not long after the court hearing.

So, once again, we were in a new place and in a strange, new neighborhood. Once again I had to start all over again at another new school. But everything was a lot worse than before because I had no job, no friends, and that horrible court incident. With that event now confined to history, I had lost my relationship with my uncle. I had absolutely no one to talk to anymore. I just couldn't stand any of it. Was it any wonder that I hated my parents? Was it really all that hard for anyone to believe that I hated my family? But even deeper still, I hated my life, and I especially hated moving again. But then, I didn't have to bother with it all for too long because living at that particular address didn't last more than just a few months either.

But that address was a milestone as my youngest brother was born while we lived there as kid number 11. That numerical definition accurately described how we were all known in our sorry family. I was number 1, and I also knew that was exactly where I was on my mother's list of things that she didn't care for. She had made that abundantly clear to me throughout my entire life. There were some things in life that simply required no guessing at all. I knew within the deepest part of me just how she felt about me. Or so I believed.

During the summer, just after I had completed sixth grade, my parents began looking at houses once again. The major difference was that they were looking for a house to buy, not just some place to rent. At first I thought that they were kidding me. I had difficulty believing that it was true. I thought that it was amazing that we were actually going to get our own place to live. In my mind I believed that it meant that we wouldn't ever have to move again. I couldn't help but wonder just where would it be? My mind kept going back as I thought about my cousins and their homes. Then fantasy over took me as I dreamt of what and where it would be. Would it be a ranch style house in the country? Would it be a big two-story house on the north side somewhere and on a nice quiet street? Just where would it be? I listened in on every conversation as best as I could. A lot of the stuff I didn't understand. But I needed answers. I really wished that my uncle had been there to answer some of those questions for me. I missed him a lot and felt so alone.

By that point in my life, just before I had begun middle school, my family and I had moved a total of sixteen times. I had experienced no stability, found no lasting friends of any kind, and possessed nothing of any real value to hold on to. Was it any wonder that I always felt so alone? Was it any wonder that I was always so desperate for someone or something that would make me feel needed, wanted, and valued? Therefore the diabolical trap had been set, and it would be sprung soon enough.

Aloft
Seventh Grade: South Harrison Avenue

It was the middle of August when my parents announced that a house had been found. I knew that my father had many conversations with my grandfather, his father, the farmer, and carpenter. During the evenings while he was on the telephone, I had heard the two of them talking all about structure, flooring, furnaces, and a bunch of other boring stuff. It sounded as if everyone was going to meet the following Saturday afternoon at the new house just to check it out and then decide if it was the right place for us. For some strange reason, one that I didn't even understand, I was informed that I was to go along. But curiously, none of the other kids were. I wondered to myself why? Were my parents just trying to make me feel important? Was I supposed to be a part of the decision-making process? Did my opinion actually count, but if it did, then why? Was there some sort of plan in the making? I figured that I would find out soon enough.

As I sat in the backseat of our old sedan, dozens of questions about the house kept running through my head. Where was it? What did it look like? Was the yard big? What school would I be attending? My mind just ran off with it, and I conjured up all sorts of things. I envisioned that the new place would be just like my cousins' homes with nice big yards, living in a ranch-style house, having nice clothes, and living the good life. But something in the back of my mind kept telling me that it just couldn't be. But still, I certainly hoped that I was wrong. I really began to wonder what was going as we drove straight through the downtown area and then past the newspaper building. That wasn't the way to any of the nice neighborhoods; they were in the opposite direction. Then as we turned south past the school that I had attended in the third grade, I felt myself getting depressed.

At the light, we turned left on East Market Street and past the two places near the river where we had lived before. We crossed over the bridge and then turned right onto a skinny, little brick-paved street. That was when my depression really set in. All of the houses on that street were the two-story type, tall, narrow, and really old. If I were to have guessed, they were, at best, in average condition or worse. Therefore none of it was the stuff that my dreams were made of. Perhaps my ideas were all wrong, but when someone bought a house, shouldn't it have been in a better neighborhood than where you were renting?

Our car came to a halt at the curb of a house on the west side of the street with an alley that ran on the south side of the lot. I looked out of the car window in total disbelief. It was a complete dump. Even before I got out of the car, I could tell that the place needed a lot of help and then some. It had all of that fake brick shingle siding on the outside, the screens in the windows were all torn out, and everything else had paint peeling off in chunks. It was obviously vacant and appeared to have been so for quite some time. It was also apparent that the previous resident had left quite a lot of their stuff behind. I had questions about their actions as well. In particular, I wondered why had they left in such a hurry, and had they been evicted too? Or maybe it was just easier for them to leave all of their trash behind for someone else to clean up. It wasn't as if my family hadn't ever done that before. With that, I got out of the car, leaned against the rear fender, and took it all in. I knew that I wasn't really hoping for a mansion or anything close to it, but somehow I actually thought that it would be at least a little better than what was before me.

But then, as I thought about everything, I decided that maybe I should just give the place a chance and take a quick look around. I walked around the front of the house and to the left, then down the alley, and into the backyard. What a beautiful setting that was! It looked like an actual junkyard! It was as if it the entire neighborhood had dumped all of their unwanted stuff there. As I took it all in, I made a mental list of my visual survey. A lean-to garage was poorly attached to the back of the house. There were all kinds of boards and other lumber in piles strewn all over the place. Halfway back in the yard was a ten-year-old compact coupe-style car that sat on blocks with no wheels on it at all. The entire place looked pathetic.

Then I stopped and looked at the tree. At first I couldn't believe what I saw. It was the most perfect tree that I had ever seen. There were a half dozen other trees there in the backyard, which kept most of it in shade. But just past that old car and toward the back alley that ran north and south was a huge oak just thick with branches and leaves. Then my brain suddenly woke up, and it hit me, those piles of lumber!

I rushed up to the house and now looked at everything in a completely different light. I quickly put together quite an impressive inventory. There were two-by-fours, a lot of planking, a barrel full of nails, and even two rusty but usable hand saws. The place was a gold mine in disguise! I couldn't believe my luck! I had to look at it all twice. There was everything in that yard that I would ever need to build a proper tree house. Additionally, there was even tar paper for the sides and shingles for the roof. It was just too good to be true.

With that accomplished, it was time for a good look at that tree. As I stood beneath it and then climbed up into it, there at the halfway point were big, thick branches that spread out perfectly for just the right-sized place for me. It was even better than I had thought, and it was much more than I had hoped for or had dreamed of. That tree was really it, the real deal. Then I dropped back to the ground and headed back up the alley past the old car. Then just as I had walked past it, I stopped.

I turned and walked up to the car, wiped the dust off the window with the bottom of my shirt, looked inside, and it was then that the idea came. It stirred around inside of my head, and then all at once, it quickly became a plan. All of the windows were still in place so I opened the doors to check out the interior. It had red bucket seats, a nice backseat, and everything was in good shape as there wasn't a tear to be found. Every house needed furniture, and it appeared that I had discovered the perfect furnishings for a tree house.

Then my planning reverie was broken as I heard her calling out my name. I always hated it whenever she did that. So I put on my usual performance as I strolled slowly up the alley as if I were surveying everything until I returned to the front yard. There she was, standing there with her hands on her hips, all impatient and ticked off. What did she want this time? But before she could speak, I informed her that I thought that the house was just great. Then I asked just how soon could we get it and when could we move in.

It was just at that moment and before she had a chance to respond that another car pulled up to the curb behind our sedan. It was my other grandparents, my father's parents. As they parked, I looked from their car and then to my mother. It was always interesting to watch her reaction to their arrival. It happened the same way every time. Just as soon as she recognized the car, she always bristled. Her eyes would squint, her nostrils would flare, and then she would clench her teeth in pure anger. But when my grandmother got out of her car, their eyes locked as if they were mortal enemies. I could always tell what that meant as the next battle in their personal little war was just about to begin. The hatred between those two was something that you could literally feel whenever you were near the both of them. It was almost like watching two old alley cats as they squared off over territory.

But there was something very important about the situation that was understood by our entire family. My father was my grandmother's absolute favorite as he was a true momma's boy if there ever was one. The whole incident was quite strange, it was oddly funny, and it happened all at the same time. But I knew my audience all too well. So, I played the part of a young gentleman, said my hellos to them all, and then left the adults to their stupid little games. Then I went around the corner of the house and down the alley to really eyeball that inventory once again. It was then that I began to seriously put together plans for the tree house. Those plans also included much more than just the structure.

I spent the entire month of September in full-blown construction mode. My first step was to use a saw to remove the little branches and to clear an area in the upper part of the tree for my new residence. Then I measured off two-by-fours and hauled them up into the tree. I measured them out for the floor, for the roof, and made certain that I had enough slant for the rain to run off. Then I brought the sheeting boards up into the tree one at a time. They were big, bulky, and heavy, which made for muscle-aching work for a short, skinny, little kid. Once they were nailed in place, I covered them with tar paper to keep the wind out and any warmth in. Then I added shingles to the roof in order to keep the rain off. After every ounce of daylight had been used up, I had accumulated more than a few blisters and scrapes. Once a whole bunch of sweat had also been spent, it was finally finished. From the back of the house, or even from the alley at ground level, my little dwelling could barely be seen as the branches and leaves were so thick. Someone couldn't even get a good look at it until they were standing almost directly beneath the tree. It was just the sort of privacy that I had planned for.

Once inside, the layout was designed in the form of a lopsided rectangle, but with enough room for two or three people to bunk out. The walls consisted of three solid pieces, a doorway, and one window where I used a roll of tar paper for opening or closing. It was absolutely the best tree house that any kid could have possibly had.

But a house needed furniture, and it was then that I set my sights on the abandoned car sitting in the yard below. Since it was a compact-sized car, I believed that the interior pieces would be perfect for the job. I didn't have too much trouble unbolting the front bucket seats, but the rear bench seat was quite a chore. Once I had it out of the car, it was fairly easy to haul all four pieces up into the tree. By putting a nail through each of the holes in the seat frames, I was able to position my new furniture exactly where I wanted it. A shallow wooden box that I had found in the lean-to garage made for a good bookcase, and a couple of old quilts made the place seem like a real home. It felt so good to have a place of my own. It was so incredibly relaxing to just to sit up there, away from everyone and have the breeze gently rock me to sleep. It was great just to be left alone and to do whatever I wanted to do. What more could a guy possibly ask for? In my heart I believed that I could have lived there for the rest of my life.

But the age of twelve years was a strange time of life to travel through. Everything changed quickly, and everything seemed so much different than before. It was also a confusing and frustrating time. Everything was different, but everything was, in a fashion, nearly the same. It was almost as if the entire world had been painted with a different brush or with different paint or something else that was unknown. It was more than just puberty and the associated body changes. It went far beyond all of that.

Admittedly, in the days ahead, it was true that the tree house provided opportunity for illicit actions, which created issues of their own. Therefore, in order to answer my questions and with no uncle to advise me, I had to make quite a few trips to the public library. That, in and of itself, was quite a new event for me. Before, whenever I had wanted an answer to any of my questions, I had just asked my uncle for anything that I wanted to know. But those wonderful days were gone.

Although I happened to see him once in a great while, he always seemed too busy as he now had a family of his own to attend to. At least, that was the reason that I told to myself. Every encounter with him was now brief and had nothing but a few polite words spoken. It pained me beyond belief. All of the closeness that had been so prevalent between the two of us for years had disappeared. It was obvious that I just didn't fit in with his life after everything that had happened on Euclid Avenue. I believed that I really was the one to blame for all of that.

Another part of that problem was that I just wasn't comfortable around anyone in the family. I really didn't understand it, I really couldn't describe it or define it, but I felt like a complete stranger to the extended group of people that comprised my family. It just felt too weird. I felt so very much alone and completely isolated from everyone. I knew that a good portion of it was my own doing. I knew that I gained more comfort when I sat up in my tree house and read a novel than I ever did spending time with my family or even hanging out with any of the kids from school. I just knew where I was the most comfortable and felt the least amount of pain.

But there were other, more public changes that went on as well. My father had made it possible for me to get my first real job. At the newspaper, he had obtained the position of mailroom supervisor. This was the department that took the finished newspapers, sorted them, bound them, and shipped them out to destinations within a ten-county area. On Sundays, every customer received a newspaper that was big enough to be a log in a fireplace. At least half of it was made up of the weekly color comics and advertisements from stores around the city and at the mall. The setup within the mailroom was that high school boys stuffed those advertisements one by one into the comics. Then they were bound by twine and then delivered to paperboys all around the area. The more advertisements that there were, the more stuffing that was required to be done, and therefore, more money was to be made. It all operated off a weekly deadline, and sometimes that meant working right up to that deadline late on Friday evenings.

On an average, the mailroom recruited about a dozen or so high school boys. The unwritten but always understood and honored rule was that every employee was to be sixteen years of age due to all of the machinery in the department and the subsequent safety issues. But since my father was in charge and a few of my older cousins already worked there, he bent the rules so that I could begin when I was actually four years too young for the job. However, it sounded like a great plan.

It was as if the job had been specifically designed for me as I caught on to it quickly, as if I had done it forever. I then crafted a method and plan of my own once I had begun the task. I watched the other boys very closely, observed the things that worked for them as well as the things that didn't. I paid close attention to their habits that increased their production and especially the ones that didn't. All of those things were of greatest importance as we were not paid by the hour, but by the amount of work that we produced each night.

Therefore, the harder and faster that I worked, as well as the fewer breaks that I took, greatly affected the amount of money that I earned. None of those lessons were lost on me as I threw myself into it with everything that I had. There were other reasons for my intense drive. That had to do with the new financial arrangements devised by my parents as soon as I had been given the job. They told me that all of the circumstances were right for me to grow up and to enter the adult world. I was excited about the opportunity.

After a brief discussion with them, I agreed that a new program was necessary. Within the first few weeks, I had quickly gotten to the point where I was making more money than the other boys in the department. In fact, I made more money on an hourly basis than did the adults who worked there during the day. Basically I earned in thirty to thirty-five hours what they had to work forty-five to fifty-hours a week. However, none of it was even remotely easy. It meant walking in the door immediately after school and hitting it as hard as possible with few or no breaks for five to seven hours straight every night. But to me, it was worth it, and the act of simply working just felt so incredible. That satisfying feeling of working hard and earning money gave me peace of mind and raised my self-esteem. It also changed my spending habits to a great degree.

My parents observed those changes and cornered me for a discussion one evening in the mailroom. It was an intense lecture. It was a verbal lesson about bills, budgets, and economics in general. One of their points was due to the fact that there were so many children in the household. I therefore had the opportunity to not only operate as an adult, sort of, but also to set things into place for my future. It was something that the two of them knew was near and dear to my heart.

With that in mind, every week on Friday I went to the office and received my pay envelope from the secretary. I then met with my mother, separated my expenses for the week, and gave her the balance. She then took the deposit to the bank and put it into a special account that they had set up specifically for me. That was the plan.

It had been on a Thursday night at the newspaper just one month after I had started the job that we had that meeting about my finances. They had informed me ahead of time about it, and as they had asked, I had done my homework on the subject. It was well after nine o'clock when the two of them showed up in the mailroom for our discussion.

Actually, it wasn't much of a discussion. My father just sat there and nodded as usual, as I spoke of the data that they requested, and my mother did most of the talking. Generally speaking, from that evening on, I became responsible for very nearly all of my living expenses. Once I had put it all down on paper, it turned out to be quite a list.

It included all school fees, book fees, and school supplies. That list also had school clothes, gym clothes, and personal health supplies such as toothpaste, soap, and deodorant. The list also extended to all school lunches and supper after work since I stayed there until well past the normal hour. Curiously, it also included dentist and doctor appointments as well as paying for whatever fees were incurred.

That account was set up specifically so that when I turned sixteen in three and a half years, I would be able to not only buy a very nice car, but also to have enough money to maintain, license, and insure it. As far as I was concerned, it was a great plan. The type of car, age of the car, and condition of the car ultimately depended upon my ability to save money. It was a simple plan as the more money that I gave my mother to put into the special account, the better that I would have it when that time arrived. She had set the account up and entered the amount given to her each week into the bankbook. But just to protect myself, I also entered the amount into a notebook of my own. I also used that book to record all of my other expenses. I recorded every single penny that I earned and spent. After some trial and error and some extensive homework, I quickly learned how to make every one of those pennies count.

Within ninety days after I had begun working, I achieved a rate that surprised everyone, including myself. Through various means, I found the speed and dexterity to outperform every other boy that worked there. The standard expected rate of work was approximately one thousand pieces per hour. Some of the older boys could put out fifteen to eighteen hundred pieces per hour.

However, before my thirteenth birthday, I achieved a sustainable rate of three thousand pieces per hour. I could accomplish that rate every hour and every day. By succeeding at that task, I had gotten to the place where I was earning two and a half times the minimum wage. That made for an unbelievable paycheck every Friday.

In the beginning, I had to admit that I did go overboard with my expenses as I ate out for supper every night and also ordered double lunches at school. I had also spent far too much money on school clothes in an effort to distance myself from my previous appearance. I cannot possibly put into words just how good it felt to not only get those new clothes, but also to take the tags and stickers off them. It just felt wonderful. Just to know that I was the first person to wear those clothes, what an incredible feeling.

By reading the weekly advertisements and want ads in the newspaper, I quickly learned that there were many other ways to effectively manage my money. I soon learned that I could achieve basically the same results, but with far less money. So, instead of eating out for supper, I learned of a place on the northeast side of the city that handled damaged and bulk foods and also health items like soap and shampoo. Why would I have cared if the cans of tuna and other quickly heated dinners were just a little dented? So what did it matter if the shampoo bottles were scratched or the labels torn? All of these items, on average, sold for about 20 percent of what they would have cost on the regular grocery store shelves. I also found another bargain farther out on the same state highway, which was a bread and bakery place. They sold all of the baked goods that had been returned from the regular stores after a certain date. The bread and pastries were still quite good. I was able to buy breakfast items for a week at the price that the regular stores charged for just an item or two.

The real savings was finding fantastic bargains with books, car magazines, and needed items by shopping at garage sales throughout the city. There were new ads of that sort in the newspaper every week. There I found things such as a fan for work, an iron for my clothes, a couple of radios, and other wonderful things. The best part was that my mother, having approved and understood my expenses at the start, never paid any attention to what I did, purchased, or anything else from that point forward. With that in mind, she never knew that I had found other ways to get what I needed for far less money. That allowed me to stash money in a secret location at the newspaper, which in itself, also led to a very interesting discovery.

Once winter had set in, it began to get very cold outside, making the tree house practically uninhabitable. I stuck with it for as long as I could until I couldn't stand it any longer. Among some of my garage-sale purchases were a sleeping bag, a wind-up alarm clock, a couple of small lamps, and about a hundred feet of extension cords. I had gotten more than a little sick and tired of getting off work at ten o'clock at night, getting on my bike, riding through the rain or snow, climbing up into the tree house, and shivering myself to sleep under a quilt. So I attempted something one night, a bit of an experiment. I just didn't go home.

That evening, I finished my work and went to the locker room when everyone else had left for the evening. I took a nice, hot shower in peace and simply stayed there in the building. After I made certain that everyone had gone, I went back into the mailroom and unrolled my sleeping bag out onto one of the metal tables between stacks of comics. Then I fluffed up my pillow, set my alarm clock, got comfortable, and quickly went to sleep.

My alarm went off right on schedule at five o'clock in the morning. It felt so nice to wake up not only in a warm place, but also in a fairly clean one. It really didn't matter much to me that it was a newspaper mailroom. As I sat there on a metal table, eating some donuts for breakfast, all of a sudden it just hit me like a ton of bricks. I had never seen it before and couldn't believe that I never seen it before. It was an absolutely amazing discovery. I just couldn't believe my luck.

The company had designed two sets of double doors for the mailroom. The first set of double doors brought you in from the outside and then immediately into a small eight-by-ten-foot room. Then you went through another set of double doors and into the mailroom itself. That design kept strong winds from roaring into the mailroom and scattering newspapers and such all over the place. Immediately next to the inside double doors on the left was a soft drink machine. Next to that was a large metal table that was about four-feet-by-sixteen feet and about waist high off the ground. The fascinating thing was that the mailroom itself had very high ceilings that had to be at least eighteen feet off the floor. The little room with the dual double doors went all of the way up to that eighteen-foot height. So the question in my mind was, what was above the ten-foot ceiling inside of that little room between the double doors?

As I sat there and looked at it, I could see that it was an easy step to go from the metal table and then to the top of the pop machine. From there it was just a bit of a reach to a small three-by-three-foot solid wooden door. It was painted the same color as the wall, which made it nearly invisible unless you were looking for it. What was in there? Could it actually be what I had thought that it was? There was only one way to find out. There wasn't time to waste as my father was due to arrive just after six in the morning.

Getting up to the little door was very easy, but opening the door itself proved to be a bit of a challenge. It had been painted over more than once, and it took quite a few tugs before I could get it to open. I had run extension cords and had one of the lamps ready, but even so, I just couldn't believe my eyes. It was a room. It didn't look as if it had ever been used and appeared to have a thick layer of dust over every surface. My inspection revealed it to have a solid floor with a vent in the outside wall that could be opened for air, and electrical plugs had already been installed on two of the walls. It was as if someone had built the room long ago and then had completely forgotten about it. But all of that really didn't matter. It was now mine.

That evening, once the shift was over, I began cleaning the room after everyone else had gone home. I knew where the janitors kept a shop vacuum in the building, and I made full use of it. When I had finished, I just sat there on the floor and couldn't believe my luck. It was far better and much more permanent than the tree house, and it was all mine. I knew that it would always be there no matter where the family might decide to move. At long last I had found some measure of stability.

It wasn't long before life became a ritual as one day just seemed to follow another. I awoke every morning to my alarm at five o'clock in my new little room. It felt so incredible to wake up in a place of my very own. It was good to know that my things were always where I had left them. I didn't have to worry about vulture brats, ants, or birds getting into my stuff. It was also nice to wake up in a place where it was always warm, somewhere that I didn't have to worry about the heat being turned off because someone didn't pay the heating bill. Best of all was waking up to complete peace and quiet, with no screaming kids, no blaring television, and no parents shouting and fighting. It was quiet enough, I could even hear myself think. Could anything possibly be any better?

In the mornings I always checked outside of my little room for people and then headed for the locker/shower room. Once ready for the day, I sat down behind stacks of comics, ate my breakfast while reading a book, and then headed off for school. I made sure my new room was secured, grabbed my jacket, hopped on my bike, and headed south through the downtown area to the middle school on South Pine Street. There I usually spent a very noneventful day in studies, lunch, and gym class. But by far my favorite time was always the hour that I spent in the library. I always wondered just what it would be like to own a large house with one room in it that had nothing but books lining the walls.

If it were mine, I would put some comfortable chairs in it with a cupboard for snacks and then spend the time reading.

Something did happen in seventh grade science class that proved to be quite interesting and more than a little confusing. Our teacher had given us an important assignment. We were also informed that it would count as a large percentage of our grade for the semester. We had to get all kinds of information about our families regarding the topic of genetics. By using siblings, parents, aunts and uncles, grandparents, and great-grandparents on both sides of our families, we gathered information on body type, hair and eye color, height and weight, and other important items. We then charted the data on papers that the teacher had given us and then condensed it into formula that spoke to who we were genetically.

I did the work exactly as instructed and placed everything into its necessary order. It was a very enjoyable project. It gave me a chance to learn a lot about my family as well as how to organize. I had it all done before the deadline and quickly turned it in to the teacher. But then a curious thing happened.

Two days later she quietly called me to her desk as my classmates were still working on their own projects. She informed me that there was something wrong with my assignment as I had turned it in. She wanted to know if I was certain that I had gathered the information properly. She also asked if I had recorded the information properly. Then she added, was I certain that I had calculated the charts and formulas properly? I told her that I was absolutely positive that everything was correct. I added that I had gone over all of the data three times and had asked questions of many relatives in order to acquire the data. She then stated that she would have to call my mother as the project was, at best, an average grade for my semester. I truly didn't know how to respond. I was hurt, I was upset, but then I just became determined. I knew in my own heart just how well that I had done.

The next day when I walked into class, the teacher wore an expression on her face that I really didn't understand. She never said anything to me specifically, but every now and then I noticed her looking my way. Then just a few minutes before the bell rang at the end of the class, she called me to her desk.

She appeared to be sympathetic and almost pitying, but again, she was always very nice to me. She informed me that she had spoken with my mother and that my project was just fine just as I had completed it. By the end of that week, the entire class had turned in their projects. Then two weeks later we got them back with our grades on them. At the top of the first page on mine in bright red ink was a very large *A*. I guess I had done a good job after all, but I still really didn't understand what the big problem was all about. It would take a few years, but the answer would make itself known in an incredible way.

After school, I always followed the same routine as I rode back to the newspaper. Upon arriving at work, I always walked my bike inside the mailroom, set it in a corner, waved to my father, and immediately started to work. He never actually said anything to me about anything, nor did my mother. My parents never asked about school, grades, homework, classmates, or anything at all. In my heart I believed that they just didn't care. But then maybe they were just too busy. Maybe there were too many other kids in the house. Perhaps they believed that if I didn't complain about anything, then there wasn't anything for them to be concerned about. I just didn't understand them and wondered if they ever bothered to understand me.

However, other adults in the mailroom always asked me questions about my personal life. One of them, the senior motor route driver, always asked about my day, about school, and about my hopes and dreams. Not only did he ask such questions, but he also had little bits of advice for me. They were always important things to know, and when I acted upon his advice, good things seemed to happen. He gave me instructions on how to maintain my bike, helpful advice about money, and how to save every spare penny. His advice covered a number of common sense items. However, what surprised me most of all was that he offered that advice and never once asked for anything in return. He always seemed to go out of his way to say at least a little something to me every day. It felt as if he actually cared about me. He and his wife were completely different people than my parents.

When school was out and summer arrived, I discovered that my work schedule had changed. During the summer the high school boys worked during the daytime just as the regular mailroom workers did. But we were allowed to start working as early as we wanted. But also during the spring and summer, I still kept to the tree house during the week, since it was nice outside and only used the secret room on the weekends or when thunderstorms tore through our area. The room wasn't well ventilated, and it became very warm during the summer months. But I also had other reasons for keeping both places. The most important of those reasons was that the tree house was a much better place to entertain "guests."

We usually worked until four or five o'clock in the afternoon, which for me made for a ten- or eleven-hour day as I started working as early as possible. By working those hours, we finished our work much earlier in the week. That worked out well for everyone because it gave us all more free time. We generally finished somewhere around noon or one o'clock on Thursdays. Once we were certain that all of the work had been completed, my cousin and I rode the seven miles to his house out on North Cool Road. I always believed they were rich since they had a very nice house and an in ground pool. As soon as we rolled into their driveway, we parked our bikes, ran around the house, and jumped into the cool water. That was the life. My cousin sure had it made in more ways than one.

I never ceased to be amazed by the condition of his home. It was always neat, clean, and tidy. Everything was where it should have been, everything was dusted, and nothing was out of place. It wasn't immaculate in the way that a museum would be, but it was spotlessly clean and incredibly comfortable. I knew that there was a difference between housing three kids in the house and a dozen, but I always believed that it was much more than that. I believed that his was how a house should be, and I knew full well that ours never was. What really amazed me was that even though they lived in the country, I never ever saw the first bug in that house. But there was more to it than just the things that I saw with my eyes. In his house, I always felt welcome, comfortable, and relaxed. Whenever I was there, I never wanted to leave. In my heart I decided to myself that someday, somehow, someway, I would live like that too. But I didn't have a clue how to get to such an enviable place in life. How could I possibly make such a thing happen?

One Saturday morning I was actually at our house in the front yard near the porch. It was just after ten o'clock, and I was putting a new chain on my bike when they showed up. That bike was my only mode of transportation, so I had to take really good care of it. They didn't pull up in a car, so they startled me a bit as I was engrossed in my work. They were a nice couple, a husband and wife. By their appearance, they were probably a little older than my parents. He wore a short-sleeve shirt and tie, and she was in a nice dress. It looked as if they were going to a wedding, a funeral, or something. He introduced himself, gave me time to wipe the oil from my hands, and shook my hand like a real gentleman. Then he announced that they were from a church just around the corner. I knew which one it was, I had ridden past it about a hundred times or so, and it looked like a nice-enough place.

He asked me questions about our family, my hobbies, and other things of that sort. Then he talked to me about something he described as a church camp, which wasn't at all familiar to me. He depicted it as a really nice place in the eastern part of the state where I could camp out and enjoy activities with other kids my age. The camp also had classes where kids listened to adults as they talked about Bible stuff. It all sounded pretty good to me at the time. I figured that I could have tolerated somebody talking about Bible things and all of that if it meant that I could get away for a free vacation. I hadn't ever been more than thirty miles from home. Nor had I ever been on vacation anywhere much less to a camp was on the other side of the state. They made it sound as if it were very interesting and a lot of fun. The only problem that I had was that I would have to take a week off from work and miss out on all of that money. Now that was something to consider. They stated that all of those things weren't a problem and that I could let them know my decision by attending their church that Sunday. That stopped my brain in mid-thought as the first bits of fear crept into my heart.

I had to go to their church? I didn't say it out loud, but that had to be the worst part. I knew what my grandparents, my father's family, were like, and they went to church every week. I also knew that you had to get dressed up, and I didn't own anything close to that sort of attire. But by the end of the conversation, I agreed to go. But deep inside I wondered if they had some hidden scheme or plan or something that they wanted me to join. After all, I knew that it would be a neat time to get away and that it wouldn't cost me anything. But I also already knew, by experience, that anything that you get for free is always worth what you pay for it.

My parents weren't at all pleased when I informed them of my plan. Amazingly, my mother in particular was downright angry. She and I got into quite a debate about the whole ordeal. I suppose that I pushed harder for going to the camp simply because she was so opposed to it. Why didn't she want me to go? What did she have against churches? What did she have against those people? She didn't even know them. After all, they weren't her in-laws, so maybe they were actually different. Why was it such a big deal for me to miss one week of work? The more she argued, the more convinced and determined I became. There wasn't anything that she could have done or said to stop me.

Sunday morning, I had ridden my bike to the newspaper early, somewhere around seven o'clock. I figured that was the best time to have the locker room to myself, as I believed that no one else would be there. I took my time getting ready, ironed my very best outfit, took a nice hot shower and attempted to make my hair look decent. With more time available, I would have scheduled a haircut at the barbershop. But then, I just as well have gone to my aunt's beauty shop as she would have been more than happy to cut it for free. At every family gathering she always had some smart remark about my hair. If she had her way about it, she would have cut it right down to the nubs. As I looked at myself in the mirror, I decided that my best would just have to do.

I returned to the house and chained my bike up to the tree beneath my little tree house. I really didn't know what to expect as I walked the two blocks to the church. I had seen churches on television, read about them in magazines and newspapers, but I hadn't ever been in one. When I walked in through the front door, a man who wore a weird-looking suit shook my hand and welcomed me to the place. He was really old and even looked older than my grandparents. He looked as if he was older than dirt as he was even a little dusty. But he was nice to me, and when I told him my age, he directed me to a room down the hall. I stood outside of the door for a minute to decide if I really wanted to go through with the deal.

When I walked in that door, I was completely unprepared for who and what I saw. There were at least two dozen or more kids there that I went to school with. To make matters so much worse, there were at least three girls in the room who had spent more time than they should have in my tree house. I instantly became nervous, began sweating through my clothes, and wondered just what everything was about. My mind raced down various dark alleys within my head. The questions that arose within my mind tormented me.

How much did these people know about me? What would I do if they forced me to stand in front of everyone and tell of all the bad things that I had ever done? Would they force me to confess about my activities that involved the tree house with some of the people in the room? At that moment, I wanted to get up out of my chair and run for the door. But just as I was about to make my escape, an adult stood up in front of the group and announced that the meeting would begin by singing. That seemed harmless enough and served to calm my nerves a bit. The singing only went on for a few minutes, which was a good thing as the music was very slow and boring. It nearly put me to sleep. It had no beat to it at all and was dry as an old bone. Then the same adult made a few announcements and talked about the church camp. Then as he looked at a piece of paper in his hand, he suddenly asked me to stand up and introduce myself.

I was terrified and scared out of my wits. I know that my voice cracked when I spoke as at least two of the girls in the room laughed out loud. I sat down just as soon as I could, and only then did I finally begin to breathe.

If I hadn't been bored enough during the singing, I certainly was after he began speaking. He rambled on and on what seemed almost forever about a number of things. He spoke about the world, just how evil it was and about all of the hidden traps that it had in store for teenagers. He spoke about the fact that someday we would be confronted with those traps, and then he spoke specifically about those traps.

As he continued, I knew there were at least three pairs of eyes looking at me. I could almost see their faces out of the corners of my own eyes. With that I knew that my actions were known and that they were going to get me! They knew what I had been doing! They knew about the tree house. They knew about the alcohol and the girls. They knew! In my mind I even figured that they purposely came to my house with the church camp invitation just so that they could get me in that place. I was nearly ready to stand up and run out of the door when he suddenly stopped. That was all that there was to it. He just stopped and told everyone that our packets about church camp for our parents to sign was up at the front to be picked up. That was it? I couldn't believe it. After all of that intimidation, to just walk up, grab a packet, go home, get it signed, and then return that afternoon to leave for camp. I was amazed at all of that church stuff. First, they tied my head into a knot, and then they shoved me out the door. In the end I decided that it was nothing but confusing and frustrating nonsense. Naturally, I signed the paperwork myself.

However, church camp wasn't at all what I had expected. We rode on a big bus, which was kind of fun and was something I actually enjoyed. When we arrived at the camp, the adults herded us into a big tent and proceeded to give us a stern and very serious lecture. At first I thought that it was just hysterical. I didn't know what anyone else thought, but those adults acted as if teenagers had no idea about the things that they labeled as evil. But what they tagged as evil were things such as gossiping, hurting other people's feelings, leaving others out of the fun, snobbery, and lame acts.

What were they talking about? People had done those sort of things to me throughout my entire life. Those mild attacks had been foisted upon me just that school year and by the very kids that sat all holier than thou so very close to me in that very same tent.

When they first talked about evil things, I thought for certain that they would say something about cigarettes (which I had brought) or alcohol (which I hadn't brought) or about sex (which I knew for a fact was available). They didn't bother to say a word about any of those things as it was merely about little petty, stupid things. I knew right then and there that I would have some kind of a week ahead of me.

We were actually at camp for a total of four nights and five days. By the end of the second day, I knew who most of the kids were in the camp. By the second night, I was sharing cigarettes with a few of them and letting them know exactly what the consequences were for talking. By the third night, other illicit actions occurred there as well. It was the kind of behavior that would have gotten me sent home in a minute had we been caught. In my mind, church camp proved to be hardly any different than life at home, at work, or at school. But then, before I knew it, the week was over, and we were all back on the bus and headed back for home.

After we had returned, I experienced a significant view of human relations. In the church parking lot, as everyone gathered their belongings and met with their families, I instantly felt ignored and alone. I stood there with overwhelming jealousy and envy as parents and kids greeted one another as if it had been ages since they had last seen one another. It was an incredible thing to observe. Then everyone got into their cars and went their separate ways. I just shook my head in amazement, picked up my sleeping bag and my other belongings, and headed east down the alley for the tree house.

Once I got to the house, I went inside and attempted to say something to my mother over the always-blaring television. All she did was to wave me off as she was watching one of *her* shows and obviously didn't want to be bothered. So I went back outside, grabbed my stuff from the front porch, and headed back down the alley to the tree house.

As I sat up there, feeling the tree swaying a little in the wind, emotions suddenly swept over me with such a force as they never had before: sadness, depression, loneliness, and an entire truck load of guilt. The guilt was by far the worst of it all. I had never experienced very much of that emotion before, at least not since Euclid Avenue and certainly not for things that I enjoyed.

A lot of things had happened at that camp and very little of it had to do with church. Actually, for me, none of it had anything to do with church, not one bit. I just really didn't get it. Just what was the whole God thing all about anyway? What in the world was that sin stuff all about? That was the part that I really didn't understand. It was the exact opposite of everything that my uncle had told me about life. But yet deep inside, I felt empty, very much alone, and so desperately and completely lost. The worst of it all was that I knew that I was alone, empty, unneeded, and most certainly unwanted. The episode in the parking lot when we had returned from the camp really drove those emotions home. However, despite my struggles against it, that week had changed things within me somehow, and I really didn't care much for it. It caused far too much turmoil inside and brought about too much confusion as well. So that night, within the security of the tree house, with uncertainty reigning supreme, I simply cried myself to sleep.

Separation
Ninth Grade: South Harrison Avenue

I was desperate for advice, and I discovered that the older guys in the mailroom at the newspaper had a lot of interesting ideas, fascinating habits, and worthwhile advice. In general terms, I had heard the majority of it from my uncle many years before. However, they helped to fill in the necessary details I required at that time and answered some of the more pressing questions as well.

After the adult staff had left for the evening, a few of us worked until ten o'clock at which time one of those employees returned to count our production and lock up for the evening. During that private time, our little group discussed the normal topics of life such as drinking, drugs, and girls. But it was the conversations about girls that intrigued me the most. I learned that it was best for me just to listen, learn, and remember the important details. After each conversation, I resolved to use the information that I had gained and act upon it. It was by far the very best advice that I had received to that point.

During school hours, beginning in seventh grade, whenever I was in the company of female schoolmates, a certain general conversation always led to another. The next thing that generally occurred was that either they invited themselves, or I made the invitation. With that, I began entertaining guests at the tree house. In a fashion, it became a secret-society type of thing. There was never a word spoken in public between any of the individuals who consented to those very private parties. No one ever discussed their actions with another, and no gossip regarding the tree house was ever knowingly passed within the school walls. I was the only commonality between them all. I assumed that their motivation was probably in order to either retain that haven away from parents or the guilt of it all, or most possibly both. They arrived one at a time and stayed for as long as they wished, which meant that there were never more than two of us in the tree house on any occasion. Interestingly enough, those arrangements turned out to be the only thing that wasn't ever complicated.

But what wasn't complicated was how it began. It always started with small talk, where they generally did the talking, and I usually just listened. The conversations almost always began with statements about their parents. To hear any of them, no one in the world had very good parents, not even the best ones or the ones that lived in the big houses with all of the money. Nearly every girl always said the very same thing. They weren't understood by their parents, weren't listened to, were always ignored, and therefore felt unwanted. I always listened patiently, understood completely, and filled that void, I suppose. I informed them that I understood their problems, as their worst days were my best days and always made certain that they understood my situation in general as well.

Those talks about parents always led to sharing cigarettes, wine, or whatever else happened to be available. Within a short period of time, those actions soon led to tears, hugs, kissing, and clothes removal. Those particular acts proved to be everything that my uncle had said they would be, but actually it was so much more. However, there were a few things that both he and the guys at the newspaper had left out.

They were things that were really hard to describe. In those years on Harrison Avenue, there had been quite a few of those guests. As I considered my actions, I suppose there were far more of them than there ever should have been. Individually, they were different in a score of ways, but in many others, they were nearly the same. As a group, they were for the most part older than I, and a couple of them had even driven to the tree house, parking in the back of the lot where the weeds were the tallest. I knew full well that nearly all of them had real boyfriends at school as I observed them together on a daily basis. Those same girls passed by me in the halls, never uttering a single word, not even a morning greeting or acknowledgment. What happened in the tree house was never spoken of outside of the tree house. Partially, it seemed to be the price paid for living in the wrong neighborhood as most of them lived in far better neighborhoods and homes. But despite anything that any of them ever said, I knew full well that they all had better parents. They truly had no idea of just how good their lives really were.

But it was always the same general story with each one of them. They set up the meetings secretly, arrived at the tree house secretly, and I was understandably sworn to that secrecy. During their time there we smoked, drank, and did far more than was ever permissible. Afterward, they always left in the darkness, but only after restating and demanding that the terms of secrecy be upheld as well as the consequences of breaking that secrecy. I never knew if any of them knew each other, but the interesting point was that they nearly all said the same exact thing. But there was still an awful lot about the whole ordeal that I just didn't understand. It completely confused me.

If they had boyfriends during school who accompanied them to activities, then why did they bother to come to the tree house? If they belonged to all of the right social clubs at school and at their churches, then why did they go to such lengths to meet someone like me in such an unacceptable neighborhood? If they were from good families or had the "right last names," then why did they involve themselves with someone of my type and family background? Why did they ever bother with me at all?

The free cigarettes, booze, and drugs were good enough as far as I was concerned, and the rest of it, as I figured it, was good enough or even better. There was certainly no debating the enjoyment of those activities. However, it was the confusing aftermath that I could barely tolerate. Once the activities were over, they were brutally over. The clothes went back on, followed by a quick kiss good-bye, a mandatory reminder of secrecy, and then suddenly they were gone. I was yet again alone. With every instance it was always the same. Every visit always ended the same way as my emotions then went through the same almost sickening roller-coaster ride once they had departed. It actually had gotten to the place where I hated it so much that I nearly ended the entire program. In the dark and quiet aftermath, I always felt empty, used, and completely depressed. The majority of the time I stayed awake until dawn, smoking what cigarettes were left and asking myself dozens of questions.

Why was I doing it? Had I ever considered the results of what could come from my actions? Didn't I realize that my life could be ruined? Wasn't the prospect of physical violence from the girls' boyfriends or family a very real possibility? Did any of them actually care about me? Did I really care about any of them? Was I just being used? Was I just using them? Were those physical actions really all that there was to love? Was there anything more to it than that? Was that really all that there was to life? Was there actually more? Were my actions right or wrong? Had I actually hurt anybody? After all, I always waited, never pressured, forced, or coerced anyone. They always made the offer to come to the tree house, and they always brought stuff. No adults to that point had ever discovered my secret, and as far as I knew, no one has ever gotten into any trouble that I was aware of.

My own parents certainly weren't the best examples or even mediocre ones. But they hadn't given me the first clue that they had any idea of what went on in the tree house. But then again they had proven time and again that the only people they ever really cared about were themselves. I believed that they cared only about what directly affected them, and that certainly had very little to do with me. I supposed that I always had realized that much to be a fact. In actuality, the only time that I ever talked to them was on Friday afternoons when we discussed my banking transactions. I had gotten in the habit of reviewing my personal bank records with my mother, who always agreed with my numbers as she hurriedly returned to whatever was important to her at the moment.

At that point in life I never permitted anyone close enough to fully trust and discuss my issues of loneliness and depression. I didn't really know which path to take, so I chose the easiest way out and changed nothing. But the emptiness and loneliness that I experienced after the tree house actions were the hardest to tolerate. On the one hand, I had to have that feeling of being needed fulfilled even if it were for just a short while. I concluded that a few stolen minutes with someone and for something was better than not having any time with anyone at all. If indeed, that physical act was really all that love actually amounted to then I believed I could accept it. In my mind, I supposed that I would have done nearly anything to feel loved and wanted. Finally I decided that grabbing crumbs from the meal was better than having nothing at all. I convinced myself that suffering through the depression and having gained a piece of attention was better than complete emotional starvation. But despite my decisions and supposed self-understanding, I knew that my life was a wreck and heading in a dangerous and unknown direction.

I continued to spend the winters in my little hideout at the newspaper. I followed the same routine as I had previously and as before my parents never asked the first question concerning my whereabouts or actions. More and more as time went by, that little room at the newspaper quickly became my permanent place of residence. It wasn't long before I had removed everything of value out of the tree house and secured it there.

I also found it shocking that I had actually made it into the ninth grade while still attending the same school and still living at the same street address. With that I had just begun my third year in a row. Although it might not have been a world record, it was certainly a record in my tumultuous life, and it registered with fireworks for me. But while on the surface everything seemed the same, a host of things had changed within the family, and they had changed dramatically.

Every night that I sat either in the secret room, I had nothing but questions. They were never ending and, unfortunately, were always unanswered. But it was on that night, despite the weather, I sat alone in the tree house. That night I looked across the yard at the back of a dark and empty house. On that night it was empty of people, but it was chock full of trash, junk, and other garbage that my family had once again chosen to leave behind. When I had walked through there earlier in the evening, it was full of clothes, assorted junk, and other trash that had been thrown all over the place. Despite the cold temperature, the garbage and filth produced such a stench that I nearly threw up. There was absolutely nothing inside of that building that I would have ever wanted. The place was infested with roaches, mice, and rats. They were everywhere that you cared to look. Our family had come to be known for such things. Wasn't that just an incredible thing to be famous for? Once, I was even teased by a female classmate about that very subject. She had seen roaches crawling on my sister's clothes as she sat behind her in class. Was it any small wonder that I had never kept anything in that house? Was it so difficult for anyone to understand why I had never spent any time there? Who in the world would have ever wanted to live like that? Who would have wanted to eat a meal in such a place? How sickening was that? Who could possibly have ever slept there, knowing that bugs crawling all over everything and everybody? There just wasn't any way! There simply wasn't any way that I could tolerate that lifestyle even for a moment. I actually sprayed the tree house regularly to keep the ants out of my stuff! I simply never understood my family and probably never would.

On my own, I had learned how to keep things clean, how to store food in containers, and how to make myself presentable. I even went to the laundry and learned to clean, fold, and press my clothes. However, I did receive assistance and instruction from the ladies who worked there. They were quite helpful, understanding and probably took pity on me. So, just what did I need my family and especially my parents for? They had become nothing more than a nuisance and an embarrassment to me.

But on that night, my mother and the other kids were long gone from the house. But I knew where they were. My father was gone from the house as well, but I hadn't the slightest idea as to where he was staying, even though I saw him every day at the newspaper. He looked awful as he smoked one cigarette after another and never spoke to anyone unless he had to. It was kind of scary, and I had no idea what would happen to him from that point on. Through all of those strange days, neither of my parents ever asked, demanded, or requested any information regarding any of my actions or whereabouts. It was life as usual.

But it was to be the last night that I would spend in my tree house. I knew that I would really miss the place. It had been something that I had built with my own two hands, and I just didn't want to leave it. I was angry just thinking about it. I was certain that some neighbor kid would probably take it over and not take care of it. That situation played out just as every other scenario in my life ever had. No one had ever talked to me, and no one had ever informed me of what was going on. They simply did what they wanted to do and left me alone to deal with handling however their decisions ridiculously affected my life.

But I certainly didn't want to move again and change schools. I knew for certain that I didn't want to go to the other side of town. I knew for certain that I didn't want to live with my mother and her new boyfriend. I was fully aware that it wasn't the lame cover story she had told everybody. But I knew exactly what was going on. I had watched it all happen as it happened, and the end result was really of no surprise to me.

It had happened just as it had every other time before. I believed that everything was going along just fine. It was as fine as it could have been for our family anyway. As for me, ninth grade was going just great. School was good, my grades were good, and I had come to believe that I finally had my life under some kind of control at last. My routine was pretty much what it had always been.

As soon as school was out, I got on the bike, headed for work, and hit it hard just as soon as I walked in through the double doors. I worked for three solid hours like a madman, out producing everyone else. It was one of the few things that allowed me to feel good about myself, and it was also one of the few good things that actually lasted. Then I stopped for a quick snack and a smoke and then hit it again until eight o'clock. There had been some changes in the organization as that was when an adult employee called the shift to an end and verified our production counts. I always helped him to record those counts and to see everyone out the door. As soon as they had left and I was alone once more, I would hit it again and work until about eleven o'clock. After all, it was all about the money and I needed every dime that I could earn.

Then I attended to my own needs as I ironed my clothes for school the next day, grabbed a shower, set my alarm clock, and read until I fell asleep. But I confess that oftentimes, I did ride to the tree house and wait for company to arrive even if it meant sacrificing a little sleep. After all, it was always important to keep my priorities in order.

In those months my parents had become more than a little strange in their habits. My father, who already worked seven days a week at the newspaper, suddenly decided that he needed a second job. For some reason, both of my parents began going down the street to the auction house. It was a short distance away on our little street, to the north and almost to the corner near the bridge over the river. According to my brothers and sisters, they spent nearly every evening of the week there. That left the kids completely to their own devices. Not a very good plan.

The house, which had always been a total mess before, had, with no one in charge of the place, turned into a literal garbage dump. The last time that I bothered to walk inside it was so bad that the floor couldn't be seen. The kids were all over the place, and the noise and smell were so intolerable that you had to hold your hands over your nose and ears.

From the tree house late on Friday and Saturday nights, I observed my father as he hurriedly walked home from the auction house. Then he spent about five minutes in the house before he jumped into the company van and drove off to the newspaper to manage the next morning's production. I rarely saw my mother at all. When I did see her, she was always in the company of some tall older guy who always walked her to the house. I had been informed that he was only making sure that she arrived home safely. I knew that this was the story she had told to my father. I also noticed that after he had walked her home he always stayed for a while. I wasn't stupid, and since I certainly wasn't innocent, I knew what men and women did in private. I may not have known a lot about a lot of things, but I certainly understood those actions.

Our family went through that sorry routine for a couple of months until well after winter had set in. When that happened, I did what I had always done and stayed in the secret room at the newspaper. I left there for school in the morning and returned there in the afternoon. The only time that I deviated from that routine was when I bought groceries for the week or went to the laundry. It was also during ninth grade that I began working weekend nights at the newspaper stock handling on the loading dock as I helped the rural motor route drivers. It made for some very long hours, especially on Saturday nights, but the money certainly helped.

Then it happened. Not with a flash, a bang, or even a small explosion. Although I had chosen to live at a distance from my family, I could easily see that everything was unraveling. It was very early in the spring on a Thursday evening as I was suddenly interrupted by the sound of a police officer's voice. I was busy entertaining a guest in the tree house, and I was instantly terrified. My guest was at least as scared as I was. We were caught dead to rights, and justice was about to be served, or at the very least it was going to be. If they came up there and checked the place, I knew for certain that I would go straight to jail. A list of questions raced through my head. How old was she? Did that really matter? How much trouble would the cops create for me over that sort of thing? More importantly, what about the alcohol and drugs? Once I reached the ground would they be able to smell it on my breath and on my clothes? They couldn't really send me to jail, could they? Then I heard his voice as it became angrier. So I climbed down the tree as slowly as I could. When I reached the bottom, the cop began yelling, asking me questions, and used his baton for a question mark just an inch from my face. They were the usual kind of questions that the police always seemed to ask.

Where were my parents? What were their names? Who was in charge? Did I have any idea as to just how upset our neighbors were? Did I know what my brothers had been doing? Then he wanted to know what I had been doing up in the tree. Was there anybody up in that tree with me? I answered his questions as best as I could and lied through my teeth about anything concerning the tree house. He was furious with my answers and yelled into my face that all of our neighbors hated us. He added that they didn't want our kind on their block and that they would have run us out if they thought that they could have gotten away with it. Then he added that maybe, just maybe he would help them do it. Then he turned on his heel, left his squad car sitting there in the alley with all of its lights flashing, and then walked down the street to the auction house. He wasn't gone very long. I walked up the alley to the street to confirm his actions and awaited his return.

He returned after just a few minutes, and he never said a word to any of us. He just gave me a glaring shot of a look, got back into his car, and screamed out of the neighborhood with gravel flying everywhere. No sooner had he left when my siblings started in on me. I responded with all of the anger that I had built up within me. I told all of them in no uncertain terms just what I thought of each and every one of them. I told them how I hated our family and how I wished that I wasn't forced to have anything to do with any of them. Then I walked away from them in disgust and headed back to the tree house. Once back inside, I discovered that it was completely empty, which was really no surprise. It was certainly no shock that no one was there, but there wasn't even a little note. But then again, since she was at least as scared as I was, she had probably left as soon as she had the chance. Sweet, it was the perfect ending to a perfect day.

But things weren't getting along any better at work either. At first I noticed that my father was acting differently, even a little strange at times as he then became all weird paranoid or something. I could tell that something was really messed up with him. He was a big guy, not tall at all, but stocky like most former football players tend to be. But by that time, he somehow seemed smaller and weaker, almost whining whenever he spoke. It became worse with each passing day, almost as if it were a growing and living thing as it then took on a life of its own. But at almost three hundred pounds, I suppose that it was good that he wasn't eating as much. But he also smoked one cigarette after another. He looked terrible, and I could tell by his eyes that he wasn't sleeping very well either.

Then the big news hit the family. It was a very rare case when my father ever bothered to have a conversation with me, but on that particular day he did. It was shortly after school, and I had been working for about a half an hour. He walked up to my table and then just looked at me, not even saying a word. It was downright creepy. He stared at me with eyes that looked like he wanted to die or something. It was as if I were looking directly into his soul. Then he began to speak, but for some reason couldn't and then stopped. All he could do at that moment was to just stare at the concrete floor. When he gathered himself together again, coughed, lit another cigarette, and hurriedly stated that my mother would be there soon and that the two of them had something very important to tell me.

Then he turned quickly and left with his head down, and directly out the double doors he went, crying. However, I couldn't believe my own luck. My mother was coming there just to talk to me. I knew ahead of time that it would be a real treat, especially since it was obviously something that was of great importance to her. I could hardly wait for the happy event to begin.

About an hour later, I looked up from my work to see the two of them as they walked towards me across the mailroom. As I observed the differences between them, I knew that bad news was imminent. My father was walking slowly with his head down, in apparent defeat as he continued to stare at the floor. He stopped about six feet from my worktable and just leaned against the wall by the water fountain and looked off into the distance at nothing in particular. My mother on the other hand was exactly the opposite. Her hair was all done up, had about a pound of makeup on her face, and smelled as if she had been doused with a gallon of perfume. Actually, that was what had gotten my attention when they were coming as her perfume showed up well before she did. She was all decked out in some new outfit and strutted across the mailroom as if she were a queen visiting her subjects. She walked right up beside me, tried to kiss me on the cheek, and snorted when I turned away. Then she then lit up a cigarette and began her speech.

She started in on her spiel, as she never really could just say what needed to be said. She was taking on a new job. It was a very important job. It would be her responsibility to take care of the bedridden wife of a local businessman. Whoever the woman was, she was in very bad shape, and because of that, she required constant care. Then she dropped the bombshell that I knew was coming. I hadn't any idea of what the specifics were, but I was soon to find out. She would have to live in the house in order to provide that special kind of care. Then the questions just ran through my head.

What businessman was she talking about? Oh yeah, some businessman, that auction- house guy. He was the same guy who had walked her home all of those nights. Wasn't he the man that she spent her weekend nights with as my father was away at work? Then I lashed out in anger. What should I care what she did with her time? What should any of that mean anything to me? She always did whatever she wanted, so why bother me with a phony announcement and the added drama? I never bothered to consider her or any of my family's problems. I was too busy just trying to take care of myself to ever be worried about her and her nonsense. But through all of the discourse my father remained unmoved, completely silent, never saying a word, and never looking up.

Then she smiled. I knew that smile and knew exactly what it meant. I had learned to hate that smile. It always meant that whatever she was about to say was not going to be good, at least not for me. Then she just said it as she dumped it onto me like a bucket full of vomited words. What! What was that all about? What did she mean that we had to move again? It had been the first time in my life that we had ever stayed in one place for more than a year. I liked not having to change schools all of the time. But then, not only did she want me to move, but to also change schools, and once again it was during the school year. I really hated every possible thing about it. But I wasn't finished as I had other questions and statements of my own.

Why wasn't my father moving with the family, as if I wasn't already aware of the plain facts? Did she really think that she was talking to a complete child? Did she really believe that I was that stupid? Didn't she understand that I knew exactly what was going on? Did she really believe that I didn't have eyes and that I hadn't watched and had observed everything? I knew exactly what she was doing and knew precisely just what she was up to.

Then I did something that I just couldn't resist. I asked her the questions that I knew would really set her off. Why did I have to follow along? Why couldn't she just leave me alone and not bother me anymore? Wasn't I already taking care of myself? What did I really need her for? It wasn't as if she ever cared about what I was doing, where I was or whom I was ever with. So, why did she even try to perform the caring parent act on me? However, I was most suspicious about the way she was acting.

It was as if she were the perfect, caring mother and all of that other phony nonsense. Please, when did she ever even begin to care about me, my brothers, and my sisters or anyone but herself. She never paid any real attention to me. But despite what I had said, she ignored me and kept rambling on with her prepared speech. Then she just said it. We were all moving; it was all said and done. There was no discussion or debate as it was finished. I had to get any of my belongings that I wanted to keep from the house. I looked past her shoulder to see that my father was still staring at the floor wearing a face of a man convicted to die.

It made me mad, it made me angry, it made me sick to my stomach, and I just wanted to scream. Then she smiled at me again with that same sickening smile. I really hated that smile. It was the smile that always declared that she had won and no one could possibly stand against her. She was the ultimate victor as we were all her victims. One more look at my father's face confirmed every word of it.

Four days passed since the meeting, and once again I sat in the tree house. I was alone as it was sure to be the very last time that I would ever be there. The backyard was quiet, but it certainly was not empty as it was full of trash and other stuff that none of them wanted to take with them. The last time that I had seen my brothers and sisters, they were happy and excited about going to the new place and our supposed great new life. I hadn't set one foot in the new place. But just how great could it be?

How could she just trade my father off for someone else? How could she act as if she were simply making a deal for a new car? Perhaps that wasn't a very good analogy, but it was the way that it seemed to me. I knew what she had told everyone. It had all gotten back to me through various people both at the newspaper and elsewhere. But if anyone believed that phony cover story, then they had to be really stupid. I may have been only fifteen, but I already knew what was going on.

I had already packed all my books and belongings and had taken them to the secret room at the newspaper. But this was the day she had demanded that I show up at the new place. Although it was nearly eleven o'clock at night no one had even bothered to come by to find me. I guess that I half expected someone to check on me or to even yell at me for not following her orders. I guess that for some reason I almost wished that someone would and then even demanded that I go with them. But it was late, I was getting hungry, and so I decided that I might as well go.

I climbed down the tree with a small sack of items to take and just sat there on my bike. I would really miss that tree house. I knew that a lot of things had happened there, and I suppose that some people would even say that they were bad things. But they were the only times that I felt needed, wanted, and worth something, even if it were only for a little while. I had lived in that place for two and a half years, the longest that I had lived anywhere. There had been many discoveries, many lessons learned, and since I was being honest with myself, I also knew that there also had been many regrets.

As I sat there on the bike and wondered what to do next, I suddenly heard tires screeching from somewhere around a corner. I rode east on the alley for a few feet to the street in front of the house. There to my left and toward the corner came a van as it screamed through the intersection, nearly on two wheels. Then I watched as it fishtailed wildly up the block. Who was this nutcase? Then it came to a screeching halt in front of our house and bounced halfway up onto and then over the curb. I could tell immediately by the color of the van and by the lettering on the side of it that it was a company vehicle, driven by my father.

What in the world was he doing? Had he finally lost it? I watched from the shadows as he flung open the driver's door and came out cursing, shouting, rambling, and not making any sense at all. Had he finally lost his mind? Was he drunk? He made it halfway to the front porch of the house and then dropped to his hands and knees in the yard while sobbing hysterically. He had no idea that I was there watching it all. Suddenly he stopped, wiped his nose on his shirtsleeve, gathered himself together, and then went into the house. I didn't know what to do or what would happen next, so I just stood there by my bike and waited. I didn't have to wait very long.

From somewhere inside the place, I heard him as he shouted and screamed. Then I heard crashing noises and the obvious sound of a window breaking. It wasn't but a moment later as he came out of the house still shouting and crying with tears streaming down his face. Then, still talking to himself, he stopped and growled something about just driving the van into a tree and ending it all. Then suddenly, he noticed me standing there. He stopped and stared while not saying anything, not a solitary word. He simply looked at me. Then our eyes locked onto each other. I had never seen a sadder look on anyone's face in my entire life. It made me want to cry, and I really didn't know why. He was the most pitiful and helpless thing that I had ever seen. Only a few seconds passed, but it seemed to last forever.

Then he let out a raging, roaring, bellowing scream and half-ran for the still open door of the van. With the roar of the engine, a lot of tire smoke, and noise, he was quickly gone. I watched as he drove through the red light at the other end of the block without bothering to slow down. Where was he going? What was he going to do? Would he really run the van into a tree? Was he really capable of suicide? I believed in my heart that he was. He certainly had been through enough with my mother. But should I have called someone? Who should I have called? Just what would I tell them? Would they even believe me? Would they even care? None of them had ever listened to me before. I guess there was nothing that I could really do about anything. Maybe he would have been better off if he had done something to himself. I secretly wondered that about myself sometimes.

Confinement
Ninth Grade: West Wayne Street

West Wayne Street. Our newest place of residence was just one block north and two blocks east of where we had lived immediately following "the event" during the second half of my sixth-grade school year. At times I felt as if I were a human Ping-Pong ball, as we bounced from one neighborhood in the city to another, but naturally never ended up in any of the good ones. However, this particular neighborhood didn't seem to be all that bad and actually appeared quite decent at first glance. However, looking at it from the outside, it was obvious that the new house was very small considering the fact that a man and his invalid wife were already living there. With the addition of my mother and our brood, it was certainly going to be cramped quarters.

I had been sternly ordered to bring all of my school clothes, which I complied, although I had stubbornly brought nothing else. All of my other belongings had been safely stashed within the confines of the secret room. I had also been informed that there would be new rules for everyone to follow and that they would be followed to the letter. But since I had never experienced a household with rules, I couldn't wait to see just who the person was that would attempt to control me. I wasn't about to willingly fit in to anyone's program.

I had no sooner parked my bike, locked it, and grabbed my bag when they both met me on the front porch. It was my mother and her latest boyfriend, the auction-house owner. As I looked him up and down, as my father's obvious replacement, only one thought crossed my mind. She really did know how to pick them. His name really wasn't any more important to me than any of the others had been. But for my own purposes, I called him Yellow Teeth. I had labeled him as such primarily because he had the largest, ugliest, and nastiest coffee- and cigarette-stained teeth I had ever seen. It was hysterical and sickening all at the same time. She had been kissing that? Physically, he was probably the exact opposite of my father. He was tall, gangly, smelled bad, and dressed funny.

As I walked toward them he smiled at me, tried to make nice, and shook my hand as if he were some kind of gentleman. We walked inside the house, and the three of us took a seat in his living room. It was interesting to notice just how quiet the house was. What really amazed me was the fact that all of my brothers and sisters were inside the house at the same time, and yet it was quiet. I wondered just what sort of threats it had taken to achieve that result. I wasn't sure, but I was certain that I was just about to find out. Additionally, I observed that the two of them were sitting together on the sofa and far too close to each other, which told me a lot about the situation. At that moment, I figured that I had better hang on to my shorts, because there was bound to be an entire list of unwanted rules coming my way. I had no sooner completed that thought when from his shirt pocket he produced an actual written list. What was even more interesting was that my mother sat there in absolute silence. He carried the entire conversation. That really had to be a first, and I had to admit that I was impressed. Then he began to put me in my place.

There was a mandatory curfew. I was required to check in with him every evening as soon as I arrived at the house. There was to be no more roaming around the city in the evening doing whatever it was that I was doing. I also had to inform him in advance by Friday afternoon just what I had planned for the weekend. Then there was a big surprise, I was to keep my entire paycheck, but I also had to account to him for every penny that I either spent or saved each week. He informed me that he would be watching my every move and that it was for my own good. It sounded as if I just joined the military.

But after two months had passed, I had to admit that the arrangement was tolerable. Although I had learned a bit of discipline and ways around those roadblocks, I had also gained absolutely no respect for most adults. They set up standards for me that they never attempted to achieve within their own lives. They constructed rules and regulations for me to follow and then violated them before my eyes every day. They also tried far too hard to interfere with my own personal plans. I had maintained my own lifestyle for far too long without any adult supervision and resented their intrusion. But in looking at the entire package, it certainly wasn't the worst situation or location that I had ever been in.

However, the new school proved to be quite an interesting place. I easily maintained my grade-point average and socially it quickly became a fascinating exercise. Due to the newness of it all, I had made a few serious and life-altering decisions. As my full paycheck was suddenly freed up, my spending priorities changed. With that, I chose to dress in a certain manner and began to carry and conduct myself in ways that I had observed in adults that I had admired. They were men at the newspaper who had become my leaders, mentors, and role models. These men were from good families, had stable homes of their own, and were what I wanted to be upon reaching adulthood.

But choosing such a direction put me at direct odds and in daily contradiction with my family and their pathetic lifestyles. As a freshman, I had both a brother and a sister who attended the same middle school along with me. Their attire was strictly dictated by mother's budget, which was admittedly, meager at best. They also had personal habits, which weren't socially acceptable either. It was really sad and disgusting as I knew there was always soap and shampoo in the house. But then again, it was their personal choice. Therefore, by my personal choice, we looked, smelled, and acted differently. It was not a matter of right or wrong, but about very personal choices. However, there were other things that set us apart, and they came about as a result of choices as well.

One of those choices was the free-lunch status, which our household easily qualified for. While both of my siblings naturally participated, I fiercely refused to comply despite any budgetary benefits. Pride was my overriding motivator as I had paid for my own lunches for three years, and there wasn't any way that I would be labeled as some kind of a worthless welfare case. There was too much at stake in the mandatory social games that were always in play within school society. I purposed in my heart that I would do whatever was necessary and whenever possible in order to set myself apart from my family.

The social structure within school society demanded that I set about on a carefully prescribed course. I knew from experience that a new person to a school always generated intense interest from within female classmates group. Knowing this, I determined to take full and complete advantage of any opportunities as they were presented. Therefore, I simply chose the easiest and most believable route available to me. Although I never made an official announcement, I casually released the same statement to anyone who inquired about my family. When asked I always responded gently and firmly, but with added pity, that the two people where indeed, related to me. But, despite anything that anyone might have heard, they were not my brother or sister, but only my cousins and that our families worked for the same business. It proved to be quite effective.

It was easy enough for everyone to believe. Within days the tale became apparent to all and was accepted without any difficulty. It proved to be an easy fit, made perfect sense, and certainly made me feel better about myself. The story made me feel quite proud of myself and even superior to my siblings. However, once the words were said, it was done, over with, and there was no going back. I continued to keep quiet about the matter, appeared to be a private person, and everyone accepted my stated situation at its apparent face value. For the most part, it appeared that everyone respectfully understood and appreciated me for the person that I declared myself to be. The deception worked perfectly.

Home life, on the other hand, proved to be another sort of event. The biggest part of the equation was due to the fact that I rarely spent any time in the house. However, I was also shocked to find that the place was much cleaner than what I had been used to, but then again, that certainly wouldn't have required too much effort. Although it was crowded and cluttered, I never saw a single bug running around anywhere. That one item was a major event to me.

Each day after school, I went directly to the house, changed into work clothes, hopped on my bike, and headed off to the newspaper. By that time I had become the leading producer in the mailroom, and as a reward, management permitted me to set my own hours. Therefore, I worked as many as I possibly could. Normally, I ended my workday at ten thirty or so in the evening. Then I grabbed a shower in the locker room, got dressed, got back on the bike, and enjoyed a long and leisurely ride to the house. Once there, I locked up the bike, walked in, said a few mandatory hellos, and then went upstairs for bed.

However, bed was a very liberal way of describing my sleeping arrangements. Technically it could have been called a bed, but actually it was only a thin folding cot mattress a mere six inches thick. It completely filled the three-by-six-foot closet floor in the boys' bedroom. It was very tight with just enough room to read a book by a battery-operated lamp before dropping off to sleep. But at least I had it to myself, as it was probably the best arrangement to be had, considering the circumstances. My six brothers had to share two beds in their small nine-by-twelve-foot room, so I was lucky enough just to have had my own little bit of a place. But even so, that closet was worlds away from what waited for me at the newspaper in the secret room. But it was still there, it was still mine, and my secret was still safe. I really missed it as it was the only place that had ever truly felt like home.

But on Friday nights my schedule changed as I stayed on at the newspaper beyond my normal hours. I met up with the regular mailroom crew as they arrived at eleven thirty to produce the Saturday-morning paper. My task was to work the loading dock helping the routes drivers with their loads. That shift usually ended at four thirty or five o'clock in the morning. When it was all wrapped up and the mailroom was shut down, I went with the other guys to a bar just a block away that served coffee and breakfast. We talked, laughed, and joked as I listened to whoever had the latest advice on how to fix whatever national issue we had just printed in the paper.

After that, a bike ride usually got me to the house just about the time the sun came up. I always went upstairs to my little closet bedroom, closed the door, and then slept until nearly noon. Once awake, I got around, did my laundry, and then went shopping for whatever I had on my list of necessities for the week. After just a few hours of goofing off with the guys in the neighborhood, I returned to the newspaper at ten o'clock that night. That was the production run for the Sunday-morning paper. When those papers were rolled for delivery, they resembled a small log for a fireplace. Their weight required extra handling, naturally heavier loads, and the opportunity to make a decent amount of money. But working on the docks required working harder and faster. It called for back-breaking hustle, but the rewards were always worth it.

The shift usually ended around six or seven in the morning. We piled into the delivery trucks, drove to the storage lot, and then went to the truck stop for breakfast. Spending time with adults and being an integral part of their conversations were much more enjoyable than the petty stupidity and childish drama I experienced at school. Those kids always acted as if they were adults with tons of experience in the issues of life. Then they spent most of their time trying to prove it to everyone. With the guys in the mailroom, we all knew each other too well and for the most part respected each other. To be sure, some of the guys did shovel it a bit, but that was to be expected. There at that truck stop, I felt as if I belonged with them. They never ever treated me as some kid and never thought that any of my questions were stupid. They always gave me advice and occasionally it was great advice. It was almost felt like having family to talk to.

On Sundays, I usually arrived at the house sometime after nine in the morning. Unfortunately, I always had to listen to Yellow Teeth make some smart-mouthed remark about where I had been and what had I been doing. It was idiotic because he knew full well just what my activities were. But for some reason, he really seemed to have an issue with me and always had to lip off about it. Each week in that house became increasingly worse than the one before. It didn't help that frequently during the week, my mother—using her fake, phony, and sweet voice—declared that I had better watch my step because he was such a bad and tough guy. To me, none of it meant a thing as I had no fear of him whatsoever.

But I had to wonder, just what sort of schemes were the two of them up to? Just who did they think they were? They had been busy playing their own sorry little games and had obviously never thought for a moment if anyone noticed. But then they wanted to give me grief about my working hours. I was completely sick of these hypocrites! I decided that I would do whatever I wanted, whomever I wanted, wherever I wanted, and whenever I wanted. I was more than happy for the opportunity to give them directions about just where they could put their demands. But I also knew that I was headed for a serious confrontation. I could feel it, welcomed it, and waited for the opportunity to arrive.

School was less than two weeks away from being out for the summer. I could feel the tension in the house growing in intensity each night after work. On many occasions as I walked in through the back door, Yellow Teeth and my mother could be heard having words, which often lasted late into the night. It was obvious that there was a little trouble brewing in paradise. It sounded as if the honeymoon might have been over by that point. But as far as I was concerned, it served them both right. It just made me want to laugh out loud. Wasn't all of that just too bad? Weren't they getting their just reward? But I was also very curious as I wondered what the details were. In my own mind, I wondered if I had anything to do with their newfound unhappiness. I certainly hoped that to be the case.

The following Sunday morning after I had awakened, I could tell that Yellow Teeth was in a really foul mood. I heard him downstairs cursing and shouting as he walked about the house. A few minutes later, as I lay there in the closet in the darkness, I heard the back door slam. I then left the closet, and from the boys' bedroom window, I looked out and saw the kids as they scattered out into the backyard. I could tell by their actions that they had left the house in fear.

Who did that worthless jerk think that he was? When I went down the stairs to check it all out, he met me at the bottom of the steps as if he had purposely waited for me. He told me in no uncertain terms that he was totally fed up, with me, with all of my nonsense, and that he had had enough. Then he just turned and walked away without giving me any explanation of any kind. What had I ever done to him? I was never in his house long enough to do anything , much less anything wrong. What in the world was he so angry about? What could I have done differently if I hadn't any idea of what the question actually was? Then I discovered the other part of the equation.

It was my mother. Where had she been as all of that had happened? A quick glance revealed that she had just stood there in the living room while Yellow Teeth tore into me and never said a word. She had witnessed the whole thing and never bothered to open her mouth. What kind of mother was she, and why wouldn't she do anything to protect her children? A lot of help she was. But when I caught her eye and glared at her, the truth revealed itself without a single spoken word. She simply turned her back on me while wearing that same sorry smirk on her face. It was obvious that none of what went on was going to be good for me or for anyone else. Therefore I knew that I was in some sort of trouble although I didn't know what I had done or what the discipline would be. But I knew from past experience that I was going to get blindsided somehow. Wonderful, wasn't that just wonderful? I decided that I had better set some serious plans in place.

Finality was reached the following Saturday morning. I had made a decision and had spent the night in the secret room. I had really gotten sick and tired of sleeping on the floor of a cramped little closet when all the while I had a better place of my own. There really was nothing like waking up in my own bed and in my own place. It just felt so good and so perfect. It was life as it should be.

As I rolled over and looked at the clock, I could see that it was almost nine in the morning. I figured that I had better get my act together, get on the bike, and head for the house. As I rolled my bike out onto the loading dock, I was greeted by a gloomy and dreary morning with drizzling rain for added effect. To myself I thought, great, now I could get a free shower as I rode my bike. However, there was no sense in waiting, as the weather obviously wasn't going to get any better.

By the time that I arrived at the house, the drizzle had turned into a full downpour. I probably could have wrung a full bucket of water from my clothes. I was absolutely miserable and not in a good mood. All I wanted was a nice hot, relaxing shower, some peace and quiet, and a good book. After all, wasn't that what rainy days were best made for? I really was in need of time to relax and unwind. I was certainly not in the mood for dealing with my family or any of their nonsense that day.

As I wheeled my bike into the driveway, I was presented with an interesting sight as my mother's car wasn't there, which was quite strange at that time of the morning. I wondered just what she was off doing or where or with whom? Whatever the case might be, it certainly didn't matter. I locked my bike up on the back porch, stripped down to just my jeans, and left all of my other clothes in a heaping wet pile there on the back porch by the door. I wasn't in the mood for anyone's attitude. I already had enough of my own.

But as I entered the house, I got no farther inside than the kitchen. It was Yellow Teeth. He sat there at the kitchen table in all of his glory as he drank coffee and smoked his cigarettes. He looked at me with eyes that were filled with pure hatred. There were no signs of that former gentleman to be found anywhere. As I stood there, I felt the adrenalin as it began to flow within my veins and wondered just what had I done to anger him. But at the same time in the back of my mind, I clearly heard my uncles' voices saying to get ready, get ready, and get ready.

Something very serious was about to happen. In my mind I anxiously wondered if it was about to be what I thought that it was going to be. Evidently my intuition was correct because he didn't ask but ordered me to put my sorry hide in a seat at the table. It seemed that he and I were about to have it out, once and for all. I figured that I had better make the best of my situation and set the scene to my advantage. Therefore I refused his order.

That act of refusal angered him so badly that he completely lost his temper. He stood up so quickly that he knocked his chair backward onto the floor. Then he launched into a foul-mouthed tirade, as his spit flew with every word. I had certainly had enough of him and his nonsense, so I shouted back with a few well-chosen words of my own. Two could play this game. Then he suddenly chose a few topics that for some reasons, he must have believed would have caused me pain. Obviously, he was sadly mistaken.

He simply gave me information that I had already possessed. He informed me that my mother wasn't going to protect me from him anymore. That caused me no anxiety as she had never protected me from any assailant of any kind, including herself. Then he added that he was sick of me living in his house, being forced to deal with me, and that he couldn't tolerate the sight of me. I told him that I really didn't care. Then he informed me that I was going to learn some respect and obedience from him even if it took a few bruises to get the job done. I responded by telling him that I was through taking orders from trash such as he was or from any other worthless person in his house. Having uttered those words, I simply turned from him and began walking away. That really set him off. He began yelling that it was his house that I was living in and I would listen to him or else. Then I turned around and asked the inevitable fight starter—or else what? I told him to just go ahead, just bring it on, and give me the "or else." He suddenly was silenced by the statement, as if no one had ever stood up to him before. He simply didn't know what to say to that. He had no response at all.

In the momentary silence, I grabbed a garbage bag from the kitchen cupboard and pounded my way up the stairs. I put everything into it that I hadn't already moved to the secret room a few days before. But I also prepared myself for what I had assumed was coming my way. I knew that when I returned to that kitchen, it would be far from over. I knew that a confrontation was waiting. My only decision was whether I wanted to be a victim or not. After I had finished gathering my belongings and headed downstairs, he was still there in the kitchen. But he had changed his position to a place of standing as he blocked my path to the back door. It could have been so very easy. He could have just gotten out of my way, and I would have walked out of his house, never to return. He would never have to be bothered with me again. He and my mother could have gone on living their lives however they saw fit. I really didn't care. But he hadn't chosen the easy route.

I told him to move, and in complete stupidity, he stood there in defiant silence. Then I told him again. In my mind, I figured at the least he had been warned. He wouldn't be able to deny that. Then I told him once more to get out of my way, and once again, he stubbornly and stupidly refused. I calmly sat the bag down and then repeated myself for the fourth and final time. He still refused and thereby proved himself to be a very foolish man.

Then suddenly he let loose with a string of profanity and added a few names, with some detailed physical threats thrown in for good measure. I knew for certain that at least one of them had to be physically impossible. I stopped him in midsentence and told him that as far as I was concerned, he was nothing but an old fool. Then I added that if he had a brain in his head, he would get out of my way or else. He didn't say anything, not a word, but just stood there and glared. I knew that he was begging for a fight. Then I instructed him once again to move out of my way and that he wasn't going to like it if he didn't. He didn't believe a word of what I had said to him. He just laughed at me.

Flashbacks of third grade and my uncles' voices raced through my head. I took two steps toward him as my eyes swept the room for weapons. As I did so, he brought his fists up to chin level and reminded me that he had once been a boxer. As he positioned himself in that stance, he uttered a crass, disgusting remark concerning sexual acts that had occurred between himself and my mother. Why had he thought for one moment that I cared about anything what the two of them had done? He just didn't get it. I didn't care what they did or where they did it. Nothing about the two of them mattered to me. He obviously never expected those responses or the actions that immediately followed. For just those few seconds, he was caught completely off guard. It was just enough, it was perfect timing, and it went exactly as I had been instructed.

As he watched my hands, he should have been watching my feet. The side of my left foot struck him firmly in the jaw and instantly dropped him to the kitchen floor with a loud, heaping thud. I calmly walked over to where he lay on the floor on one elbow as he continued to run his foul mouth. I knelt down beside him and remaining silent, double punched him in both the mouth, and nose. The blood splattered everywhere as he collapsed the remainder of the way to the floor. There was blood on the cupboard doors, on the kitchen table, and all over the floor. There was a lot more of it than I had expected. I stepped over him to the sink and washed the blood from my hands and then angrily threw the wet washcloth into his rapidly swelling face. Then I stepped back over him, and as a bundle of anger still raged within me, I drove a well-placed foot into his ribs for added effect and punishment.

With that accomplished, I picked up my bag of belongings, walked out onto the back porch and put my wet clothes back on, and was instantly chilled. I got on my bike and rode toward the downtown area and to the newspaper in the rain. It was still a gloomy, dreary day, but I never felt better. I hadn't felt that good about myself for a long, long time. But I never looked back as I was through with that place and with all of those people. There was no one that could ever make me go back there. I was finished with them all. I was finally free.

I spent the few days that remained of the school year living in my secret room. I went to school every day as required and returned to the newspaper each afternoon. No one ever bothered me, and no one ever questioned me about anything, which made me very curious. In actuality, I knew that I had committed a crime and that fighting was against the law. But evidently someone talked because my uncle surprised me with a visit at the newspaper. He had stopped by just to check on me and to see how I was doing. It was so good to see him again, to sit, and to have a real conversation with someone. He never asked any of the questions I expected but did say, with a wink of an eye, that he was very proud of me. We quickly caught up on each of our lives and talked as if nothing had ever happened between the two of us. Neither of us mentioned the events of Euclid Avenue.

However, he did provide me with some very interesting news. It was told that Yellow Teeth had suffered a broken nose and a fractured jaw when falling from a ladder at his house. Evidently my mother had found him in the backyard, and the rescue squad had taken him to the hospital. It was an interesting story and quite a good one. But it also appeared that I was completely off the hook. Perhaps he was simply too embarrassed to tell the truth or a dozen other reasons, but none of which mattered to me. I was through with them, and they were out of my life for good.

But there was more news, although it was of a far different nature. At that point it was all hush-hush and unproven, merely the basis for a rumor. The unconfirmed news was that my mother was pregnant again and with child number 12. It would have been easy to assume just who the father was, but with her, that was not always the safest or wisest choice. I had to wonder how she would explain it, what scheme would she use, and what cover story would be set into place to depict the situation. I knew that it would be so interesting to watch as the drama unfolded. It would be interesting to see the events and all of the players in her next little game.

It was Tuesday and the second week of summer vacation. Staying in the secret room permitted me to begin my workday earlier, usually before five or six in the morning. That enabled me the greater opportunity to earn more money. It also looked to be a busy week as the area merchants were gearing up for the holiday week with additional advertisements, which created additional work in the mailroom. That always translated into a very good paycheck on Friday.

An hour or so into the workday, my father arrived, and surprisingly, he was smiling. That was certainly an amazing thing to behold. I found it hard to believe that he was actually in such a good mood. I wasn't even sure that he still had teeth in his head; it had been so long since I had seen him smile. But then I also wondered if he had been drinking and at that hour of the morning. Nobody with even half a brain smiled like that so early in the morning. Unless there was something else that was going on and it was then that I began to wonder. As he walked toward my worktable he appeared to be in a genuinely good mood. I also noticed that he had two coffees in his hands, apparently one for himself and one for me, which instantly raised suspicions.

My mind quickly chased itself in circles as I attempted to figure out what in the world was going on there that morning. He never did anything for nothing; he never had and not for anyone. It was all very suspicious, curious and more than a little weird as well. As he sat the coffee down, he began talking about a lot of nothing, just goofy conversation, and it struck me that he was giddy, almost stupidly happy. I just didn't understand. What was up with him? He hadn't been in a decent mood for half a year or more. The truth was that he hadn't been hardly human for quite some time, always growling and snapping at everyone and everything. Then just that suddenly he simply walked away from me, said that he would talk to me later, and began whistling a song as he went.

I was instantly confused and on alert. I wondered just what was going on and what had just happened. It was strange, very strange. Something was up, and whatever it was, I knew that I had better put my guard up, get ready, and be prepared for what was certainly coming. I knew without actually knowing that surely my mother had to have something to do with all of it. With that in mind, I lost myself in my thoughts, questions, and fears for the next couple of hours as I worked.

As part of the daily mailroom process, a bit of relative calm ruled over the mailroom for nearly an hour once the first production run was completed. It was the time of day when employees either took a break, grabbed some lunch, or found a place to take a nap before the next run began. As I watched people heading out, I heard my father calling my name, and as I looked up, he motioned for me to join him out on the loading dock.

He was still far too excited about something, and I found it unnerving. Then he said that he only had a minute or two as he had to get ready for the next run. In conversation he was the exact opposite of my mother. He had no tact or delivery whatsoever, and so he just let me have it with both barrels and with absolutely no warning. He and my mother were getting back together. We were all going to be a family again. They had been seeing each other for just a short while and had worked everything out. They were also getting a new and bigger house in a very nice neighborhood. He then added that there was also going to be structure in the family, and the two of them had a plan set in place for just about everything. There wasn't anything that I had to worry about anymore. Then he stated that my mother would be there shortly because she was the best one to talk to me. She had all of the details, and then he dropped the real bombshell on my head. She would also begin working at the newspaper that very afternoon. Then he just walked away as he whistled that same stupid song.

What? What? What was that all about? Had he completely lost his mind? Why would he let that miserable excuse of a wife and woman back into his life? I would rather be alone and depressed than to have someone like that running, controlling, and ruining my life. There wasn't any doubt in my mind of just what she would do. According to the rumor, I knew exactly why she had been "seeing" him for a little while. I wondered if he even knew about the pregnancy before she had begun snuggling up to him. *Fool!* What a sorry fool! She was just going to bury him in debt again, dump him again, and then leave him hanging again. What an idiot!

Then there was the other problem. Just who in their right mind had given her a job at the newspaper? Just what kind of job would she be doing? I knew at that moment that my life wasn't going to be worth living for a minute with her around all of the time. My father was always very easy to dodge and avoid. But she was exactly the opposite, as she would want to know my every move. It was pure stupidity, and it was really going to throw a wrench into everything that I did and wanted to do.

Why was my father so stupid? Had he forgotten why she had left? I just wondered what sort of story she had spun for him. There wasn't any way that I would ever let any woman pull that kind of trash on me! It was just as my uncle had always said: life was far too short to be wearing used shoes all of your life. She was for certain a pair of well-worn and used-up shoes. I had seen her in action, with my own eyes and far too many times. I didn't really care if they did have a new house to move into. I really didn't even care how big it was or even where it was. They could do whatever they wanted. I had been doing just fine taking care of myself by myself. They hadn't bothered with me for two months even though they knew full well just where they could find me every day of the week and every hour of the day.

Then there was the other nonsense. What was that business my father spoke of about a plan and structure? It all smelled like a pile of horse stuff on my grandfather's farm. Those two couldn't plan a picnic together much less anything else. It all reeked like the house that we used to live in. My life was fine just the way that it was, and I liked it just the way that it was. I liked my privacy, I liked my solitude, and I didn't care for any of them, not a one of them. They could have all fallen of the end of the earth for all that I cared. I had suffered through enough of their nonsense for an entire lifetime and then some.

Then the bad news herself strolled through the double doors in all of her glory and honor. There she was in the mailroom, my own personal and private domain, and it angered me to no end. Just before she arrived, I had asked a few questions of the young ladies on the newspaper office staff who readily supplied me with all of the answers that I needed. She had somehow managed to obtain one of the afternoon country motor routes. That meant that she would be there in the mailroom seven days a week. My entire life had just been completely invaded.

From my worktable, I observed her. I watched as she talked to everyone as she acted all smug and victorious, prim and proper as my father naturally stood off to the side. I thought that I was actually going to be sick. Then the two of them began walking toward me, she was all charming, and he was all stupid and happy like an idiot schoolboy. Better yet, in my eyes, he looked as livestock might have as they were headed off for the slaughter.

She wasted no time at all and announced to me that as my mother, she was completely in charge as she then presented me with her new list of rules. We were all to live in one house, and I was expected to be there every night. I would have my own room in the house, and she would be keeping an eye on me there at the newspaper as well. There were many other details to discuss, and she would take care of all of that later as she preferred not go into it there in public.

What was actually going on there? I wasn't in need of any more rules, another boss, or, least of all, a babysitter. She obviously had some hidden agenda, thinly veiled to be sure, but it was there nevertheless. I just knew it. She never operated without one. I could see it on her face, and it was very easy to read it in her eyes. But just what exactly was it? Evidently she could read my face just as easily because her mood changed in an instant. Just that quickly, she became angry, ugly, and with a finger in my face she informed me that there would be no more discussions. There would be no debates, and there would be no questions. She would give the orders, and I had better learn to follow them. Then there was nothing but glaring silence, total and complete silence.

But it was the loudest silence of all as pure hatred surged between the two of us. She was in for a fight, and she knew it. But then again, I knew that there wasn't anything that she wouldn't do to protect herself and her private and secret little agenda. It really didn't matter what she was up to. I just wanted to make certain that I survived it. Incredulously, through it all my father just stood close by, stupidly oblivious, as he reveled in his own little dream world of what he thought his life to be. Didn't he care about anything but himself? Was he that single-purposed? Was he that blind to the obvious? He was willing to accept the fact that his wife was back into his life after she had lived with another man and was now pregnant with that man's child. To me, that wasn't living. I wasn't even sure that it was beyond mere existence. I would have preferred to live alone, totally and completely alone. I really hoped that someone would be decent enough to put a bullet in me if I ever became close to being that stupid.

Decision
Tenth Grade: West Elm Street

It actually was a large house on a slight rise from the street as were all of the houses in the neighborhood. It had three large bedrooms, but only one bathroom that had to handle the needs of a dozen people. A discovery awaited me on the very first day as I walked into the new house. There I discovered that one of the bedrooms had a large six-by-seven-foot walk-in closet. That evidently was what my mother had meant when she stated that I was to have a room of my very own. It was much smaller than the secret room at the newspaper and that by a considerable amount. However, it was just like any other promise that she had ever made. She always made it sound good, but reality was always something much less and also revealed her true motives. It was the nature of everything that she did as I was due to find out so much more in the days ahead.

But my father was correct in that there was also a big living room, a dining room, and a full basement. It all sounded good enough, and I supposed that it suited the purpose, but again twelve people had to share that living space. I supposed that *big* was a relative term, especially when it came to descriptions and discussions within our family. However, the neighborhood was also nice enough, and there really wasn't a doubt that it was the best house that we have ever lived in. However, on a very interesting note, I observed that the new house was just around the corner from the house that we had lived in when I was in the fourth grade. It was the house where we had been evicted by the sheriff's department after my father had not gotten that anticipated promotion. It seemed as if it had happened a lifetime before, but it had actually occurred only a few years. There had to be some sort of irony in all of that somewhere.

It was a normal Monday morning, and after I had gotten out of the shower in the locker room, I found a message scrawled on a piece of paper and taped to my locker door. It was from my father, and the note stated that I had to move all of my things into the new house that night and that he would accept no more excuses from me. Well, as far as I was concerned, he could just take a flying leap. I knew without even asking that he had done only what she had told him to do. But I had already made my decision and was ready to stand by that decision. I determined that I was going to stay in the secret room and keep all of my belongings right where they belonged. I had determined before I had even read his note that I was going to take only what I absolutely had to when I went to the new house that night.

After quitting time that evening, my father stopped me in the parking lot and offered to put my bike into the van and drive me to the new place. I declined and said that I would rather ride the dozen blocks or so. Upon arriving at the house, I discovered that everyone was sitting in the living room for a mandatory family meeting, and my mother was visibly ticked off. But seeing her upset always made me smile inside for some reason, and I always fought to control my face from allowing it show. I declined an offered seat and stood against a doorway as she once again began her speech.

She went through a huge list of who was to do what, and she even had charts for chores and responsibilities for my brothers and sisters. I had to admit that it was very impressive, but privately I wondered just how long it would all last. None of her ideas and schemes ever did. There was never enough discipline or leadership within our family to have ever made such things successful.

When my sister complained that my name wasn't on the list or on any of the charts, I quickly discovered just exactly what my role in the whole ordeal was to be. From that point forward, I was required to help my mother on her new motor route on all weekends and holidays. I knew then and there that my life, both socially and otherwise, was about to be trashed. I knew that I would be forced to listen to her stories, listen to her flap her lips and brag for seemingly endless hours every day. I just couldn't believe my sorry luck. No matter what I did, no matter which way I turned, I either ran into a dead end or found myself cornered by her and her schemes.

It was all done under the premise of her giving me driving lessons in preparation for obtaining my driver's license. But my uncle had already taken care of that as I could have easily taken my test that very day if I wanted to. But I knew as I stood there in the living room before her that my fate was sealed. Despite the circumstances within or surrounding my life, it was always the same. She was in complete control, and according to her and that sickening smile there was nothing that I could possibly do about anything that she had set in place. But I had plans of my own, and I wasn't about to become another one of her doormats.

Within the first two weeks, life at the house actually turned out to be not all that bad. Since it was the summertime, I still woke up around dawn and headed out of the house for the newspaper well before the place erupted into total noise and chaos. I did attempt some semblance of participation before the family that I wanted to be part of everything and had changed my solitary ways. I went so far as to put an old desk that I had found at a garage sale into the room/closet. I then constructed a bunk bed over it, which allowed me just enough room to install a dresser where I allegedly kept my clothes. But it was all a charade as I only stored there those things that I had grown out of. Anything that I owned of any value, I naturally had secured at the newspaper in the secret room. There wasn't way that I was going to take the chance of getting bugs into any of my stuff. It didn't matter at all that I hadn't seen any in the new place, but I really didn't care as it simply wasn't worth the risk.

But that closet/bedroom of mine that my mother had so graciously given to me had charms of its own. There was a window that opened onto the front porch roof, and from there it was an easy couple of feet to a wooden trellis on the east side that extended all of the way to the ground. With that arrangement in place, I had my own private entrance, which meant that I didn't have to come and go through the house. That meant that I didn't have to bother with all of those blasted kids or especially with her.

Since I was fifteen and would be turning sixteen within a few months, I then began frequently checking with my mother about my car fund at the bank. Over the course of those few months, she had given me quite a bit of information about certificates of deposits, my account balances, and how they were tied up for a designated period of time. She had even given me literature about it from the bank, which described the general process. She then informed me that the certificates would be available sometime near the end of February. That time frame gave me about six months or less to find the car that I wanted, so I began the search immediately.

In preparation for the car purchase, I discovered that I had gone a little over budget on school clothes and supplies in preparation for my first year of high school. Therefore, I knew that I had to shave money by either eliminating double school lunches (my only hot meal of the day) or by the elimination of other luxuries of both legal and illegal in nature. But somehow I knew that I would find a way to get it all figured out. I always had before when it had been necessary.

September arrived and with it, the beginning of my high school days. It was something that I had waited my entire life to arrive. I had longed to arrive at that place in life and had great expectations for it. I believed that high school would be the place where I would be able to lay a decent social foundation that would at last separate me from my family. It was to be a place and time where I would recreate myself and begin building my dreams for the future. I thought that I had a great plan.

However, high school revealed itself to be exactly the opposite of what I had expected it to be. Truthfully, I wasn't exactly certain of what it was going to be, but in actuality, it was practically the same as middle school. It had the same scenarios, pitfalls, snares, and other difficulties. The rich kids were still the rich kids with all of the self-centered arrogance that came along with it. The kids who were always out to prove something remained the same with their self-destructive and selfish acts. After all of the assumptions and observations were taken in, the reality of the situation was that nothing had really changed. The only difference was that there were simply more kids to fit into each of those self-named little groups.

I found that it was easier and simpler to just not belong or join with any group at all. The simple fact remained that I had a job immediately after school, which helped out in the question department. Whenever someone asked something of me, be it time, money, or whatever the reason or cause, the answer always came easily. Working after school was mandatory every day, and since my dad was my boss, I had no opportunity to slack off. It worked every time, and it actually worked rather well. That tactic permitted me to pick and choose specifically just who, what, and where of what I wanted to become involved in. I felt as if I were in total control of nearly everything around me. The combination of those items caused me to indulge in some measure of quietly enjoyed pride.

At that point in time, the new school was fine, my classes were better, the teachers were great, and so were my grades. I managed to get along well with most of the kids, had not gotten into any altercations, and all appeared to be acceptable. But due to other decisions and circumstances, secretly my life still reeked, and I hated it. Even though I initially believed that I had everything under control, I quickly realized that the old habits had never left and it wasn't long before they arrived knocking at my heart's door. With that, I soon was reminded that everything came with a price.

It happened during the second week of school on a Thursday night, or actually very early on Friday morning. Someone that I had known quite well made a special and serious request. It was the sort of request that no self-respecting and motivated young man would have ever turned down. The two of us had discussed the entire matter over the phone and set everything into place. The supposedly foolproof plan was to meet the young lady at one o'clock in the morning at her house. Actually, the meeting was to take place at her pool house, which afforded even more privacy. I had my own thoughts about that privacy as her relationship with me was secret from everyone at school, just as the days in the tree house. Nothing had changed, not the people I encountered and neither had I.

During school hours she was a rich and affluent student involved in all of the correct societal groups that I never cared for and was in turn publicly shunned by her as well. But she was always very, very different on the phone, as she then became a completely different person. However, without any discussion, the same statements and unwritten rules that had been the normal course of events in the tree house became the same regimen in high school. For her and the rest of them, it was all about secrecy, their needs, wants, and desires. However, because of my desperate and insatiable need for attention, I stupidly agreed to any and all conditions. I told myself without ceasing that it was simply an innocent game and that no one had ever actually gotten hurt. I convinced myself that I had to discount my own emotions, their value, and settled for foolish self-delusion.

However, there was a very real obstacle that nearly cancelled the entire arrangement. There was a strict curfew in effect for the entire city, and it was very much enforced by the local police department. There had been riots in some of the older and poorer neighborhoods and even at the high school that I attended. The police would and did arrest anyone on sight caught in violation of that curfew. I read their names almost daily in the newspaper. The other part of the problem that went along with the curfew situation was the fact that her house was just outside of the city limits in the suburbs. That meant that I had to ride my bike about five miles in the dark, through unfamiliar neighborhoods and avoid the authorities at all costs. Not to mention, of course, there were all of the other obvious dangers that such activities always brought about. I thought about all of those things, weighing the good, the bad and the good and after much contemplation about all of those consequences, out of my bedroom window and into the night I went.

The bike ride to the girl's house was uneventful even though I spotted one cop car, but it was a few blocks away from my carefully laid out path. I was always very careful to keep to the shadows and had gotten quite good at that sort of stealth. Once I had arrived at her place, the experience at the pool house went as expected and as those activities tend to do. After a specified period of time, it was over as statements and promises were made as I then began the long trip back into town. That ride also gave me ample time to fully engage the emotional fight that always raged in the aftermath of those encounters.

The first mile or so went well enough, and then just as I crested the railroad overpass, there was obvious trouble ahead. An officer had someone pulled over with lights flashing and all the visibility that went along with it. Having my way blocked, I was forced to take what appeared to be a shortcut through a grocery store parking lot. Normally the parking lot was well lighted, but thankfully on that night it was completely dark. However, it wasn't but a few minutes later when I quickly discovered just why it was so dark. As I neared the eastern entrance of the lot and was nearly out to the street and far away from the cop, the surprise suddenly appeared.

It was sudden, quick, and terrifying as my bike dropped into an excavated depression two to three feet deep and nearly six feet across. In the split second before it happened, I had wondered why there was a bright-yellow backhoe sitting off to my left side in the parking lot. However, before another thought passed through my brain, the unexpected happened. As the front wheel of my bike suddenly dropped, it slammed into the floor of the hole and then against the opposite upright side with a tremendous amount of force. At that instant, the bike and I began to perform acrobatics through the early-morning air. Both of us then slammed incredibly hard onto the pavement as we each bounced a few more times before coming to a crumpled stop. I could do nothing but lay there moaning out loud in the most unbelievable kind of pain.

I wasn't able to move at all. Every inch of my body ached as if someone had beaten me with a ball bat and had done a very good job of it. As I attempted to raise my head, the right side of my face brought gravel up with it. When I attempted to brush the gravel off, I then realized that it was bleeding, and I had scraped it badly. I crazily stumbled and staggered to my feet and stood upright, but only for a brief second. I instantly lost my balance and sat back down on the asphalt in a miserable and painful heap. My head seemed to be chasing circles around the rest of my body. I was completely disoriented, nauseous, and felt that I was on the verge of blacking out. At that point, I almost wished the cop would have come along and arrest me. My head and the rest of my body hurt so badly after a few minutes that I just sprawled on the pavement, gazed at the night sky, and waited for everything to just stop spinning. I guessed that I must have lay there on that cold parking lot surface for half an hour to forty-five minutes. Just how ironic was that? One minute I was dodging the cops, and then when I wanted one to stop and get me, nobody showed up. That was just the kind of luck that I always seemed to have.

As I attempted to stand upright, I discovered that I was able to stand fairly well and then checked to ensure that all of my body parts were intact. With that inventory complete, it was then time to check on the bike. It was as bad as I had expected. It appeared to have become junk, something now completely worthless. The front wheel was no longer a circle as it looked as if someone had taken a bite out of it. The handlebars were bent in a very curious way, and it appeared that one of the welds on the frame had snapped. I had to ask myself out loud just what to do, and with nearly three miles left to go, the bike and I began to drag each other back to the house.

By the time that I had finally made it back to our neighborhood, the sky in the east had begun changing colors. I laid the bike down in the backyard, quietly went in the back door, and cleaned myself up as best as I could at the kitchen sink. Then with all of the stealth that I could muster, I went up the stair steps, climbed the short ladder to my bed, and lay my head down for just a short while.

It seemed as if I had only blinked when suddenly, I heard my brothers tearing around their bedroom just outside of my door. A fearful glance at the clock on my desk told me that I had less than an hour to get ready and get to school. I was usually out the door and had begun my day by that time. So I waded and shoved through the little brats and then locked myself in the bathroom. It was then that reality paid me a very startling visit. The mirror just said it all. My face was scraped from eyebrow to chin and it was pretty deep in some places. It really looked bad. But, there wasn't much left to do at that point other than to just live with it. But even so, I knew that I had to hurry and attempt to avoid the constable of the house. I also knew that at least one of the little brats had probably complained about locking them out of the bathroom. I knew that she was up and about because I heard her barking orders at everyone downstairs. I realized that I had to make some sort of appearance, so I declined to use my normal route of departure by means of the porch trellis. After I had done the best that I could with my face, I headed down the steps.

I really had the worst kind of luck. I was only but two feet from the front door when I heard her voice as I then tried to act deaf. Then she proceeded to announce all three of my given names with the voice and intonation that I had heard many times before. I knew then and there that I had better stop. I waited at the door with one hand on the open frame and braced myself as she met me there. She took one look at my face and let rip with a long string of profanities that instantly silenced every other voice within the house. Everything within those walls came to an immediate standstill as I realized that I had immediately become the family spotlight.

At first she thought that I had been in another fight and instantly assumed that I had been out running with my uncle at the bars. I replied that it was a ridiculous idea since it had been a school night. Then she settled down a bit and with an all-knowing eye looked me up and down and from head to toe. It made me very uncomfortable, much more than I had ever felt in my entire life. Then she began the all-knowing, standard parental game as she asked questions and I gave answers. It quickly became a verbal ping-pong match. Who was she? That wasn't important. Where did she live? That really wasn't important either. Then, as she looked at the other kids who had gathered nearby in the living room, she ordered me out onto the front porch with a curiously playful shove. It puzzled me that she wore a smile unlike any that I had ever seen before. It was a smile that seemed to radiate admiration and approval and it immediately caught me completely off guard.

It was then that I heard the most incredibly amazing statement that had ever reached my ears. It had taken her forever to say it of course, but the intent was crystal clear. She declared that if I was going to be involved in those sort of activities after curfew hours, curiously she couldn't seem to bring herself to say the actual words, then there were some things that I had better understand.

I then thought to myself, great, as I assumed I would be forced to then listen to the pregnancy speech, the responsibility speech and all of the other hypocritical nonsense that she so loved to declare. But I was wrong. I was so very wrong. It was the most ground-shaking, mind-bending, and outrageous thing that I ever heard any adult say to a teenager. It was utterly unbelievable that a parent, any parent, would have ever considered such a thing, much less to have actually said those words.

She stated that if those were the sort of habits and actions that I had committed myself to, then so be it. But there would be rules about the entire matter. She reminded me that there was a curfew in effect in the city and she knew that I knew everything about that. She then added that she didn't want me out and about all over the city, as it would only cause her trouble. She didn't have the time to deal with it and she didn't want to be bothered with juvenile court dates, penalty fines, and other issues. That was only one of the two rules that she had for me on that subject. The only other rule was that I was to wait until after all of the younger kids were asleep, and then I was to simply bring the girl into our house. Then she looked me directly in the eye with that same weird sort of pride, as well as something else that I couldn't define and wanted to know if I had understood everything that she had just stated.

Of course I understood! Anyone with half a brain would have understood an obvious blank check when it was waved in their face. Once the discussion was over, she suddenly appeared to be in a very strange and unusually good mood as she simply turned away and walked back into the house as if nothing had ever happened. I stood there on the porch and attempted to sort out my thoughts.

But in the back of my mind, as I headed off for school, the questions formed within my mind. Why had she made a statement such as that? Was the possibility of my getting into trouble with the authorities actually more important to her than giving me proper guidance? I wasn't stupid as I knew full well that my actions were wrong and against all of the socially acceptable rules. But then again, when had she or my father ever given me any guidance? That was what I looked to my uncle for. For as long as I had ever known, he was the only one who had ever cared.

But what if the younger ones ever found out? How would I react if they ever saw something? What if they heard something? Wasn't all of that important as well? Then there was the other issue. I realized just how obvious it was that she really didn't care if the girl got into trouble for curfew violation or for anything else for that matter. I often wondered if there was anything that she really did care about. What in the world ever went on inside of that head of hers? There was also that strange and creepy feeling about her smile that completely unnerved me as well. It was at once unsettling and disturbing at the same time. I simply shook my head in amazement that morning as I walked up the steps to the high school.

November arrived, and it was early in the month as I had unfortunately developed another serious problem that I naturally had to deal with on my own. However, the problem wasn't about curfew, girls, wrecked bicycles, work or money. Actually I had two problems, one that I eventually worked out by myself but the other I had no idea what to do with. It literally turned my entire world upside down and inside out.

I had arrived at a place in my life where I thoroughly enjoyed high school as well as the new routine that went along with it. I experienced no problems with my schoolmates and I actually enjoyed most of my classes. But a real problem came up regarding my second semester schedule. That schedule revealed that I had gym class right dead in the middle of the day and just before lunch. In middle school, gym class was something that I had barely tolerated and only suffered through it because it had been at the very end of the school day. Gym class itself was fine, participating in the workouts and the other activities were acceptable, and I even enjoyed some of them.

However, it wasn't the actual class that bothered me. It was the entire demeaning locker room process. The smell of the place was almost as bad as the house that we had lived in on the east side. That was a little tough to take at times. But by far, the very worst part was being forced to undress in front of thirty or forty other guys, who as teenagers of different ages, were in various stages of puberty. Some of them, being the blazing idiots that they were, had a tendency to be very vocal about things they observed. I grew to hate it so bad that it almost made me sick to my stomach at times. I just couldn't stand it.

As I then realized that I had to endure that same trauma all over again and worse still, that it was during the middle of the day, I decided that I had to do something about it. I considered one idea after another but none of them provided a way of escape from the dilemma that was before me. Then I simply made up my mind. I absolutely wasn't going to do it. I flat out refused to do it. The more that I thought about it, I figured that they couldn't make me do it. What would they have done? Would they have tied me up, bodily drug me into the locker room and then forced me at gunpoint to get undressed? I didn't think so. But somehow there just had to be a way around that entire mess. It was then that I hit upon what I believed was a brilliant plan.

I made an appointment with my family doctor under the guise of needing a physical for sports. I kept the appointment, made some noises about the school track team and then made my move. Once he stepped out of the office for a moment, I went over to the table where he kept his writing pad and looked at it closely. I observed that his signature was neatly imprinted onto the paper, almost unseen by the force of the pen. I quickly grabbed the top two sheets and put them into my pocket. When he returned to the exam room, he shook my hand, wished me luck in all of my endeavors, and sent me on my way. I paid the bill, got onto my new ten-speed bike and headed off to work as quickly as I could. By that time of the day I was an hour late and time was always money.

After everyone had left the mailroom that evening, I went into the secret room. Under a good light I carefully traced ink into the depression that his signature had made into the paper. It looked really good, almost as unreadable as a doctor's signature should be. I was quite proud. Then I wrote some lame medical excuse and then added that an additional study hall would be beneficial to my studies for college preparation. I felt the smile spread across my face in approval. It was an absolute masterpiece.

I took the document into school with me the next day and received permission to go to the office. I went in, sat down and then presented the document to the guidance counselor. She checked my schedule, looked at the piece of paper, then my grades, and with a smile, announced that I now had an extra study hall before lunch. Mission accomplished! There was no more gym class for the balance of my high school career. With the extra study time available, I was then also able to complete all of my homework and other studying during the school day. With that positive turn of events, I was then able to devote more time to work and making more money. Everything was working out perfectly.

The second problem wasn't any fun or even close to it. Part of the family's grand new deal was that I had to help my mother with her motor route whenever I wasn't working in the mailroom. The only good part of the forced enslavement was that I was allowed to drive on the route once in a while even though I didn't have a permit. I knew that it was illegal and would be seen as irresponsible, and so did she. But then again, when had she ever bothered to follow any rules about anything?

It was very early on a Saturday morning, well before dawn while on the motor route and as usual she was running off at the mouth. Then for some unknown reason she began talking about her pregnancy. As she spoke, she kept trying to make it sound as if she wanted me to believe that nothing had ever happened between her and Yellow Teeth. Then she cleverly attempted to twist the story to bend places and dates in order to cause it to appear as if she had gotten pregnant immediately after she and my father had gotten back together. I knew for a fact that she was lying as any grade school kid could do simple math. They had gotten back together by all accounts sometime in late July and the baby was due in late January to the first two weeks of February. When I tossed that technical bit of data in her face, she instantly became angry. I then purposely followed a previously known formula as the more questions that I asked, the angrier she always became. As her anger increased, the more I enjoyed it and consequently, the more questions I asked. After ten or fifteen minutes of fierce intensity, it was obvious that she had reached her breaking point. At that particular point, all of her restraint vanished, and she finally exploded.

That was when she let me have it with both barrels. It was a brutal verbal assault that hit me harder than anything physically ever had. However, it was obviously that she enjoyed every minute of it as the look on her face clearly told me everything that I needed to know. The tables had been instantly turned as I slumped into the seat of the car in completely unanticipated shock. It was then her turn to be amused. She really enjoyed the look that her cruel and confusing words put on my face. Suddenly, in that moment, it just wasn't so much fun anymore. In a vicious battle of wits, I was hopelessly outgunned as she was a seasoned opponent.

It was then her turn to ask all of the questions. Did I remember my seventh-grade science class? Did I remember the debate over my project grade? Well, those circumstances were quite similar to the events of the current day and the child that she carried. She allowed the questions to sink in and stir within my mind for just a moment. The next barrage hit me like a fist in the face.

The man whose last name that I carried was not my father. What? What? I shook my head in puzzled disbelief. What sort of nonsense was all of that? As she spoke the words, my mind spun such as it had never done before. It was nearly more than I could take and I instantly became nauseous. I had difficulty catching my breath and as she sat there in the driver's seat and watched me, she wore her trademark smile in quiet amusement. Then she proceeded to speak once again as she was far from finished.

She and my biological father had split up very early in the summer the year before I was born. She then met the young man whose last name I bore shortly thereafter. He had never dated and was naïve to the point of absurdity. She had been his first physical encounter which she fully used to her advantage. She seemed to be very proud of that accomplishment. Immediately thereafter, she announced her pregnancy as if it were the news of the day. As he was from a church attending family, he chose the moral route and dropped out of college and entered the workforce. They were married within a few short months later in a forced and contentious ceremony. I was born early in the following month of March. She then informed me with dripping sarcasm to just do the math on that one and check it all out in the family album on the shelf at home, the names, and dates were all there.

The emotions that had been boiling inside of me throughout her conversation came out with a blizzard of questions that were so strong and forceful that she immediately stopped the car and screamed at me to just shut my mouth. In the shock of the moment, I did what she asked, but she also looked at me with those eyes that I had seen plenty of times before. I knew then and there that I had better hang on tight, for the real punch, the real fist in the face was but seconds away. I knew that it was coming. I knew that it would rip my heart out just by the vengeful look on her face. But I just sat there in the passenger seat immovable. Even though I dreaded her words and feared them, I had to hear what she had to say.

When she spoke, she issued a condemning statement that forever changed my world. It reduced me to complete and total worthlessness. Her statement rocked me back into the seat of her car and literally sucked the air out of my chest and seemingly my life with it. As she spoke the words, I literally felt the blood drain from my face and instantly became weakened. I was horrified beyond any known words. It was far too much to bear.

She bluntly stated that if abortion had been legal when she realized that she was pregnant or if it would have been inexpensive enough, then I never would have been born. I wouldn't have had any chance of sitting there in her car that day. I would never have existed. Then she stated that it was well known fact within the family that I was not wanted. In fact, I wasn't wanted by anyone and certainly not by anyone in my father's family. Then as if to thoroughly drive the point home, she said that because of me, her life had been ruined and all of her hopes and dreams had been crushed. It was all because of me. Then as if she had not inflicted enough pain, she then added that if she had it to do all over again, she would have found the money and would have gone through with the procedure.

Then there was silence, nothing but total and complete silence. It wasn't welcomed, it wasn't needed, but it was still far better than to hear any more of her poisonous words. There was also no noise to be heard but the sound of the engine idling as neither of us said anything else. I couldn't do anything at that moment other than to just stare at the floorboards of the car. I obviously knew everything that I needed to know and then some. That moment proved to be the beginning of the end between the two of us. Perhaps it was somehow necessary and possibly even long overdue. But then, without another word spoken, I calmly stepped out of the car and quietly shut the door. She looked at me through the open window with seemingly all of the anger that the entire world itself possessed. Then without having said another word, she simply drove off down the country road and out of my sight.

My mind was in complete and utter turmoil as the questions and statements first closed in and then chased after me in mind twisting circles as a dog fruitlessly chases its own tail. They were questions that reached down to the core of my being and viciously attacked the very foundations of my existence itself. It seemed that I was nothing more than a mistake, an error and a lifelong series of regrets. I was never meant to have happened. I should never have existed. I was far worse than unimportant as I had been nothing but an intrusion into her life. I was never wanted or even considered? If she had the choice, I would have been thrown away like a worthless piece of garbage. I was nothing more than an unwanted bit of flesh. Then the questions reached even further.

If my father wasn't my father, then who was my father? What was his name? Did he know about me? Had he ever been told that he had a son? Did he ever think about me? Had he ever asked about me? Did he ever want to know anything about me? Since he lived in the same immediate area, had I ever seen him by accident? Then I became angry.

Why was it my fault that her life was a mess? Was that also one of the reasons why my grandmother, my father's mother, openly hated me and had abused me so badly? Was that why she went out of her way to treat me so cruelly? Was that why both sides of my family always seemed to look at me the way that they did? Was that also why I physically looked so much different than any of my brothers and sisters and indeed the majority of the rest of my family? Just who was it that I belonged to? Who was responsible for my existence? What was I? Who was I? Was I really worth anything to anyone?

It was nearly a nine-mile walk if I returned to the family house from that spot on the lonely country road. But in reality and the far more logical choice was the shorter walk to the newspaper and the secret room. So I obviously decided to go to the only place where I had ever felt at home.

February. Other than for the most obvious reason that had caused the never-ending tension, both of my parents acted as if nothing had ever happened. It was as if there had been no event and no discussion had ever taken place as neither of them appeared to be bothered by my feelings and emotions. By all outward accounts everything quickly settled back into the same routine that had existed previously. I went to school, went to work, went on the motor route and worked the docks on the weekends. I simply went through the motions of my life with as little emotion as possible. However, I still knew what I knew and decided to simply tolerate her in silence whenever I had the misfortune of being in her company. I decided to focus on much more important things to concern myself with during those dark and lonely days. I always tried to look for a bright spot in my life wherever I could find it. It oftentimes required a tremendous amount of searching, but I had one item that became the focus of my attention.

I had been spending quite a bit of time looking through the want ads for months and believed that I had narrowed my list of the cars that I wanted to buy to just three. My uncle stopped by the newspaper one evening after he had gotten off from work. He and I went over the entire list. He had me write down all of the pros and cons to each car that I was interested in. Once we reduced it to the final three, he reminded me of all of the things that I needed to look for and I wrote them all down as well. Then he told me to put down a deposit to hold it, but only if I was certain of the car and to be sure to get a receipt. Then the two of us would go, take it for a test drive and he would check out everything else. As far as I was concerned, everything was in order, and I was good to go. I could barely contain my excitement.

With something as important as my first car purchase, I decided on that particular morning that attending school could just take a back seat for the day. The next day of the week was Wednesday and I knew that I could just take in a slip into school to cover for the day off just as I had done my entire life. As I left the house at the usual time for school, I turned left instead of right as I reached the sidewalk and then headed off on my great adventure.

A private owner had the first car that I went to check on. It was only a mile or so away on the city's north side and in a nice neighborhood. It was just one of the things that my uncle had said was an important detail to consider. But leaving at that time of morning had also given me plenty of time for fresh donuts and coffee, which was always my favorite breakfast.

I had arranged the appointment for nine o'clock, which left a little time to waste, but the waiting itself was nearly unbearable. I had ridden past the car just the night before prior to going to the house. It was incredible looking and in great shape. It was dark jade green with black racing stripes, special model wheels on raised white letter tires with beautiful black leather interior. It was the most beautiful car that I had ever seen. I couldn't wait to sit in it, to feel my hands on the steering wheel and to shift the gears. I could just see myself driving it. The waiting was almost more than I could stand.

The long-awaited time finally arrived. I knocked on the door of the house, and a very nice older gentleman introduced himself. He discussed every detail about the car and fully explained everything. It was his son's car and he was going through a divorce. Due to that fact, he simply couldn't afford it any longer. I explained my entire situation to the gentleman and related all of the details about my job, my savings and my uncle's involvement just as I had been instructed. The man actually appeared to be impressed and even took me for a short drive in the car so that I could get a good feel for it. Then he went through the entire car with me from nose to tail. His son had kept perfect records from the first day of purchase. As the car was very nearly perfect. I decided not to look at anything else.

I explained to him what my uncle had told me about a deposit, a receipt and a full test drive. He agreed and seemed to be quite impressed with the transaction. It was just after ten thirty in the morning as I rode away on my bike with my emotions running like the wind. I couldn't believe it! I had bought a car! It was the happiest day of my life.

I rode my bike directly to the newspaper, walked into the mailroom and immediately began working. My father tossed a question at me in passing about getting out of school early and didn't bother to wait for the answer that I didn't give. It evidently wasn't that important to him either. At lunchtime I called my uncle at the wrecking yard and gave him all of the details about the car. I described the man that I had talked to and reviewed all of the other arrangements. He said that he would stop by the newspaper about seven o'clock that night.

With all of those items of importance wrapped up, I hunted my father down. I told him that I needed to talk to him and my mother about something extremely important. I then asked him if the two of them could meet with me just as soon as she had finished with her motor route that evening. When he asked about the details, I responded that it was very serious and that both of them needed to be there. He reluctantly agreed and as luck would have it, stated that they would be there at seven o'clock that evening.

The three of them, both parents and my uncle, all arrived in the mailroom within a few minutes of one another. My father had gone home to eat supper and supposedly to check on the kids. My mother pulled into the parking lot just as he was getting out of the work van. As they walked into the mailroom together, I observed strange and puzzled looks on their faces. I had hoped for such a response, as I had purposely not wanted to tell them just what the nature of the meeting was. I figured that it was their turn to wonder what was up.

The two of them had no more than walked up to my worktable when my uncle strolled in through the double doors of the mailroom. They both became a little angry and upset as they were visibly displeased by my uncle's sudden appearance. They obviously hadn't expected him to be there and it didn't appear that they wanted him there either. It also appeared that at that instant, my mother suddenly tried especially hard to be ignorant. I had not made any secret of my car search and assumed that she knew why I had called the meeting. Her actions puzzled me as red flags began popping up inside of my head. I suddenly began to have a very bad feeling about it all.

But when she asked about the reason for the meeting, my father sheepishly spoke up and added that he hadn't paid much attention to anything that I had said to him earlier in the day. He had concluded that it was a matter of life and death by the way that I had acted throughout the day. Then it was as if a light suddenly came on inside of her head as a barrage of questions erupted from her mouth as if the topic was about a girl.

What was her name? Who were her parents? Caught off guard, I was without an answer. Since she heard nothing from me, she then dropped the bombshell. Was she pregnant and how long had I known about it? Just what did I expect her and my father to do about it? She just went on and on, gaining stupidity by the moment as she never let me get a word in anywhere along the way. My father just stood there with the same stupid look on his face that he always wore on those occasions and most others. Meanwhile, my uncle sat on the metal table just behind them and out of their line of sight. He motioned to me with a finger on his lips as if to be silent. He apparently thought it best to just wait until my mother wound down her tirade to a tolerable degree.

But she never did wind down, but just kept going on about how irresponsible and impossible that I was. Then she added some additional nonsense that I never thought about anyone but myself. Then she told me that, by my own selfish actions, I had put the entire family into jeopardy. After that statement, I had finally heard enough. It had become more than I could stand. Something inside of me just snapped. I stepped directly in front of her and with my face just inches from hers, I told her to just shut up and to just listen! Then, before the shock wore off and she had a chance to respond, I informed her that I had only brought them together to talk about a car. It was only about a car.

Then I related to them just what had happened earlier in the day. My uncle then quickly spoke up and spoke of how I had researched the whole thing very carefully and that he had given me plenty of instructions. Then he added how the two of us had planned to go on a test drive the next day. In addition, he added that he would personally make certain that it was the best car that I could buy for the money. While I had been speaking I looked back and forth at all three of them, but as my uncle spoke, I focused my attention solely on my parents. I really didn't care much for anything that my eyes observed. The looks on their faces stirred up very unpleasant feelings within me. Something was very, very wrong.

My father simply refused to look at me. He stared at the floor, the walls, the ceiling, at anywhere, or at anything but at me. Something during that meeting had taken a horrible turn as the alarms went off loudly inside of my head. I instantly felt that the situation was really just that bad simply by looking at him. I also felt it inside of me. But my mother, on the other hand, acted completely different. All of her normal confidence and arrogance had suddenly and uncharacteristically vanished. She immediately took on the appearance of a convicted criminal in a courtroom or perhaps more appropriately as the conversation progressed, a cornered rat.

When she began to speak, it was in a quiet and strange voice that was completely out of character. It was completely unnerving, and I was instantly on my guard. When she had only spoken a total of three words, and one of them was the word *bank*, my father looked at me for the first time that evening during the course of the conversation. He then quickly turned his face, walked away, went through the double doors and then outside. When I returned my attention to my mother, she was still making the same sort of noises while not actually saying anything. She made statements about the family's finances, that there had been some tough times, that there was no other way around some of it and other things of that nature. My frustration, patience, and tolerance had reached its limit. I angrily stopped her in midsentence with a simple raised hand. Then I plainly asked her just when I could get my money.

The truth was more than mere ugliness or criminality. It was reprehensible and nearly beyond belief. There was no money; there was absolutely no money. In fact, there had never been any money, not one thin dime; it had never existed. It had been a manipulative scheme, and it had been very carefully planned out. From the very start, I was an integral part of the purchase of their house on Harrison Avenue. It was why they had felt compelled to bring me along when the house was first looked at. It was the only reason that I had gotten the job at the newspaper four years before I should have. The two of them had devised, schemed, and carefully constructed the entire ordeal. They had known what motivated me and had focused upon that want and need. I had been thoroughly used and savagely taken advantage of.

Additionally, there had never been any bank account, certificates of deposit, or anything of that nature as it had all been a complete fraud. It was the most horrible and debilitating sort of a lie. It had been a methodically planned heap of lies. It had been constructed, designed, and fashioned that way before I had received the very first paycheck. The two of them had planned it even before I had gotten the job in the mailroom. They had crafted the entire ordeal from beginning to end.

The money that I had given her on Friday evenings never lived to see Monday morning. She had spent it all, every penny and every last dime. She claimed that she had spent it on food or to pay utility bills so that the family would have groceries, lights, and heat. Then, to add insult to injury, she further claimed that if it hadn't been for me through all of those years, my brothers and sisters wouldn't have had any presents at Christmas or sometimes not even any school clothes. To hear her tell it, it was the only way that the family could have possibly survived. What they had accomplished, even without my knowledge, had financially saved the family. In her scheme of things, the entire matter should have generated a tremendous amount of pride within me. Those were not, however, the sort of emotions that welled up within me.

That meant that I had actually purchased my own Christmas presents. It was a vile, vomit-inducing trash heap that she attempted to toss upon my head. As far as I was concerned, the both of them were nothing but worthless and lying trash. The reality of it all was incredibly clear. It was stealing, it was theft and truth be told, technically, it could be considered slavery. In my opinion, she was nothing more than a filthy, scheming liar. There had to be laws against that sort of treatment of children.

Then in an instant, as she looked me in the eye, her appearance instantly changed. She then smiled that all too familiar and sickening smile. I then responded to that smile with everything that was pent up within me. I was loud, I said it out loud, and the words were as profane as I could possibly utter them. *Lies, lies, lies!* I then let her know that as far as I was concerned, she was nothing but a liar! As far as I was concerned, she was a completely worthless parent as well. How did she dare to do something like that to me? What right did she have to do that to me? Just who did she think that she was? How had she ever managed to live with herself? Did she possess any conscience at all?

Then, as if it were the only answer that she had, she simply shrugged her shoulders. She stood there in front on me, stared at me wordlessly, and curiously looked at me with great intent for those long moments. Then, just that quickly, she gave me that same blasted smile, turned, and casually walked out of the mailroom. As she strolled out of sight, my uncle and I just stood there and stared at each other in wordless amazement.

As soon as she had walked out the double doors, I nearly broke down in that very instant. My constant dream and years of hard work had vanished before my eyes. My face instantly turned red as I desperately fought back the tears that welled up in my eyes. I couldn't and wouldn't cry in front of him.

But my uncle seemed to be in at least as much shock as I was. But it was also obvious that he had been thinking in those few short minutes. He walked up to me, put his hands on my shoulders, patted me on the head, and then gave me instructions. He told me to go back to work, take my frustrations out that way, make some money while he got busy, and made a few phone calls. That much I knew that I could do. So I worked like the angry madman that I truly was for the next two hours as he left to go on his mission.

He wasn't gone very long. He happened to be one of those guys who seemed to know practically everyone in town. So while I worked, he had been very busy. In that short amount of time, he had located a car that he believed I might approve of. But he warned me that it needed a tremendous amount of work. He quickly added that I didn't need to get depressed because he would help with the repairs every step of the way. He had already gone to see it and he had taken the time to inventory all that was required to make it roadworthy. He had already put together the entire list of needed parts. He also had a reasonably good estimate of what it would cost to complete the project. It would be quite a project, and it would probably take a few months to finish. But in the end it would be a very good car and it would be something to be proud of. It was a promise to me and I knew that he always kept to his word.

In that short period of time, he had also gone and spoken to the gentleman who had the car for sale that I had my heart so set on. My uncle had explained the entire situation, had easily gotten my deposit back, and had the money with him. Then he did his best to cheer me up. As if to brighten my mood, he went on to say that the car he had found happened to be a convertible. He was positive that he could get most, if not all, of the parts that I needed from the wrecking yard. We talked about the details for a while longer and agreed that we would get together the following Saturday afternoon. He would meet me with his tow truck, and then we would haul the car back to the house. Although it was good news, it was still quite depressing from just a few hours before.

At that point, I really didn't care one bit about what my family thought or what they had to say. Because of those feelings, emotions, and other inner turmoil, I spent the night in the secret room. There I spent the hours in silence as I smoked an entire pack of cigarettes as I leaned next to the vent in the wall. I had never been that angry and upset about anything before in my entire life. I just wanted to hit someone. As I sat there in the dark, I just couldn't stop the tears as they flowed. First, there was all of the information about who my father was, who he wasn't and the great mystery that she purposely surrounded the entire matter with. Then there was my mother's horrific abortion statement that she had so vengefully thrown in my face. Finally there was the revealing of their planned, deliberate, and diabolical four-year practice of theft and manipulation. I hated them with everything that was within me.

During the long watch of the night, I believed that it was probably for the best that I stayed there in the room. I knew myself well enough that if I had ventured out into the streets I would have surely found someone to start a fight with. Then we both would have been the victims of my overflowing anger. Then as they always did with incredible regularity, the questions came knocking at my mind's door and demanded answers.

Why did she always pull such stunts on me? Why did I always let her get away with it? Why had she lied to me over and over again about the bank account? Why had she given me all of those banking details and had kept a bankbook that recorded deposits as well? Where had she gotten that? Why had I ever bothered to trust her about anything? After what she had done to me so many times before, I should have known better. Why had I believed a single word that she had ever said? Historically, I should have seen it coming.

The promotion out of state and leaving-me-behind scheme in fourth grade, the evil event scheme in sixth grade, and then there was that whole mess with her boyfriend in ninth grade. The precedents were all there, as were the visible facts. I simply trusted a dishonest, selfish and incredibly devious person. I was ashamed to be related to her.

It was also sarcastically comforting to know the truth about all of those sorry conversations she always had about money being tight at Christmas. The actual truth was that every year she had actually pulled off an even bigger stunt. So what little bit of a present that I had received at Christmas, I had actually bought for myself. With that fact revealed, my mother's standard holiday statement rang out as both incredibly ridiculous and horribly cruel. Every Christmas it was the same repetitious story in regards to the two presents that I always received. It was the real and obvious fact that the other kids each received five or six gifts. Afterward she always pushed the guilt upon me, that as the oldest child, she knew that I understood the family's ongoing and never-ending financial situation. She always found a way to justify her actions despite the pain, the anguish and the consequences that it brought about in the lives of others. It was fiendish, diabolical, and had obviously been very well thought out. But hadn't she ever considered or realized that she would have been found out at some point in time? She had to have known that sooner or later the truth would have been revealed. Or was the actual truth of the matter the simple fact that she simply didn't care?

Hadn't it been just a few months prior when she had informed me that my money was safely secured in certificates of deposit and that they wouldn't be due out until February? How could she have been so cold, so calculating, and so incredibly cruel? What kind of a sick person possessed within their heart the capability to contrive such deceptions? What sort of twisted person was capable of committing those types of crimes against their own children? In my mind, her crimes were grand theft, weekly petty stealing, deception, manipulation and even perhaps a type of slavery. The total dollar amount of the crime actually committed the matter to be a felony. The facts were all there and had been recorded and witnessed every week over the course of four years. The total sum of the theft was five thousand three hundred eighty dollars and five cents, plus interest. That was the accumulated total of my four years of intense work. The added insult was that she had denied nothing, but had openly admitted to it all.

She placed the entire matter under her self-designated and self-righteous cause of protecting the family. She had convinced herself and others who had knowledge that she was blameless. But I believed none of it and had agreed with none of it. She and my father had lied to me, manipulated me, defrauded me and had stolen not only the money, but my trust in nearly any human being as well. It was nearly unbelievable to me just how callous and uncaring the both of them were about every facet of the ordeal. But the truly unanswered question remained. What had they done with all of the money?

I went to school the following morning with nearly no sleep and growled like an animal at anyone who bothered to get close. I was in no mood to socialize and found it very easy to keep everyone at a distance. I made no attempt to bother with lunch, but instead spent the entire time with the Westside Smoking Club just across the street from the school. During that hour, I simply sat there on the curb, smoked my cigarettes, and said nothing to anyone. Everyone clearly understood without asking that I was in a full-blown foul and destructive mood due to that fact, everyone wisely left me alone as they had witnessed those moods before. Later in that afternoon at the newspaper, I kept to myself, talked to no one and worked just as hard as I possibly could. Neither of my parents bothered to say even one word to me, not a glance, or, heaven forbid, may the sky suddenly fall, to utter a single word of an apology. They kept their distance, not out of fear, but because they obviously didn't care. I believed they knew that my usefulness to them was over.

After I had been at it for over an hour, I took the opportunity while everyone was busy and went to the front office. There I spoke to the circulation manager who also was my father's supervisor. He easily detected that I was very upset and remarked that he had actually expected my visit. He informed me that others in the mailroom had told him that something very wrong had taken place between my parents and I. When I told him what had happened, he wasn't at all shocked or anything even close to it. He reassured me that he would make certain that my money was protected. That was especially important since we were paid in cash. As a measure of security, he added that he would personally make certain that absolutely no one touched my pay envelope. Then he reminded me that there were a few people in the office that I could always confide in and trust. He then added that I could talk to him about anything and at any time. With that, he shook my hand, looked at his watch, and told me that I had better get back to work.

Saturday after the shift had ended, in the early hours of the morning, I simply hid out in the storage area and relaxed until everyone had left the mailroom and then went into the secret room. I stayed there until daybreak without sleep. My brain just wouldn't shut down as the questions kept coming and sleep proved to be a very fleeting thing. It simply wasn't to be found that night. I believed that my raging anger was primarily responsible for driving it away.

After daybreak, I left the newspaper on my bike, went to the doughnut shop, got a large coffee, and then rode around town aimlessly. The next thing that I knew I was on Harrison Avenue in front of our old place. I should have said address, because evidently my family had left that house in such bad shape that the bank had no choice but to have it demolished. I shook my head at the irony of it all and rode down the alley to the big oak tree and stopped. As I looked up into the branches I knew what to expect. The tree house was of course in a shambles, and I really didn't know why I expected anything more. I just sat there on my bike, drank my coffee, and allowed my mind to consider everything. Although the questions flowed without ceasing, the answers themselves never came. I stayed there beneath the tree until the coffee was gone.

My uncle arrived at the house on West Elm Street that afternoon with his tow truck. When he pulled up to the curb, I hopped into the cab of the truck and off we went. He asked how I was holding up and had I spoken with my parents. When I told him no, he said that we would go and grab a beer later if I wanted to. But the conversation had barely begun when we pulled into a rundown trailer court on West Vine Street. He stopped the tow truck and announced that we had arrived. I wasn't very optimistic as the neighborhood didn't offer that much in the way of hope.

I climbed out of the truck, looked around at the dozen or so mobile homes, but didn't see a red convertible anywhere. Then he motioned to me to follow him as we walked around behind one of the mobile homes. When I first saw that car, I just wanted to sit down in the gravel driveway in a heap and cry. My heart just sank to the ground. That car looked exactly as I felt. It looked worn out, used up, obviously unwanted, and appeared to have been simply tossed away.

It was red just as he had told me, but it would take hours with polishing compound and a buffing wheel if there was any hope of ever getting that paint to shine. The convertible top itself was down and the black vinyl interior was completely shot as greenish-yellow mold grew on every surface. My uncle walked me around it and warned me that realistically, it looked far worse than what it actually was.

He informed me that the wiring harnesses for the interior, under the dashboard, and inside of the engine compartment were completely burnt. A short of some kind in the wiring had caused all of the trouble. But he had already located all of the electrical components and harnesses that were needed at the wrecking yard. He also had secured a nearly new white convertible top as well as a complete bucket seat interior with nearly new carpet. He was certain that we could score just about anything else that we needed. The more that he talked, the more excited that I actually became about it. By the time we were towing it down the street, I believed that the both of us were more than ready to get started on our new project.

As we backed the car into the driveway off of the east to west alley, all of the little brats came running out of the house. But before I attempted to start in on them, my uncle stepped in ahead of me. He let them have it in no uncertain terms just what he would do to them if he found so much as a fingerprint on that car. They were scared to death of him and always had been. After he had threatened them, they took off running for the house as he simply smiled and stated that I was welcome.

Then my father came out of the house, and I was instantly upset by his arrival. Just what was it that he wanted? My uncle recognized my anger, raised a hand, and informed me that it was all part of the plan. Evidently one of my parents had to transfer the title since I wasn't an adult. Once they had done that, then I would have to give them the money for the license plates for the same reason. He then stated, even as my father stood there, that I was to let him know if either of them attempted any more games.

From that memorable day on I worked doubly hard in order to earn every dime possible in order to pay for the car to be completed. The two of us worked on it every Saturday afternoon and as much as possible on Sundays and over a reasonable period of time it was finished.

In my youthful and very biased opinion, it was an absolute beauty. As far as I was concerned, it was the most incredible car that I had ever seen, but my ownership naturally influenced that statement. I knew that it wasn't exactly perfect and it didn't look as if it had just rolled off of the showroom floor, although it was close. However, it would have easily held its own on any used car lot. It actually had turned out much better than I had ever expected. That buffing wheel had done an incredible job of bringing out the shine in the paint and the chrome had polished up very well also. The interior with bucket seats and console turned out so well that it looked as if the factory had installed them. I could hardly believe my eyes every time that I looked at it. It provided me with a tremendous sense of pride. I had accomplished something magnificent with my own two hands.

My uncle had also managed to come up with a really nice set of nearly new, raised white letter tires on chrome rims that had cost me very little money. I knew that it was far less than what they were worth. Actually, I didn't really want to know exactly where he had gotten them as I knew that he had contacts of different sorts all over town. He had accomplished quite a feat of work. All of the electrical work had also been done, everything had been tested, and it all worked perfectly. The engine ran as if new and the newly installed exhaust made it sound just oh so good.

After we had bolted on the new license plates, I handed my uncle the keys and told him that he had the honors. He refused, cracked a big smile, grabbed me by the shoulders, spun me around and shoved me toward the car. He would take a drive with me later. All that he wanted at that moment was to see me drive off down the street in my new car. So as we stood there side by side, I took the keys back from him as the tears welled up in my eyes. He really was the best friend any young man could have had.

I positioned myself behind the steering wheel, put the key into the ignition, started the engine, and put the convertible top down. There wasn't anything comparable to sitting behind the wheel of a convertible, or the exhaust note from a convertible with the top down. Then, with a reminder from my uncle to be sure to treat it like a baby, I was off for the day.

I drove that car everywhere, up one street and then down another. I drove past peoples' houses that I knew and into some of the neighborhoods that I had never dared to ride my bike through. After an hour or so of that, I made the decision to drive out of the city and southeast to the lakefront cottage that my grandparents, my father's parents, owned. That drive took a casual half an hour, as I was both pleasantly surprised and very thankful to find the place temporarily deserted. I parked the car, got out, and looked back at it as I walked to the water's edge at the dock. I chose one of the half a dozen deck chairs all scattered about near the boathouse, sat down in one of them and just looked out onto the water. I was amazed at just how perfectly quiet and calm it was there. It was completely relaxing and tranquil, a most unfamiliar feeling at best. I would have given almost anything to live in a place like that. It seemed as if it were the perfect place to sit, to think, to contemplate, to plan, and to even dream if I actually dared to.

As I sat in a chair and looked out over the water, I went over every detail of every problem, of every hope and of every dream that I had in my life. I soon became so lost in my thoughts that before I realized it, the sun had dipped below the tree line, and there was practically no orange left at all in the sky. But by that time I had also come to grips with the reality about my parents, my entire family, and most importantly, about myself. A balmy summer's drive back to the city that evening also brought an introspective, but good finish to what had become, an enlightened day. All of my newly made decisions, which would change my life completely, had been made. I just had to discover a way to carry them out.

I enjoyed the mailroom so much better in the summertime. It was much hotter, much noisier, and far more hectic. But I was also allowed to put in much longer days. With that change in the schedule, I usually had my week's work done well before noon on Friday. There were other benefits to working during the daytime hours as well. While I had ceased speaking with my parents if at all possible, there was one gentleman that I did enjoy talking to.

He was the senior motor route driver and had been at the newspaper since before I was born. He took care of the machines, was a very good friend of the circulation manager and owned a home out on the boulevards on the west side of town. He was a good man, well-known for his integrity and honesty. He worked seven days a week, seemed to be quite normal, and enjoyed a good cup of coffee just like the rest of us. From my point of view, it appeared that he had his life in control, was someone that I gained advice from and, more importantly, was someone that I could model my life after. I desperately needed and wanted a role model as I knew that this was one area where my uncle just did not fit the part.

I discussed nearly everything with him that troubled or concerned me. We debated the pros and cons concerning the decisions that I had made that day at the lake. He was always careful to tell me that our conversations were in full confidence and that he completely understood my situation, as he knew my parents very well. He revealed to me that it was more than obvious to him just exactly what they were all about.

There were dozens of financial, social, and legal questions that I had for him. I didn't actually shock him about anything but some of my questions did set him back a bit. We discussed the issues of renting, leasing, savings and investments and a host of other things. We talked about high school, college and girls. We reviewed the hundreds of pitfalls that surely awaited me along the way. He also added a number of personal stories that really drove the point home. We sat down over coffee and worked out budgets as he taught me how to manage a household and how to balance a checkbook. He walked me through all of the things that were necessary for a person to live on their own. I found him to be an amazing person who obviously had won my admiration. He offered his advice freely and practically begged me to rely upon both him and the manager for anything that I needed. He in particular had kept to his word and forbid my parents from attaching themselves in any way to my job or my paycheck. The both of them also promised me assistance in any way that they possibly could. It meant the world to me to have someone to rely upon. It set me free to embark on those decisions that I had made at the lake.

Having previously searched the newspaper for a car, I then put those same skills to use as I sought to find a place of my own. I had more than the obvious at hand to motivate me. Within me, I knew that sooner or later, something would happen that would make the secret room a place that I couldn't use anymore. That secret had been kept safe for too long and I knew that the odds of it not being found out weren't very good. Realistically, the prime reason was the simple fact that what I really had wanted was simply a place that was truly my own. I wanted to be viewed as being upfront, honest and someone with integrity. The instructions that my mentors had given me were much more than simple facts or methods. They had taught me a tremendous amount about respect, about honor, decency, and maturity. I wanted my home to be something that I had paid for because at times as I lived in the secret room, I felt guilty for using it. I had been a victim of crime and wanted no part of it.

I spent many hours during those days as I searched the newspaper, circling the want ads and making telephone calls. Within a short while, I successfully narrowed my search down to a mere handful. During the course of a few telephone conversations, one of those prospects appeared to be much better than any of the others. It was a three-bedroom mobile home in a restricted suburban home park just outside of the city limits. Perhaps it was the prospect of living outside the city proper that appealed to my sense of pride more than anything. I would never have admitted it, but I had developed a measure of snobbery that should have been repulsive to me.

I scheduled an appointment to see the place and immediately notified my trusted advisors at the newspaper. The home revealed itself to be very nice and was actually far better than I had expected. The landlord himself proved to be a very nice man who spoke openly about my appearance, my car and his appreciation of the contents of my application. It took a great deal of effort for me to conceal my shock that someone was actually impressed with me.

On the rental application, I naturally included my employment at the newspaper for four years as well as casually mentioning in a very generic fashion that I was attending school. As he spoke, I never attempted to alter his belief that I was attending college while holding down a full time job. All of the facts and near facts that I had presented appeared to have impressed him, and I never corrected any of his statements. I handed over my first month's rent, a deposit and received a receipt as the transaction was completed. He also informed me that I had to have the utilities changed over into my name within the next few days. He shook my hand with a smile and left me standing there in my new house with keys in my hand. I had my first real home. With that, I felt as if I were an actual adult. I had my own house, real freedom and real responsibilities as well. I was scared to death.

The Real World
High School: Maumee Drive

It was close to four o'clock on an early Monday morning when I gathered together my belongings inside of the secret room. It all felt every bit as depressing as it had when I had packed up the tree house just a few years before. Perhaps it was because I felt as if I had grown up quite a bit while living in that little room. It almost felt as if I were leaving home. Perhaps it was due to the fact that it had been my only place of refuge and solitude for all of those years. It was almost as if I were saying good-bye to an old friend. It had to have been the most comfortable place that I had ever known. I had never felt more relaxed, protected, and safe than when I was tucked away within those walls. During the evenings I simply closed the little door and the world behind me in complete safety and security.

I had probably read over a hundred books and had eaten nearly all of my meals there within those last four years. But I had also anguished over nearly every major decision in my life within those walls. However, unlike the tree house, I had never invited or entertained the first guest there. I never shared that room with anyone, it was solely mine and mine alone.

As I began to make the move to my new home, the circulation manager permitted me to use his own company van to accomplish that task. With that vehicle at my disposal, I spent an entire Saturday scouring local garage sales to equip my new household. All of the appliances were already in my new home, but I had to purchase just about everything else.

At one such sale I found a dinette table with four chairs, a full set of dishes, glasses, and all sorts of other kitchen items. At another I found two chairs for the living room, an almost new iron and ironing board as well as a very nice stereo. At the third sale I also managed to purchase an older bedroom outfit, which included two dressers. It was a good thing that none of the items were outrageously large, as I would never have gotten them into the mobile home by myself. I spent the majority of the day Sunday shopping for kitchen utensils, pots and pans, towels, and such necessities for the bathroom and kitchen. Then and only then did I stop at my parents' house for the very few items that I had left behind in the little closet-bedroom.

They were both there at that time of the day and were sitting in the living room watching television. Neither of them bothered to utter a single word as I walked in the front door. Not once during my few minutes there did they attempt to discuss my moving out or to speak a single word. They didn't bother to ask for the address of my new place or even a phone number, although I hadn't gotten one at that time. They simply carried on as if it was just another day, nothing of any consequence, excitement, or concern had gone on. It was as if I didn't exist to them.

It was as if having refused them access to my money, I had turned my back on them in their time of greatest need. It was as if I had become a traitor to my entire family. They acted as if I had abandoned them. Where was the irony in all of that? The two of them just sat there in their chairs and ignored me, as if they hadn't seen me as I stood there in the living room doorway. It seemed that I was completely invisible to them. But at that point, as I stood there before them in their house, I couldn't have cared less. I was completely finished with them as well.

If I was upset with them that Sunday, I became a raging inferno by Monday afternoon. As soon as I had gotten out of school after just half a day, I made my rounds to all of the utility companies, gas, electric, telephone and cablevision. As I traveled from one business to the next, I experienced the same sorry, bewildering, and outright-disgusting story. At each and every office I ran into the very same brutal red tape barrier as I struggled through my dilemma. At each place, I was informed that I had seriously past due utility bills. I nearly lost my temper at the very first stop.

At every stop in my tortured journey, I found myself in conversations with a series of department heads. Once I had jumped through all of those hoops, I then ended with up the top manager, vice president or someone with that sort of title behind his name. At my insistence and usually with some reluctance, that individual then made the requested telephone call to the circulation manager at the newspaper. By the time I had arrived at the third utility on the list, I simply bypassed the front counter and asked for the supervisor of the past due department. By the time I had arrived at the last such place I went straight for the manager's office. Throughout the course of that frustrating afternoon, I smoked more than my usual quota of cigarettes and my nerves had become completely shot. I needed a drink in the very worst way, and I was as angry as I could possibly be.

The added fuel at each stop only furthered to inflame the firestorm of anger that I already had in my heart for my sorry parents. At each and every stop along the way, I heard the same exact tale. At every office, I was informed that I was not permitted to have any utilities turned on at my new home because I had a seriously past due bill. Each utility had also sent every bill with my name on it to a collection agency for forced repayment. At each institution, it was the same sad story but it also had the same ending. At each instance, I had to show the manager of that utility my driver's license, which proved my age. I then recited my entire story and requested the obligatory telephone call to the manager at the newspaper. There was no possible way that I could have run up a gas bill, an electric bill or whatever bill at the age of only nine, ten, or twelve years old.

In the days that followed, the process was explained by each of the utility managers who passed the gathered information to me by way of the circulation manager. It was discovered that upon further investigation that those two deadbeats parents of mine had seriously past due accounts with every possible business in town. Therefore, in order to get around those obstacles, they simply had used their own children's names and had practiced that tactic for years.

Since they had already used my name and had successfully ground it into the mud, they had then gone down the entire list of my younger brother and sisters. They had used their names at every address where they had ever lived. It was nearly unbelievable. Just who did those two think they were? How long did they expect to get away with their crimes? What caused them to believe that they had the right to destroy someone's credit rating even before they were capable of having one? What made them ever believe that they could have ever possibly have gotten away with it? As far as I was concerned, they didn't even deserve the title of parents. To them, children were apparently nothing more than tools to be used. I believed that it was time for justice.

But, unbeknownst to them at the moment of my utility ordeal, they actually hadn't gotten away with it. In each and every case the utility manager, after having spoken with the circulation manager at the newspaper, treated me as if I were the brand new customer that I actually was. They also informed their collection departments about the entire situation and made the necessary corrections in my favor. In at least one particular case they informed me that my parents would receive a very personal visit in the near future. My parents' private little scheme had been brought into a very public light. Everyone who had need of that information had been made aware of it. The two of them were about to go down for their manipulating deeds, and I enjoyed every bit of it.

At the newspaper the following afternoon, I located both of my parents and called them off to the side for a private conversation. I informed the two of them personally and then individually that they would never, ever get another dime from me. I informed them that I had put measures into place to prevent them from ever gaining any sort of access again. I let them know in no uncertain terms just how serious I was about everything. I laid everything out in clearly and sternly told them exactly what could be expected from me from that point forward. Then I let them have it.

I didn't care if they were broke, busted, or even completely destitute. I didn't care if they had suddenly found themselves to be homeless. I didn't care if they and the kids were starving. No matter what the situation, there weren't to bother me about anything, ask me for anything or even consider contacting me for help. It was over. I further added that if they knew what was best for them, they had better just keep their distance. I wanted it to be a valid warning due to the anger that raged within me that had become a seemingly unquenchable fire. It had me in total control. With those lasting words, I let them know that I preferred to live the remainder of my life without either of them. It was an ugly end to a very one-sided discussion.

I truly believed then and there that I had finally won a battle against those two scoundrels. The truth of the matter was that although I had indeed won that particular battle, the real war with those two diabolical schemers was far from over. As I naively basked in my victory and the self-glory, I became over confident about my two lifelong adversaries. I was about to get completely blindsided by them. I simply never ever saw it coming.

It was my junior year of high school, well into the fall season, and my routine had settled primarily into what it had been for some time. I went through my daily habits at home in the morning, drove off to school and then went to work in the afternoon. As before, I usually got off work late in the evening, went home, and then relaxed in newfound peace and quiet. However, I also found myself immersed in a number of questionable habits that had begun to fill up my days and nights.

On the weekend evenings there was always money to be made on the docks at the newspaper. During the week there were always those same visits that I had participated in at the tree house. As before there existed a shamefully embarrassing list of guests. On most occasions, it was just simply conversation. At other times it was innocently working on homework together. Often it was nothing more than the fixing and sharing of a meal. But frequently it ended up as the predictable something else type of activity. The twists, turns, and decisions throughout those visit always led to that intriguing something else. As momentarily enjoyable as those times were, the aftermath was always as brutal to my emotions as it had always been. Sooner or later the guests were gone and the debilitating loneliness always returned.

It was the same sad story as it had always been. I permitted it to continue in that decrepit fashion for years, ever since I began the immoral practice in the seventh grade. The emotional roller coaster was always the worst part just as it had always been. Others would have believed those accomplishments to be a great badge of honor. Still others would have used it for something to boast about. Some would have used it as a stepping-stone for prominence within the strange social society that was high school. The entrenched emotions that I felt, however, never reached those grand heights. At times it was nearly intolerable, but curiously not crippling enough for me to cease my actions. My emotional requirements were rudimentary basics at their best. I only wanted to be needed, desired, and to be found of some sort of worth to someone, perhaps to anyone, through whatever means and time possible. It was all in vain.

Those guests were never gone very long when the loneliness, and the depression always set in. I soon believed it to be the ugly and necessary payment for those brief moments of enjoyment. When the bill arrived, the payment of the debt came at me hard, fast, and with a horrible ugliness. It was as if I were on a fevered and high-pitched rush. But then the coming down afterward happened just as quickly and was almost violently fierce. The intense emptiness that always followed was nearly more than I could emotionally stand. It was as if someone had ripped my soul from my body, as if my heart had been ruthlessly torn from my chest. It was emotional vomiting and I hated it with every fiber of my being. However, it was still not enough to stop.

At times though, I wondered if all of the nonsense, intimacy, and subsequent emotional turmoil were really worth all of the effort. Was it was really worth all of the risk? Was it really worth all of the grief that erupted inside of me afterward? With each and every instance, I also knew that it had become more and more dangerous. I knew that the odds were rapidly rising against me. With one wrong move, with just one small slip, with one error or with one mistake and it would be over. The house of cards that I had created for myself would easily come crashing down upon me at any minute and certainly without any warning. I knew that those matters were true deep within my heart. However, I foolishly chose to ignore it all.

As I thought about all of those issues, it prompted me to make a change that I erroneously believed to be an incredibly brilliant and adult decision. Therefore, it turned out to be just as poor a one as all of my other social decisions had been. But as I made the lifestyle change from dating high school girls to young adult women who worked at the newspaper, restaurants, banks, and elsewhere, my problems never lessened. I foolishly believed, without reason or sufficient information, that I had taken a step up the social ladder. What I hadn't considered was the fact that it all came with a substantial price. I soon discovered that in addition to everything else, it also required a moderate degree of subterfuge. They included such items as the omissions that I had permitted with my landlord and other pathetic games with the truth. I had convinced myself that I had chosen a proper route. I had simply permitted people to believe whatever they wanted to believe about me.

But as I made those changes, I realized that the problems weren't at all different as only the locations and the players in the game had changed. Those decisions had also intensified the alcohol and drug problem that I had foolishly believed had been contained. But with that adjustment in lifestyle, I was then thrust headfirst into the adult world. I then had problems that were even far more heinous than any of those that had knocked at my door before. I unwisely chose to walk into that society without advice, consultation, and certainly without any critical thinking or concern. I literally had no clue of an idea of what was just about to happen. I never admitted it to anyone, but I knew that I had piled up an emotional debt that I would certainly have to face someday. I simply chose to ignore the obvious reality that was directly in front of me. But I also had battles on other fronts to contend with.

It was a Wednesday, the day before Thanksgiving, and the alarms in my head began going off early that afternoon. I attempted to write it off as a guilty conscience, conviction of the heart or some sort of intuition. But even as I considered those possibilities, none of them seemed to fit. The emotions started in just as soon as I had walked into the mailroom that afternoon. I really couldn't put my finger on it, but something was just not right there. The first red flag flashed before me as my father walked by my worktable and asked how I was doing. Where in the world did that come from? He and I hadn't spoken in quite a while. Why would he have cared about how I was doing? When had he ever bothered to care about anyone? Actually, I had begun to believe that I didn't exist to the two of them anymore. But then again, I had given them orders to keep their distance.

With my brain on full alert, I began watching everything and everyone in the mailroom with great anxiety and intensity. I noticed that as my mother made preparations for her motor route, she suspiciously seemed to be in far too good of a mood. Something was up for certain, and I knew from experience that some poor victim somewhere was about to get nailed. I wondered at that moment just who it might have been. From my vantage point, I had, over the years watched both of my parents. I had watched them make their little plans. I had seen them kiss up to the managers at the newspaper and had observed the intricate details as they embarked on one underhanded scheme after another. There were schemes and there were schemes within schemes as she frequently pursued one male victim after another. It was a truly disgusting thing to watch.

But on that particular day, she was in too good of a mood and just seemed to be far too happy. But then, just as she was about to walk out of the double doors, she turned, made sure that she had my attention, looked directly my way and then gave me that devious, smirking smile of hers.

At that moment, it looked as if the victim had already been selected, and the bull's-eye was centered directly on me. The questions raced through my mind once again. What was she up to? Had the utility companies finally gotten in touch with them about their delinquent bills? Had they realized that I had initiated the whole ordeal and had demanded that justice be done? I was aware that the two of them would be extremely upset about the whole matter. That word had discreetly gotten back to me through various individuals in the mailroom. But the real question was, just did she have planned?

What was she going to do? What in the world was she up to? What sort of plan had she concocted? But then, I wondered, what could she possibly do to me at that point? I knew full well that she wouldn't dare call the authorities and inform them of my living arrangements. That announcement would have immediately put the spotlight on her, the rest of the family, and would have resulted in a full investigation. I knew that she didn't want that sort of an intrusion into her life.

But, as I gave further thought to the topic, that scenario would have been fascinating. I wondered just what sort of dirt something of that nature would have dredged up from the secret closets within her life. My uncles had revealed things to me during other conversations that if they were true, would have sent her directly to jail. Their own childhood stories of victimization regarding her actions was more than merely revolting; it was criminal. Therefore, with all of that in my mind, just what could she possibly have been up to? With her track record, it could have been anything. I figured that I just had to hang on to my shorts as I waited for the nasty little ride to commence. I was certain that it was going to be amazing.

It was seven o'clock that evening, and the double doors had been chained shut for about two hours. The only way in or out of the mailroom was through a door at the far end just inside of the dock and past the wire baling machines. My worktable was at the back of the room at the far opposite end. It was near the water cooler, which was quite a distance away from that door. But it was also at a vantage point where I could observe everything that went on within either of those two very large rooms. It was from that specific location where I watched it all unfold before my very eyes.

Initially I only heard a noise coming from that door far at the end of the room. Someone had unlocked the metal door and had walked in. There was yet an hour left to go in the shift for the other kids in the mailroom. Therefore it was far too early for any of the mailroom guys to have returned to lock up for the night. I naturally stopped working as I wondered just who it was and what it was all about. I had no sooner thought that thought when the answer came much quicker than I could have possibly believed. It wasn't even close to whom or what I had expected.

The three of them walked into the mailroom together, my father, my mother and Yellow Teeth himself. Just what was he doing there? There was no possible way that his appearance there that night was of any good at all. At that point my mind raced as I truly began to wonder just what in the world was going on. The three of them just stood there near the door, in obvious plain sight, as they talked quietly in a huddle for a few minutes. Then just that quickly, they ceased their discussion, turned in unison, and looked directly at me. With an obvious prompt from my mother, my father began walking toward me while the other two simply stood there with their arms crossed and watched.

My father motioned for me to leave my worktable and to meet him at a distance from the other workers. But as I walked toward him, I noticed over his shoulder that the other two were watching intently and smiling. Whatever it was all about, it certainly wasn't something of any benefit me.

As I stood before him face-to-face, he began talking about the family, about blood ties, and about personal sacrifice. It was a really nice rambling story, but it was an absolutely boring and dead-end speech. When I had finally heard enough, I stepped back, lit up a cigarette, raised a polite hand, and requested his silence.

I informed him that his silly speech was unnecessary and that he should just plainly tell me what he wanted. He was instantly at a loss and just stared at me blankly. Then he started to mumble, refused to look at me, and simply stared at the floor. Then, with his carefully prepared speech suddenly interrupted and in obvious confusion, he slowly turned away.

No sooner had he done that, my mother then came stomping angrily toward the two of us with a raging fire in her eyes. It was almost comical, as if it were happening to someone else. She stopped him in his tracks just long enough to say something quiet and angry to him. Whatever she said, I was certain that it both degraded and humiliated him. It almost looked for a moment as if she had actually spit on him. Having summarily dismissed him, she completed her stomping act and then stopped directly in front of me. I waited silently, coolly, and patiently as she shook visibly and forced herself to put her emotions under control.

When she began speaking, it was all about just who my youngest sister's biological father was. With a pointed gesture of her thumb backward at Yellow Teeth, she then declared what his parental rights were. She went on to state that his intentions were to disrupt the family just as she was attempting to put everything back together. Well, that certainly was an earth-shattering shock: Yellow Teeth was my little sister's father. Any schoolkid could and actually had that one figured out. The whole sordid matter was probably the worst-kept secret within our extended family, at the newspaper, and, indeed, the entire city.

So, just what were they doing there in the mailroom that night? It seemed that the three of them had convened a meeting about parenting, responsibilities, and finances. During that meeting, the three of them together had arrived at a conclusion. It was an agreement that my mother believed was in the best interests of everyone involved. But why had the three of them bothered to have a meeting about such things there at the newspaper? Why had they interrupted my work to inform me of any of their nonsensical problems? Hadn't I already informed them that I didn't care about them or about any of their issues? Hadn't they already done enough damage to me? Then she politely asked me to hold my questions and allow her continue. I gave her the floor.

Yellow Teeth decided that he was willing to walk away, to leave the family alone, and to legally sign off all parental rights to my littlest sister. However, there was a catch, and it was a big one as he would only surrender his rights for a certain price. During their recent meeting, the three of them had agreed upon something in exchange for the amount of money that he had initially requested. She then quickly informed me that the entire price issue required something of value from me. My mind then raced uncontrollably.

Price, what kind of a price was she talking about, and just what had she meant by an exchange? What in the world was she talking about? What kind of nonsense was going on there that night? The entire incident was rapidly becoming physically sickening to me. Were they suddenly selling children? Just how could someone hold a family hostage in exchange for money or something else, whatever that was? But the better question was just what did I have to do with their whole mess. It was their problem and I had no involvement in their stupidity whatsoever. Then once again she smiled the smile that always disgusted me. Once again, I was blindsided, and it hit me right between the eyes. She really let me have it. But the very worst of it all was the pride that she so openly displayed.

Standing there before me, she appeared to revel over my reaction much more than she had ever enjoyed any pain that she had caused me before. She even drew the words out slowly as if to only prolong my agony. Her dirt bag boyfriend's asking price to permanently leave the family alone was for me to hand over my red convertible.

MY CAR! MY CAR! MY CAR! What a group of sorry, worthless excuse for human beings! Just who did they think they were? After all that the two of them had already done, then they wanted to just take my car from me. There wasn't any way that I was going to allow that to happen! I believed that I didn't have to let it happen! As I thought of it, there wasn't any sound reason as to why I had to let it happen. As far as I was concerned, she could have just have just stuck it in her ear or someplace further south if she really wanted. There just wasn't any way that I would give up my car for her, my sister or anyone else on the planet for that matter.

I was more than willing at that point to shed blood or break a few bones over their ridiculous demands. What audacity! What arrogance! But she also knew full well just what I was capable of and of what I was willing to do. There wasn't any way that I would give my car, which I had practically built by hand with my uncle, up for anything or anyone. So, then just what was she going to do?

Then she smiled that same sickening wicked smile that I had really grown to love to hate. It really wouldn't have taken too much for me to hit her right then and there. I had no more than thought about actually doing it, when from her purse she produced a yellow and very official-looking piece of paper. It was the title to my car. She had placed the title to my car into her name. I instantly realized at that very moment that I had absolutely no legal right to my own car. Then she added a litany of taunting words that were designed to fully irritate me. She always knew what it took to really cause me pain.

Legally, she could literally do whatever she wanted to with that car. I could have called the police at that moment if I really wanted to. They would have stopped by the newspaper, and then they would have told me the very same thing that she had just smilingly stated. Then, as if to really turn the knife into the wound, she even offered to dial the number for me.

There was nothing that I could do but to just stand there in raging fury and suddenly cry uncontrollably. I felt the anger rise within me as it came to a full boil as the tears streamed down my face. But all that she did at that moment was just stand there with that same smile on her face. She was the victor, and I was most certainly the vanquished.

Then as she held her hand out demanding the car keys, I took them out of my pocket and threw them onto the floor. Then, through a choking voice, I informed her that somehow, someway, and at some point in time, she would get exactly what was coming to her. I only wanted to be there to see it all happen. Then she just turned her back on me and laughed loudly as she picked up my car keys and strutted away. She then met up with her cohorts, and the three of them walked outside. As I stood there in the mailroom, I heard the rumble as my car started up and then left the parking lot. There wasn't any way that I could have looked out of the window and watched. I couldn't bear to see it go. I felt as if I had just lost my very soul.

Needless to say, I was finished for the evening as there wasn't any way that I could have worked anymore. Then I realized that I had a full audience for the entire episode. Behind me, there was no longer any noise of newspapers snapping as the guys worked. All activity in the mailroom had ceased as all of their attention had been focused on the drama that had unfolded there before them. I couldn't turn around and didn't dare to as I wouldn't allow any of them see my face. I was in full emotional overload and on the verge of collapsing into a heap there upon the floor. The entire ordeal had left me physically exhausted and emotionally spent as I shook uncontrollably. Therefore, I walked away from my co-workers without looking back. As the tears continued to run down my face, I went to the phone at the opposite end of the mailroom near the wire baling machines and just stood there. In that moment, I wished that I were dead.

I called my uncle and told him exactly what had happened. Within the hour, he picked me up and took me to his favorite bar where I got thoroughly trashed. After we had been there well after midnight, he drove me home and promised that he would see me in the morning. Before he left, he asked me how much money I had available and that somehow, together we would find a car by the weekend. I remembered hearing him lock my front door as he left, but little or nothing after that.

When I awoke the next morning, I couldn't do anything but sit there on my sofa as my emotions smoldered unchecked. How could someone be so cruel and callous? How could the two of them perform such a stunt knowing that they had to look me in the face at work every day? Had they ever thought for even one minute just what irreparable damage their actions had created? I had heard stories and rumors of physical abuse within our family and others and had seen the toll that it had taken upon its victims. I reminded myself once again that my own uncles had previously revealed stories that had shocked me almost beyond belief.

Although she had never attempted to carry out such acts on my person, I almost felt that the schemes that she had perpetrated upon me were even worse. That sort of mental, manipulating, and torturing kind of abuse was, as far as I was concerned, even more diabolical than the putting of hands on someone. But then perhaps, it was really all the same. It all took planning, cunning and then staging the entire act. She had to gather all of the pawns at her disposal together in order to pull off the wanted end result. She was so completely methodical. It was obvious to me that she had planned the entire event for months, perhaps from the very day that I had bought the car. I believed her to be the most evil person that I had ever known.

It took longer than both of us had thought to find a decent car for the money that I had available. Therefore, I had to find rides to get around everywhere. But with some generous help from the guys at work, it wasn't too difficult to accomplish for the remainder of the week. But what a degrading and depressing mess that my life had become. I hated having to explain to those who asked, just what had happened to my car, my pride and joy.

But my uncle had managed to locate a fairly nice two-door dark-blue hardtop. It was in good shape, and we picked it up a few days later in the week. By the following Monday, I had also discovered that the title department could have cared less about my age. All that was necessary for the transaction was a driver's license and enough money to pay the sales tax. I then had a car that I knew for a fact was mine and that no one could ever take it from me.

But that newfound fact couldn't possibly have detracted from the emotional turmoil that boiled within me daily. I was so roaring angry that I could have spit nails had it been physically possible. My emotional stability degenerated quickly to the point that, at a moment's notice, I was willing to pick a fight with just about anyone. I had neared the place where I had realistically lost control of my temper and all the anger inside. I found myself in a very dangerous place, but had no idea of how to escape from it.

Despite my ongoing battle with anger and other questionable habits, I had somehow managed to avoid serious trouble despite those stated activities. However, there were minor skirmishes that caused more than just a little excitement in my life. There were the occasions when a father or a brother came to my home looking for their daughter or their sister. That always produced quite a bit of drama, which I tactfully talked my way out of.

But there were also the unfortunate incidents when the police had gotten involved. Those occasions happened when they had smelled something drifting out of my car or when someone had reported that a group of guys were drag racing on a two-lane highway out in the country. But for the most part, I always seemed to get away from the event without any heavy-duty action on the part of the authorities.

With an unhealthy amount of pride, I considered myself lucky as I believed that I presented myself well, spoke well, and went out of my way to be respectful. Naturally, it was all an act only for the selfish sake of saving my own skin. I tried very hard to emulate the adults that I had chosen to observe every day. However, I had chosen only those traits that furthered my habits rather than those that built character. But I always knew deep within without having thought much about it, that sooner or later, the odds would be against me and that my number would be up. I had accumulated a substantial debt and payment for my actions was long overdue. It was inevitable.

It was March of my junior year, and my number certainly came up. No matter what I had done or what I had gotten myself involved in, there was one thing that I knew that I could count on.

I knew that I could only at best just barely keep my anger leashed and retain everything else in my life under control. It was like a boiling pot on the stove. Every now and then it simply spilled over the mental fence that I had constructed to contain it. Then I had to fight with everything that I had to rein it in. I simply could not get past just how callous, ruthless, and manipulative that my parents had been. I had begun to blame them for everything ugly that happened in my life. I tried my best to make sense of it everything. However, I was completely unsuccessful.

But the fact that my mother was willing to use people, especially her own son as a slave or a piece of property, just to get whatever it was that she wanted was repulsive. Additionally, there was the fact that my father always stood idly by and watched it all happen. Every time I turned around they seemed to prove that my worst thoughts about people were true. It devoured me from within every single day. It was never ever far from me and it truly never ever left me alone. The raging anger had taken over my life. It ruled me, mastered me and I knew it. I just never constructively did anything about it. But even with all of that in my life, I also knew that I actually couldn't blame my parents for everything. They were who they were and there wasn't anything that I could do to change them. I could only change myself but I didn't have a clue of just how to accomplish that task.

It wasn't as if I hadn't any understanding of right from wrong because I most certainly did. It was crystal clear. If I hadn't believed that what I had been doing wasn't wrong, then why had I gone to such incredible lengths to hide my habits and to keep them secret. I always knew when I had made decisions that were acceptable as well as those that were not. I was responsible enough to have recognized that. I simply chose the wrong path and I did so deliberately.

All of the decisions that I ever made were completely and totally mine. It was always more than obvious to me just which side of the morality fence that I generally chose to stand on. I understood that it was completely about choices. From that standpoint of honesty, it also really didn't matter what kind of childhood I had or even how my parents had raised or treated me. This was deeply understood despite the painfully obvious fact that I had indeed been dealt a very lousy hand. I even believed that I had probably just stood in the wrong line when God, whoever he was, had passed out parents to children or vice versa. But I always knew deep within when I had made my mistakes and when I had responsibly done what society expected of me.

But my problem was twofold, and I managed to live my life under that duality for quite some time. On many occasions, instead of first making the right decision, I knowingly made the wrong one. I then spent an enormous amount of time and effort as I attempted to concoct a scheme that would circumvent the rules and regulations that rewarded correct behavior. I wanted the reward for good societal behavior, but I was unwilling to pay the price for it. The decisions that I made were never for any noble cause, as they only served to satisfy my own very selfish desires. But no matter how grand the plan, no matter what the goal may have been, the end result was always the same. Depression always arrived like a familiar bill collector at the door, demanding payment for services rendered. I would then spend days sifting through the outcome of my stupidity and then make determined decisions to never repeat those actions. But I seemed completely powerless and always failed at the attempt.

But those decisions and commitments that I had so strenuously and seriously made to myself never lasted very long at all. No matter how I attempted to resist the daily assaults, I always submitted myself to the very next temptation that presented itself to me. The very habits that I had chosen for my own personal pleasure then seemingly ruled over me. Then, to make matters worse, I simply added another one to join the others, which then added to my personal bondage. But it all had its temporary benefits as it caused the pain to retreat out of my life for at least a short period of time. However, my anger had to be the most demanding and dangerous master of them all.

Even though I sometimes exerted all of the effort that I had within me, the raging anger always triumphed. Like a wild animal on a leash, it took off and careened down strange and unforeseen paths as it ran rampant with me. But I never seemed to be smart or wise enough to simply let go of that leash. I always felt helpless to resist that decision as I allowed the pleasure of the moment to be my guide. But as it had always been, the emotional destruction afterward was the worst. It invariably scattered my tortured feelings to the wind and admittedly vented all of the pent up frustrations that lay within. But unwanted guilt always returned as it requested payment that I could and would not make. I knew that real disaster was imminent and that it impatiently waited for me. I knew that at some point I would turn a corner and the situation would be waiting for me. And wait for me it certainly did.

I met my uncle for dinner that particular evening for my seventeenth birthday. He happened to be the only one who had ever bothered to remember my birthday as my parents certainly never had. Even as a little boy, they chose to ignore my day, but always celebrated those of my siblings. It was a Saturday night and we had enjoyed a good meal at the truck stop. He had also gotten a little buzzed, and since they refused to serve me, he decided that we had to go somewhere else. His immediate choice was one of his favorite hangouts on South Main Street.

We both walked through the front door of the bar laughing and carrying on as if we didn't have a care in the world. He had chosen that bar despite the fact that we both knew that it was a rough joint and was a place with quite a reputation. However, we had been there before on occasion and had watched the occasional bar fight so it wasn't unfamiliar. As a matter of fact, I had delivered newspapers there during the fifth and sixth grades. Even then I remembered watching from a distance, as a few really nasty fights had broken out and had observed the real action when the police had arrived. But even though we both knew better and even though the place was packed and even though it was a little crazy that night, we stayed anyway.

On the way there, he took the time to talk as he sternly reminded me of his personal and standard bar rules. They were the obvious rules as I knew them and had been familiar with them from his previous warnings. They were the normal topics such as bar fights, getting away before the cops came, and other great advice of that nature. With that speech fully locked within my head and with both of my uncles' training under my belt as well as my whole angry-at-the-world attitude, I believed that I was up for anything. With the first look around it was obvious that we were in for quite a night. The bar was crowded, but there were a few empty tables lined against the back wall. It was the perfect vantage point to sit, drink, and observe. I sat there at the table and looked over the place, thick with cigarette smoke, blaring music and very loud people. Those tables were the best spots to watch human nature at its absolute worst as it unfolded before my eyes.

Naturally, it wasn't long before a few fingers could be observed pointing our way as my uncle drank his beer and I had tequila shots. But all seemed as calm as it could have been until a couple of women stopped at the table and the mandatory conversations soon began. Within just a few moments, the placed changed and everything happened incredibly fast. It was nearly unbelievable.

It all began with a familiar remark, then a shout, which proceeded into a standard argument as others characteristically showed up. The shouting, pushing, and shoving began as the next thing I knew beer bottles and chairs began flying through the air. Over the racket my uncle could be heard laughing right out loud. He really lived for that kind of excitement. It was his very favorite form of entertainment.

It was crazy and insane as people shoved, punched, hit, and kicked. I was right in the middle of it all, especially when someone decided that he should take it upon himself to throw the kid out of the bar. It all happened faster than I had ever thought possible. A man was in my face yelling, cursing, and making threats. But since I was half-drunk or probably more and mad at the world and looking for any excuse to fight, it was a horrible combination.

The actions that followed were completely expected and were also all too familiar. I felt it coming just as I always had on previous occasions. It was a runaway wall of water that came, grabbed me and took me with it. Under normal circumstances, I would have fought back those feelings, but there were no such inhibitions to be found this night. There were kicks, punches, and blood flying, as I suddenly found myself on top of him on the bar floor. Abruptly everything within me simply exploded. The next thing I knew my uncle was grabbing me by my shirt collar as we ducked, cursed and shoved our way through the back of the bar, out the rear door and into the dark alley.

We stood there, looked at each other for a second, and then sat down in the gravel in a heap. We were acting goofy and stupid, asking each other about injuries and laughing about the whole mess. Then sirens and screeching tires were heard as we looked at each other and then laughed even louder. Then we began a roundabout path around buildings, over fences, and through back yards in order to get back to his car before we managed to get ourselves arrested.

I awoke somewhere near noon the next morning and felt strangely better than I had in a long, long time. I curiously had no headache, no hangover, and didn't seem to possess my usual mad at the entire world attitude. I had a very strange but awkwardly guilty peace within. A casual investigation also revealed that I had a nasty scrape on my right knuckles, but other than that everything appeared to be fine. Then I gave meager thought to the night before and considered exactly what had happened.

I knew that it had been crazy and completely stupid, but I had deviously enjoyed it all. I knew full well that a bar wasn't the proper or even a remotely safe place for me to be that night, or any night. I knew that it was wrong and even illegal for me to have been there, but what real harm had been done? It hadn't really been that big of a deal, had it? The people that went there always drank, always got drunk, got stupid, and fights broke out there on a frequent and regular basis. I reasoned that I didn't need be bothered or worried over the whole matter. But something inside reminded me that I should have cared, that I had been irresponsible, but I just shoved those unwanted moral and logical thoughts out of my head.

Monday morning was as normal as any Monday school morning could be. I awoke, got myself together, cleaned the house a bit, got into my car and headed off for coffee. Once at school, everything seemed to be as it always was, perfectly normal and boring. No one talked about or discussed anything that was of any importance to me. I heard nothing of bar fights, arrests, or anything of that nature. That would have been the topics for adults that I would hear later at the newspaper and certainly not for high school kids. I just sat there in bored amusement and listened as they recounted their usual lies and fairy tales about their own grand exploits over the weekend.

I always let those embellished boasts go in one ear and out the other. I never attempted to upstage any of my class mates although I easily could have done so. Therefore I stayed with my self-imposed and steadfast rule that kept my secret life a secret. I knew that if I desired to continue in my chosen lifestyle, then everything about it had to be kept quiet. It was not only the order of the day, it was mandatory, and with me it was of the greatest importance. But just a few moments later, my world would be rocked to its very core. All of my careful precautions turned out to be not so careful and were in fact, completely worthless.

My third class of the day had just begun when someone knocked on the classroom door. It was one of those stereotypical kids of the type that worked in the school office. As he spoke quietly with the teacher, all of the class looked on in curiosity and with undivided attention. As he stood there, a slip of paper could be seen in his hand. Everyone in school knew what those particular slips of paper represented. It always meant that someone was about to receive an unwanted invitation to the dean's office. It was always a cruel kind of a game to watch everyone in the class, observe who was nervous, and then wonder what crime had been committed as they were escorted out of the room. It happened regularly enough that it was never a real cause of alarm for most of the school population.

I myself had never been in any kind of trouble in high school and had never been sent to the office for any occasion. But as the teacher solemnly turned away from the door and headed directly for my desk, the red flags immediately went off inside my head as the fear began to set in. I believed that there wasn't any way that the slip of paper could possibly have been for me. I was incredibly mistaken.

I felt every eye in the room scrutinizing me as I fearfully stood to leave. All of my false bravado left me as the fragile and fleeting emotion that it truly was. Then a few unexpected quiet gasps were heard as the teacher instructed me to take everything with me. She seemed to have a bit of sorrow in her voice and on her face as she informed me that I would be gone for quite a while. My mind raced completely out of control at that moment. My thoughts chased themselves in dizzying circles as I searched for an answer as to what sort of trouble I was about to experience. The events of the morning simply wreaked unbelievable havoc with my emotional stability.

As I walked into the school office and realized that two police officers sat just inside of the door, I nearly jumped out of my skin. I knew at that very moment that I was in desperate trouble. I fortunately had a proper state of mind that kept my facial appearance as innocent as possible, which required a great deal of effort. It became nearly impossible when both officers stood up, walked toward me and found a place on either side of me as I stood there at the office counter. As someone called out my name, I then received another surprise as both officers took up places directly behind me. A door opened, the dean spoke my name, and the three of us walked into the office in unison as it closed shut behind us. I was scared to death. I just wanted to run for my life.

We each found a seat as I kept my mouth tightly shut as the dean made the obligatory introductions. He then began a dialogue pertaining to the evils of drinking and just how dangerous that frequenting bars could be for anyone. Then he motioned for one of the officers to speak. With that the fear inside me escalated to a screaming roar.

The officer gave a crisp, concise, and very accurate account of the happenings at a certain bar on South Main Street over the weekend. He stated that there had been quite a fight that nearly resulted in a riot. Due to that, over twenty people had been arrested for a variety of different offenses. He related that unfortunately a few people had also been hurt badly enough to be transported to the hospital. Then the officer quickly turned, looked me squarely in the face, and bluntly asked if I had any knowledge of the matter. I stared directly back at him, without blinking, and declared that I had no idea of anything that he spoke of. Then he made two statements that convicted me to the point of nearly confessing. At that instant, it felt as if the walls had closed in on me. I was suffocating to the point that I nearly stood up and ran.

The officer revealed that he had interviewed a number of witnesses, and those reports had led him directly to my uncle. The two of them had apparently carried on quite a conversation. That conversation revealed a great deal of information about not only himself and the bar incident but also a tremendous amount of data about me. The officer reported that he had also informed my uncle that just the act of taking me into a bar would have been a violation of his probation and could have him thrown immediately into jail. As those facts stared him in the face, my uncle caved in and had told the officer everything about that night. He confessed that he remembered having gone to the bar and that the two of us had been served alcohol. He recalled that someone had started a fight, but that it hadn't been either of us. He remembered that when the opportunity had presented itself, he had grabbed me and the two of us had gone out the back door of the bar. But something in the officer's voice caused me to believe that the he had a measure of disbelief over my uncle's telling of the story.

Then the officer reported that one particular patron from the bar had been transported to the hospital and was still there due to his injuries. The officer had the hospital report in his hand and quickly proceeded to state the medical issues. The report listed that the man's injuries were fairly serious, but not overly severe or even remotely life threatening. He had sustained a broken nose, a fractured jaw, six cracked ribs, and a possible concussion. The medical experts stated that he would recover with little lasting effects of the experience. But, as the officer related it, the victim was naturally angry, upset, and was bent on serious revenge. The officer once again looked me in the face and forcefully demanded an answer.

I responded by stating that if there had been a bar fight and that people had been fighting, then who could have known who had done what to whom? The officer replied that the victim distinctly remembered a very young man in the bar and that he was probably far too young to be there. He further recalled that the young man was in the very midst of the fight and could easily identify him. As the officer continued to state the facts, it was obvious that he had everything necessary to convict me of the crime. He had a couple of sources that had spelled out far too many details. The struggle within me over my impending doom had me at the point of mental and physical collapse. I needed all of my resources within me to keep my face stony straight. I desperately struggled to maintain my composure, but I knew that I was desperately outmatched. Those men in the room knew without a doubt that I was guilty and there was nothing that I could do to get away with it.

The officer then revealed his greatest source. He added that my uncle had informed him about my family and my upbringing. He had told him about the street fighting training, the martial arts lessons and a number of other items of interest. As the officer droned on about other non-important points, I thought of other things. Had the authorities actually known everything that had been stated? Had I actually been specifically identified as the culprit? Had I truly been sold out by my uncle and just why had he done it? Were the police just playing games with me? Had I really inflicted such injuries to someone? Was I truly responsible for all of it?

What had happened to that man certainly wasn't a prideful item as I certainly never wanted to put anyone into the hospital for any reason. Deep inside, I was aware of my guilt and there was no doubt about it. But even so, I didn't want to face the consequences of my actions. The officer's question broke me from my reverie. He stated that he had everything necessary to arrest me on the spot. Was I willing to simply admit to the crime? That had sealed the deal as my future was obviously set, and I was now doomed. They had me just where they wanted me, and there was no way out. My only recourse was to admit my guilt and throw myself on the mercy of the court. It was the only proper and decent thing to do at that point. However, I was not in the habit of doing what was proper and decent.

Therefore I just said no. I point-blank, cold-faced, and bluntly said no. I denied any involvement in anything and at any time. Had I said yes, it would have put an end to of all my future plans, especially those concerning my college dreams and goals. At that point, I reasoned that I had to do whatever was necessary to get out of that mess. With that immoral decision made, I immediately slipped into my standard defense mode instead of simply just telling the whole truth and getting it over with. I followed my irresponsible gut instincts instead of making the correct, adult, and difficult decision that I should have made. I was such a fool.

But then as they pressed me further, I decided to surrender, but only to a point and took instead the path of partial admission of guilt. I had no desire to go to jail and no sense of false bravado about it either. Just the thought of being behind bars scared me to death. That fear reached into the deepest recesses of my being. My uncle had told me a number of horror stories about what happened to some people in jail. I had no intention of submitting myself to that sort of abuse.

So I told them that it was indeed true that I had been there that night, and I admitted that I had a drink due to the fact that it was my birthday. I admitted that I had seen the fight begin and had observed as beer bottles and chairs flew through the air. I stated that I was just a kid, had wanted no part of that mess, that my uncle had found me, and had taken me out of the back door of the bar. I didn't know anything about that man in the hospital and didn't want to know anything about him. I certainly didn't want someone coming after me for something that I did not do.

Having made those declarations, the officers looked at each other, stood up, and immediately ordered me to remain seated. Then the two of them, along with the dean, went outside the office and shut the door. Within minutes, the dean returned and motioned for me to follow him. Once again I found myself sitting on a chair outside the office and in the hall. Once again, I was stuck in one spot, doing nothing, and allowed to go nowhere. For what seemed like an eternity, I simply sat there and waited, with nothing but thoughts and questions to torment me.

What had I done? Why had I allowed myself to get into such a mess? Why did I always permit my anger to control me? Why was I so out of control? Why was I so stupid? Then the practical questions arrived. Would they make me pay for everything, the damage at the bar as well as the hospital bill for that man? Would I be arrested? Would there be a trial? Would they put me in jail? Would everyone in town find out about it? Would it cost me my job? What would I do about it? I sat there for well over an hour before they finally returned.

When they did, one of the officers literally took me by the arm, and once again the three of us were seated in the dean's office. I was dead, just dead and I knew it. I tried very hard not to shake, but that came about anyway. But despite my foolish stubbornness, I was scared spit less. I knew at that moment that I was to be hauled off to jail. My life as I knew it was over, and I was ruined.

Then the dean spoke, which interrupted my tortured thoughts and once again motioned for the officer to speak. The officer replied that he had conducted discrete interviews with the hospital, my parents, and with specific individuals at the school. The school itself had reviewed my records with him, had reported that they were quite good, and that I had been a student with no previous problems. When he had spoken with my mother, she stated that as far as she could remember, I had been at work on the dock that night as usual. When he had spoken with my father, he stated that I never missed any work, and that as far as he could recall, I had been there in the mailroom that night. Obviously, there were contradictions at hand. Initially, I was quite confused.

The officer also spoke at length with the victim in the hospital. He had related the full details of the situation to the gentleman. He had also revealed to him that the person that they had believed most likely responsible for his injuries was merely a teenage boy. With that statement, it was obvious that everyone had been spoken to, everyone had given their statements, and the officers were prepared to finalize the entire matter. I had also come to my own conclusions. My mother selfishly protected herself as was her usual and expected action, and my father had covered everything up as well. My uncle was quite simply scared to death of jail and perhaps still held a bit of a grudge over what had happened on Euclid Avenue. As I sat there on that hard chair, with an armed police officer on either side, my future perilously hung in the balance. Therefore I was certain that my fate was sealed.

With all of the bewildering contradictions in place, emotional turmoil, and imminent disaster spiraled downward within me as there was revealed a very sudden shock. I literally gasped when I heard the words. The police had decided to simply release me. Neither of the officers personally agreed with the decision, and they certainly appeared to not like it one bit. The man in the hospital had apparently decided that the public embarrassment of the situation wasn't worth the effort. I was a juvenile, and the punishment that I would have received would have been very minor and of little consequence. The majority of the alleged fault of the incident would have fallen upon both my uncle and the bar owner. The officers had spoken with their own superiors and a decision had been made.

However, the actual fact of the matter was incredibly simple. I was guilty, I knew it, and everyone else in the room knew it as well. The only necessary but missing piece of the puzzle was my confession. It would have been the decent, honorable, and moral thing to do. However, deep within me roared a deafening and finalized decision as I simply refused to do it. But I was far from being let off the proverbial hook, as much was about to come my way. It was then that the earth-shattering warnings, statements, and decisions were officially announced. They were not empty words as the officers ensured me that they would be as real in my life as their authority permitted. Their statements proved to be true as I witnessed them as they were carried out over the remainder of my high school career and then some.

I was to be watched like a hawk by anyone who possessed any sort of authority over my life. The owner of the bar had been given my school photograph. I wasn't allowed inside of his place of business for any reason and he had been ordered to contact the police if I ever did so. The school itself had also been instructed to watch my every move, and an officer had been assigned to check on me unannounced at the newspaper from time to time. The adults resolved that it was their place to ensure that I stayed in mine. However, as I was a juvenile, the entire matter was kept private, confidential, and if I managed to stay out of trouble, it would remain entirely off the record. I was asked if it was all perfectly clear and if there was anything about the resolution of the matter that I didn't understand. With all of that life changing drama shoved into my life I was then released to return to class back just in time to make the last one of the day.

But once I was outside of the school office door, in the hallway and all alone, I just leaned up against the wall and attempted to breathe. I needed a cigarette right then and in the very worst way. The shakes came on with an incredible fierceness, and they didn't stop even as I slid down the wall to the floor. My nerves were totally shot, and it was of a certainty that there wasn't any possible way that I could have returned to sit in a classroom. I just stumbled my way out of the building, to my car and that awaiting cigarette.

What in the world had I done? Why had I allowed myself to get into such idiotic situations? STUPID! STUPID! STUPID! I had been completely responsible for putting a man into the hospital. A man, someone whom I had never known and who had never done the first thing *to* me, suffered because *of* me. It was what I had allowed my anger to do to me and how I had allowed it to control me. I had given it permission to rule over me supremely, and it had nearly destroyed me.

What a mess my life had become. My parents had both covered for themselves, but all that they had really done was to protect the remainder of the family by not informing the police that I wasn't living at home. But the worst of it was that my uncle had given me up when the cops had pressured him hard and had threatened to put him back to jail. I knew how he felt about the place, and he had told me just how horrible his jail experience had been. But he had turned on me! But then once again, a disturbing and revealing thought ran through my head. Wasn't that justice of sorts? I then gave the matter time for real contemplation.

Could that have been my repayment for what had happened to him five years earlier on Euclid Avenue? That could have been it, deep down inside of me I knew that it could. I really didn't believe that he had been cruel or vindictive about it. He simply did what everyone did when they were backed into a corner as he merely took the easiest route of escape. He merely chose the one that protected himself and his immediate family. He had made the obvious and logical decision. There wasn't any way that I could have blamed him. However, the entire scenario really brought my relationship with my entire family to a final close. With them, the door to my heart was permanently shut tight. But the truth of the matter was that my practical dealings with them were far from over.

School had been out for only a few days when the circulation manager stopped by my table for a very brief moment. He was there only to ask a short and simple question. He did it almost silently and so very quickly. It was as if he didn't want anyone in the mailroom to know that he was doing anything more than simply asking about my day. Even though it was short and sweet, it carried a tremendous amount of weight with it. He wanted to know if I would be willing to meet him on Saturday morning for breakfast at a certain restaurant on the north side of town. With a mixture of fear and much curiosity, I agreed, asked for the time, and so the appointment was made. He walked away as the entire matter was completed in less than sixty seconds. Even as I heard his footsteps fading away, the questions raced inside of my head as my brain went into overload once more. As I worked, I allowed fearful scenarios to play out within my mind.

Did it have anything to do with what had happened at that bar and the situation that followed in the dean's office? Was it about the unauthorized key that I had been given to the mailroom door? Had he finally found out about the secret room? Did he have concerns about the extra money that I had been making on the loading dock on the weekends? Then the real fear crept into my heart. Was it about any of the office girls? Had something happened there? Was there something going on with one of them that I hadn't known about? As always, it didn't matter how many questions that I asked myself, I simply had to be patient and wait until the day presented itself. It proved to be an extremely long wait until Saturday morning.

However, I continued to work that morning as if nothing had ever happened. But something truly had happened and was about to happen, and I knew it instinctively. What had transpired in those few seconds was a very big deal. Something was up there in the mailroom, there was absolutely no doubt about it, and I knew that it would prove to be huge. His appearance at my table certainly wasn't just a social thing or something of coincidence or happenstance. He wanted or needed something that only I possessed and could give. More revealing and more than obvious was that whatever it was, it absolutely couldn't be talked about in public. But what in the world could it be? I was certain that it had something to do with the mailroom, the more that I thought about it. But I was worried more than anything that my job was somehow in jeopardy because of it. It was pure torment, and I worried about the situation endlessly.

By the time that Saturday morning arrived, I was so keyed up about the issue that I had trouble sleeping at night since the day that he had made his request. No matter how much I thought about it and also do to the fact that I couldn't discuss it with anyone, I was totally in the dark over its possible topic. I managed to go through a couple of dozen scenarios but only one that really made any sense. Unfortunately, it was the one that would really create a rift in the family. Therefore, I just had to wait for that breakfast appointment.

I arrived at the restaurant about ten minutes earlier than necessary in an effort to calm my nerves more than anything else. He arrived a few minutes after as we then went inside and found seats. Through the ordering of breakfast and coffee, the conversation was normal enough. It centered around standard topics such as, school and classes, my car and cars in general, my living arrangements, and those related sort of issues. It helped to settle me down a bit, but I could barely wait to get the real conversation, as I believed that I had it all figured out. I hoped that my assumptions were correct as I had brought a surprise along. However, it was still comforting to have a conversation with someone about nothing more than simple daily life. But once the waitress had taken our orders and had then served our meals, his entire attitude quickly changed. He then became very, very serious, and even the very tone of his voice became quite ominous. I was so intrigued that I had difficulty eating and simply put my fork down and listened. Then the real questions began.

Would I be willing to discuss anything that went on in the mailroom, anything at all? Would I be willing to discuss any conversations that I may have overheard? Would I be willing to reveal to my real superiors anything that I had seen? Would I be willing to answer any questions of any kind that he had about anything or anybody that pertained to the mailroom and its operations? I responded yes to all of his questions, and then it came. It wasn't at all what I expected, as it really hadn't been that was high on my list. However, it was on the list, and I was prepared. Then the detailed questions came.

He wanted to know if I had a good working understanding of anything pertaining to my mother's rural motor route. I replied that I knew the route, the customers, and such details. But it was not about the practical knowledge of the route itself that interested him. His inquiry was about the method in which she operated the business that most concerned him. He reminded me of the fact that all of the motor route drivers were actually independent contractors who were responsible for managing their own business, particularly their vehicles. Their contracts required that they actually purchased the newspapers from the company and then sold them at a set fee to their customers. He naturally wanted to know if I understood that and I replied that I did. Then he began to dig a little deeper.

Had I been aware of the fact that my father was in the habit of using the company van and company gasoline to run my mother's route on the weekends? Did I know how often he had done that? Was I also aware that the act actually constituted theft? Did I know that both of my parents would probably lose their jobs over the matter and that if the company wanted, they could both be charged with a crime and jailed?

Yes. I answered yes to all of it. He was quite startled by my response and actually stopped eating as well. He then motioned for the waitress to refill our coffees and then asked her for some privacy. He then motioned for me to continue. I went on to inform him that not only had my father used the company van but had also filled my mother's vehicle with gasoline on numerous occasions with the company's credit card. I then added that the company had also paid for repairs to her vehicle on at least three occasions that I was aware of. As he stared at me, I then informed him that I had kept a detailed listing of all of the dates and details of each and every instance. I went on to state that my notes included the company van use, the gasoline purchases for her station wagon, and even which mechanic had performed the repairs on her personal vehicle where the company vans were stored.

That detailed information literally rocked him back into his chair as he just stared at me in amazement. He was totally shocked. Then he asked just why had I done all of that. I initially made a very nice speech about doing the right thing, which appeared to be both please and impress him. Then I added for good measure that there was a lot that the two of them owed me and that they deserved more grief than he could ever possibly know. He asked once again if I had realized, with the information that I had given him, that in two days on the following Monday morning, that both of my parents would probably be without a job? The final proof would be gathered by observing their actions throughout the weekend. But what he really needed more than anything were those detailed notes that I had discussed.

As I reached for my wallet he mistakenly assumed that I was going to pay for breakfast because he politely stated that the meal was on him. But instead of money, I pulled out a folded piece of paper that contained those very dates and other pertinent notes. As I handed it to him, he acted as if I had just given him a gift of incredibly great value. As he reviewed it, he was nearly speechless and only uttered a quiet thank you. With that accomplished, I stood to my feet as he quickly followed suit. As we shook hands he looked at me with something that I could only describe as pride and approval. I then turned and walked out of the restaurant. As I stood on the sidewalk outside of the building, I lit up a cigarette and took a long steady drag and enjoyed what had to be one of the most fulfilling Saturday mornings of my life.

As I sat there in my car with the key in the ignition, but the car not yet started, I gave into a number of thoughts. Had I done the right thing in revealing the truth about my parents? After all, in my defense, I had been asked those questions by my supervisor who had requested by help. What they had done and had been doing was wrong, illegal, and immoral. But I had observed those character traits in both of them throughout my entire life. But did I have the right to give the information that I had in my possession? Should I have been collecting that data for nearly a year? Were the actions that I had taken really any different than what my parents and my uncle had done regarding the incident at the bar? Was I really any different than them? Had I simply operated out of revenge? But it was too late to question my actions as I had already played out my options. There was nothing left to do but to take an observer's stance and watch as it all unfolded before me.

It was a typical summer Monday morning in the mailroom. Outwardly it had actually been a typical and boring weekend as well. I had worked the loading docks on Saturday night just as I always had and my parents ignored me just as they had for some time. As was also my habit, I hung around after the shift in order to go with the other mailroom guys for breakfast. Just as with other early Sunday mornings, my mother never showed up to run her route. That tactic always ensured that my father would be doing it for her as soon as he had the mailroom shut down. He was always so completely predictable.

Sure enough, just before I left for breakfast, I observed the proof in action as he and two of my younger brothers loaded up the company van with the contents of her route. Somehow, somewhere I knew that someone else watched as it happened as well. I reasoned that the circulation manager hadn't stayed up all night to observe it. Someone else had been handed the assignment. I just wondered who it was. Whoever it may have been, so much went on that weekend and I was purposely and thankfully kept out of it.

Again, it was a normal Monday morning, and I had worked for nearly four hours when the real drama started. It was nearly nine o'clock as I watched as a young lady from the front office walked through the mailroom. It was unusual to see any of the ladies in the mailroom, as it always meant something serious was going on. She never bothered to look my way but walked directly towards my father. Once there, she spoke gently but professionally as she took him by the arm and then walked with him off to the side. There she spoke to him privately for just a few minutes, turned away, and then walked back toward the front office. The look on my father's face told me everything that I needed to know.

It was that same terrified and defeated look that he had worn on his face when my mother had moved the family to her boyfriend's house a few years before. He was obviously in deep and awful trouble, and it was clearly revealed on his face. His life was about to be turned completely upside down, and he knew it. I was certain that he didn't know exactly what the details were, but I was just as certain that his guilty conscience had provided him with a long list of possibilities. I watched as he walked deliberately to the telephone on the wall, visibly swallowed hard, and then dialed a number. Not even once did ever he look my way, which allowed me to observe him and his every move.

It was apparent by his body language that he was talking to my mother. I had no specific idea of what he said to her, but it was apparent that she was not pleased. Their conversation was all very quiet and serious as he then suddenly snapped and yelled into the phone. He had never raised his voice to her, not even once as far as I could recall. I would have been shocked by his display of bravado, but actually I believed that I had seen him click the phone off first. But even at that, it was all bad, very bad. I realized at that moment that it was certainly going to be some morning. I wasn't at all disappointed.

Less than fifteen minutes passed when she came stomping in through those mailroom double doors. I easily observed that she was as mad as she could be. To the casual observer, she was ready to fight. But I also observed that she was scared out of her wits. She was clearly uncomfortable and desperately tried very hard to hide it. She quickly found my father, and the two of them walked toward the front office as they spoke closely in angry and frightened whispers. Then, just as they had almost walked out of the room, she glanced to her right and looked me directly in the eye. I didn't blink, but I looked back at her with all of the hardness that I possessed within my heart. As I shot that look their way, I watched in amusement as her eyes widened in understood expectation and unanswered questions. Only a few seconds had passed, but much had been said without any spoken words as they walked out of my sight.

Once they left the mailroom, I worked as I did every other day, like a person crazy for money. However, my mind wandered, as my hands were busy as I just thought about everything as it raced through my mind. Most pressing of all, naturally, was that I really wondered just what was going on up front inside that office and behind a closed door. Then just after ten o'clock, my introspective reverie was broken. I heard it loud and clear. It sounded as if someone had kicked a door open, as you would when you're angry or in a big hurry. It happened to be the door that was just around the corner, to my right and to the back, the one that led to the front office. Then I heard her. It was my mother. There was no mistaking her loud, demanding, and forceful voice. She was obviously not very happy.

Then I saw her. She walked in a fast-paced, deliberate motion and was followed by my father, the circulation manager, and his superior, the operations manager. Then for some unknown reason, they stopped as a group at the center of the mailroom. I heard one of the managers sternly inform my mother that she had better be quiet and go willingly or things would become far, far worse. I was amazed at the drama and immediately stopped working.

It was real, it was actually happening, just as I had hoped that it would, and best of all, it was taking place right there before my long-awaiting eyes. It was justice and it was the best unasked for gift that I had ever received. The conversation with the circulation manager suddenly became reality right there before me. It was perfectly clear to everyone in the mailroom just what had happened in the front office. They had both been fired from their jobs, and it was effective immediately. Then, just before they had to be almost physically escorted out through those double doors, I heard my father voice as he mentioned my name in a question.

As I heard his question, I stepped away from my table and stood less than fifteen feet away from them all. It was then that I heard the circulation manager speak as he informed my parents that my job wasn't in any kind of jeopardy. He then added, possibly for the benefit of all twenty or so people that were there in the mailroom listening, that I was in no way tied to anything that the two of them had done. At that very moment, I had been given reason to be proud of who I was and what I had become. That was more than enough vindication for me. I had obtained long overdue justice.

But he had no sooner uttered those words as my mother turned and look directly at me. At that moment I was overwhelmed with emotion, and I swear that I just couldn't help myself. The emotions that had risen within me during those few moments were just too great to stifle. It just came over me and truthfully I really never bothered to contain it. I smiled. I just smiled. I had waited a very long time to smile that smile. There was no doubt in my mind that she knew exactly what that smile meant. Justice was so sweet.

September arrived, my senior year of high school. I was finally a senior. It was about to enter my very last year of school. I had waited all of my life for it. I knew for certain that I was on my way to college and believed that I had everything completely figured out. I dwelt upon the fact that I was nearly through with high school and had endured more than enough of the politics, games and certainly all of the social stupidity that high school had to offer. Even though I knew that it was months away, it felt as if it were just around the corner. It felt so close that I could almost taste it.

School had been in session for only a few weeks as I attended my second class of the day. I looked up from my desk only to see that there was another kid at the door from the office. Once again he had another slip in his hand and once again, it had my name on it. What did I have to go to the office for? But thankfully the look on the teacher's face wasn't nearly as condemning as it had been the previous occasion. That helped to calm my nerves a bit. But even so it was still certainly very puzzling.

I ran a couple of dozen possibilities through my head concerning what it could have been about. I considered my occasional houseguests, the infrequent visit to college parties and a smattering of other smaller, but unknown crimes. I had wisely chosen to stay clear of the bars and had confined such activities to my home. I nearly bruised my brain as I considered every conceivable possibility as I walked the halls toward the office. But I couldn't for the life of me figure out what in the world it could have been about. As I walked into the office, the girl behind the counter directed me once again to the dean's office. I really hated going into that man's office as nothing good ever became of it.

I knocked on the open door frame and heard his stern voice as he called me inside. I was curiously surprised to discover the school nurse sitting there in one of the chairs. I tried to be polite and asked if I had interrupted anything and the dean simply said no. He then added that it was necessary for her to be there for the meeting. I became more than a little confused and then felt the familiar stress as it raced to the forefront inside of me. The tension and anticipation quickly filled me from head to toe. It was the unknown of it all that tore at me the most. What in the world was it all about? Then an idea, a light of sorts came on inside of my head. It didn't help my inner trauma at all.

Perhaps they had discovered the phony excuse that I had turned in from the doctor during my sophomore year. That had to be it. I was convinced of it. I was so dead. I was so busted. I just wondered what they were going to do to me about it. What could the punishment be for that type of crime? But whatever it was all about, I could just tell by the look on his face that the dean was thoroughly enjoying every minute of my obvious discomfort. He purposely allowed the silence in the room go on far longer than necessary. Then just when I thought that I couldn't take it anymore, he began to speak.

I wasn't in any real trouble. At least I wasn't in what was generally understood as trouble. Thankfully, at least it wasn't the kind of trouble that required intervention from the police. Then he stopped for a moment just to allow his statement to sink in. What had he meant by all of that? Then he went on to say that he was also very pleased that there hadn't been any further instances since we had our other little visit. He paused and then stated that he firmly believed that we would be able to clear up the current situation without any difficulty. I wondered just what in the world he was talking about. He had some sort of hidden scheme, but whatever it was, he didn't reveal the first clue.

Then he motioned for the nurse to speak. Evidently there had been health reports that concerned alleged incidents of bugs and lice on people. Since the reports had originated from within the school, it was her responsibility to investigate such issues. I quickly became embarrassed and felt it instantly as my face rapidly changed colors. I knew without having heard another word just who the reports were all about. Once again there was a pause in the nurse's speech as the dean held up his hand and asked her for a moment of silence. Then with another motion of the hand, he permitted her to continue. That man truly loved drama.

She then stated that she had conducted numerous physical exams on several suspected students. Three dozen students in all had been examined but only two of them had tested positive for head-lice infestation. Then, without any warning or visible sign, she paused once again in the conversation. Then, as if for effect, she continued on with her statement. The two students were my sister and my brother. My sister was a junior, and my brother was a sophomore who attended the same high school. Naturally, I had played the same game in high school that had proven so successful in middle school. I had declared them to the school population to be only my cousins. That particular incident that morning had placed my entire social life at the school in jeopardy. It was an embarrassing blow that I knew that I wouldn't recover from. The information from that meeting with the dean was bound to raise through the school within the day. There was no possible way to recover from that sort of attack upon my reputation. As I sat there in bewilderment, my mind began to chase itself in vicious little circles.

I attempted to speak in an effort to defend my position, but simply couldn't. The words just wouldn't come out. I was irreparably embarrassed, and I hadn't any idea as to where to begin. I certainly didn't know what to say. It was more than obvious that the dean was thoroughly enjoying my obvious turmoil. He then stated that the procedure required for the nurse to inspect my head by the same process that she had performed on my siblings.

It actually only took a minute or two as the dean had permitted her to conduct it there in his office. I had agreed to the ordeal, but silently wondered why the dean was required to be there. I had questions for him as well, but he merely chose to ignore me. He simply motioned for my immediate silence as he instructed her to proceed.

She ran her fingers through my hair as she checked every single strand, inspecting my scalp as if she were looking for buried treasure. When she finished her task, she reported to the dean that her examination was negative. She had found nothing, nothing at all. She reported that there wasn't anything to be found, not even the first sign of an issue. He nodded his head in unsurprised understanding, as he then dismissed her and she left the room. I knew without knowing that having passed that examination was only the beginning of my troubles. Then the dialogue became curiously strange.

The nurse had no sooner left the room when the dean arose from his chair and walked around the corner of his desk. He then sat on the edge of it directly opposite from me as he was obviously about to either prove a point or to put me in my place. Why I had ever found a special place on his list was far beyond me. But I intimately knew by the way that he was enjoying the situation immensely. Obviously, he had something of special importance to impart to me.

With his standard and fully expected superior attitude, he informed me that my brother had been examined first and had already been sent home. My sister had then been examined, and as stated, she had produced the same exact results. But when the nurse had informed her that both she and our younger brother had tested positive, she volunteered an additional bit of family information. As the nurse brought my name up in the conversation as the next to be checked, my sister informed her that I would probably test negative. The nurse was naturally curious, and when she asked, my sister then spilled the entire story. My carefully kept secret about my living arrangements ceased to be a secret from that point forward.

It was the real reason why the dean was in such a good mood. Having possessed that sort of information, he had me exactly where he wanted me, and I didn't have a chance of getting out of it. As we went through the ritual of questions and answers, I admitted that I did not live within the city school system and that I did not live with my parents. Then, whether it was out of defense or curiosity, the dean then asked if there was anyone that he could speak with that might be able to help to explain the situation. I inwardly sighed a bit of relief as I immediately suggested my mentors at the newspaper. Perhaps the morning wasn't going to be a total disaster after all.

In my mind I believed that perhaps that conversation would straighten everything out and perhaps even impress the dean to some degree. With that he gave the circulation manager a call. After the normal course of pleasantries, chatter and nonsense, the dean then hung up the phone, and actually appeared to change his tune a bit.

Then he made the grand announcement. He would permit me to attend the high school and complete my senior year, but only at a price. He let that sink in for a moment before issuing his ruling. In order to stay at my current school, I would be required to pay tuition, which was required of all out of district students. Then he informed me of the amount. As far as I was concerned, it was far in excess of what attending that school could ever have been worth. Fine used cars had been purchased for less money. I politely declined his not-so-generous offer, asked him where to sign the paperwork, and allow me transfer out of his grand little domain.

I just couldn't believe my luck. One of the many reasons that caused me to move from my parents' house was to avoid just this sort of nonsense and turmoil. However, I realized that it had all been a result of my own decisions. I knew that I could have paid the money and stayed. But I felt victimized and wondered why that sort of nonsense always happened to me. Then the reality of the situation hit me.

I had to face another change of schools, and once again, it was during the school year. It was the fourth time in my twelve years of education that I had to do such a thing. I immediately was reminded of just how much I hated the stupid game. But it was also high school where the stakes were incredibly higher and everything about such a change would be completely different. I would therefore be required to reveal a good portion of my life to a new group of strangers. But that was the least of my concerns.

The fact of the matter was that I would now be required to attend the richest and most affluent school in the county. It was an institution where two out of three students were the offspring of doctors, lawyers or other professionals. The school had a well-deserved reputation about divisions, private social groups, and it all revolved around money. It was plainly obvious to me or to anyone else with a working pair of eyes, as to just where I would fit in. I couldn't wait for the sorry little game to begin.

The truth of the matter was that the remainder of my senior year was actually one of the most uneventful and boring times of my life. There was a bit of trouble the very first day when I neglected to put out my cigarette and nearly walked into the school with it. Admittedly, there were also a few difficulties with girls in my classes who apparently *belonged* to my male classmates. Anyone attending a high school understands that sad social process, as well as territories, people as property, money as a badge of honor and all of the other assorted and standard nonsense.

There was also my only fight, which occurred in senior study hall. An idiot football player woke me up from a hangover and very needed nap. The ordeal was stupid on both of our parts and was over nearly before it even started. But other than those petty actions, the balance of the school year remained fairly calm. I studied hard, achieved good grades, and, as always, went to work every day after school. A routine was simply a routine and the months went by quickly.

What I had really looked forward to was the trip that I had planned to take as soon as the school year was completed. All of the necessary arrangements had been made and the preliminary work for my college of choice had been approved. Within days after graduation I headed for the coast to take my entrance exams for the college of my dreams. It was the field of work of which I had dreamt of for a lifetime. That planned course of study was intended to place me into a career which would take me far from my hometown and my good for nothing family. Within a short period of time I believed that they would become nothing more than a distant and forgettable memory.

Once I arrived on campus, I just knew that I would do well. I already knew that I had the gift. I had always known it. I even privately permitted myself to dream about it. I believed that perhaps I would be able to finish school early and be recruited by one of the big name companies. Then, in just a couple of years, I would be living in a world class city, perhaps with a nice ranch-style house in the suburbs with a sports car for the summer and something else for winter. Life would be great and it would be better than I could ever possibly imagine. I believed in my heart that I was long overdue for something good. I couldn't wait for my new life to begin. Therefore, I was ready for anything.

I graduated from high school on a warm June afternoon, on the first day of June. Unfortunately, I celebrated that special event in my life alone. There wasn't a family member in attendance to witness the event. Additionally I also made a few serious decisions in preparation for my trip to college. I had sold my car and had purchased another, an economical one that was much better suited for the trip. However, once I arrived at the school and had begun the entry process, life struck me with a hard and unforgiving reality. Truth arrived at my doorstep with an eye opening viciousness that I was completely unprepared for. It set me back with a cold and brutal finality. Depression, deep, life-numbing depression embedded itself within my mind and came home to stay in a very real and permanent way.

Once I had arrived in the big city on the coast, things were far more different than I had ever realized and were much more difficult than I had ever anticipated. I had taken the entrance exams for college just as I had planned. With some subjects I did quite well, but on a number of the others, about all that I got right was my name on the paper. When the entire process was completed, college then became a non-existing option for me. I was defeated, branded, and became a self-described total failure. I was lost.

The Precipice of Hell
West Wayne Street, South Cole Street

I had barely survived my first real test of adulthood as I returned home to our little city in utter defeat. It was not the glorious picture that I had once intended. It was not how my life was meant to be. I had assumed that one day I would return to my hometown, but it would have been as the conquering hero. I had dreamt that I would have become a leader in my field and known to all. But such was not the case. So little was it the case that I never even started on that special road of which I had dreamt of my entire life. That path was closed and it was closed for good, never to be reopened. There wasn't a loophole to be chased after, and there wasn't another worthwhile path of any kind at that time that I could have taken. There wasn't even a roadblock that could have been fought, clawed or gotten around. The road that I had dreamt of, that had been at the very core of my existence since childhood, the one that I had known so well, simply ceased to exist. In actuality, it had never existed, at least not for me. That depressing realization was perhaps the worst of all.

Have you ever had a dream? Has your life ever taken a cruel, hard, and occasionally wicked turn? Have any of your dreams simply evaporated before your very eyes as you watched helplessly as they died? Have your dreams ever exploded into a million pieces as you stood there in horror and watched it all happened?

Did it feel as if the whole world had changed? Didn't the air itself even smell differently? Wasn't it all the more depressing to shamefully discover that the awful truth was that the world hadn't actually changed, but that it was only you? Was it yet even more depressing to find out that to the entire world around you, the earth-shaking explosion that ruthlessly ripped through your life was nothing more eventful to them than a tiny bug hitting a windshield? Did your heart sink when you finally realized that it actually only mattered to you?

I returned to our city late one Sunday evening in August. The only thing to be found lower than the amount of money in my pocket was my self-esteem. Just as a novice in the boxing ring, depression hit me hard and mercilessly, again and again. But the greatest punishment was the endless questions that I dumped upon myself. I granted myself no mercy of any kind.

Just what had happened? Why hadn't I bother to prepare myself better? Why hadn't I investigated all of the college requirements better? Why hadn't I counseled with someone at school? I had plenty of opportunities to do all of those things. I simply never took anyone up on it. Why had I been so stupid in attempting to handle it all on my own? What could I have done differently? I believed that there were thousands of things that I could have done differently. Why had I wasted all of that time on all of those other worthless things? The drugs, the alcohol, the girls and all of that wasted money. And then it was not only the money, but all of that lost time. Why was I so blasted stupid? Why had I been such an idiotic fool? Why did I ever believe that I could have left my town? I guess that it was all in my head. But why had I even bothered to hope? Why had I even attempted to dream? Why had I ever thought that I could have become a better person than those in my family? Was I really destined to be just like them? The life that I had dreamt of was over before it had ever started. That certainly seemed to be the case. I was cursed to live a life of mediocrity, in a low life, wrong side of the tracks kind of prison sentence. It looked as if it existed without an end. I appeared to be doomed to such a future.

I pulled into the newspaper parking lot, which was always deserted on Sunday evenings, turned the car off and just sat there. It was only then that I truly felt as if I had returned home. But at the same time it was the most horrible feeling in the world, and it literally caused me to be physically sick. Getting out of the car, I stood there on the loading dock and wondered just what to do next. With my mailroom keys still in my possession, I went through the door just as I had done a hundred times before. As I walked inside, I stopped and for an incredibly long moment, looked around, and took in the all-too-familiar surroundings. Then, as I stood there in that quiet and darkened room, the recent events instantly crashed down around me. As I stood there trembling, the room spun as I sat down in a miserable heap on a bundle of newspapers. There in that spot, I cried myself into a fitful sleep. After what I had thought to be only a few moments, I awoke with a terrifying start to discover that it was five in the morning. As I attempted to clear my head, a seemingly unending parade of questions marched through my mind.

Why was I so lost and completely without direction? Why did I feel as if I were worth nothing? Why did I feel so completely worthless? Everything in my life that had claimed any sort of value was now gone. Everything that I had deemed worthwhile in my life had vanished and all hope in my life along with it. Who or what was I supposed to be after my dreams had gone down in flames? I couldn't be who I wanted to be. I couldn't even be who I once was. According to the world, I was just another worthless and nameless loser. What was I supposed to do with myself? How was I supposed to live? How could I possibly face everyone at the newspaper or anywhere else for that matter? Was life really nothing more than self-survival? Was it all only about me? Was there anyone that cared enough to stand with me? Would I have to go it alone for the rest of my life? I took a deep breath and felt a coldness within that I couldn't describe as it entered my lungs and filled me completely. It felt inhuman, otherworldly, and I resisted it as best as I could with what meager strength that remained. I then had serious questions to ask myself.

Could I become that cold and callous? Could I put myself first at all costs and then forget all about everyone else? Could I forget about real friends and care less about whether or not I made enemies? Could I forget about real relationships and selfishly promise myself to live only for the moment? Could I take a no prisoners approach to life? Could I promise myself, more than anything, to never allow myself to be used by anyone again? Could I decide not to ever care about anyone or anything?

With all of those unanswered but seriously considered questions, I made a strict vow to myself that day. It was a vow to do those very things, to simply just not care any further or about anyone. It was also a firm vow to never be used by anyone again. It was a promise to selfishly make the most of every day and to never live beyond that day. I vowed to not care about anyone, anything, and not at any time. I decided to use the world to serve my own selfish desires and to give absolutely nothing of value in return. I decided that I would not worry about the next day when and if that day ever bothered to show up. I determined that I would become hard, coarse, mean, and tough as nails. Most of all, I purposed that I would allow no one to get near enough to cause me pain ever again. No one would ever be allowed to get close enough, not even for the briefest of moments and that was a certainty. As far as I was concerned it was the only way that life was going to be. With that, the decisions were set into place, and I was on my way. I was blinded and stupid.

Later that Monday morning, I sheepishly walked into the front office of the newspaper. It had to be one of the most humiliating and degrading experiences of my entire life. However, everyone was unexpectedly nice, polite, and caring. But the very first thing they asked were questions about college and if I was I home for a visit. I tried to be polite enough as I gave each of them a brief thumbnail sketch of the whole matter. That information brought about a lot of sad faces from people who I then realized indeed cared about me. That was a realization of a different and totally unexpected sort. It caused me to retreat even further into my self-diagnosed depression. They obviously had such high hopes for my life, and unfortunately, I had then let them all down as well. I had not known that they had been that interested in my affairs or that any of them had actually cared. It was a very unfamiliar emotion.

I sat down with the circulation manager over coffee as we discussed a number of subjects. Fortunately, there was still a job available at the newspaper, and he informed me that I could begin as soon as I wanted. He was also aware of an apartment that could be rented cheaply and was more than willing to advance whatever I needed. All in all he was much more than kind and far more than helpful. It was almost as if I had watched a scene on television and had an actual father figure of sorts to talk to.

That afternoon I went to look at my new home. It could not have possibly been more ironic. I parked the car and stood on the sidewalk in front of the building and actually laughed out loud. That apartment was on the very same street and less than a block west from ol' Yellow Teeth's house. It seemed that I just couldn't get away from my past no matter how much effort I put forth or how hard I tried. It was just another step farther down the dark ladder of depression. It was just another move downward and into a far deeper and darker pit.

My new apartment was on the second floor of what had been a very large house, which had obviously been home to quite a large family. My new living quarters consisted of a small living room with a couch that turned into a bed, an end table, and one chair. It had a tiny bathroom that had once been a closet and an even smaller kitchen. It was a long way from the mobile home that I had lived in just a few short months before. But even so, I reluctantly informed the landlord that I would take it. He handed me the keys and unknowingly left me with all of my depression and despair in those three empty and very lonely rooms.

I made a desperate grasp for reality, knowing that my mental state was fragile at best. However, I felt stranded in my position as every worthwhile path to the future was seemingly blocked. I found myself in a terribly dark and confusing place that I couldn't climb my way out of. How had I ever gotten to such a depressing place in my life? What was I going to do with the mess that I had found myself in? As I sat there in my new and nearly miniature apartment, the anger within me raged once more. This was *not* how my life was supposed to be! I had planned and hoped for much better than what I had received. But why had I become such a miserable failure? Was my future set into place? Would I ever succeed at anything? It wasn't what I had planned for my life! I was supposed to have achieved far better than where I had found myself. Then I once more, I gave into reason as I boiled the entire matter down to the place of decision. I had made those decisions, and there was really no one to blame but myself.

I realized that I really had only two choices at that point. It was just that simplistic. I could have crawled back to my family as a loser and begged for their help and support. That decision would have required the absolute destruction of my ego, the submission to their endless ridicule, and the open admittance of defeat. They would have thoroughly enjoyed that particular decision.

Or I could have taken the other route as I hardened myself and made whatever sacrifices necessary. With that, I decided to roll with the proverbial punches and take each miserable day as it arrived. It quickly became an incredibly easy choice to make as life soon became just as I was used to. Having that sort of basic street logic in place, I simply preferred to become hard, nasty, and ruthless. That decision ensured that I would never have to experiencing the pain of relationships and the deep seated hurt that went along with it. In the end, one solitary item forced my decision far more than anything else. I knew without any kind of a doubt, that my family would have only gloated in sickening pleasure over my failure. It was their nature, and I had seen it happen in other people's lives before. I was not about to become another one of their victims.

With those decisions set in place, life became boring, pathetic and downright predictable. One day simply led into another and then into another as I purposely withdrew further and further from everyone around me. I quickly learned to put on a hard public face. It permitted me to conceal the intense inner turmoil that raged without ceasing inside of me every day. It coursed through me as if it were a living thing from the moment that I awoke until I went to sleep at night. It was always there, it never let up, and it never ever relented.

All of my lifelong regrets caused anger and the hostility to build up within me. It always sought an outlet and when it was found, it erupted with pure and absolute rage. It seemed that the only thing that I successfully accomplished was creating an increasingly harder shell about me. Those ingrained habits drove everyone that cared for me very far away. However, I maintained polite conversations and civility with my coworkers in the mailroom and front office. But I allowed no one to become emotionally attached to me, no matter what enticement may have been offered.

However, that was not to say that my selfish and worthless old habits had been neglected. I worked hard in the mailroom as I always had before and in the evenings returned to the little apartment. During the weeknights I just snacked on junk food, watched television, and often drank tequila until I passed out cold. In the mornings after I awoke, it was generally a breakfast of leftover cold pizza, a couple of pills, marijuana, and another big glass of tequila mixed with orange soda. If that didn't get the body started in the morning after a horrible and self-destructive evening, then nothing could. Then there were the obligatory social issues that always had to be considered.

Even without my having asked, there was always an invitation to a party, somewhere, with someone or anyone. Without a second thought about the event, my actions or the consequences, I always went. I never turned down a single opportunity. At those parties, without any set program of any kind, I occasionally stayed a while if it interested me and if suitable temporary companionship presented itself. Many times those parties went on until the sun came up. It was completely crazy, absolutely stupid, and insanely ridiculous throughout its entire scope. Nothing worthwhile of any sort occurred during those events as common sense, morality, and any hint of decency went right out the window. I was well aware that sooner or later that sort of nonsensical and idiotic behavior would get the best of me. I knew full well that it would catch up with me and that it would be in ways that would cause deep regret.

But I always pushed that sort of rational logic aside and continued on with those bad habits as if tomorrow would never arrive. However, it never kept the deep-seated and familiar pain at bay but merely dulled them to not much more than an afterthought. I believed that it was the best prescription for my sorry life that I could devise. Those habits for the most part certainly made my awful existence at least sufficiently tolerable. When I was loaded, drunk, stoned, or all of the above, I was at the point where I just didn't care about anything. Perhaps it was because the problems just seemed to get smaller or perhaps, had simply faded from my consciousness for even a brief period of time. But no matter what my excuse I might have used, anything was better than being sober. I simply couldn't tolerate the truth about my life.

On the rare occasion that I addressed myself honestly, I knew that it wasn't such a good idea after all. I knew deep down inside that I had only fooled myself as I had actually gotten to the place where I hated looking in the mirror. I knew that it was internal conviction, but I never possessed the honesty to admit it to myself. But I also realized without having known the specifics that sooner or later a life-altering wake-up call would find me. I also knew that when it came, it would hit me hard, fast and in the ugliest and most unwanted form that it could possibly take. But even though I knew that danger was imminent, even at my heart's door, I still chose to ignore it.

It was late in December, and I voluntarily spent yet another Christmas alone. I sat in my apartment and watched all of the happy people on television. It sickened me as I was secretly and selfishly envious of them all. Deep within, I desperately wanted that seemingly unobtainable sort of normal and decent life. It was the type of life that I had seen played out in the lives of my cousins and countless others. But I didn't have any clue as to how to achieve those heights or even where to begin. I didn't possess the necessary drive to create or involve myself in even a semblance of a normal relationship. I was also far too stubborn to spend the holidays with my family, in their filthy house, and their stupid drama. I was also too bored and depressed to do much of anything else. It was a simple and effortless decision, it was mine, I owned it, and I was more than aware of it.

It was early on a Thursday evening when the phone call came. There was to be a huge party the following evening, and it promised to be an event like no other. The obligatory but unnecessary question was asked and answered. Of course I wanted to go and they could count on my being there. With more than a little anticipation, I then committed myself to serious intentions of a very detrimental nature. Not the least of which included plans to just get totally blown away in an attempt to forget about everything that had happened recently.

As it had turned out, it really was just that kind of party. It was held at someone's house far out on the west side of the city in the midst of the boulevard. It was an incredible scene. There must have been five or six dozen people in that three-story house. It was quite an ordeal, and it was simply total and complete insanity. The music was deafeningly loud, almost violently so as it pounded its way straight through my body. It was crazy intense as the smoke, cigarette, and otherwise was so thick in the place that it nearly looked as if the fog had rolled in. It quickly became a demented game to experiment with one thing after another. Drink this, smoke that, and put a little something under your tongue. It wasn't long before the night quickly became a complete blur. There wasn't much about the events of the remainder of that evening that I remembered.

When I awoke, sunlight had just begun to pour in through a window in the room. I could feel its warmth on my face as I kept my eyes tightly closed. As I lay there, I thought about what a night that it had been. But at that moment, I wasn't able to even begin to retrace my steps. In addition to the standard and obvious difficulties, my head and eyes hurt so badly that it was nearly impossible to open them. But bit by tiny little bit, as I strained and squinted against the incoming sunlight, I opened my eyes slightly until they were barely more than a mere slit.

As I painfully took in my surroundings, I recognized cheap wood paneling on all of the walls and realized that the ceilings appeared to be lower than in a regular house. I then recognized that I was in a mobile home. It all looked familiar but only in a very general sort of way. As I attempted to sit up, I found that I couldn't as my body simply refused to respond. As I further attempted that strained movement, it was then that I realized that I was indeed lying in a bed. That was a relief as I usually ended up on someone's floor after such nights. That was very hard on the back and the rest of the body. Once, I had even found myself in someone's front yard.

But I was in agony, such as and to a degree that I had never experienced before. What in the world had I done the previous night? I couldn't even have begun to name everything that I had mindlessly tossed into my poor old body. I remembered how the party had started with a huge bong with pot, hash, and other ingredients followed by incredible amounts of tequila shots and other alcohol. The remainder of the evening was a very vague and foggy memory. It was simply a blur, with only tiny somewhat remembered pieces of a very large and forgotten puzzle. Then, as I lay there in my lost and confused state, my brain slowly began to regain its functions.

Then as the first real rational thought made its presence known, I paused for a moment and waited as cruel reality sunk in. Then a question posed itself within my head as I wondered just whose place had I awakened in? Suddenly fear and anxiety mixed with terror rushed into my head. Nothing about it looked at all familiar. I wasn't able to recognize a single detail in the place that could have given me a clue. I decided that I had to force myself to sit up in order to figure everything out.

Where in the world was I? I had to physically struggle with everything that I had in order to raise my head off of the pillow. My brain didn't want to consider much of anything and my eyes didn't want to focus very well either. After an incredible amount of effort, I struggled and successfully sat upright on the edge of the bed. Once I had achieved that position, I then had to wait for a few moments for my head to stop spinning. Then suddenly an awful and terrified realization hit me like a ton of bricks. It was desperately unnerving. Fear struck at me just as real as a knife would in the heart.

Where were my clothes? Why didn't I have them on? Then that same intense fear gripped my heart as if it were in a vise as I then heard a soft snoring noise coming from somewhere immediately behind me. I turned to my right ever so slowly, even gingerly as I held my breath and looked over my shoulder. On the other side of the bed, mostly covered by the sheets and other bedclothes was a woman. A woman, there was no other factual description. I simply had no idea as to who she was. As I carefully pulled the bedclothes back to reveal her face, she was completely unfamiliar to me. I had no clue whatsoever as to her identity.

Then reality, followed closely by overwhelming panic, set in fast and hard.

HAD I LOST MY MIND? How blasted stupid had I actually become? She could have been someone's daughter with a father somewhere nearby who probably had a gun! Then my thoughts quickly worsened. What if she were someone's wife? My sorry and pathetic excuse for a life could have been over in a minute! What in the world had I done? What would I have done if someone, at that moment, had walked in through that bedroom door? Those convicting and damning thoughts forced my head to spin even more intently as I fought back the urge to be physically sick. I desperately needed to focus, as I was literally scared out of my wits and then some. With that, I began to shake uncontrollably.

I took another look around the room as I forced my eyes to fully open. There were a few clothes scattered about in various piles on the floor. I found those that I thought were mine, they looked as if they were mine, and I hoped with everything that I had within me that they were. But so long as they fit, I truly could have cared less at that moment. I then began to speak quietly to myself. Quiet, quiet, quiet, think, I just had to think. Get the clothes on, grab my shoes and head for the bedroom door. I never realized that the act of getting dressed created so much noise. I accomplished it as quickly and quietly as I could. No one stirred there in the bedroom or anywhere within the home as far as I could tell.

I opened the bedroom door inch by mere inch and with all of the stealth that I could muster. I then slipped out of the room and walked on my tiptoes breathlessly down the narrow hallway. My suspicions had been correct as it was a mobile home, but as I looked out of the nearest window, nothing outside appeared familiar. As I stood there in the kitchen and took it all in, I finally allowed myself a moment to breathe. I was relieved, as there didn't seem to be anyone else in the place. As I looked about the trailer, I took a quick and careful inventory of the place. I discovered a jacket thrown over a kitchen chair, which appeared to be mine. I reached into the pocket and with great relief, my fingers brought out a familiar set of car keys.

Having achieved that goal, I took one more look around and listened with all that I had for sixty seconds. Then I quietly slipped out the front door. Once outside the trailer, I quickly located my car. It was parked in a way that only an idiot would have done, half off the driveway, well into the grass and nosed into a shrub. Then the entire fear scenario raced back within my head with record-breaking speed. I argued with myself as I hoped that the engine would start, as I had to get out of there. I opened the car door, got inside, and then quietly pulled the door closed. I held my breath as I twisted the key and the engine started. I threw the car into reverse, and I was flat out gone.

But where was I? I had no idea of any kind as to just where I happened to be. I truly didn't have a clue. But it didn't take very long to discover that I was in the smallest of small towns. It was only four blocks square as I quickly drove around them all. I feared most of all that she, whoever she was, would have come out of that trailer. But which way should I have gone? I then realized that the sun was on my left and therefore, as it was obviously morning, I took the road that I believed headed south. I knew that it was a gamble, a chance decision as I was either heading toward home or directly away from it. After a few miles I happened upon a recognized state highway and made a right turn onto it. Within a mile or so of the trailer, I recognized enough landmarks that I understood just exactly where I had been. I was horrified to the point where I almost didn't want to believe it. The questions raced through my head and scoured my brain in raw pain as they rolled out.

I had awakened well over a dozen miles north and ten miles to the east of the city. How had I allowed something like that to happen? What was the matter with me? What was wrong with me? Had I lost all control over myself? Hadn't I a shred of dignity or decency left within me? The self-tormenting questions came one right after the other. Then once I had arrived at the interstate highway, I relaxed a bit and ceased to be so hard on myself. As the conversation with within me slowly turned to a small degree of self-justification, an additional group of questions quickly set in.

Who had I actually hurt by my actions? We were all adults at that party after all. Besides, just whom did I have to answer to? Just who had the right to question my actions? Just whose standards did I really have to meet? Was what I had done really all that important? Wasn't it all just an act of human nature? After all, no real harm had been done over those few hours at the party and afterwards. I had convinced myself that all was right with my world. I had convinced myself that I really wasn't such a bad guy after all. Having made that decision, I lit up another cigarette and turned on my favorite radio station. It was then that the cold, hard, and brutal truth of my stupidity hit me with a force that I had never known before. It was as if I had driven into a brick wall. The casual justification of my actions immediately ceased. As the radio made the announcement, I lost my capacity to breathe and had to pull over to the side of the road.

STUPID! STUPID! STUPID! How could I have become such a horrible and idiotic person? How could I have allowed myself to sink that low? At that very moment, I didn't even feel remotely human. I was so truly and completely disgusted with myself that I actually wanted to vomit. The radio station had informed me of the awful truth that I needed to know. The time of day was certainly correct. That much was true as the radio had announced that it was almost eight o'clock in the morning. But it also pronounced the most sickening fact of all. It was then that I discovered it wasn't Saturday morning at all. It was Sunday morning. I had somehow managed to lose nearly thirty hours out of my life. Fool, fool, fool, I was a complete and total fool.

Late February. I had almost immediately ceased going to the parties, even when the nearly irresistible temptation to do so pulled at me with an incredible force. What had happened in December had terrified me unlike anything else had in my entire life. I had been completely out of my head and had driven miles to a place where I had never been and with someone I had never known. Although it was bad enough to barely remember what I had done, it was the unknown that unnerved me. The terrifying fact was that I had no idea whatsoever, of just exactly what had happened during those lost hours. All that I managed to reconstruct were foggy bits and small pieces that amounted to nothing. Therefore, with all of that pile of nonsense packed into my shining resume, I decided to avoid the party scene. However, I hadn't given myself a complete ultimatum about the situation.

But as the unfamiliar guilt attacked my conscience, I made other decisions. I simply chose to hang out with the other guys in the mailroom. It was a standard-shop-floor type of atmosphere, and it appeared that most of them were as resigned to their meaningless fates as I was to mine. It was a comfortable place to be.

We all were all fairly similar in most respects. Our basic mutual premise was that we all just lived for the moment. We simply existed from one lousy day to the next. But those days were not without their questions or issues. They ranged from the mundane to those that struck at the very core. Was that all that there was to life? Was there nothing more than a dead end job with little or no hope for advancement? Was it about making just enough money every week to keep you hooked on whatever bad habits you possessed? It made me angry that it was just a job, certainly better than none at all, but it certainly was not a career.

As I pointed a great deal of the anger at myself, I was reminded that I had promised myself a long time before that I would have a career. That was what college was supposed to have brought about. The very last thing that I had ever wanted was to become just like my parents. Was I cursed to live a life of mediocrity? Had I been sentenced to a worthless and boring life of simply existing and never actually living? Was I doomed to that sort of lifelong failure and defeat? Then the anticipated depression set in. Should I just let whatever happened to me, simply happen? Should I simply resign myself to my fate? Should I even bother to care about my future?

It was early on a Monday morning when I arrived at the newspaper. As I walked in the through the double doors, I noticed that my coworkers were quite excited. They were carrying on about something of some importance, which had apparently jump-started their day. A half dozen of them were huddled at a metal table and a few of them had their wallets out and opened. Curiosity instantly got the best of me, as it always had, and so naturally, I inquired. They nearly fell all over themselves as they practically blurted out the news.

There was a new waitress at the little sandwich shop next door to the newspaper. That sort of announcement was always the type of thing that either raised or lowered the conversation level among the male workers in the mailroom. But even so, it was a break from their steady diet of sports data and trivia, government corruption, schemes to fix the world, and the obligatory know-it-all debates. Therefore, either singly or by pairs, every guy on the mailroom staff stopped into the little restaurant that morning in order to check out the latest victim.

The term *victim* was appropriate, because as long as she didn't have a face that scared dogs or weighed more than the average truck of the pickup variety, the guys usually involved themselves in a little bet. It was a wager, a game of sorts, very cruel but somehow it was also at the same time perversely entertaining. It was a strange and admittedly sick test of manhood. It was a test not only those who put their money on the line, but also primarily to those who participated in the contest. It was a game that didn't present itself too often, but when it happened, it created more than a bit of disgusting excitement. It sounded cruel, mean, somewhat sickening, and even a little weird, but I found myself hopelessly fascinated by it. Therefore, I too opened my wallet and announced that I was in.

The bets were then made, secrecy was sworn, and then the sorry little game began. It was more than just who could get the girl to go out on a date as it was far more involved than that. Heathens had to be the only title that accurately fit what we were, as it was truly a heathen's game. In order to claim the prize, the winner would have to get the girl, not only into his bed, but also be able to prove it. It was a cruel, vicious, and disgusting game. But truth be told, we were cruel, vicious, and disgusting young men. It was something that we only quietly and secretly admitted.

Therefore, with just over a hundred bucks on the line, four of us had decided to put our names as well as our reputations all on the line. What a group of selfish fools we were as stupid and disgusting as the whole thing was. I had not only placed a bet but had agreed to participate. I was strangely drawn into it, as there was a degree of intrigue with a mysterious motivation about it. But I also had a desperate but private need to prove myself to the men that I worked with. Secretly, I needed to belong, and I needed their respect.

Sometime near the noon hour, all four of us walked into the restaurant for lunch in order to size up the victim for our little game. It proved to be a quite amusing one from the very start. The entire process instantly captivated me. The first two guys to try for the prize were shot down immediately, almost before they had even started. I could tell as I watched and observed her actions that she had a huge boatload of attitude. Not only had they not gotten her phone number, but were also lucky to have even gotten out of there with their lunch orders. Whatever pickup lines either of them used evidently ticked her off. Apparently, she had seen their types before. With that the remainder of us observed that we had experienced prey on our hands. The game suddenly appeared much more difficult than we had ever expected.

It was then that guy number three saw an opportunity, took his chance, and actually carried on a brief conversation with her. It also appeared that he made some progress as afterward we learned that he had gotten her telephone number and a date for the following Friday.

He was the kind of guy who acted as if he knew everyone in town. Once we were back to work in the mailroom, he gathered us together and informed us that he had indeed secured the date. But there were a few things that he had to do first. Through his many resources, he planned to have her checked out immediately after work that night. Privately, I was relieved that he had accomplished so much as that meant that I was off the hook. I could then sit back and merely watch and enjoy the game.

On Thursday morning, he came into work a few minutes late and announced that he had blown the engine in his car and asked one of us to loan him ours. There wasn't any chance that I would let him borrow my car. It seemed that no one else was able to help him out either. However, the rules of the game were still the rules, as he had to find his own way to complete the wager or forfeit. So by lunchtime, as he appeared to be in defeat as he went next door to the restaurant in apparent shame and canceled their date. Inside I instantly but privately panicked as the game was now focused squarely upon me.

That meant that it was my turn. But I quickly decided to wait until the following day. My coworkers believed that I was purposely trying to lose or that I was scared. They wondered if I had known something about the girl that we should have called the whole bet off. But it wasn't anything like that. I just had never done anything that crazy or stupid before, at least not on purpose. But maybe, just maybe, I should have bailed out of the sorry game right then and there when I had the opportunity. But I took a fool's advice, which was my own and let my pride make the decision for me.

I walked into the restaurant for lunch the next day, placed my order, and never said another word. I waited until she looked my way for about the third time and only then did I speak to her. After all, it really was just a game. We talked for quite a while, and during the course of my lunch, I obtained quite a bit of information about her. But in my head, throughout the conversation, the red flags went up everywhere along the way. But I ignored them as it really wasn't a date, and I certainly wasn't in the market for any kind of a relationship. It was, after all, merely a game.

It seemed that we had a number of things in common. She came from a big family just as I had, but the background was somewhat different and even a little strange. Her family actually seemed to be in some ways, worse than mine. There was also something about the way that she described them that was somewhat unnerving. She was two years younger than myself and had dropped out of school sometime during the tenth grade. When I asked for her telephone number, she informed me that she didn't have one. Then she then revealed that she lived just across the street in a single room at the old hotel.

I then became all the more suspicious, recalling that the other guy stated that he had already gotten her telephone number. Had he actually gotten a number from her, was she lying, or had she given him a false number or had he not gotten one at all? Then in the midst of the conversation, she quickly changed subjects and brought the matter to a close. It was an unexpected thing to have heard, at least as far as I was concerned as it was a series of questions from her. She asked when I would pick her up after work that night, where would we go, and what would we do. She was somewhat forceful and appeared to be somewhat desperate, but I stupidly discounted it all. From somewhere in the back of my mind, an unknown and unfamiliar voice softly brought up a single word question. Why?

Flags. Flags. Flags, red flags. Red flags were all over within my head. As I walked into the mailroom and went back to work, I rapidly ran the list through my head. I quickly became more than a little nervous about the entire game and intensely questioned my involvement in it. There were questions about her and there was something very strange about her and her family. She wasn't even eighteen yet, which was a huge issue, and was possibly the reason I believed that the other guy had bailed out. She was a teenage girl, living on her own and in a single room in the worst hotel in the entire downtown area. It was home to all sorts of people, the types that even I didn't care for. It was all very important information, but it seemed that they were only pieces of a much larger puzzle. But then I decided why did I care about flags? After all, it was only just a sad little game! There was some money to be made and my first real opportunity to earn respect and a reputation among the men in the mailroom. Therefore, I simply chose to ignore the obvious issues.

I picked her up after work. We stopped for fast food, drove around, and listened to music for a while. At a specified time, we then stopped in at a semi-respectable party that I had already known about and had planned to attend. We had been there for less than two hours when she bluntly asked if we could go to my apartment. To me it appeared as if the game was going to be easier to win than I had ever expected. Within a few minutes, we were back in my car and heading for the apartment. Once there, she quickly made herself comfortable, made a decision to stay the night as everything progressed along a most predictable course.

The following morning I awakened with a start as I unexpectedly was with company. I wasn't used to company staying until morning. However, it was a long thirty seconds before I found my bearings. I slipped out of the apartment and went around the corner for coffee as I attempted to clear my head. I returned to the apartment, and within less than a half an hour later she began to spill her entire life story.

She told me everything from her earliest years as a little girl up until that particular point in time. She revealed to me that her father was an alcoholic, loud, and physically violent. She described him as an evil, awful, and wicked man who kissed his daughters as if they were his girlfriends and had put his hands all over them. As she related the story, she and her siblings had lived lives of pure terror. But their lives had gotten better in recent years to some degree.

Her mother had left their father just a few years before and had moved in with a seemingly very nice man who had treated them very well. But she had issues with that situation as well. As my guest so tactfully put it, once her mother had gotten what she had wanted and her life had improved, it appeared that she didn't want any part of her children anymore. She tearfully told me that one by one her mother had succeeded in shoving almost all of them out of the door. However, she admitted that two of her sisters still lived there. But to hear her tell it, their days at home were as numbered as it had been for the remainder of her siblings. As an additional footnote to her family history, she further added that almost all of her brothers and sisters had not finished high school and that most had left home long before their eighteenth birthday.

As she was in such a mood of self-revelation, she admitted that she herself had been in trouble with the law more than once. Because of those infractions, she had been arrested and had spent time in juvenile detention as well as in foster care. Her life had become a total mess, as she was flat broke and completely desperate. —She had literally nowhere to go, and there wasn't anyone that she knew of who could or would help her in any way. Then, without warning, she dropped an unexpected bombshell on me. It came out of nowhere, and I truly never saw it coming. She asked if I would allow her to move into the apartment with me. She then offered every conceivable advantage imaginable as she continued to talk and repeated herself endlessly.

It was all quite unexpected as I had never considered having a roommate. It brought about questions that I never had to deal with. Did I really want someone living with me? Could I tolerate sharing my space, my privacy, and all of my time, day in and day out with someone else? Would I be willing to give up all of those things that were so important to me? Was I really making that much of a sacrifice? But then, after all, I reasoned that it really didn't require any kind of real commitment from me. With all of that in mind, I only thought, just what sort of problems could there possibly be with it? She could help with the cleaning, she could cook once in a while, and since she had a job, she could share some of the expenses. After all, the deed itself had already been done, so I seriously doubted that there would be any real surprises left in that arena to be discovered. I cared so little about everything that I obviously didn't care enough about anything important.

Later that afternoon I moved her into the apartment. It was sad, almost pathetic, and it should have spoken volumes to me. I should have listened to the internal warnings if I had only bothered to care enough. She didn't even have enough belongings to even begin to fill the backseat of my car. All that she possessed fit within just two small garbage bags that contained her clothes and a few odds and ends. She literally had next to nothing, and what she did have was of very little value. I had always thought that my life was a total mess, but by outward comparison, hers was far, far worse. I almost found it hard to believe that someone in our little city was that destitute. But it was really of no matter; I couldn't think of a single possible reason why she would be staying at my place for very long. In my mind, it was a temporary situation. The entire arrangement was in a state of flux, as my life had always been. I wanted and needed nothing more. I figured that at the very worst I only had to put up with her for a short period of time.

Suddenly it was the first of May, she hadn't left, and my life was nothing short of miserable. Short of throwing her belongings out into the street, there seemed to be nothing that I could do to get rid of her. What a difference a few months made as she had decided that we were a couple almost from the first day. As such, we were without a doubt, the most incompatible pair in the world. She created a fight about something every single day without bothering to take a day off. It was idiotic, stupid, and ridiculous in its scope and nature. I went to the apartment directly from work and arriving home afterward in less than ten minutes. If for any reasons she thought that it was later than what she believed that it should have been, then the fight always began. If it weren't those issues, it was a hundred other things.

Why did I have to listen to my music every day, or why did it have to be so loud? Why did I do this or that to the car? Why did I drive the way that I did? Why did I put so much ketchup on my food? Why wouldn't I ever try anything new to eat? Why didn't I sleep very much? Why did I get up so early in the morning? Why did I use so much toothpaste? Why did I use a certain kind of razor when I shaved? The only questions that she didn't ask were the ones that she hadn't thought of.

No matter what I ever did, no matter how minute or insignificant, the decision that I made about any subject was always, always wrong. I was never ever right about anything. No matter what the subject, we always found ourselves on opposite sides. Conversely, no matter what, she was always right as I was the stupid one who was always wrong. She was incredibly resourceful. She found an argument everywhere that she looked and about anything on the planet. I hated her voice, the looks on her face, and everything about her. She had no redeeming qualities that I recognized. I hated every minute of my sorry and miserable life. I cursed myself because of her intrusion into my life. I had made the stupidest decisions of my life. But after all, they were my decisions, I couldn't run from them, and I had no one that I could possibly blame but myself.

I could have just kicked myself for having allowed such an unbelievable mess to infiltrate my life. Why had I chosen to live that way? What kind of desperate stupidity was it anyhow? Why did I tolerate that sort of idiocy and abuse? Who did she think that she was? I had never let my own mother talk to me like that. The last thing that I had ever wanted or needed was for an unqualified person to walk into my life and then put it under a microscope. I didn't need to be studied, scrutinized, or bothered. I certainly didn't need someone like her to take my life apart and then attempt to mold it into whatever she thought that it should have been. Besides all of that, just when had she become such an expert on what a perfect life was supposed to be? I didn't need to be changed, and I certainly didn't want to be changed either! How had I ever gotten into such a mess? Why had I allowed my life to deteriorate so badly?

I had no sooner moved her into the apartment, when she suddenly quit her job at the restaurant. She did it completely without warning, notice, or discussion. She then informed me that since we had slept together, she expected me to completely support her. After that, it seemed that all she did was sit in the apartment all day, smoke cigarettes, and watch television. It was like a bad dream set on rerun. There were also occasions when she suddenly disappeared and apparently ran around town all day long doing who knew what. What a bunch of trash my life really had become. By what right did I have to put up with all of that?

When we weren't fighting about such things, something else could always be found. There was always quite a long list to choose from as it grew almost daily and seemed to take on a life of its own. It ranged the gamut from money, who it was that controlled it, to the demand that she wanted a better place to live and then it even became an argument about my car. My car was completely paid for, licensed, and insured, but I was listed as the sole driver and never loaned it to anyone. She, on the other hand, had never bothered to obtain a driver's license. Then she believed and even demanded that I should allow her drive my car without question. A fight broke out simply because she assumed that what was mine was hers for the taking. Didn't she understanding anything?

Was she that ignorant of the law or was it that she simply didn't care? Was she really that callous about the workings of society? But in the end it was just another of a seemingly endless line of examples that daily marched through my life. No matter what the topic, the fighting never ceased, but only intensified with each passing day.

However, the fighting wasn't the half of it. With each passing day I became more and more suspicious of her habits and actions. It wasn't my imagination that when I walked in the front door of the duplex we had recently moved into at the end of the work day that the red flags went off inside of my head. I knew that I had heard the back door close shut on more than one occasion as she sat on the sofa in the living room and feigned innocence. But whenever I questioned her about it, she attempted to maintain that alleged innocence and treated me as if I were completely stupid. She resorted to the same excuse nearly every time. She hadn't heard a thing, and I most certainly had to be mistaken. Those statements always created another fight as she turned the argument around and focused on my obvious lack of trust. Once again, she posed herself as the victim. Then she resorted to the old standby that I was just like everyone else and that no one had ever trusted her. The conversation then deteriorated into just how hard that her life had been and how that I couldn't possibly understand her pain. She played the part of the innocent victim to the hilt.

Then there was the incident that I would never have believed had I not seen it with my own eyes. One evening as I had parked the car at the curb after work, I turned it off, just sat there, and watched. In amazement I observed her as she climbed out of the first floor window of the house next door. Sitting there in unbelief and bewilderment as to what my eyes had just seen, I began to wonder just what was she doing? I then got out of the car and met her halfway across the yard. When I questioned her actions, she instantly became loud, irate and nasty. Then she matter-offactly informed me that the people who lived there had recently moved out. She was only looking to see if anything of any value had been left behind. But she openly admitted that she hadn't received anyone's permission to enter the building. Then she became quite upset as I informed her that it was still burglary, a felony crime, and that she could be arrested. With that, she then became stone faced as I argued that it was still wrong and against the law. But none of those details mattered in the least to her. It was as if right and wrong had ceased to have any meaning within her mind.

Whenever I bothered to say one word about something that pertained to her or if I questioned any of her actions, then the gloves came off. During those fights, she picked my life apart anyway that she wanted, but I was forbidden to touch hers. Day after day and night after night, it was always the same and it never changed. Life quickly became a pathetic and never-ending ritual of fighting and arguing about everything thing imaginable. There was never a break in the battle about anything and certainly never a moment's peace. Complain, complain, complain, and complain some more. It seemed as if the stupidity would never come to an end. My life had rapidly become a literal living hell on earth. It was almost to the place where I couldn't stand any of it any more. My life had become far more than merely ridiculous as it had deteriorated to the completely absurd. Something absolutely had to change.

Then just when I thought that my life couldn't get any worse, I was suddenly provided with a prospect of hope. I had previously applied to a governmental agency for a position in a grant program that would allow me to attend an adult vocational school to learn a trade. It was a very good opportunity. The program paid for the entire cost of the schooling, including books, fees, and lunches. It also had a provision which provided a fairly decent living wage while attending the program.

But perhaps the best part of it all was that it was located in a very large metropolis, eighty miles away, to the south of our little city. Although it wasn't that far away, it contained the promise that it would remove me from our town and all of my personal baggage. I believed that I finally had the chance to put some distance between myself and all of it. Most importantly of all, I would be leaving behind this leech of a woman who had so painfully attached herself to my life. The entire relationship had become far too familiar, downright sickening, and was stifling the life from me. It had progressed to the point where I never wanted to spend any time in my own home anymore. The unspoken reality was that each day was filled with another life draining fight about some stupid, idiotic thing or another. There was never any closeness, never any tenderness, and assuredly never any peace and quiet in my house. There certainly wasn't ever any love or anything remotely close to it between the two of us. As I recalled how bad my life had become after the college fiasco the prior summer, I never for once had imagined that it would have gotten any worse. My life had degraded to the point of utter hopelessness, self-pity, and I was completely miserable. I felt as if I had been locked up in jail.

But it appeared as though the school opportunity would provide a means of escape from the mess that I had made for myself. Therefore I accepted the offer just as soon as the paperwork had shown up in my mailbox. Once I had finalized the decision, I delivered my two-week notice to the newspaper and couldn't be more relieved. I was leaving my life and my past behind. I immediately began my planning and dreaming as in just three short weeks I would be gone. Then I would be out of the city, away from her and all of her nasty little schemes and games. In just that short amount of time, I would be in school learning a viable trade and would finally be creating a career for myself. But the best part of all was that I would be alone again.

But there was one thing that I knew for certain. There wasn't any way on earth that she was going with me. Just prior to giving my notice at the newspaper, I had made that fact crystal clear to her. I knew that I hadn't been very nice about it and was more than aware that I had announced it to her crudely. But it didn't matter, and I didn't care as I didn't feel at all guilty. There simply wasn't any possible way that she could have misunderstood my intentions. She knew exactly what I meant.

However, it brought on the nastiest and most eye-opening fight of all time. It was horrible, and it was awful. It was incredibly violent, and from that point on, I bore the marks on my body to prove it. It was a record breaker. I had my first name changed more times than I could count during the ordeal. But through it all, it didn't actually matter because I simply didn't care. When she finally realized that I was just that serious, she became even more violent, as she threw household objects and punched me repeatedly.

Then in the blink of an eye, she instantly changed, broke down and collapsed on the floor. As she sat there in a miserable heap, she cried and wailed and then said that she was sorry about everything. But it really didn't matter as I didn't deserve that kind of abuse in my life. It was worse than being in jail. It was as if I had been tossed into prison. But at that point, I knew exactly when my self-inflicted sentence would be over. I just walked around her, went out the front door, got into my car and left. However, the days before my departure just seemed to last forever. I kept telling myself that I would soon be rid of her and then she would be gone out of my life. Gone and gone forever, that would be the end of that. I couldn't wait for that wonderful day to finally arrive.

It was an ordinary summer evening, certainly no different than any other night after work. I had driven home with the windows down and the music playing loudly as I just needed time to unwind. But I was in a very good mood. After everything that had gone so wrong in my life, it seemed that things were finally going to change. Maybe, just maybe I thought, my life was about to turn a corner. But unbeknownst to me, at that moment it was certainly about to turn a corner, but it just wasn't the one that I had expected. I foolishly hadn't planned for it and I truly never saw it coming. Once again, I was blindsided simply because I never bothered to watch for the obvious signs.

On that night she waited for me on the front porch steps as I parked the car at the curb. I instantly felt uneasy. It was all strange, very strange as it was totally out of her character. She had never done that before. She also had a very odd and disturbing look upon her face. When our eyes met, she placed a smile on her face that gave me chills as it only served to remind me of my mother. It both frightened and angered me even before the conversation began. Then as she spoke, she attempted to be all sweetness and nice, using that lousy and phony voice which I truly hated. As the alarms began going off inside of my head once more, I wondered just what sort of scheme had she concocted for the evening? I had already informed her on numerous occasions that my decision was final and yet she remained. However, there was absolutely nothing that she could say or do that would convince me to take her along to the big city. There wasn't anything that would have changed my mind.

My face evidently betrayed to her precisely what I thought of her desperate little act. Then she tried the clingy, leech-type move, but with an outstretched hand, I stopped her. As I backed away from her, she boldly produced a piece of paper and waved it with great theatrics before my face. She then asked if I wanted to hear her good news. As the questions filled my head, terror immediately gripped my heart. What good news could she possibly have? Was she finally going away on her own? Had she finally decided to actually leave? Had she found another boyfriend to mooch off of? Just what in the world was this piece of paper all about? Was it some kind of bad news for her, perhaps a life threatening disease? But there was no such luck; however, it was exactly the sort of nonsense that my life seemed to be made of.

She handed the paper to me, and the first thing that I noticed was that it was from the local hospital. My first thought and subsequent emotion was anger. She had probably given me some kind of disease that she had contracted from who knew where. Only her sick sense of humor would have thought that something like that would qualify as good news. But what she had in store for me wasn't even that good.

I read it. Then I read it once more. Once I had read it for the third time I observed that the smile had vanished from her face. Then she crossed her arms and informed me that I needed to give it my instant thought, understanding, and had better not even bother to think about asking *that* question.

She was pregnant, and it was official; the paper that I held in my shaking hands verified it. She further went on to claim that the child was mine. She then informed me that I had just acquired serious responsibilities and then angrily added that I had better think hard about changing all of my well-made plans. My life was instantly turned upside down as it was the worst thing that could have possibly happened to me. I had spent my entire life growing up around screaming, yelling, and nasty-smelling little brats. I never wanted any part of them as a child, and I certainly didn't want any part of them in my adult life. I just wanted to scream.

How had I gotten into such a mess? I quickly changed my foolish thought process, as I fully understood just how easily I had gotten myself into the mess. It was the decisions, and it was all about the decisions, just as it had always been. But I also knew, deep within me, that each and every one of them were mine. But then I also wondered just how could I get out of it? I really couldn't go through with it. There had to be some way out of the hole that I had so conveniently dug for myself. I didn't want to be a father and I certainly didn't want any part of being in a family. I enjoyed living alone, and I had set plans into place to do just that.

However, all of those plans had suddenly been reduced to ruin. My mind was in utter turmoil.

But she was still standing there before me with her arms crossed, her foot tapping, and her face dressed in a victor's smile. She just stood there and patiently waited for me to answer her baited question. What was I going to do? Obviously abortion was completely out of the question given my past and due to my battles with my mother. However, it was also something that I would never consider. It was also something that I knew that she would never consider, but her motivations, however, were far different than mine. She didn't care about the child, for the child was only a means to an end as she was as selfishly motivated as anyone could possibly be. She always did whatever she wanted merely to get what she wanted. Pregnancy had suddenly provided her with a ticket, and she would use that ticket to the fullest extent of her abilities. Even as she spoke I could feel the chains as they wrapped themselves around me. I didn't have to go *to* the prison, it had come looking for me, and it had found me. The fight was over. I now surrendered to the fact that *we* were moving south to the big city.

There were only ten days left to go before the big move. I had mistakenly believed that she would have calmed down after having won the battle. I would have thought that life would have been at least a little more peaceful. But there wasn't a chance of that or anything even close to it. She complained about every tiny, minute detail ranging from where we would live, to what we were taking with us, to what she would be doing once we arrived. The real explosion went off as I discussed the topic of her possible employment once we arrived in the big city. How dare I ask such a thing? What was the matter with me? How could I possibly expect a pregnant woman to work for a living? Had I lost my sorry mind? It was completely out of the question. It was then that the real nagging and punishment began.

She wanted and then demanded to get married. She stated that it was the only proper thing to do. Proper? If being proper had been the case then we should have thought about what was proper a long time before. If she wanted to argue about things being proper, then she shouldn't have spent the night with me on that first date. But had I also been proper, we would have also never moved in together, and then I wouldn't have had a pregnancy that had to be dealt with. Proper, I had serious doubts about her abilities to even spell the word. However, I had no cause to set myself on a higher level as I was just as guilty of life's sorry games as well. However, from that day and with every day that followed, she never found out about the mailroom game or about the wager. That was forever to remain my own private secret.

With discussions between the two of us about marriage began, it was also when she and her mother started their own scheming nonsense. As the conversations were private, I immediately wondered just what they were up to. Why her mother believed herself to be in a position that she could possibly give advice about what was proper was laughable. She was living with a man that she hadn't bothered to be married to, but she insisted that her own daughter get married. So just exactly what was her deal? Her oldest daughter had accomplished that feat and had her own family and had done well by all standards. But the remainder of her offspring were each a train wreck just as was the one that I had gotten stuck with. With that personal history firmly in place, just when had she become such an expert in what was proper? As far as I was concerned, it wasn't any different than asking my own worthless mother for advice. What a horrible joke it had all become as I felt as if I had traveled the identical path that nearly every male within my own family had trod. But I believed that somehow there had to be a way out of the trap that had been set for me. I decided that I would just as soon pass on advice, suggestions, and any other nonsense that her family might have had for me. I reasoned that I would stubbornly do whatever I wanted.

Within days my plan had evolved into my leaving the following Sunday, staying in the city for the first week, get the new apartment in order, and then pick her up the following weekend. But then the Friday night before I was to leave, the guys from the newspaper called to inform me that they were having a party to end all parties and that I was the guest of honor. Every last one of them hated her guts, secretly believed that I was weak and had completely lost my mind. Most of them had already tagged her as a loser, but then with the recent change of events, I had actually become the loser. However, it was still a party and I was expected. It was to be a send-off of sorts for me and she was certainly not invited. It embarrassed me that at least one of them felt that they had to say those words to me. I felt lost and humiliated.

When I arrived back at the house and announced my plans for Friday evening, it really set her off. That created yet another argument on top of the daily "we have to get married" drivel that she shoveled upon me without ceasing. So I made the smartest decision that I believed was necessary at the time. I simply went to the party without her and never bothered to say good-bye or good night. After all, what could she have done to me that could have made my life any worse? I just needed to escape.

It really turned out to be quite a party. It was the stuff of both dreams and of nightmares. The music was deafening, the people were crazy, and the smoke was so thick that you could have cut it with a knife. It was hysterical lunacy at its best, and I enjoyed myself immensely. Anything that anyone could have possibly wanted to try was available there that night. It was my means of escape, no matter how temporary. I never recalled having seen the clock make it to midnight.

Sometime during the early-morning hours, my friends poured me into the backseat of my own car, drove it to the house, and parked it at the curb. They locked the doors and tossed the keys onto the front porch after ringing the doorbell. They ran out to a waiting car to observe, but she never came to the door. No one answered the chime because no one was there. Evidently she had found a party of her own to attend as I discovered later. When I awakened, it was obviously sometime in the morning as the sun was brightly shining. As I took in my surroundings, I realized that I was indeed in the backseat of my car. I wondered just how I had gotten there and felt as if I had been run over by a truck. I felt horrible as my head felt as if it were going to explode. But I hoped that I had fun the previous evening.

As I staggered in through the open front door of the duplex, I discovered that it was nearly ten o'clock. I noticed that she was sitting in a chair talking to someone on the telephone. I was surprised to observe that she was actually in a good mood. I had no idea who she was talking to, as I didn't possess the mental faculties to begin to deduce something like that. She seemed curiously excited and quite pleased about something. She didn't even appear bothered or even angered that I had been out all night. I had expected a fight, and it seemed that for once, I wasn't going to get one.

I only made it halfway across the living room as I crashed headfirst into the sofa and simply lay where I had fallen. In my sprawled-out state, I waited for the room to stop spinning as I then felt every ounce of my pain. But even as I attempted to grasp my convulsing surroundings, I heard her voice as she talked. It was obvious that she was speaking with her mother. All that I understood were bits and pieces of their conversation. I overheard as she spoke about the very real fact that I was trashed, but that I seemed to be coming out of it. She then added that it really wasn't important because she had figured everything out. Then I caught a bit of something about one thirty that afternoon and that all of the paperwork was completed. Then she became extremely upset as her mother informed her that she wouldn't be there for the ceremony but that one of her sisters had agreed to stand in as a witness.

What was going on? What had she and her mother planned? Why wasn't she angry with me? Why was she in such a good mood? What had she figured out? What was planned for one thirty that afternoon? What sort of paperwork she talking about? What was it that they had planned that her mother wouldn't show up? Which sister was going to be there and for what? Her telephone conversation just went on and on as I slipped back into unconsciousness.

I had slept for another hour or so before she attempted to get me up and around. She had prepared hot coffee to drink and something to eat. Once again, the red flags went off all over inside of my head. She was being far too nice. What was it all about? What was happening there? My head was in a fog and it felt as if someone had been taking golf swings at it. Things just weren't very clear, not in the slightest. I had never hurt myself so badly before.

Then, as I sat there on the sofa with a coffee cup in hand, she revealed what had been planned. She informed me that she and her mother had contacted various preachers and churches throughout the entire morning. They had opened the phone book and had started at the top of the list and worked their way down. They made nearly thirty calls before they had found one pastor who had agreed to rush through the paperwork and the ceremony. That particular gentleman was willing to take us through the motions that afternoon and didn't require any counseling or discussion of any kind. It seemed that all of the other preachers had such stipulations or even more. The one that she successfully contacted seemed only concerned about his fee. It was just one more reason for me not to ever bother with church or religion. As far as I was concerned it was all a fraud.

However, she was still upset with the fact that her mother had decided that she was too busy to attend. That left it up to one of her sisters and the pastor's wife to stand in as the legal witnesses. She had completed the arrangements and was so very proud of herself at what she had accomplished. But what could I have possibly done about it all? I still wasn't completely certain of the entirety of their scheme. But I still understood enough of the details. It just felt as if it were happening to someone else. It had taken a fourth cup of coffee before I had fully recognized the totality of my situation and that I had now trashed my life. I had made quite a mess of myself and I was about to pay dearly for it. Bit by bit, the information began to register, but despair and depression were the only emotions that rose to the top of my chemical and alcoholic hangover. The fact of the matter was that I had reached the point where I just really didn't care anymore. She could do whatever she wanted. I was lost.

We had less than two hours to meet the appointment. As the deadline approached, she practically forced me to me eat and continued to pour coffee down my throat. Then she herded me upstairs and shoved me directly into the shower, clothes and all. As I leaned against the shower wall and felt the water run over me, the same words ran through my mind. My life was ruined. I was just like every other member of my family. The same thing had happened to my father, to my uncle and to others. Therefore, it appeared that I was condemned to my fate. My life was over and there wasn't anything worthwhile to look forward to. There wasn't anything that I could do about it. I just didn't care as it wouldn't have changed a thing.

Within a half an hour before the blessed event, I had finally become sober enough to dress myself and believed that I could actually drive the car. But by then I understood just what was happening to me. I suppose that I could have somehow put on end to the whole charade, but then again, why should I bother? It was the clearest evidence that revealed just how disgusting, worthless, and depressing that my life had become. I also had become disgusted with myself for the decisions that I had made. It was exactly the sort of dead-end, life-draining rut that my father and my uncle had gotten stuck with. But other considerations and questions marched through my head as well.

Since I was trapped with a child on the way and more importantly, since I was stuck with her sorry hide, then what difference did a lousy piece of paper make? But still I wondered why I bothered with a worthless and useless ceremony? It was all completely meaningless, even though all that was required of me was a short drive to someone's house, a person who just happened to work at a church. Once we arrived, we talked for less than five minutes and answered a few social questions. We then went through some sort of quick formality and a seemingly stupid kind of a ritual. I was back at my house within in an hour. It seemed, as if it had all been a mere afterthought. It just didn't seem to be that big of a deal.

As society depicts the lives of people, I supposed that I had turned a corner and in its eyes had finally become a man. But none of it was even close to the path that I had chosen for myself. Within just the course of a year, I had graduated from high school, failed at entering college, and had returned to my hometown. I had then chosen to become mired in a foolish dilemma so desperate that my life had literally become a living hell. But even so, the decisions were entirely mine and, unfortunately, were seemingly irreversible. But the incredible fact was that the pain and anguish that I had endured throughout my life would soon pale in the face of what I was just about to experience. I was doomed.

The Five-Year War
Hillrose Avenue, Marian Avenue, West Wayne Street, Allentown Road, Sherman Avenue

Wars are ugly. They are horribly ugly. It doesn't really matter just who the final victor may be as no one really ever truly wins. Even the winner knows in the end that they really haven't gained all that much. The victims are, however, many, and they are usually the most innocent and vulnerable of us all. The pain may eventually subside or even fade to a great degree, but it never ever completely goes away. The scars themselves always remain forever and sometimes find themselves as unwitting tools in the hands of others. Oftentimes they are used for the expressed purpose of keeping someone within their designated place. But it is the old ghosts that are by far, the very worst of all. They bring about incredible division, despair and destruction. They always seem to rear their ugly heads at the most inconvenient, irresponsible and unwanted times. It takes much more than a mere lifetime to even begin to put them in their proper place. It is not a task fit for mere humans to accomplish.

It was September. I was twenty-four years old, but it felt at times as if I were nearly ninety. As I sat there in the backyard of my bungalow-styled home, I was incredibly amazed at just how five years could be both quickly experienced as well as horribly long and drawn out. It was a mind-bending ordeal and being retrospective gave it a flavor all of its own. My life had changed immensely in those five years. Although I was lost and had been found, I was far from safe.

I had gone to the big city to the south and began vocational school in order to learn a new trade and to finally gain for myself a career. I was soon amazed to learn just what path that new trade would lead me to. It would take me to places that I alone would never have expected or would have included into my plans.

I had gotten married in a pitiful excuse of a ceremony that lasted from door to door and including the pastor's conversation less than an hour. I had driven back to the house and just as soon as we had walked in the door, we dove into yet another argument about packing. I ignored her, went upstairs, and then slept until eight o'clock in the evening. I stayed up the rest of the night, completed the packing, and then organized everything for the move. The following day required a trip to her mother's house for lunch where she was to stay for the week. I left as soon as I possibly could and then headed south early in the afternoon for the big city.

The drive took an hour and a half, as I had no difficulty finding my way once I arrived. The apartment itself was very easy to locate as it was at the end of an off ramp from the interstate highway. The new place took some getting used to, as it was much different than where I had just lived. The duplex that I had rented in our little city was a nice three-bedroom place and most importantly was only three blocks from the boulevards. It consisted of two floors with a living room, a dining room, a kitchen and even a basement. It was the nicest placed that I had ever lived in.

The new apartment in the big city was on the second floor of a fairly large building. It was comprised of a living room, a bedroom, a tiny kitchen, and an even smaller bathroom. It was smaller than some garages, at only about six hundred square feet. But then again, it had its conveniences, as it was only about fifteen minutes from the school. Throughout the course of the week I had been able to locate the nearest shopping areas for supplies and all of the other necessities in life. It seemed as if for the most part, everything was working out fairly well. I actually began to hope that my life finally had a chance. Once again, I was mistaken as I never saw the train wreck approaching.

It was a Thursday night, and since I was in the big city and alone, I decided to take in a concert in the downtown area. One of my favorite bands was playing and I had waited for the opportunity for quite some time. I had driven through town, instead of using the freeway, at less than the speed limit as I looked at all of my new surroundings. It had just gotten dark enough for headlights and I switched them on. But with my interest focused on the city, I neglected to notice that I had the bright headlights on. I would never have known it had I not passed a police car going in the opposite direction. He flashed his lights at me and since my attention was focused elsewhere, I didn't get them turned off as quickly as I supposed that he had expected. It wasn't until he had been right beside me that I had even noticed that it was a police car.

My blood chilled as in my mirror, I saw him turn around and come after me with red lights flashing. I intimately knew just how the police could be and that they didn't take well to my kind for whatever reason. It had always been my experience and it was especially true when things went wrong or when something bad had happened. At times, it simply could be as innocent as the neighborhood where you lived. But I had no idea whether the cops in the new city were decent and honorable or prejudiced and nasty. I only knew that I was about to find it all out in a real and wonderful way.

As the officer walked up to my car, he shone his flashlight everywhere, in the backseat, in my ashtray, and then right into my face almost blinding me. Then he began giving me a bunch of grief about irresponsibility and was aware that I was from out of town and wanted to know where I was going. When I informed him that my destination was a concert, he loudly declared that I must be one of those and immediately ordered me out of my car. He then forced me to stand at the front of my own car with my hands on the hood. He then proceeded to methodically go through every inch of the interior of my car in what I knew to be a desperate and fruitless search. It was a very good thing that I had vacuumed and shampooed the entire car just the week before in preparation for the trip.

He was obviously angry and upset about the lack of contraband because he slammed the car door as he walked to the front where I stood. Once there, he ordered me to stand up straight, tapped me three times hard on the chest with his flashlight, and demanded my driver's license. Then he ordered me to remain where I was, not to move, and that he would return directly. I quickly discovered that it had been a good decision that I had pulled my car into a grocery store parking lot.

When he returned, he smiled as if he really enjoyed his job and then ordered me to follow him. He then placed me into the backseat of his cruiser. Once he had me thus secured, he proceeded to inform me that my license had been suspended and that I was in big trouble. I responded that it was impossible because the last time I had gotten a ticket I had been a senior in high school, and it had been before my eighteen birthday. I added that I had also gotten my new license after my eighteenth birthday and hadn't even had so much as a parking ticket. Something was terribly wrong. It all had to be a mistake.

But there was no mistake, he was not in error, he was correct, and he had the facts to back it up. It was all true, but strangely enough, as the facts would present themselves, I was also telling the truth. Therefore, he wrote a ticket on the spot and impressed upon me the importance of my upcoming court date. He then warned me of the consequences if he caught me even trying to drive my car out of the parking lot. That act alone would have earned me a trip directly to his jail. It was a wonderful way to wrap up my first week in the big city.

I walked around the neighborhood for more than three hours as I wondered what to do. I then carefully drove my car back to the apartment despite the officer's threats. That weekend I also drove back to my hometown just as I had planned and loaded everything up for the move south. She and I got into a huge fight just as soon as I stepped out of the car. The two of us then drove back in complete silence to the big city. She was furious about my traffic ticket, but I had no answers to give. I was at a total loss as I knew that I just had to wait until the court date.

I had been to juvenile court for a speeding ticket and even once for drag racing. On that particular occasion, the judge had torn into me good and hard for my foolish actions. With that experience behind me, I figured that I had a decent idea of what to experience in the upcoming court date. Once again, I believed that I had everything under control and had it all figured out. Once again, I never sought out any advice or assistance and once again, I never saw it coming. Therefore, I really got my clock cleaned for holding fast to my ridiculous pride.

This courtroom was far different than anything that I had ever seen before. I sat in a room with nearly a hundred people. Most of them appeared to be just like me, secure, a little boastful, but anxiously waiting for the judge to arrive. When he did, it was quite an arrival and with that, he laid down his courtroom rules from the very start. He spelled out his procedures, cut no corners, and gave no change. There were a dozen police officers in the room to maintain order and once it began, it simply became an assembly line. I was twenty-ninth on the list and was instantly worried about my situation. That judge cut no one any slack whatsoever as very few people left the building on their own as most were escorted to jail. Each of those individuals went through the back door of the courtroom with an officer at their side. All reliance upon my experience and any sense of my bravado quickly disappeared like a vapor. I was scared to death.

When they called my name, my legs were weakened as I visibly shook as I walked forward to the bench. That judge looked me up and down as if he had the ability to see right through me. Then he fired off questions in rapid succession. In general, they were about such topics as why didn't I believe that I had to obey the law? Why had I thought that I was so special and just who did I think that I was? I tried to be polite as I stammered, sputtered, and tried to spit out the answers. But it seemed that he really didn't care for any of my answers. Then, in irritating and angry detail, he proceeded to tell me the actual reason as to just why I was in his courtroom.

Did I recall the incident where I had been in an automobile accident three years prior? Did I recall being cited for the offense? Did I recall the damage that I had caused to the other vehicle? I politely answered yes to all of his questions. Then he proceeded. Whose car had I been driving? I answered that it had been my mother's sedan. At the time my uncle and I hadn't completed the work on the convertible. But again, that had been three years prior and the matter had been processed in juvenile court. I had paid my fine and had believed that was the end of the matter. Once again, I never saw it coming.

The trouble, as the judge revealed the situation to me, was more than a bit complicated as he proceeded to enlighten me in the ways of the world. He revealed through documentation that my mother hadn't bothered to insure her vehicle at the time of the accident. Consequently, she had been sued by the driver of the other vehicle and had by that date, refused to make any kind of payment on the debt. It appeared that she had gone through her standard litany of broken promises and excuses. But somehow, since I had been the operator of the vehicle, the state had decided to revoke my driver's license. It seemed that it just took a while for such things to be processed. But it had been three years and therefore, I asked a few questions of my own.

Why was I, as a minor at the time of the accident, responsible for whether or not my mother had insurance on a vehicle that she owned and had been titled in her name? Why was I legally responsible for her actions? Shouldn't it have mattered that I personally owned a car that was titled in her name and that it did have insurance on it? As I asked those questions, the judge's face actually softened just a bit as his voice then took on a fatherly tone. He stated that he would give me just one week to do something for both him and for myself. I needed to obtain a statement from my mother that the car that I had wrecked was indeed hers, was actually titled in her name and that she did not have insurance on it at the time. She also had to acknowledge that I had no knowledge of whether or not she had insurance coverage on the vehicle. She had to agree to those statements in writing, sign the bottom of the letter, and then have it officiated. If I obtained such a letter, he would let me off the hook, fully reinstate my license, and clear my record. To me, it didn't seem to be an extravagant request as the authorities had already contacted her on numerous occasions on the matter. Therefore the judge believed that it should have been an easy task to complete.

I called my mother on the telephone as soon as I returned home and explained everything that the judge had described in detail. I then told her exactly what the judge had said that my punishment would be if she didn't follow through with his request. I informed her that I would have to pay a fine and then be forced to spend two full weekends in jail. Then I opened up a bit and let her know just how much jail frightened me. I added that all that she had to do was write a simple letter and tell the truth. She stated that if she did what I had asked then she would be admitting her guilt to the world. Then she somehow reasoned that the court would then do something to her in retaliation.

Therefore, as far as she was concerned, it was a case of too bad, too sad, sorry about your luck and then she just *hung up* on me.

Just what kind of person was this woman? Was there anyone that she cared about apart from herself? Why was it always all about her? Didn't she have any idea of what jail would be like for me? Did she possess any portion of a conscience at all? Because of her decision of inaction I now had to spend time in jail. All that was required of her was but a simple letter which stated the facts and the truth. She had already been sued for the matter and had been found guilty. It was all because of my mother's financial and moral irresponsibility. How could she be so callous? Hadn't she any idea what sort of fear gripped my heart over going to jail? Why didn't she care enough to do the right thing? I was her son, her eldest, her flesh and blood—didn't that mean anything to her? Or was it because of those details? She had told me previously that I had ruined her life just by my birth. Was her decision just a small sliver of revenge? Was it a chance for her to now cause me pain? Was she really that twisted? Once again I was doomed.

A surprising turn of events occurred on the day that I had to report for my first weekend in jail. I was thoroughly shocked to discover who knocked at my apartment door. It was my father. I had never called him about the matter and had never let him know much about anything that happened in my life. But there he was anyway. He drove me to the jail and handed me four packs of cigarettes in a brown paper bag. He then repeated some detailed words of advice that my uncle had given to him.

My uncle had advised that the first order of business was to find a bunk in the middle of the cellblock. He suggested to find a top bunk bed and to stash the cigarettes inside the pillowcase. I should also take along a couple of books, which I already had and then carefully follow the unwritten rules. Never smile at anyone. If at all possible, do not eat the food. If at all possible, do not go into the bathrooms unless the guards are inside. Reach deep within and tough the whole thing out. It was then that I knew that the entire extended family had been told what had happened. But I would have bet my last dollar at that moment that none of them truly knew the real reason for my unwanted weekend getaway. As dozens of thoughts raced through my head, my father dropped me off at the gate and declared that he would see me on Sunday evening.

I thought that I had seen it all in my short life, but I was never more terrified of anything else before in my life as I was herded into a room with sixty other men. Everyone had their name called off along with their reason for being there. It was so ironic, pitiful, and desperately unnecessary. There I was on a lame traffic violation locked up with thieves, thugs, drug dealers, pimps, and even two child molesters. There were three guys in the room who had been hauled in for having nearly killed a gas station clerk and one man was there for raping an old lady. My uncle didn't have to worry about me smiling at anybody in that sorry place. After my name had been called, I grabbed a coffee can for an ashtray, found an upper bunk, stashed my cigarettes as I had been instructed, and stayed there for the entire weekend. From Saturday morning until Sunday evening I never moved from that spot. I didn't eat anything, didn't drink anything, and that being as it were, I didn't have to go anywhere.

But by not talking and not doing anything else also had the added benefit of making me appear more than a little bit mysterious to the other cellmates. They couldn't believe or understand that I didn't want anything to eat or drink and that I never seemed to sleep. Without saying so much as a word, they took that to mean that I was some kind of really bad dude and that there had been much more to my traffic violation than what the official records had revealed. By responding to their questions with single words answers and sometimes with just a glare, it only managed to reinforce that belief. The fact that I had a raging inferno going inside of me, and that I was furious to the point of violence with my mother made it almost comically easy to pull off. Within very little time, everyone had seen fit to leave me alone and went on about their activities, which was exactly the way that I wanted it. It was almost a relief.

The following weekend was exactly the same and my father did just as he had done the week before. I had no idea whatsoever of just where that streak of generosity appeared. But when I got out of his car the second time, he stopped me, shook my hand, and told me to take care of myself. That was probably the closest that he had ever gotten to me and they were certainly the kindest words that he had ever spoken to me. I finished my second weekend at the jail just as I had with the first. It was just one more item to add to my illustrious resume.

Activities at the vocational school were just the opposite. Everything there went very well and I actually completed the full course of study three months earlier than scheduled. Having obtained those results, I then planned for an apprenticeship in my new trade at local businesses in the big city. The problem that rose almost immediately was that there were no openings anywhere in that city in my field, much less an opportunity for an inexperienced apprentice. That scenario then set the stage for my return back to my hometown once again. It brought back more than one reminder of my college failure of just over a year and a half before.

However, it was a great delight to *her* because she never stopped nagging me nearly every waking hour about how bored she was and how she missed her family. She hit me with it as soon as I walked in the door after school and never shut up about it until I had gone to sleep. It had even gotten to the place where she had stayed for a week at a time back in the hometown. That required a drive north after school to pick her up on Friday nights even though her family had the means to do it and the very real fact that they were less than two hours away. However, it did permit time alone and with it, much needed peace and quiet. But even so, my life was such a mess.

Thankfully, I had received results from the numerous inquiries that I had sent to businesses in the hometown and had secured a place to work in order to complete my training. But once more I had to move within a year and it felt far too much like the nonsense that I had to endure as a child. I hated moving. I just hated it. It almost felt as if someone else had made all of the decisions for me and that I wasn't in control of anything. It seemed that I literally had little or no idea of what was to happen to me next. I really couldn't stand all of that uncertainty. I wanted planning, order, and structure. I wanted to be in control of my own life. I wanted to be in charge.

After having stayed with one of *her* sisters for two weeks, which was nearly unbearable, I found an apartment suitable for a young family. It was on the city's northwest side, which pleased me, and it was in a good, middle-class neighborhood. It was a row apartment at the corner of two small streets with very little traffic. There was a supermarket grocery store nearby, and it was just off the state highway that led to the mall and the other shopping centers. It was a nice two-story townhouse sort of place. It had a living room with a kitchen and eating area on the first floor and two bedrooms and a bath on the second. It had nice hardwood floors throughout and a beautiful oak stairway that led from the living room to the upstairs. It was a very nice place, and it was certainly something that gave me a sense of pride.

I quickly fell into the routine of work, as I usually put in ten-hour days but only five days a week. I didn't make a fortune and actually in comparison, my high school job in the mailroom earned just about as much money. But it was all training for a career as I figured that it was simply the dues of life that I was required to pay. As I kept to a tight budget, which caused many loud arguments itself, I was able to still put back a little money each week. But the problem was that it somehow always seemed to get spent on something. By that time I was less than two months away from being a father, and every dime that I managed to save always seemed to go toward something for the nursery. I could never use it for something that I wanted.

She used every bit of it for blankets, diapers, outfits, and who knew what else. How many things did a baby need? Why did a kid need an outfit for every day of the week for two weeks? Was that what I was working so hard for? It all seemed to be purely stupid excess. As far as I was concerned, no one needed that much stuff. The kid would just grow out of everything and then what would I do with everything? Then I would have spent a pile of money on things that couldn't be used anymore and then I would just have to go and buy even more! I found it all to be very irritating and frustrating.

Did this sort of nonsense ever have an ending? It was just one of a hundred reasons why I had never ever wanted any kids. They absolutely ruined your life! They just made everything in life so completely miserable. All that I had to do was look at what having all of those kids had done to my parents. Their lives were a total disaster. They had gotten divorced and were both broke and completely destitute. As separated families, they were living in worn-out, broken-down rented dumps of houses. They were pathetic, and I had no plan to follow their example.

And then there was *her*, the woman that I had been stuck with for the rest of my life. She had been bad enough before and had been nearly impossible to live with before she had gotten pregnant, but afterward, life with her was absolutely unbearable. I hated going home at night. I wished that I had somewhere else to go, but I just didn't. She started in the moment that I walked in the back door, and she barely stopped for air the remainder of the night. You would have thought that *I* had been the one that had made *her* life a living hell on earth. I simply never understood her.

I worked every day, always came home, always stayed home, and did everything that I could to make sure that we had what we needed. What more could she possibly want from me? She should have been happy that I did what I had done since I hadn't wanted any part of the entire mess from the very beginning. Besides that, she knew full well and then some from the very start just how much that I hated kids. She knew exactly what I thought of them and that they didn't have any place in the plans that I had for my life. She should have been happy that I had done what I had.

Then the day came. It was nothing but pure chaos as she yelled, ordered, and treated me as if I were a worthless servant. She cursed me all the way to the hospital, which didn't better my mood as I was furious anyway. I pulled the little station wagon into the emergency room parking lot and was shamefully nasty and repulsive with everyone that I came into contact with. My temper was out of control and I made no attempt to rein it in. I hated everything as it was happening and my life in its entirety. I observed just that kind of nonsense as it ruined my family through and through. It was my uncle's case in particular that had especially struck me as he had ceased to be the sort of person that he had always been.

His story was nearly identical to mine as he too had married due to an unplanned pregnancy. Because of it, his personality had changed overnight. He had always been fun to spend time with, but from that point forward, he was just hateful, bitter, and nasty as he turned into a full-blown alcoholic. Unfortunately, it appeared that I had chosen the exact same path. Every decision that I had made since high school, every corner that I had turned had proven to be a mistake. I watched as it had all happened right before my eyes. My life had become simply one fiasco after another. Therefore, that day at the hospital became one of the most depressing days of my life. I was desperately and hopelessly lost.

I sat in a waiting room with about a dozen other men. Without exception they were all happy, joyful, and seemingly beside themselves with anticipation. But they were also obviously anxious as well. Each and every one of them had family and friends there for companionship. I literally felt their excitement in the air. It was nearly a full-blown celebration every time one of them had been called out of the room. Since I seemed to be the direct opposite, I wondered just what in the world was so wrong with me. Was I merely selfish and immature? Why didn't I feel as they did? Why had I chosen to spend the occasion alone? Why hadn't I bothered to call anyone? But then again, just whom would I have called? What would I have said? There was really no one that came to my mind. My decisions had set the stage for me. Therefore, I spent the event alone.

It was then that I heard my name, and as they had used the *mister* part, it caught me off guard. I was quite pleased to hear it as I then felt like an actual adult and not simply a nineteen-year-old pretender. The nurse that had called my name smiled brightly as she took me by the elbow and led me down a brightly lit hallway. We came upon a very well-lighted glass wall, and once there, she tapped on the window.

A nurse on the other side of the window stepped forward as the nurse at my side mouthed my last name. The nurse behind the glass turned, walked to the back of the room, and picked up a little bundle of white blanket and walked toward me. As she stood at the window, just inches away from me, she pulled the blanket back to reveal the face of the most beautiful little baby girl I had ever seen. She was absolutely incredible and very nearly beyond belief. I was asked if I wanted to hold her and stammered out a yes as they led me to another area. There they put me in a gown with a mask and an odd sort of a hat. Once seated, the nurse gently handed her to me.

I was absolutely amazed. All of those horrible and nasty thoughts that had so filled my head evaporated from my mind like the fog on a sunny morning. In a mere instant, they were suddenly gone, forgotten, and had been replaced with something far greater. Even though I had grown up in a very large family with kids and babies all around me every day, I had never seen anything like this little one ever before in my life. She was incredibly tiny, soft, and clean; and she smelled absolutely wonderful. How could all of this possibly be? My mind was transformed.

I was a father. Suddenly something welled up within me and the emotions that previously had been so confounding were mysteriously gone. The new feelings were of such a nature that I had never felt before. It was an entirely new type of pride, a most incredible impression of tenderness, followed quickly by an almost overwhelming feeling of responsibility. I had to care, provide, and protect her. She was now my responsibility.

Then the questions coursed through my mind. How would she grow up? What sort of little girl would she turn out to be? Who would she look like? What kind of things would she like? What kind of things would drive her crazy? What sort of habits would she have? Who would she grow up to be? What kind of personality would she have? What would she grow up to be some day? Would I be the sort of father that she needed?

But of greater curiosity was a new and incredible feeling that grew so rapidly within me. What was it about this tiny little baby that moved me in such a way? It was more than just merely responsibility as it was far deeper and yet somewhat mysterious in its nature. I had never felt anything like it before. What was this new burden, this binding tie that I suddenly felt as that little person lay quietly sleeping in my arms? Why had it come on so quickly and in the way that it had? Everything just seemed warmer and kinder. I just couldn't fully understand or grasp it. I was pleasantly, but curiously confused. But in that very special moment I had also found true hope. I had discovered a reason for living and a purpose for my own future. Had I finally discovered what love actually was?

I took her home from the hospital within a few days and put her in her new bed, in her new bedroom, and into her first home. I had an unfamiliar and impossible to define feeling of pride. For the first time in a long time, I actually began to dream of what the future may hold. Perhaps hope was there to be found. Perhaps it was merely waiting for me to find it. Maybe, just maybe, I had finally found real purpose in my life.

Throughout that first evening and for many that followed, I awakened during the night for no other reason than to look in on her. I found myself doing it, on average, at least once an hour. I checked on her blankets, made certain that she was covered, ensured that the room was warm enough and always made certain that she was breathing. As I stood there in the darkened bedroom, I watched her as she slept in complete amazement. As I did so a multitude of items ran through my head. I actually began to believe that the depressing gray clouds that seemed to have covered my life had begun to lift. I thought to myself that perhaps my life actually had a chance to become better, maybe even normal.

But as wonderful as this little one was, the other female in the house was exactly the opposite. We quickly became entrenched into a completely unbelievable, unforeseen, and horrific argument on the way home from the hospital. She wasn't even diplomatic about what was on her mind. She came right out and accused me of having an affair with someone, an unknown someone, during her stay in the hospital. It didn't matter to her at all that I had divided all of my time between work and the hospital and could have documented my actions down to the minute. But obvious facts didn't mean a thing to her and never had. She was dead set upon having me tried, convicted, and sentenced for a crime that I hadn't even thought about committing.

It didn't matter in the least that no one had informed her of such actions. It didn't matter that she didn't have a name nor could she describe the alleged person. She only reasoned that men always committed those type of acts as their wives were busy having babies. Therefore, I was guilty simply by being male. In her twisted logic, it was simply the way that things were. In her mind, it was mere human nature and a simple fact of everyday life. She held fast to these beliefs despite having absolutely no facts of any kind to support her accusations. There was simply no proof, no witnesses, and not the first shred of evidence. She admitted that she didn't possess the first hint of a rumor. There was no rhyme, reason, or logic of any sort behind her tirade. There was no truth or logic whatsoever to her fantastic accusations.

But none of that mattered as she claimed she instinctively knew what it was that she knew. According to her, sooner or later the truth would be made known and then she would discover with whom I had been having the affair. It was then that she informed me that once she had accomplished that task, I would be very sorry. From my point of view, it was far too late for that, as I was sorry already and had been for some time. Once again, I was reminded that I was stuck in a marriage that I never wanted any part of. I was forced to live with someone that I just couldn't tolerate, stand to be around, or to even share air with. After all, I had personally witnessed what sort of destruction adultery had done to my parents. I had seen firsthand, what the pain and agony of having an adulterous spouse had done to my father. Not only did I not want to inflict that sort of thing upon someone, but I also certainly didn't want to drag any more drama into my life than what I already had to deal with. I was thoroughly sick of it all.

It didn't matter to her just how innocent I had been about any subject and especially that one. She was hell bent on making certain that I paid dearly for my supposed crimes. But the fact of the matter was that I regretted being with her more than she could ever possibly imagine. I had endured enough of her psychotic, idiotic, and off-the-wall nonsense. Her actions already provided me with much more than I had ever bargained for. I had already put up with enough of her idiocy and as she had thrown that sort of insulting stupidity into my face, she had finally crossed the line. There wasn't any way that I intended on putting up with her accusations that I was the same as every other guy on the planet. It didn't matter to her one bit about my innocence and that I could prove it with a dozen verifiable witnesses. She had already decided that she was going to do whatever she possibly could to make my life miserable. But it was far too late for that threat. She evidently hadn't realized that she had already accomplished that task.

However, during the following month or so, my household actually settled down a degree, but not by very much. She had ceased to accuse me of any further crimes but made certain that I knew in any other way possible that she was still angry and that the argument was far from over. She slammed doors in the apartment, cursed at me as if I weren't in the room, fixed meals only for her, and frequently locked me out of my own bedroom. She was as mean as a snake, and I just didn't deserve it.

One particular evening upon arriving home from work, I noticed a strange car in the driveway. Upon entering the apartment, I discovered that the vehicle belonged to one of her sisters. As I walked in through the kitchen door, the unmistakable sound of sobbing could be heard from the living room. It appeared that the two of them were engaged in quite a conversation. It was never safe for any male on the entire planet whenever she and one of her sisters gathered together for a talk. From their peculiar storytelling ways, all men were the sons of the devil or worse.

As I overheard the two of them describe it, men were simply evil. They just used women, took what they wanted from them and then they always abandoned them. Those firmly held beliefs however, never seemed to inhibit them as they pursued one poor victim after another. Almost without exception, every one of them had chased after any number of men who, as immoral women, believed would raise their standard of living or gain them something of any value that they desired. They were convinced that it was a fair business venture, as they didn't have to actually give up anything more than their bodies. They were also completely unbiased, as they willingly pursued nearly any man. It didn't matter if they were taken, spoken for, engaged, or even married. Any breathing male was fair game to these women in their selfish pursuit. As such, they were quite the experts at laying traps for the foolish and unexpected.

That particular sister was one of her older siblings. Something terrible had just happened in her life, and she was in desperate need of help. Evidently her current boyfriend had reached his limit with her and had simply decided to end the relationship. But then again, perhaps his wife may have had some say in the matter and influenced the man's decision. But no matter what had happened or what the cause of the problem had been, she suddenly found herself homeless. She had discovered that he had quit paying the rent for her apartment as well as the utilities. Since she didn't have a job, had never worked anywhere, she herself couldn't pay the bills and had been forcibly removed from the premises. But if only to make the situation even worse, she also had a daughter who was just over a year old.

As was usually the case in such families, her life was a mess and she was out of options. I silently wondered as to why she had landed in my apartment. It really didn't make too much sense and something seemed quite odd about the entire ordeal. Additionally, red flags of warning began going off with regularity inside of my head. Then reality revealed itself as the two of them had already concluded that she could stay at our place.

Our townhouse had a basement, and the two sisters decided that the needy older one could put her all of her belongings down there. With what little she had she was able to arrange a workable living room and bedroom. So between the two of them, it had all been agreed, settled, and done as I didn't have a say in the matter whatsoever. But I also didn't want to be labeled as cruel, insensitive, and uncaring. There before me was a woman with a small child, and although she was someone that I barely knew, the two of them evidently had nowhere else to go. I hated to see someone abandoned, as that particular situation struck me in the heart in a way that few understood. I also believed, at least at that moment that there really wasn't anything to worry about. As I conceded to the entire arrangement, I honestly believed that no real issues could arise from it. I also believed that it wouldn't last more than a few days and decided that I could tolerate it for a short period of time. I also believed that it would give the spouse someone else to talk to and would permit me to be alone and gain some peace and quiet.

I stayed upstairs in my bedroom the majority of the evening with a novel as the two of them kept to themselves, talked, and did whatever sisters did together. It was nearly eleven when *she* came upstairs. Once in the bedroom, she immediately discussed her sister and the miserable situation that she was in. I actually didn't care to hear anything about it, especially at that time of the night. I was desperate for sleep, so I put my book down, turned out the light even as she spoke, and was asleep within minutes.

I awakened with a sudden start as my brain went on full alert. I didn't understand at first what had caused it, but I knew from experience that it was something real and not imagined. Once I shoved the cobwebs out of my head, it didn't take long to figure out the disturbance. The pain in my side had forced me to sit up instantly in the bed, and my ribs were quite sore from her well-placed and wicked elbow shot just the moment before. A glance at the clock revealed that it was well past midnight.

Through clenched teeth, I angrily asked her just what her problem was, as she suddenly hushed me into curious silence. In barely heard whispers she stated that she had heard a noise, and it was coming from downstairs. I angrily and profanely informed her that it was probably her sister, that it was best if she left me alone and allowed me to go back to sleep. She immediately became angry, nasty, and then practically shoved me out of the bed. I responded with my standard and enthusiastic response and carried on no further conversation with her. With a degree of stealth, I walked out of the room with clenched teeth and a seriously furious attitude to begin my unwanted detective work.

I quietly left the bedroom and with one carefully placed footstep at a time walked the hallway to the stairs. At the first step, I stopped and strained to listen with everything that I had within me. But I heard nothing, not a single unrecognizable noise of any sort, merely pure silence. At that point, I wanted nothing more than to go back to bed and go to sleep. But I knew exactly what was to be heard if I attempted to pull that off. It was just another manifestation of the control that she believed was her right to force into my life minute by minute throughout the entire day. I knew it meant that I was to gain no more sleep for the remainder of the night which made for seemingly endless work hours the following day.

As I walked down the hardwood steps one at a time, I held my breath on each one and tried very hard not to make them squeak. At the bottom of the steps was a landing, which then turned left, went down three more steps, and emptied into the living room. As I reached the bottom of those steps, I stopped and permitted my eyes to adjust to the room. The living room area was somewhat illuminated by the streetlamp outside of the window. As my eyes scanned from the window and then left along the wall, everything seemed to be in order. Nothing appeared out of place until my eyes fell upon something that left me completely dumbfounded.

The sofa was on the wall directly opposite the stairs and the light from outside the window shone across its entire length. On that sofa was her sister, and as she lay there, I assumed and then hoped that she was sleeping. But I don't believe that many people sleep posed in the position that to me obviously appeared to be staged. She lay there with all of the blankets removed and thrown upward onto the back of the sofa. She had her underwear pushed down halfway down to her knees and her nightgown top was pulled up to her neck, completely exposing herself. It was more than obvious that everything she possessed was freely offered. In all of her crudeness and boldness, I clearly understood that it was precisely and exactly just that, an offer. It was as obvious as a nose on the face. It was divisive, humiliating, and more than a little pathetic. A fire raged within me as I was instantly and irreversibly angered.

I had never heard of anyone sleeping in that manner, especially when it was below freezing outside, and the apartment had been kept purposely cool. The only room that I really kept warm overnight was for my new little daughter. It was all obviously staged and as I stood there, the questions raced through my head. Why? Why had she acted like that? What was she trying to accomplish by that stunt? Was she so bold as to attempt something like that with her sister just upstairs? But even if it hadn't been staged, I certainly wasn't interested. However, there was certainly something that I could do about it.

I pegged it as just another game in an endless series of games that these sisters played against one another. It wasn't the first time that one of them had gone after someone else's husband. It had happened previously with others and unfortunately a few of the attempts had been successful. But I defiantly determined that there was to be no such nonsense in my house. Not as long as I had anything to say about it. And I had everything to say about it.

I hadn't a clue of just what went through that sister's mind as I simply turned away and went back upstairs. But it allowed for me to take a moment in an attempt to discern just what had happened and why. With each step up the stairs, I became angrier and far more than simply upset. Throughout my life there had been at least one thing that I completely realized and understood. There were many ways to fix conniving, manipulating people when they played their stupid little games.

Once I returned to the bedroom, I informed *her* precisely and in full detail of the downstairs scenario. I then informed her in no uncertain terms that both of us were going down there and that *she* was to follow directly behind me and match my every footstep. She knew without asking that I was very angry and near the ragged edge of losing my temper. For once, she actually kept her mouth shut and followed instructions.

We went down the stairs in unison as our footsteps sounded as one. At the bottom of the steps I instantly adjusted my eyes to the light only to discover that the living room scene had changed and certainly not for the better. I didn't bother to think of her sister's thoughts as I walked down the stairs, but her position on the sofa was completely altered. With *her* standing directly behind me and looking around my shoulder, it was plain to see that by this time, her sister was wearing absolutely nothing. Her underwear and nightgown had been discarded, her head was turned toward the wall, and she had one leg up on the back of the sofa. It was a ridiculous and disgusting sight.

At that precise moment I stepped from in front of *her* and motioned for her to remain silently where she was, just in front of the sofa. I then went to the doorway, flipped the light switch, and instantly illuminated the entire room. The two women gasped and screamed at once as I stood facing the window with my back to them. After I had given them both a moment, I turned around to observe that her sister had sufficiently covered herself. I looked back and forth at the two of them as they both sat there stupidly in silence. To me, they appeared as a pair of criminals that had been caught in the act. Or perhaps I was simply too angry to think logically.

At that moment though, I felt as if I were a judge holding court. I sternly informed the sister that although her child had a place to stay for the night, she had to leave the apartment and that she had to do it immediately. I wasn't going to give her another moment. As they both began to argue, I told them that I didn't care if it was one o'clock in the morning and that I really didn't care at all. She had ten minutes to get out of my apartment, or she would be thrown out. When neither of them moved, I yelled at the top of my voice and ordered her out the door immediately. Then to *her*, I stated that if I heard one word, just one word, then she would be gone as well. There wasn't any way that I was about to put up with that sort of nonsense. My life certainly didn't need any more drama than what it already had.

For one solid week after that early morning eviction, *she* refused to speak to me. However, I never bothered to even attempt to force the issue. The standoff created the first week of peace and quiet that I had experienced for a long, long time. But even as I enjoyed that benefit, I privately failed to understand why she had a problem with my decision. Why was *she* so upset? Why was she so angry with me? Additionally, why was her family also furious with me? They acted as if I had committed a criminal act for evicting that woman from my home. Just exactly what had I done wrong? I quickly realized that making a stand with these people also brought about a serious cost.

However, she had seen with her own eyes just what her sister had been up to. I secretly wondered if something else went on behind the scenes. Had there been a scheme of some kind or another? I simply hadn't any idea, not even the first clue. But one thing was certain as I had thoroughly angered everyone in her family.

Despite my background and upbringing, or perhaps because of it, there was one thing that was of importance to me and that was my integrity. I didn't have much else in my possession, but I did have that. I had learned much from the men that I had chosen to emulate in the mailroom and that one item rose above all of the others. I had learned that integrity and honor meant more than anything else in the world, even if it were only your public face. It wasn't something that you were born with, but you also couldn't buy it. It was a personal choice that required the utmost dedication and either you decided that you wanted it or you didn't. It was probably the only thing of real value that I attempted to possess.

But what happened nearly a month later tested every fiber of that decision and pushed me to the utter limit. I arrived home that afternoon actually a little earlier than usual only to discover that she and the baby were gone. I frantically searched the house in vain. I didn't understand why she had left or where they could have gone. She didn't have a car, and therefore someone had to have picked them up. As I stood in my living room and wondered just what going on, I then heard the obvious sound of a car. As I heard it pull into the parking lot, a car door slam, and then heard the engine race as footsteps hurried to the back door. The back door quickly opened and closed as I realized that it was her. As I walked into the kitchen, I asked her just where she had been and who had dropped her off. She set the baby down and immediately shoved a finger into my face and began yelling and screaming maniacally. It was her typical reaction to revealed guilt. She was so predictable, or so I thought.

Then her standard practice of interrogation reversal began. She always turned everything around in her never ending attempt to make me the bad guy. It was the usual litany of questions. Why did I always want to know where she had been? What business was it of mine? Why did I care who had given her a ride? Just who did I think that I was to question her actions? Why was I always getting into her business? Hadn't I always known that she could do whatever she wanted? Didn't I realize that she never had to answer to me about anything?

Then through the course of the argument, it was revealed that she had visited an infamous area doctor in a small town to the west of our city. It was well-known that anyone could go there and get whatever they wanted. It only required a short interview process, and then you walked out with a prescription for diet pills. It was always great stuff to take and was highly effective. I knew about the scheme, had been there myself, and was anything but overweight.

She sternly informed me that she had to have those pills in order to shed the baby weight. As always she proceeded to remind me that it was my fault that her body was in such a mess.

That particular argument carried on as all of the others before always had, unceasing for hours until well after the baby had been put to bed. It had gotten to the point where I was hardly able to stand it. It was so oppressive that the very air in the apartment felt overwhelmingly heavy with the stress of it all. It was as if as I walked in the door, someone had set a hundred-pound weight on my shoulders. Each day steadily became worse than the one before it. It was nearly more than I could physically take. Within me I knew that I was nearing my limit. There were times when I was more than just tempted to get into my car, fill the gas tank, and drive as far away as I possibly could. But there was just one small thing kept me from it, my little daughter.

Over the course of the following month, the atmosphere in my household went from stupidly bad to ridiculously worse. The apartment itself suffered as well and by the end of the second week, it was disgustingly filthy. There wasn't any way that I was about to step back into time to relive my childhood. I simply couldn't be expected to tolerate, much less to live in such conditions. As I verbalized my concerns and complaints, the arguments again became extremely heated, quite loud, and worse than they had ever been before. Unfortunately, we had both gotten both stupid and loud enough on occasion, which resulted in an unsolicited and extremely unpleasant visit from the local police department. Some of those events had involved neighbors in the apartment complex who had vocalized their complaints. It had all gotten completely out of hand. Both of us were well on our way to a short hospital stay or some jail time or perhaps a combination of the two. Disaster was imminent.

The following afternoon as I had returned home from work, I found a note conveniently taped to the television. It appeared that she had left a half an hour before, and the note further stated that she would be staying with one of her sisters for an unknown length of time. It just happened to be the very sister who had been thrown out of my apartment previously on that ugly and fateful night. I sat down on the sofa, put my head in my hands, and wondered out loud just how much worse my life could be. What had I done in my life to deserve this sort of nonsense? But then again, perhaps I had done far too much in my life and the bill for my transgressions was demanding payment. But as I argued with myself and went back and forth over it, I wondered just why it had to be that way. I also knew that although I had made a vow to the marriage, and even though my word was of utmost importance to me, I desperately yearned for a way out of the stifling marital prison that I was locked within. But since that was such an impossibility, at the very least, she was now gone. I now had an opportunity for a quiet evening alone and perhaps even get a decent-night's sleep.

My thoughts then froze in place as I then heard a heartbreaking noise that stopped my heart cold. At first I simply couldn't believe what my ears had informed my dumbfounded brain. It simply didn't register for at least the first moment or so. Did I actually hear a baby's cry from upstairs? Then the realization of the awful truth hit me like a thrown brick in the face: *she had left her there all alone!* I bounded up the steps two at a time and literally burst into tears as I entered my daughter's bedroom.

Her little face was red and tearstained, as she had obviously been crying her heart out for quite some time. I wondered if perhaps she had heard my voice as I had been asking myself those questions out loud. Then I noticed that her diaper was soaking wet as well. I quickly gathered all of the necessary items and changed her. It was then that I realized that her little face wasn't the only thing that was red. I discovered far too late that it seemed that the house wasn't the only thing that had suffered under her mother's program of neglect. I was infuriated beyond words. But I should have paid far closer attention to everything, especially to my daughter.

After I gathered everything together, I gave my daughter a bath, a clean diaper, fresh pajamas, and then took her downstairs to the kitchen. As I placed her into her high chair and began getting her food ready, she began banging her hands and waving them in the air. It was as if she instantly and completely understood exactly what I was doing. She was clearly excited, made noises, moved, and shook in her seat. I then understood that the neglect extended far beyond just diapers, as she obviously hadn't been fed properly either. One thing was absolutely certain, someone was going to pay for what had been done to my daughter. There wasn't any way possible to forgive for having so carelessly abandoned my little girl.

Once I had gotten the baby taken care of, she quickly drifted off to sleep while still in my arms. As quietly as I was able, I began cleaning the apartment. I started in the kitchen, progressed into the living room, and finished the first floor. I then went upstairs and gathered together the nine or ten loads of laundry that had been ignored as well. It was there that I found the damning evidence.

I knew precisely what I owned, and in particular, knew what I wore and just what my wardrobe consisted of. Whether it was a gift or simply human nature, I instinctively knew whenever something in the apartment was out of place and when something just didn't belong. The scope and intensity of my anger reached new heights as I cleaned the bedroom closet. When I pulled the bedsheets from the closet where they had been hurriedly stuffed, I found socks and underwear that absolutely did not belong to me. They were obviously men's apparel, but they were certainly not mine.

What had been going on there in my house? To whom did they belong? What was his name? How many times had he been there in my bed? How long had the affair been going on? One thing was for certain, as my anger reached its boiling point and then eclipsed it. I was more than ready to end someone's life. I had been humiliated and wanted someone to pay dearly for it. *I would not allow myself to be made a fool of!* It was garbage, nothing but garbage. At that moment, I didn't care about the marriage vows. I didn't have to tolerate her nonsense.

But what was I going to do about it? I had to find out everything. Despite the emotional upheaval that raged within, as well as the real understanding that more information would only cause it to worsen, I had to know his identity. Somebody was going to tell me what had happened. I was going to make them and was more than capable of accomplishing that feat. I didn't care what it was that I had to do. I determined that I would destroy anyone's life that had anything to do with her deception. Someone had to pay, and they would pay dearly for everything as I knew I wouldn't stop until I had all of the answers.

She had turned out to be exactly like my mother, a nearly perfect copy. It was exactly the same sort of crass and selfish actions that I had observed my mother commit against my father for years. As I stood there in the bedroom and took it all in, I felt as if I were watching history repeat itself. I felt as if, and indeed was in fact, a miserable and trapped man. There was seemingly no way out of the mess other than divorce. But that presented serious problems as well as I considered my daughter and her future. That singular item stopped me in my tracks. No matter how poorly she had conducted herself as a wife and mother, the courts would never award custody to a father. It just wasn't done, and I wasn't even certain that it was legal. But there also wasn't any way in the world that I dared to leave my daughter alone with her in that situation. Therefore and once again, I was a defeated and condemned man with no way out, at least at that moment. But I still wondered just why she had done it.

What had I ever done to her? What had I ever said or done that was so wrong? Why and when had she decided to replace me? How long had the affair been going on? How long had she been unfaithful? Had she ever actually been faithful? Perhaps that was the better question. Had she ever been truly honest with me? I had carried questions and suspicions within me for the entire length of time that I had been stuck with her. I knew without having actually known that she had probably cheated on multiple occasions before we had gone through that sorry excuse of a marriage ceremony. Then there were her questionable actions during that first week when I had moved to the big city for school, and she had stayed behind. Added to that were her constant requests to return to the hometown for a week at a time and on a continual basis. Due to her condemning attitude toward her entire family, I knew that she wasn't homesick for them. She had lied to me about everything, and I knew it.

But why had I tolerated it? I had sworn to myself so very long before that I would never allow someone to treat me as my father had been treated. It was so ironic that I found myself in the very same situation. But what was I going to do? How was I going to handle the matter? What would I say to her? Would I confront her or act as if nothing had happened? I then decided that I couldn't simply ignore the obvious facts, as she needed to be confronted. It had nothing to do with a broken heart or anything of the sort as I certainly didn't love her in any way shape or form. However, it was betrayal and I didn't deserve that sort of treatment, not from her and not from anyone. However, I was so completely confused and suddenly felt dead inside. It was as if I were a man condemned to die.

She arrived home the following Sunday night at seven o'clock. As she walked in through the back door, she wore, of all things, that same blasted smile my mother displayed on her face whenever she was victorious. She walked right up to me, stood there for just a moment, looked me straight in the eye, and slapped me in the face. She instantly became loud and angry, as she demanded to know why I had been checking up on her. Someone had informed her that I had contacted her entire family in looking for her. Why didn't I trust her? Why hadn't I ever trusted her? Why didn't I ever believe her? She had only wanted to get away with her sisters for the weekend. She needed some time to vent, time to relax after having a kid forced on her twenty-four hours a day and seven days a week; she needed that time away. With that said and done, she simply stood there and waited for me to speak.

Then as I bluntly questioned her about what I found in the laundry; her eyes widened in amazement and guilt as she just went completely off. She screamed, yelled, and stomped around the kitchen in a circle as she said things that I couldn't even understand. It was almost like gibberish, as an idiot would speak, and I couldn't make any sense of it at all. Then suddenly and without warning, she grabbed the freshly washed dishes out of the kitchen strainer and threw them at me. She didn't seem to care in the least that the baby was in the room. The pottery and glasses just shattered everywhere. She simply lost it.

Then for an unknown reason, she screamed even louder, cursed, and then made all sorts of crazy animal sounds. It was far more than I could take or understand. She grabbed plates, pots, and pans as quickly as she could and sent them flying as she created debris everywhere. Anything, everything, and anyone were her weapons and targets. One coffee cup grazed my head, and I purposely stepped in front of a cereal bowl that was headed directly for the baby. She had become a full-blown screaming maniac. Nothing was going to slow her tirade, much less bring it to a halt or diminish it to any degree. On previous occasions, I usually waded into the mess, took upon myself whatever pain was necessary, and physically put a stop to the insanity. But since there was a child in my life, that changed everything.

It was a split-second but logical decision. I quickly reached for the nearest blanket, kept myself between the baby and the screaming psychotic, wrapped my little girl up, and burst out the back door. After I had made it halfway across the apartment parking lot, I stopped with my daughter in my arms and turned around. She was still screaming her way through the apartment and was as loud as she ever. I heard the obvious sound of one precious household item after another being broken. Evidently she was set about destroying everything that I owned. I wondered if she even realized that the baby and I had left the apartment. She was extremely loud, and I knew that it was only a matter of time before the neighbors called the police once again. There was nothing that I could do as there was no sane or safe way of stopping her, and I wasn't about to leave my daughter. With that in mind, I simply walked to the back edge of the parking lot near a row of bushes, sat down on a rock, observed, and considered everything.

Why did I allow this nonsense to happen? Why did I allow my life to deteriorate into such a horrible and apparently never-ending mess? It had been less than two years before that everything in my life had looked so incredibly bright. I believed that I had my life under control as I was on my way to college and my future couldn't have looked any better. But I had been such a complete fool. I had thought that I had accomplished everything and that I had done it all on my own. I had convinced myself that I could handle everything just as I always had before. After all, I had taken care of myself for years, although long before I should have. But even at that, I had been confined to just a very small circle of society. But even so, I had been fairly successful in the attempt. I had made it all of the way through middle and high school without any assistance, guidance, or instruction from my parents. Perhaps I had accomplished it despite the efforts of my parents. Perhaps I had done it in spite of myself. However, due to my accomplishments, while conveniently forgetting my failures, I was fiercely independent and quite proud of myself.

I had paid for all of my necessities, all of my needs and wants from the very first day of working in the newspaper mailroom. I had provided of all of my meals, breakfast, lunch, and dinner. I had planned out my days, weeks, and months as best as I could and had kept to my own schedule. I had also not only set up the appointments but had paid all of my dentist and doctor's bills as well. I had shopped for, purchased, and had taken care of all of my clothes. I had paid for all of my schoolbooks, supplies, school fees, and had arranged my school schedules every year. I had even taken the personal initiative of ensuring that I always had a roof over my head. Even though it was an unauthorized room at the newspaper or a drafty tree house, it was, however, far better than any of the garbage dumps that my parents bothered to call home. Incredibly, I survived all of those things, despite the obstacles. At many times, I was amazed at my alleged luck. But after having endured such turmoil, how had my life arrived at the sorry and miserable place where it was at that point? Why had I made such foolish and idiotic decisions? They were, after all, what had gotten me into the pit that I now found myself in.

But as I looked into the mirror within my mind, the facts were crystal clear. It had been my fault. There was absolutely no doubt about it. The decisions I made had delivered me to my sorrow-filled place in life. I had chosen not to properly prepare myself for college. I had chosen not to seek good advice. I had chosen to live a heathen lifestyle and certainly no one twisted my arm when I had gotten involved in that infamous wager with my coworkers. There was no one else to blame for my situation, and there was no point in trying. I was the sole person responsible for the mess that my life had become.

I had within me so many dreams, so many questions, but had made so many incredibly poor decisions. On nearly every occasion and in every instance in my life, people of wise counsel had always been there. They had always been available and therefore the advice that I so desperately needed was simply there for the asking. But I was simply too stubborn.

I had already spent my admittedly short lifetime surviving on my own and had accomplished so much that I believed that I could handle anything. It just seemed safer and wiser, at that point in time, to simply keep my own counsel and to make the decisions on my own. That precious and independent streak within had cost me dearly. I was left with nothing, only surrounded by the rubble of what was left of my pitiful life.

But as I sat there on that rock that I had been using for a seat, my baby daughter stirred inside of her blanket. I pulled a corner back, drew her close, and shielded her from the bit of cool wind that blew across the apartment parking lot. She whimpered a little as she then she opened her eyes and looked directly into mine. There was nothing in life more amazing to observe. As I watched her, I wondered, just what could she be thinking? Then she smiled preciously, as only a three-month-old baby could, closed her eyes, and immediately went back to sleep.

I had spent my entire life never being dependent on anyone. I never tried to depend on anyone and rarely permitted anyone's help. I just never wanted anyone to get close as such a thing was simply too frightening. However, this little tiny girl not only instinctively believed that I would take care of her, but also depended upon me for absolutely everything. She so believed in me that all she had to do was see my face, was comforted, and then she felt safe enough to go to sleep. The tables completely turned in my life as I was amazed beyond belief realizing just how much someone now depended upon me.

It all felt so very different, somewhat uncomfortable, and more than a bit surreal. As I had lived my life, it had been so easy to build up those solitary walls, to be independent from society and close contact with people and to walk alone. However, it had been immediately thrust upon me as my little daughter now required my undivided attention throughout every minute of every day. She instinctively relied upon me completely. It was now so obvious considering the other half's hysterical and violent actions. I then realized that I was the only one that could or would take care of her.

But as the recollection of past failures arrived within my mind, I battled over whether or not I could actually do it. I was no more certain of my own abilities as a father than I had been the day in the hospital when I first saw her. Once again, the questions came. Could I really be everything that she needed? Could I be that responsible? Could I actually be that unselfish? Could I be that sort of person and how would I do it? What if I made mistakes? What if I made decisions that would cause her harm someday? What if I couldn't be the sort of parent that she needed me to be? What if I failed?

However, it wasn't as if I really had a choice. It was as if I had been unwillingly but gently pushed into something that I had any clue of how to perform. It was completely unknown and uncharted territory. But none of that mattered in the least, as I simply had to be that person. I had to be that person for her. Therefore, despite my ignorance, my lack of training, and my own doubts, I needed to become a real father. I made that decision as I held her while sitting on that rock in the parking lot. I decided that I would do whatever necessary to keep her safe, to keep her happy, and to raise her into adulthood.

But then I considered, what would she become someday? Who would she resemble as she grew up? What would her first day of school be like? I could almost see myself walking her up to the front door. But, the real questions were even more serious and frightening. Did I have inside of me what was necessary to be the kind of father that she needed me to be? I was terrified.

As I sat there on that rock and discussed those issues with myself, I noticed that not only had the baby gotten quiet, but so also had the apartment. It was sudden and abrupt as the screaming had suddenly stopped. Perhaps she had run out of things to break. Then, as I sat there, my curiosity began to get the best of me as I wondered what had happened inside of that apartment as it was now quiet. Then as I thought about it, perhaps it was too quiet. I wondered just what had gone on inside the apartment and should I have go inside. I considered if it was safe to go in there as I couldn't go in by myself and couldn't leave the baby outside. So what was I going to do? I peeked inside of the blanket and determined that she was still asleep and therefore it was time for a decision. I stood up from my sitting place and walked across the apartment parking lot. There was really only one way to determine what the situation actually was. I had to go inside.

I had no sooner stood up, when flashing lights appeared on the opposite side of the apartment building. That could only mean that the police had arrived. That wasn't a great feeling at all, but it certainly wasn't unexpected. It was as if when my life couldn't get any worse, it always did. Since they had arrived, the cops would now be forced into the middle of the mess that I called my life. I was instantly embarrassed and humiliated. I hated having someone knowing my personal business. I hated having someone involving themselves and observing as they investigated my life. I naturally wanted to handle everything on my own without anyone's input or advice. I knew as I watched them just what the cops thought of me. I knew that I looked like an obvious failure to not only the authorities, but to everyone that I came into contact with. I felt so degraded.

As the officers stepped out of their car, they appeared to be more than a little shocked as they realized that I was holding the baby. They immediately began asking questions, which forced into the public eye the actual issues between the two of us. I revealed the laundry discovery, my ongoing suspicions, the never-ending fighting, and then the subsequent violence. I shamefully had to admit to them that nothing about my household was under control, not the apartment or our family. I had to admit that to them, these complete strangers, that my life and family structure were a total wreck and needed professional help.

They listened intently and recorded it in their report. Then one of them bravely went into the apartment to hear her side of the story as well. Then they both took turns as they questioned each of us on a variety of subjects. When that was completed, they then discussed our situation with all of our neighbors. After they had finished, both officers returned to the apartment and sat the two of us down together in what was left of the living room.

Just short of taking both of our heads off, they did just about everything else within their power. After I had placed the baby in her crib upstairs, they proceeded to let both of us have it. It was to be our very last warning. Their next visit would see both of us handcuffed, taken to jail, and then my little girl would be placed into foster care by the authorities. They were sick and tired of constantly responding to calls at our address, and it was to cease immediately. Then they ordered the two of us to clean up the mess that had been made. Additionally and just to be certain that we both understood their seriousness, they informed us that they would be back in just one hour to check on our progress. It wasn't a joke, and they obviously weren't kidding.

When they returned, they sat us down once again and ordered us to commit to a truce. They forced us to make promises to each other, and I hated every minute of it. It was indeed to be a truce as I guaranteed them that there would be no more breaking plates and such. The very next day I ensured that with a trip to the grocery store. From that point forward, the kitchen cabinets were stocked with paper plates, cups, and plastic utensils. It was just one of my brave, bold, and prideful moves. But she had a few of her own. That much I should have already known.

That next day as I had arrived home from work, she met me at the door with a letter in hand. She refused me further entrance into the apartment until I had read it. It appeared to be a letter from the laundry, and it basically stated that in the normal course of business, mistakes occasionally occurred at their facility. It wasn't at all abnormal to see an article of clothing left in a dryer and then afterward discover that it had been mixed in with another family's laundry. According to their letter, it was a common and frequent occurrence. The letter then went on to state that they were sorry for any problems that it might have caused and other pleasantries of the sort. However, something about the letter seemed to be out of place as it just didn't feel right. I didn't bother to say anything about it at that moment but simply accepted it at face value as she then went about her business as if nothing had ever happened. But despite my apparent acceptance of the document, I privately determined to investigate it as soon as possible. The whole matter made me extremely uneasy.

The next day at my lunch break, I sat down to investigate the paperwork properly. It was contained within a simple, plain envelope and was written on a plain piece of paper no letterhead or any other item that would make it official. It had an individual's name at the bottom, but curiously had no signature below it. It all appeared to be very puzzling and conjectured. When I contacted the laundry, I was informed that they had received no recent complaints nor were they aware of any sort of problems with anyone's laundry. One employee who had been working a number of years with the company informed me that as a general rule, they didn't write letters, but telephoned customers, when possible, if there were issues of any kind at their facility.

The interesting but unsurprising item contained within the whole issue was the fact that none of them had ever heard of the person whose name was typed on the bottom of the letter. With that, I thanked them for their time, sat at the desk, and wondered about the relationship quagmire that I was buried in. It was obvious that not only had she fluently lied about her actions, but had also gone to great lengths to cover them up. However, it was nothing new, unexpected and certainly not out of character. She always had a penchant for falsehoods as she added one more lie to cover up for the lie that she had already told. Then she would further add yet another lie to become a jumbled heap of words that no one could possibly sort out or keep straight. But none of that mattered as I felt myself growing harder and more callous by the hour. I just wondered what would happen next.

As expected, life with her simply never got any better. Although the raging outbursts and destructive violence finally ceased, the daily arguments, complaints, and demands continued unfettered. It never mattered what was done. I was always completely in the wrong and was deemed to be wrong about everything. It was emotionally draining, and it was downright maddening. She added to the list of things that she hated about me on a daily basis as everything was fair game.

I awakened too early in the morning. I spent too much time reading, as she wanted me to watch some idiotic television show with her. I spent too much time on my hobbies and far too little time with her. I ate too much for breakfast, or I ate the wrong things for breakfast, and it all cost too much money. I smoked too many cigarettes, even though she smoked at least as much as I did. I left for work too early, never told her good-bye, and felt that I always avoided her. I spent too much money for lunch, and when, in response, she began packing my lunch, the complaint quickly became that I took too much food to work with me. But even as I was away at work, her complaints continued.

I never called her during the day, or when I had changed my habits to suit her, I called her too frequently. But when I did call, she whined that all I ever asked about was the baby and never cared about her daily routine. Then there were the arguments about my trip home from work. Even though the drive was ten minutes or less, I always arrived home too late. But heaven forbid if I ever came home early. She really threw a fit when that happened as that always made for a special kind of argument. Her complaint was that I should have called first. What was so wrong with me?

But no matter what the topic happened to be, the arguing never ceased; it just went on and on and on as if it had gained a life of its own. However, she was extremely gifted as she could argue about anything, anywhere, for any length of time and all without the benefits of any facts or data. She argued about any detail on any subject, no matter how minute or insignificant. I believed that arguing had become the only thing that pleased her, as it was the only thing that she ever wanted to do while in my company. Truth be told, it was the only sort of actual interaction between the two of us. But I had finally reached my limit. It had become more than I could possibly tolerate. It had become far more than I could emotionally stand. I felt as if my mind was about to snap. I had to do something while believing that I was still in control at least a portion of my life.

With that I decided to take on two full-time jobs. In my mind that decision went a long way toward solving a number of problems, which I believed were of utmost importance. I was then able to save a decent amount of money, which would permit me to find a better place to live. I wanted to live somewhere with a yard, a place where my little girl could go outside and play. I wanted a neighborhood where I could put her in a stroller and take her for walks. I wanted to be just like those people that I had envied all of my life. I believed that taking on two jobs was the best answer. I became firmly convinced throughout my life that money solved all problems. I had foolishly believed that the lack of funds was the cause of nearly every difficulty and subsequent roadblock in my life.

But as I soon discovered, desiring such acquisitions cost a significant amount of money, and living that sort of lifestyle was far more expensive than I had anticipated. Without a college degree and a decent career, those self-imposed standards required that I worked a substantial number of hours. For reasons that I never understood at the time, she didn't appreciate my decision at all. I supposed that I should have discussed the matter with her before making the decision, but never considered it. She never wanted anything to do with me when I was at home. I just figured that it was the only way to maintain my sanity. Besides, I needed that sense of accomplishment.

I applied for employment at a rubber products factory, then interviewed, and obtained the position. My plan was to work there for only a year as I kept the job that I already had during the day at the shop as my permanent one. Every evening I left the house at ten thirty to be at the factory by eleven. I worked in that sweatshop factory until seven in the morning. After the shift had ended, I rushed home, took a shower, grabbed a quick breakfast, spent ten minutes with my little girl, and then blasted out the back door. My day job began at eight thirty in the morning and lasted until five in the afternoon. I believed that I had a great plan set into place. But just as my life had previously played out, it didn't last nearly as long as I had hoped for.

First, the owner of the business at my day job had decided to sell the place. Once the new owner had arrived, everything changed overnight. His first decision was to reduce the wage and benefit package of every employee on staff. That turned the entire place into chaos as people quit, and layoffs soon began. As I was the newest employee, therefore, I was the first one shoved out of the door. Therefore, I was instantly thankful for the job at the factory. But within a short period of time, that organization changed as well. Decisions made by upper management brought in new equipment and processes that created changes for the factory population. Naturally, even before the new equipment arrived, everyone understood that the likely result of those corporate decisions were serious job reductions.

Once again I realized that as the most recent hire, my position was in great jeopardy. It didn't require too much insight to observe the handwriting on the wall. As I contemplated my fate, I knew that I was in deeper financial trouble than I had been before. Within one short month, I had gone from a position of having two jobs and stashing money away, to having lost one and was about to lose the other. I was instantly angry and upset. Why couldn't I ever get ahead? Why did I always seem to run into such roadblocks? Why couldn't things ever go my way for just once? I just couldn't take it as it was nearly more than I could possibly tolerate. Once again, I felt as if I were about to snap. Something just had to change.

It was a Thursday evening. I had eaten supper and was sitting on the sofa with my daughter at my side watching television. Actually I was just wasting time for a few hours until I had to leave for work that night. She and I had already endured our required daily argument as she remained upstairs pouting in the bedroom while supposedly talked to her sisters on the phone.

It was obvious without hearing the words that I was being raked over the coals once more, as the tone of her voice told me of all that I needed to know. As I sat there deep in thought, suddenly there was a knock at the front door. It was startling, as I was not expected anyone. With more than my usual dose of suspicion, I wondered just who in the world it was. A quick glance out of the window revealed a gentleman dressed in a suit with a briefcase in hand. I quickly became worried as his professional stance instantly brought about feelings of fear and apprehension. I had never seen him before in my life. What did he want? It was certainly odd and a little strange, but I was understandably curious.

I opened the door, and he immediately introduced himself. He was a local businessman and sold insurance. Was I interested in such things, and would I allow him to come in? I didn't need or want any insurance but as I had decided to be polite and invited him into the apartment. As we talked, he politely questioned me about my job, cars, hobbies, and other items of that nature. Within minutes the conversation took on a more serious note as it then turned to subjects such as life, families, and kids. Then suddenly and seemingly out of nowhere, he began to talk about church, God, and living something that he described as a proper life. But even though the subject was entirely foreign to me, he curiously made me more at ease than anyone ever had before. I was intrigued.

I informed him that I had come from a huge family and that my childhood had been horrible at best. I let him know that my family didn't anything worthwhile going for them and due in part to that, the little one that sat beside me was the only child that I was ever going to have. Then I told him that, in my opinion, church was only for the weak, the stupid, or for those in need of a different sort of country club. He surprised me by not arguing, but by telling me that he fully understood my point. Once that topic was out of the way, we went on to talk about my crushed college hopes, vocational school, and my recent job turmoil. Before I realized it, we had managed to knock off a pot of coffee. But also by that time, she had managed to make her way downstairs. I made the necessary introductions, and she thankfully decided to put on the nice- wife act for our guest. Then the conversation turned a corner that I didn't expect.

He wanted to know if I were really in the market for a new job, and would I interested in a position at a local company with some friends of his? He went on to state that they owned a shop in the same sort of business that my daytime line of work had been. They desperately needed someone who was qualified, trustworthy and willing to work. When I had agreed to his employment question, he asked to use the telephone. With that, I committed myself and with more than a little curiosity, agreed. He made the call, spoke nice things about me, and secured an interview for the very next day. It all happened so quickly that I honestly didn't know what to think about the whole ordeal.

Having accomplished all of that, we both said good night as he happily left without making a sale, which left me all the more curious. I was more than amazed by the entire transaction and was admittedly at a loss for words. I worked through my thoughts as I prepared for another evening shift at the factory. Even though she attempted to start yet another argument before I left for work, I simply tossed it aside and ignored her. It was her belief that I should have discussed the job opportunity with her before agreeing to an interview. She fully believed that she was supposed to be in control of everything in my life. But my mind was elsewhere, and I couldn't have cared less about what she believed, wanted, or demanded. That gentleman's conversation had thoroughly intrigued me.

The next morning once I had gotten home, I slept for two hours, awoke, gathered myself together, and headed for the address the insurance salesman had given to me. It was out beyond the far west side of the city, past the new subdivisions and shopping centers. As I pulled into their parking lot, a curiously strange but pleasant feeling came over me that I couldn't describe. It was as if I had arrived at a place where I belonged, but had never been. It was a place in that I had never before seen, nor had any understanding of. It was entirely strange and more than a bit unnerving. It even felt a bit creepy, but in an odd and peculiar way that I actually liked. But since I was already there, I set my feelings aside and went on in.

It was a flourishing business, and it was very impressive. It was everything that a man in my profession could have possibly wanted. As I walked in the shop door, it felt different and strange, but quite good from the very start. As I met the two owners just inside of the building in a very dusty office, they both reminded me to some degree of the men at the newspaper that I had admired, but yet were also quite different. They weren't hard men, but seemed to be very firm and determined in their nature and quite secure about something that I couldn't exactly pin down. It was as if they knew precisely who and what they were. But on the other hand, they didn't appear proud or boastful either. They showed me around their business with a very matter of fact attitude that was unexpected. They described in detail every aspect of the business without any boasting or bragging whatsoever. They had a tremendous amount of things to be proud of, but their lifestyles caused me to focus on what the job was to be, not how great or prosperous the two of them were. I was amazed at how subdued they were about their own accomplishments.

Whenever I made a statement that normally would have generated a great deal of pride in other people, it only brought about odd and curious statements from them. They stated that everything in life was a gift, that their own lives were blessed and something about being stewards, whatever in the world that meant. In that regard, they were far different men than anyone that I had ever met before. It all felt more than a little strange and perhaps even to some degree, slightly uncomfortable. But even so, I was instantly impressed by the both of them.

On the other hand, I hadn't any idea if they were impressed with me, or what their reasoning may have been, but I was hired on the spot. Everything about the job seemed to be as near perfect as one could ask. As for a job where you worked with your hands every day, it was just about as good as anyone could have hoped for. The job itself was good, the starting pay was adequate and carried with it promises for increases in the future. The working conditions themselves were equally good as well and there were also other perks that went along with the organization.

There were business associations with a number of car dealers in the area, and the owner's father had a small used-car lot as well. I hoped that particular benefit would give me the opportunity to find something better to drive after I had turned my budget around. With my hiring, I also made an agreement to quit my job at the factory but worked there for the obligatory two-week notice. They wholeheartedly agreed, but once we had concluded our agreement, there was one curious note, at least on their part.

They both found it was rather odd that I didn't require a discussion at home prior to making an employment decision. I found their perception to be curiously intriguing. Why would I ever bother with something like that? I had always made decisions on my own and usually without advice or input from anyone. In addition, I simply believed that it was one of the best decisions that I had ever made. But there wasn't any possible way that I could have understood just how important that decision would turn out to be.

The situation at home never changed and was the same as it had always been. Within a few days I quickly settled into a comfortable routine. I awoke early every morning well before dawn for a pot of coffee, a bit of a good novel for my necessary hour of peace and quiet. It was my favorite time of the day, just to be alone and to be left alone, with nothing but a good book and my own thoughts. Was there any better way to begin the day? Then as usual, I went out the back door as quietly as possible. It was a selfish habit, if for no other reason than my desire to avoid another stupid, pointless and degrading early morning argument. In my mind, it was just an incredibly simple decision.

I quickly discovered just how enjoyable it was to pull into the shop parking lot and be greeted by people who actually appeared to be glad to see me. There were always two pots of coffee ready when we arrived and a big white box next to them full of doughnuts and all sorts of other pastries. That was certainly my idea of a first-class breakfast. During the first fifteen minutes or so, we enjoyed our breakfast as the owners went through our daily schedule. They reviewed what was expected, everything that needed to be accomplished as well as what new work would arrive that day. To me, it almost felt as if I had gathered around a breakfast table with family. It pleased me much more than I would ever publicly admit to anyone.

I never worked that hard or so willingly for anyone since my days at the newspaper. It was simply that the job provided me with a real sense of accomplishment. It was the pleasant feeling of a job well done and having completed a task that was appreciated. Then there was the added bonus of having the work of your hands openly acknowledged by someone. In that particular sense, it was far better than the newspaper. It was also better and different in other ways as well. It had turned into a very rewarding place to be employed. However, there were portions of the job that took some real getting used to.

Everywhere that I had ever previously worked, someone always had a radio playing. It had helped to keep me alert as well as to pass the hours. At the newspaper, since I had been there the longest and also owned the radio, I played the sort of music that I preferred. At the other shop that had been recently sold, they had a local greatest-hits radio station piped in over the speakers. But the music they played in the factory nearly drove me out of my mind. It was the exactly the sort of music that my parents listened to, and it reminded me of them with every song. *Boring, boring, boring.* It nearly sent me over the edge.

But my new employer played a radio station that I had never heard of before. I quickly realized and believed that its only reason for existence was to tie my brain into a knot. The music itself I classified as old fashioned, but the lyrics were another issue altogether. It was the local Christian radio station and with my experience, it was just weird beyond belief. I had never before been exposed to that particular brand of American culture and instantly found it to be quite disturbing. It bothered me because at first as I purposely shut it out and attempted to ignore it. Then a song would entrench itself within my head during the workday and follow me all of the way home. Throughout the course of the evening, it ran through my brain over and over again. I tried to shut it out, to cut it off, to drown it out with other music, but it was of no use. Nothing worked as the songs were still in my head when I awakened the following morning.

However, the format at the radio station wasn't merely music as there were also interludes of biblical discussion. At one point or another within those conversations, something caught my ear, and my thoughts would be hauled into the debate or teaching as a silent but willing witness. At times it was the topic of the programs, or it was a particular line in a song that grabbed my attention as I then actively looked forward to hearing certain bits and pieces. It wasn't long and well before I had actually realized it, that I caught myself listening to entire songs and programs without paying much attention. Within a month, I had actually gotten to the place where I actively listened to it every minute of the working day. Then soon after, it progressed to the point where I actually looked forward to the next day of work for no other reason that just to hear the next program. I never admitted it out loud or even privately to anyone, but I then soon began listening to the station in my car when I was certain that no one else was around.

But what was it about that radio station? But then, as I wondered to myself, was it actually about the radio station? Could it have possibly been about the songs? Or could it have really been about the programs, the discussions, or the topics? Or perhaps, was it what the songs and programs were actually all about? I wondered just why I had begun to find myself actually enjoying the format. I really just didn't understand it. I soon understood that there was so much more to it than just music and programs. But much more importantly, just what were the feelings that began rising up within me? Where did they come from? What was it about those emotions that cause so much tremendous guilt within me about so many different things? Then I questioned whether I should feel so guilty about everything. Why was I feeling so incredibly guilty about the events of my past? Just what was going on within me? Why did my life suddenly found itself in so much turmoil? Or had it truthfully and realistically always been in turmoil? Why did it begin to feel as if my entire world was being turned completely upside down?

However, other much more interesting, oftentimes confusing, and downright strange things went on in the shop as well. I knew full well that both of the owners believed everything that they heard on the radio with everything that they had within them. It was readily apparent in everything that they said and their actions spoke to those beliefs as well. But surprisingly, they were perfect gentlemen as they never shoved nor forced their convictions upon anyone. It was refreshing, unexpected, and certainly not what I had been used to from my previous experiences with Christians. They never attempted to push anything upon me, not ever, and not even once, I just never saw it. They simply made themselves available whenever I had questions or was in need of advice. But there were other items within their lives that intrigued me as well.

Unlike a number of my relatives, their beliefs didn't seem to be something that they put on as some would a jacket or a costume whenever it suited them. It was much more than clothes, more than carefully scripted public prayers, and certainly much more than something that was put on for show. It was a much deeper, far more involved character trait than I could possibly understand. But it was also quite observable. I saw it revealed in everything that they did. I observed it every day in the shop and throughout every situation that occurred. It never mattered if it were good, bad, or ugly; that indescribable presence always seemed to be there. Whatever it meant, whatever it was, no matter how odd or indescribable, I literally felt it. Deep down within, something was moving and changing within me. It was something very odd, very unfamiliar, quite strange, and certainly very different. I had never felt anything like it before in my life. It set my emotions on edge and completely unnerved me to the very core of my being.

But although the owners were great employers to work for and to be around, they were also men with a devious streak. While they never vocally pushed their religious agenda, they did employ other tactics. Each day after the shift, I always found a small present on the driver's seat of my car. It was something that they called a tract. It was a small piece of literature about the size of an envelope and barely any thicker. It was a little booklet of sorts. It always told a short but very important story about some facet of life that was always resolved through the intervention of God. At first, I avoided reading them and tossed them into the trash. I didn't want to read them, and truth be told, I was a bit afraid to. It was as if I knew that just by the reading of it I would be pulled into an unfamiliar lifestyle, which would change me into someone that I wouldn't like or recognize. But in the end and as was naturally the usual case, my curiosity finally got the best of me.

I had never heard about tracts before, much less had ever seen them. The stories themselves were new to me as well, but I found them to be very interesting. They were all about right, wrong, and the payment that was necessary when crimes against society and people had been committed. While not every story applied to me, unfortunately many of them did. But nevertheless, every last one of them always spoke to something deep within that had previously been unknown to me. There were actually occasions when I pulled off the side of the road on the way home just to read or to reread the stories. Those little tales captivated me in a way that nothing else in my life had ever done before. They rapidly changed my perspective about every possible aspect of my life.

I began questioning everything imaginable in my life. Between those tracts and the messages that I heard every day on the radio station, it seemed as if every problem that I ever had in my life could be fully addressed. It appeared that I had discovered a way to obtain an answer to my every question. However, it wasn't as if those people had a magic wand for everything; it was as if there was someone out there somewhere who actually cared. It was as if there was someone who, if they didn't have the exact answer that I may have wanted, at the very least they had an answer of some kind. Therefore, I was intrigued.

But there was something about all of it that was far more important than anything else could possibly have been. According to everything that I read and heard, there was someone who would always, at every instance, be there to listen to me. But that someone also knew everything about my life in advance. What was even more fascinating was the claim that this someone knew my every move and even knew my questions before I asked them.

That sort of reality was all very new to me, very strange, and very, very disturbing.

But curiously, it also proved to be the recipe for outrageously vicious and ruthless nightmares. They began shortly after I had begun reading the tracts. They were real, seemingly unending, devastating, and very, very ugly. They were far worse than the terrifying voices that had driven me out of the house when I was a little boy. But in other ways there were also quite similar and awkwardly familiar. They always seemed to find me after just a few hours of sleep. Shortly after they began, I once again dreaded going to sleep. It was as if an unknown and unwanted something was always waiting nearby as I dropped off into slumber. At times, I almost felt something nearby in the bedroom before I dropped off into sleep. Once again, just as I had in my youth, I began to despise the approaching nights. Once again, dread filled and enveloped my heart.

For two solid weeks and more, it was the same repetitious event. Night after night, it was the same mind-bending torment over and over again. I felt it as it approached, fought against my closing eyes, and struggled with everything that I had within me to stay awake. But in the end sleep always overtook me, and the dream, just as a hunter seeks its prey, always found me. It may have been a dream, but it felt exactly like reality.

It always hit brutally hard, as if I had been violently thrown against a wall. It hit with a force that literally took my breath away. It was as if I were being slapped awake, hard and quite viciously. It was as if I was awake and coherent, but knew full well all the while that I actually still slept. But then again, perhaps that was the only way that I kept my sanity. Nevertheless, the script never ever changed.

It always began with a brutal and forceful shove from behind and from someone unknown. That shove always knocked me completely off of my feet as I then fell into a deep, dark and muddy hole. The night itself was always dark and moonless with a steady drizzling rain. From the bottom of the hole as I looked upward from the ankle deep mud floor, a dim light could barely be seen far above through the misting rain. The rim of the pit itself was twenty feet or more above my head, which put it far out of my reach. Each attempt to climb out always brought about a fall back to the muddy bottom. However, as in every previous dream, the otherworldly voice arrived carrying with it heart scorching pain to my terrified soul.

It resonated with pure surging hatred, and unlike the previous times as a child, I understood every ruthless word. I was terrified of it in such a way and to a degree that I had never experienced before. Whatever it was, it always made the same degrading and debilitating statements. But worst of all, it knew that those statements defined me and that I firmly believed them.

I was worthless, and I had no value. I was beyond hope and had no future. I would never get out of or beyond my family cage. I was destined to live the life that they were destined. They were what I would become, which was something that was far less than what society expected. Everything about my life had been set firmly into place. There was no possible means of escape as my future had been fully and clearly written for all to witness. There was nothing within my means that I could ever do that would change my life. It was useless for me to experiment with any religious nonsense. Church was a complete waste of time, it wouldn't help me and it couldn't change me. It would only frustrate and confuse me. I couldn't possibly be rescued. I was hopelessly lost.

Whatever the origin of the voice and whatever it happened to be, it knew that as it spoke those defiling words, that I believed them. I knew within my heart that I didn't measure up to the impossibly high standards possessed by church people. They instinctively knew just what I was every time they looked at me. Their intrusion into my life with all of their man made rules only made things worse. It reminded me that at best, I was destined to turn out just like my father's family, and the voice knew just how much I despised so many of them. According to the voice, as bad as my life had turned out, church and its stifling rituals would completely destroy it. I would then grow to hate my life far more than I did to that point and far more than I could possibly expect. Then the conversation turned a corner.

Just as quickly as it had started, the tone of the voice suddenly changed. It then took on a new tone of kindness and endearment. It said that there were better ways out of the pit, but religion wasn't on the list. There was a means of escape and it was easier than I could possibly believe. Then just as quickly as it had arrived there within the walls of that muddy hole, the voice abruptly left as the words echoed inside of my head. With that I found myself completely alone and in complete chilling silence. With terror set deep in my heart, I always expected it to return.

But there I remained, on my hands and knees with mud past my wrists and ankles, deep in the bottom of a dark pit that I could not remove myself from. As I struggled to stand upright, I always slipped and fell back down into the mire. It never mattered how desperately I tried, I made no gains of any sort against the slippery mud walls. I dug my fingers and toes into the sides but fell backward with every failed attempt. Nothing ever worked. With each attempt, I broke down in frustration, which was immediately followed by desperation and endless tears. I just couldn't take it anymore. However, I was powerless to actually do anything about it and was at the point of surrender.

At that point I always woke up sobbing and in tears, usually accompanied with loud shouts and screams. But that always woke *her* up as well which started an argument all of its own. As my head barely cleared itself from the event, I attempted to explain the dream. But she would never hear any of it, always made fun of me and told me I was stupid and childish. I then found myself in the middle of a real life argument, complete with yelling and shoving until nearly dawn.

I became so disgusted with her nonsense that I usually went downstairs and attempted to grab an hour of sleep on the sofa. But her degrading remarks usually kept me awake until it was time to leave for work. They were cold, hard and ruthless statements that cut to the very core. Generally she stated that I wasn't a real man and that to her, I was just a little boy. I was no better than my family and was nothing but human trash. She always reminded me of the fact that she knew plenty of men who were more than willing to be a father for my daughter. Then, without missing a beat, she added her standard routine of extremely personal, crude and disgusting statements that only served to make my blood boil. It all served as fuel for a series of never-ending arguments. It was an ugly, pathetic and downward spiral. My home life deteriorated with each and every passing day.

I had spent those weeks with very little sleep, mostly attributed to the nightmares and working like a dog every single day. She added to the trauma with arguments about money, drinking, pills, marijuana use, raising my daughter, and practically everything else imaginable under the sun. Then there was the inner turmoil I was experiencing since I had involved myself with all of that church nonsense. There were the unending questions I kept asking myself about just where my life was going from that point. The stress of it all tore me apart in every sense of the term. I was even at to the place where I had become the new owner of a nasty bleeding ulcer. I was physically and emotionally spent and had become an absolute physical wreck. But even at that, I honestly believed that it couldn't possibly get any worse, at least, I hoped that it wouldn't. But once again, with amazing accuracy, I proved to myself just how terribly wrong that I could be.

Something just didn't feel quite right as I entered the apartment parking lot that evening. As I walked up to my back door, a cold chill raced through me even though it was the first week of June. Once I unlocked the back door and walked into the kitchen, my suspicions quickly became reality. All of my daughter's things that were usually in the kitchen were gone. As I took two steps at a time upstairs, the truth revealed something that only added to my torment. The baby's room was completely empty, and so were most of *her* things from the bedroom closet. As I walked slowly back down the steps, leaning against the wall and dragging my shoulder along it all of the way, I only asked myself *why*. What was it about that time? Then as I sat on the bottom step of the stairs and gazed around the living room, I noticed that she had left her standard trademark. There was a piece of paper taped to the screen of the television.

It really didn't contain anything new. It was simply another list of familiar insults. I was a horrible husband. I was a lowlife. I was nothing but trash. I was a total loser. I had a dead-end job and never made enough money. I would never amount to anything. I was worthless and would always be worthless. I never let her have any money. I never let her drive the car. I wouldn't let her buy any dishes. I never let her buy anything. We would never own a home. I didn't care about anything. I never helped her with the baby. I never helped her with the house. I was always at work. I never took a day off during the week to spend time with her. All that I cared about was my job.

Then as if that weren't enough, she dropped below the belt and delivered a few more ruthless and nasty hits to the ego. I was the worst lover that she had ever had. I was terrible at everything. I never treated her as well as her former boyfriends did. She hated every second that she was forced to spend with me. Then she finished it off with a few degrading remarks about physical issues and other insults of that nature. Was there anything in a man's life that could be more degrading?

However, it was a long list of overly familiar complaints. The note didn't reveal what she had planned nor did it indicate just where she and the baby had gone. She had simply taken my little girl and had left. I naturally tormented myself with naturally foolish questions. What was I going to do? Where would I go from that point? What was her next move? I had no idea of what she had in store for me or for herself. My emotions just ran all over the place and took me along on the painful ride.

But the real truth of the matter was that I really didn't care what she did or where or who she did it with. As far as I was concerned, she could do anything that she wanted. I was content that she was gone. The house was quiet without her there in the apartment to daily torment me. With her gone, I actually had the opportunity to get the apartment cleaned up. As far as I was concerned, she could be dead and counted as just another statistic. Nothing about her really mattered to me as I only cared about my little girl. She was my singular concern and the only item of importance to me. But where was she? How was she? Was she okay? Was she safe? Was she taken care of? How could I find her? I was tormented by her disappearance.

But what could I have done? I could go into the city and try to find them. With nine brothers and sisters, she could be at any one of their houses. Additionally, there were any of her dozen or so friends. Then there was the very real possibility that she was at another man's house and probably in his bed as well. But I was uncertain as to just how many of those possibilities there could be. But I did have in my head have a sizable number of possible suspects.

They were the men who called my house allegedly just to talk to her. It was always under the pretense that they had trouble with their girlfriends or with their wives and that they needed her valuable advice. Who would have wanted advice from someone like her? Did she really believe that I was that stupid? What a truly worthless example of a human being, much less a wife and a mother she turned out to be.

The only thing worse than the phone calls were the occasions when she attempted to explain as to why a strange man was sitting in my living room when I arrived home from work. It was always the same worthless piece of trash answer. Why did all of those guys go to her for an alleged bit of advice? I may have been a stupid heathen from the wrong side of the tracks, but only a total moron wouldn't have been able to figure that nonsense out. Didn't she know, understand, and remember what I had told her about my mother and father and all of those fairy tales and more? I probably heard every lie that a cheating spouse could have possibly told. From my youngest days, I always had a front row seat for nearly every one of my mother's disgusting little acts of betrayal. With that, it seemed that I was forced to experience the same sorry movie in my own life, in my own house, and even before my very eyes.

But what could I do about it? A trip down into the basement brought up what little was left of my stash. There was barely enough there to roll one left handed cigarette and even then it wasn't very big. I lit it up, took one long drag, and coughed like I had bronchitis or something. It was too old and dried out. I had bought it quite a few months before, just before my daughter had been born. That certainly ended that clandestine experiment. As I went back upstairs and into the kitchen, I opened the refrigerator only to find it completely empty. There wasn't any food, alcohol, and more importantly, no orange juice. In anger I opened the kitchen cupboard as it revealed that it was empty as well. When I had left for work that morning, my tequila bottle was just over three quarters full. The bottle was still there, lying on its side in the cupboard as if it had been left only to make a point and was, of course, now completely empty. I knew full well that she didn't dump it in the sink but had drank it all. That meant that she had been out running all over town with my daughter and was more than a little loaded. That, in and of itself, begged a number of questions.

Just who was taking care of my daughter? By the looks of that tequila bottle, there was no way on earth she was doing it. She didn't have a car, so who had picked them up from the apartment? Where did they go and just what was going on? What would or could I do about any of it? She could have rotted in a pit for all that it mattered to me. She could have walked in front of a truck for all that I cared so long as she did it alone and didn't hurt the truck or the poor guy driving it. However, I couldn't just sit in the apartment, trapped in my anger and do nothing. It was then that I decided upon my course of action. I had to find them and when I did, I determined that I would take my daughter and bring her back home. I made the difficult decision to take care of her myself. I could and had changed diapers. I was the one who usually rocked her to sleep at night. I frequently was the one who fed her, bathed her, and took care of her most nights of the week. I knew that I could do it. Therefore, I had to find her.

I spent Friday evening looking everywhere as I made a hundred phone calls, talked to everyone and scoured the town for leads and answers. Everywhere that I went and with everyone I talked to, they revealed the same sad story. She and the baby were gone, long gone and were allegedly out of town somewhere. That reduced my situation to pitiful hopelessness and was depressed to the point of simply wanting to die.

My very last stop that evening was at the home of one of her younger sisters. She and her husband lived on the east side of the city in a trailer park near the county fairgrounds. She was decent enough, at least for the moment, as she didn't slam the door in my face and or send me away without answers. Initially, she first swore me to secrecy to protect herself from the family and then she told me everything that she knew. Or perhaps she merely told me what she wanted me to know. She informed me that nearly the entire family was in on the dastardly scheme. In the back of my head I wondered, was this help and knowledge just part of the tired old family game? They were all quite successful at such antics.

That trailer park was on the county's main east-west national highway and was heavily traveled by large semi-trucks. It was very late in the evening when I left the sister's home. I got into my car and drove slowly to the entrance of the mobile home park. As I reached the end of the driveway, the depression simply overwhelmed me with a force that I could not resist.

There at the highway, I put the car into neutral and just sat there with the engine running. Just what was I going to do? I was so completely lost. I felt far more than crippled, I felt completely helpless. I was so worthless, unwanted, and absolutely unneeded by anyone. There was nothing at that point that I could possibly do to improve my situation. She was gone and more importantly, my daughter was gone with her. In just those last few months, that little girl had completely changed my entire life. She had become the only thing that made coming home at night worthwhile. I would never have thought in a million years that taking care of a little baby could bring about such joy. She was the only thing in life that brightened my day. She was certainly the only thing in my life that I could be proud of. She was also the only thing in my life that I could boast about. Without her I was suddenly without purpose or direction. She was gone and apparently, it seemed that I would never see her again. From all outward appearances, it looked as if *the family* was going to make sure of that.

There was really nothing left to do. I was twenty years old, and my miserable life was over, was a sorry mess, and had never been anything of worth. I had lived through plenty of things before, but at that point, I had endured more than enough. I was just tired, so very tired of struggling to accomplish anything in my life. I was tired of her and the endless and stupid arguments. I was tired of the fighting, emotional, physical, or otherwise. I was sick and tired of failure and tired of being a failure. No matter what decision I ever made and whatever hole I happened to be in at the time just became deeper. My life was becoming almost exactly as the nightmare. It was as if the hole in my life was entrenched so deeply that there was no light of any kind. I was totally and completely in the dark and was now without hope. I was completely lost.

I was just too tired to go on. There was almost nothing left in life that even made it worth living. I didn't even feel like breathing anymore. I was so very, very tired. I just didn't want to continue. I didn't want to bother with any of it anymore. Couldn't I just check out of my life?

No. It wasn't my voice and as I sat there in my car I had no visible idea of where it had come from. It was startling in its quietness and disarming in its firmness. It was unlike anything that I had ever heard before. It was strong, confident, and completely unlike anything else that I had ever experienced. But what in the world was it? Had I imagined it? Was it real? It wasn't hateful, nasty, or destructive as the others had been. But then again, was it actually reality? How did I know that it wasn't just a result of all of the stress that I had experienced? Maybe it was all a lie. Maybe I was just being kept from going to a better place. Perhaps checking out was the best possible choice available to me. After all, there had to be a better place as this could not be all that there is. Wherever that place was it couldn't possibly be any worse than the sorry excuse that I had for a life.

Incredibly, the more that I thought about it, the better ending it all sounded. It would be so easy. I knew that I could make it all happen. I then realized that I could do it right then and there. I could make the decision right then at almost three o'clock in the morning. All that I had to do was put the little station wagon into first gear, hit the gas, and allow a truck do the rest. A nice broad side hit to the driver's door would make my exit from the world I knew and then into the next almost instantaneous. I found it easy to talk myself into it. I just had to put the car into gear, press the gas pedal, close my eyes, and wake up in a better place. I convinced myself that it would be the easiest thing that I could ever do.

But what better decision could I possibly make? After all, wouldn't everyone be better off? My daughter was so young that she wouldn't even remember me. How much memory could a four-month old baby have? Wouldn't she have been better off without me? But I was so very tired, and I had tolerated far more than I could possibly stand.

No. There was that blasted voice again. It was still quiet and firm but startled me so badly that I dropped my cigarette. But I just didn't care anymore. My mind was made up. As soon as I saw the next semi-truck heading east, it would all be over in a minute. I knew that it would be so easy. I even reasoned that with a truck as my chosen instrument, I would be the only person hurt and that I wouldn't feel a thing. In actuality, I didn't have to wait very long.

The first truck arrived not five minutes after making that final decision. I watched as it moved towards me while quickly gaining speed. I heard the engine noise as the driver shifted into higher gears as he approached highway speed. My estimate was that he would be nearing fifty miles an hour or more when he arrived at my spot. I calculated that it was more than enough for the job. His truck would probably crush my little car like a pop can flattened by a brick. It couldn't have been more perfect.

I had the car in gear, one foot on the clutch and the other on the gas. The truck became closer, then even closer, then the truck was close enough to read the decals on the door, and then it happened. I buried my foot into the floorboard as the car launched forward with an incredible rush. The truck was just within feet of me as the driver lay on his air horn loud, long, and hard. Mere seconds passed as my front bumper crossed the road shoulder stripe as the truck swerved, and I impulsively screamed in terror. Without no thought of any kind, I instinctively jammed on the brakes with everything that I had while madly turned the steering wheel to the right. The little car slid sideways as I watched the semitrailer through the passenger window missing me by mere inches. The truck driver had used the entire two lanes of the highway as he fought to avoid hitting me. He succeeded in his efforts and surprisingly, continued east on the highway without having bothering to stop.

I was sickened, very sick to my stomach, and shook violently as I gripped the steering wheel. It was so bad that I was unable to do anything as I sat there in my car in the middle of the highway. After a few very long minutes, I finally found enough strength to start the engine. I turned the steering wheel and slowly eased the car back into the trailer park driveway entrance. Once there, I opened the door, stumbled out of the car and dropped to my knees on the pavement. There I curled into a ball and cried uncontrollably with my face on the asphalt. I laid there in that position for over half an hour. What a total mess I had become. But somehow, even though I was somehow forced to survive, my life was obviously destined to continue. But why and for what possible purpose could it be?

Less than a week later, she and my daughter returned home. Despite all of my searching, I never located them. They simply showed up one evening shortly after I arrived home from work. Her timing was most unfortunate, as my landlord had recently informed me that he had experienced more than enough of our nonsense and had demanded that we leave. Therefore, when she finally returned home, I was in the midst of packing our belongings. I had thankfully retrieved my deposit and had already secured another place on the same side of town. It was a duplex, with a little more room, a one-floor layout, and a small yard. It also helped that it was just slightly less money a month. I figured that any benefit to the budget was always worthwhile.

It was a bittersweet reunion at its very best. I was thrilled beyond belief to see my daughter. After an hour of holding her, feeding her, and taking care of her, she was ready for bed. It was then that the real discussion began. According to her, she simply needed time away. She was tired of the fighting and fed up with the daily conflict. She poured out her story as if I was responsible for every awful thing that ever happened. Therefore I was understandably furious.

She was tired of it? What kind of nonsense was that? She then added that while she had been gone she had made a number of decisions. She made her statements as if her side of the situation was the only one that was important. Within a few minutes she was done, and that was it—short, not so sweet at all, but very, very final. She had returned, and as far as she was concerned, that was more than enough. She believed that she was required to explain nothing to me. According to her, I simply didn't deserve any answers. She countered my every question with a statement of blackmail.

Either I accepted the situation as it was or she would simply take my daughter away permanently. If she left, there would be no chance of any return, there would be no way of finding her, and it would be absolutely final. It all sounded far too familiar, sickening, and disgusting. It was nearly the same exact speech as my mother demanded to be moved out of the slums on East Market Street.

Therefore, I spent the entire evening on the front porch with a pack of cigarettes and a bottle of tequila. The questions mercilessly raced through my mind without ceasing. Why was she so calm about everything? How could she be so matter-of-fact about life? Didn't I deserve any answers? Just where was she during that time away? What had she done while she was gone? Who had she been with? What were her plans when she left and did she only return because those plans didn't work out? What caused her to believe that she could blackmail me and hold my daughter and emotions hostage? What in the world had caused her to believe that *she* was the one that I didn't want to live without? Why did she think that *she* was so blasted important? How could she just climb into bed at night and then sleep through her guilt? Didn't she have any conscience at all? Why did she dance around every question asked of her? If she were so innocent about everything, then why didn't she just given me the straight and plain truth? I wished that she had never bothered to come back.

At that point, I certainly didn't want the first thing to do with her in any form or fashion. By what rights could she get angry and upset as I resisted her sorry excuse of a peace offering? Perhaps my head was simply too scrambled to be bothered with her little naked games. Maybe, just maybe, all that I really wanted at the end of the day was the simple truth. But perhaps the fact of the matter was that I simply wasn't interested in her. Perhaps, I simply didn't have the stomach to deal with her adulterous habits and actions.

The very simple truth was that what she had to offer and attempted to blackmail me with could be found nearly anywhere, if that was what I really wanted. It was easily found right there in the city and with very little effort. The services that she so vainly and pitifully bragged about that evening could be provided by a dozen willing volunteers. And they would have done it with far less baggage. All that was needed was a simple telephone call. But what I really wanted and needed in my life was so much more than something that simplistic. I needed safety for my heart and security for my soul. I needed peace of mind and the kind of comfort that only loving arms could bring. I needed the sort of assurances that I knew about by observation, but had never personally experienced. I certainly didn't need the mind games she was offering. However, I had made a vow before witnesses and had given my word as well. Therefore my future was set. What else could I do?

Daily life became tense, tormented and overwhelmingly stressful. I was forced to tolerate blatant falsehoods, the daily grinding denial of those lies, as well as the ongoing bouts of conflict, betrayal, and deceit. But I did it all for one solitary reason, for an innocent little girl. She was a little girl who needed me for everything, but perhaps not as much as I needed her. She became my motive, my daily purpose and my only reason for living. I often thought to myself that perhaps the situation within my household would change. However, I harbored very little belief that she would ever change. Secretly, I always hoped that someday, she would simply take off and leave my daughter and myself alone. Maybe, and I felt no guilt whatsoever over it, that perhaps an untimely disease or an accident would strike her down. Then I would be rid of her for good. She caused me nothing but pain and anguish and I had arrived at the place in my life where I just couldn't tolerate it any more. I believed that my daughter and I would be so much better off with her out of the picture as then and only then would our lives be worth living.

Although my daughter was the brightest spot in my life, my situation at the job had taking a pleasant but very curious turn. One of the personal items was that I needed a new car. When my employers discovered that need, they went completely out of their way to provide assistance. They began a search and quickly found a very nice car for me. It wasn't perfect as it was seven years old and in average condition. But the one that I had been driving was twice that age and in far worse condition. It also helped that the price was right. But there were other, far more important things that had changed.

Despite the obvious intent of the nightmares, I came to the conclusion that the religion issue might be worthy of an investigation. I knew full well that the men I worked with weren't perfect or had perfect lives or perfect families. However, they appeared to possess some sort of purpose in their lives, which was more than evident. But more than that, they appeared to have an unseen sort of guidance and direction. In my discussions with them about the things of life, they also spoke of something that was completely foreign to me. It was something that they called a blessing. It was an intriguing idea. They said that it was the benefit of obedience. But it wasn't something to be gained for wages earned. It was all about a number of things that I didn't quite understand. But there were other items of discussion that completely befuddled me, especially something that they called grace. Whatever it all happened to be, I determined that I would discover everything that I possibly could about all of it. I also wasn't entirely sure about the whole obedience issue. That idea certainly didn't fit within my lifestyle either. However, I didn't need all of the answers to every one of my questions in order to make a decision. I instinctively felt and knew that I was standing at the most important crossroad of my entire life. It was beyond frightening.

But the more that I considered the events and decisions of my awful and horrible past, the simpler the entire matter became. None of the other decisions that I ever made ever really turned out for my own benefit. But I reluctantly had to admit that I never asked for very much advice before making those decisions. I just went with my instincts and never thought about the issues at all. I just made all of those decisions on a seemingly mindless whim.

But I determined that it would be much different when it came to the religion question. I decided that I would ask of the two owners just what exactly the entire Christianity matter was all about. At that point in my life, it was all a complete mystery to me. But I was terrified of the choice, as I had already made far too many mistakes in life. If choosing that particular path was indeed a mistake by the point of view of some people, then by everything that I had already witnessed in life, it was still a good mistake to make. At that point in my life, I really had nothing at all to lose. The biggest difference was that it really didn't even matter if I was completely wrong.

The following week during lunchtime, I discussed everything that I could think of with the both of them. They each took turns as one sat with me one day, then the other the next. I went through my entire life's history. However, not at any time did they ever judge or degrade me in any way. I asked them questions regarding every year and nearly every instance of every problem and every obstacle in my past. They also managed to convince me that there weren't specific answers to every question that could be asked. They stated that many questions in our lives were destined to be answered later, far outside of our place of living and outside of our time on this planet. But many questions could and would be answered while in this life. It all plainly and simply revolved around my personal answer to one pivotal and personal question. What would I do with this Jesus question?

As these two men provided a great deal of documentation for me, along with their own personal history and experience, so very much was clearly revealed. I discovered that we all belonged to someone, despite our age, social standing, or anything else that we may try to conjure up in our defense. Then there was the real mind blowing statement. As human beings, we all answer to one of two masters. All of our futures, both in this world and the one to come, depended upon understanding that one simple fact and then making that singular and all important choice. It absolutely all hinged upon making that everlasting choice. And that choice would forever determine my eternal destiny.

They made that more than obvious to me. Everyone was created to live forever, it was simply a matter of just where did I want my eternity to be. Through all of these discussions, that choice soon became crystal clear. I could choose the one to whom I had belonged to throughout my life to that point, the one who had tormented me ever since I had been a child. Or I could simply choose life. I could choose the One. The Creator of Heaven and of Earth. The Keeper of my very soul. The one who took *my* place upon a rugged and splintered cross. It was a place that I deserved, a death that I deserved and one that *he* did not. He was the one who owed no debt, but instead paid a debt that I could never afford to pay. And all because *he* loved me and had done so since before the earth had been created. Knowing all of those things, how could I possibly refuse such a gift?

I had to reconcile myself to an overwhelming number of facts. I had to realize that he had died a cruel death for me in order to purchase my eternity. I had to arrive at the understanding that if I had been the only human on earth, he still would have done it. I was required to view him as more than a nice guy, a good teacher or even a prophet. He made a claim to be God himself, the Creator of all and the actual living Word. I had to understand that if he were not who he had claimed to be, then he was the greatest liar that the world had ever seen. It was an introduction far beyond all measure.

But at the very same time, the idea was absolutely terrifying, life threatening, and certain to be life changing. It required an incredible step of faith from me. I had to literally walk into something that I could not see with my eyes. The real fact of the matter was that I had to believe, without reservations, in someone that I absolutely could not see. It was the truest of all steps of faith. I didn't know what lay ahead of me as I took that step. But the actual truth in life was that I never had really known what would happen next and that none of us actually do. All of our footsteps are unknown to us in advance. Having that knowledge firmly in place, did I really want to walk the remainder of my life alone? But the bonus was that not only did I not have to walk alone, but, as I chose those routes, I would then have someone to walk ahead of me.

Those two good men, who had quickly become friends, helped me in every way possible. They answered all of my questions and had given me all of the instructions and guidance that I needed. They also reminded and informed me that having made that decision did not remove me from the normal course of life's events. It certainly did not mean that my life would be perfect or even close. Trials and troubles would naturally come my way as it was a necessary part of the Christian walk. The two of them provided me with everything that I needed to know. It was all very necessary and it was all very good. But at the end of our discussions, something still remained that only I could do. It was the one decision that everyone has to make alone. No one else could possibly do it for me. I had to decide. I had been informed, the knowledge had been presented and with understanding in place, I had to make the choice.

The Conversation

It was Tuesday, and it was nearly lunchtime. My employers had made it possible for me to remain in the office and completely uninterrupted for one solid hour. With that in place, I went into the crowded little room, shut the door behind me, and sat down at the desk.

I sat there quietly for a moment as I wondered just how to begin. I asked myself, just how in the world does someone have a conversation with God? My two friends had given me general instructions and some guidelines. But I knew that although it was all up to me, he was patiently waiting. I began the prayer by saying that I was truly sorry for everything and admitted that all of my mistakes had been my fault. I realized that there was nothing in my past that I could really blame on anyone else. However, as the prayer continued, the more the emotions rose to the surface and came spilling out. Then, with my eyes closed, I quietly spoke *his* name. That was all that there was to it. I simply said the name. Then just that suddenly the sentence stopped before another word could roll past my lips. I ceased to speak as I literally caught my breath and held it for a moment. Something incredible and profoundly unbelievable then occurred and before I knew it, my mind struggled valiantly to keep from going over the edge as even reality itself changed there before me. It all happened within the blink of an eye.

I opened and closed my eyes over and over again as the little office, the desk and even the chair that I had been sitting in were now gone. I was thoroughly and completely bewildered and disoriented. It felt as if I had suddenly lost my mind or had been mentally been taken hostage somewhere, somehow and apparently by something. The one thing that I knew for certain was that I was not where I had been and that I had no idea of just where I had arrived. It was as if I was in the midst of a wide-awake and very coherent nightmare. But I also discovered that I was in full possession of all of my faculties. I blinked my eyes, tested my breathing and slapped myself in the face. But still nothing in my newfound reality changed. I remained in a mystifying place of near-total darkness. My mind desperately struggled to contain it all and was very close to the point of imminent collapse.

I had been suddenly and involuntarily taken somewhere and somehow, but where and by whom or by what? It was terrifying, frightening and a shaking to your very bones sort of place. It was the stuff of horror novels or movies or something even more imaginative and surreal. I had absolutely no clue whatsoever as to where I had just arrived. There was certainly nothing in my life experience that served to give me any sort of a reference point. I didn't know if I were in a room, some sort of a strange location or just precisely where I had been placed. One item was certain. I had been forcibly taken and was strategically placed into the situation where I now found myself.

The first item that registered was that it was almost completely dark. There was a dim and feeble light, but it was very distant and far, far above me somewhere. It was very poor illumination, but it was the only thing that interrupted that dark and dreadful place. There was so little light that I couldn't see the hairs on my own arm. It was all very dim, extremely depressing as I then realized that it was also becoming quite damp. There was also just enough mist moving through the air which kept my skin and clothes wet and cold. It was very uncomfortable, mentally disturbing, and I wanted out of that place in the very worst way. I would have done nearly anything to accomplish that feat.

It was at that precise moment when I began to look around and then fully discovered the extent of my trouble. As I looked downward at my feet I observed that I was standing on an object that was, by my best guess, just over one square foot in size. It reminded me of the top of a deck piling on a dock at the water's edge. It was irregularly shaped and all rounded off as if it were very old and appeared to have seen frequent use. With the constant mist, it was also more than a little slick. After just a few moments of carefully positioning myself, I soon began to experience great discomfort. There was no hope of relaxing in that place as I couldn't afford to move much more than an inch in any direction.

But what was in the darkness around and particularly beneath me? There was no visible way for me to verify anything. Was it solid? Was it water? How far down was it? Testing with a bit of spit, I strained my ears and heard nothing, which brought no real answers. A second attempt didn't produce any better results either. As far as I observed, with what information I obtained, was that if I slipped off of that post, I was in for a long, long fall and for a very long time. What sort of place was this? Where in the world was it? But most of all, why was I brought to such a place and how had I gotten here? Who or what had brought me? Then, as my mind spun endlessly as it continued to grasp for reality, I wondered if I were actually there? Was it possible that I still sat at the office desk and was merely experiencing some kind of a delusion? Was it possible to dream, and to dream that vividly while being wide awake? What was happening to me? How could I get back to what I believed was reality? Would I ever return to a familiar place? Those questions went on inside of my head for nearly twenty minutes as my brain chased itself in fruitless circles over and over again.

Just at that moment I suddenly heard a most unfamiliar noise. Initially, I couldn't detect exactly what it was or from where it came. I had to scour my brain quite some time as I searched for an answer. I determined that it was like a click of sorts. Then after a few moments, I realized that it was almost the sort of sound that thick, dirty fingernails make on a bar counter. I had seen and observed such things as I had listened to my mother's boyfriend lecture me previously some years ago. But then there were another series of clicks, then silence, then two more, followed by additional intervals of silence and then a third. Then there was a long tension filled pause that caused my skin to crawl. Then suddenly there was an entire whole score of them as if someone were playing a silent piano to a tune in their head. Someone or something somewhere was drumming their fingernails on something. Then I determined that it wasn't quite a wood noise, as it seemed to be something different. I then decided that it more closely sounded like a stone noise, as fingernails were methodically and patiently drummed upon a stone surface. Then just as suddenly as it had begun, it stopped.

I found myself once again in complete and total silence as I caught myself holding my breath while straining with everything that I possessed just to hear something. Fear crept in with full intensity at that point and then moments later, fully confronted me. My nerves were completely on edge as my legs began to cramp from standing in one place. Then the added terror arrived as I became quite certain that I was not alone.

It was then that the voice spoke. As it did so, I trembled and was instantly chilled to the bone as I recognized it as the very same and horrifyingly familiar voice from my youthful past. I remembered it as if I had only been yesterday. It was that voice from my youth, the voice that I had heard as a little second grade boy. It was the same voice that led the entire chorus of other voices when I was driven out of the house on South Pendleton Street. It was the same voice that chased me out into the street nearly every night in pure terror. It was the same voice that terrified and indelibly marked my childhood. However, in that time and place, it was all very different. In that place where I so precariously stood, I understood its speech fully and with perfect clarity. In that dark and dreadful place, as I stood there on that small post, it called me by name.

I shook and as it spoke, I shook horribly with a full body chill. It was horrifying enough when it spoke my name as that revelation was more than terrifying enough. But it was the actual voice itself that nearly caused my heart to stop beating. With each and every word, it plainly revealed exactly what it was. It was an awful and thoroughly evil voice. It was a voice that carried with it the promise of an impending doom. It shook me to my very core while my heart attempted to forcefully beat its way out of my chest. Then it quietly and calmly spoke my name once again. But it wasn't just the obvious evil that I could hear within the voice, but also a deep seated and ingrained hatred. I heard it in every syllable that it uttered. The very timbre and quality of that voice thoroughly chilled my blood. It was at that precise point that the unspeakable realization came. There was something eerie and unworldly about that voice. It was then that I knew for certain that it wasn't human.

Then in the total silence, I suddenly heard movement. I likened it to the sound of a large canvas covering being removed from something. It reminded me of coverings used when storing cars, boats and other larger items. Or perhaps like the noise that wet bed sheets on a clothesline made when they snap in a brisk wind. However, even that didn't fully describe the sound. It was a dragging, unfolding type of noise followed by a sudden snap of a sound. It had been loud initially as it then became quieter as the noise apparently moved to my left and then past me somewhere in the darkness. Then, from somewhere to my left and seemingly elevated, it spoke once again. "I know you, I have always known you. I have been with you from your beginning. Most importantly of all, I know all of your secrets."

Was this all a joke? Was it simply a nightmare? I began to hope with everything within me that it was. Who or maybe better yet, what was this thing that spoke to me? Who or what could possibly know all of my secrets? Why would anyone want to? Who or what would want to be bothered with someone like me? I was no one of any sort of importance, not by any stretch of the imagination. But there were other issues that bothered me equally as much. None of this experience was lining up with anything that my employers ever told me about religion or Christianity.

However, that seemed to be the path that everything had traveled. After all, I did bow my head in prayer and did begin the discussion about conversion when suddenly this insanity had been thrust upon me. Besides, after how my employers instructed me, only God himself knew everything about everything. Whatever that thing was, it couldn't be the God that they had talked about. That voice, in this place full of confusion and anger, was intensely hateful and I felt it with every spoken word. It just didn't feel right. Nothing about it felt right. Then, in frustration and forced out by my own anger and fear, I simply blurted out the words. "Who are you? What are you? Tell me! Tell me! Tell me now! Do you hear me?"

Then suddenly and without warning, there was movement. It was that same tarpaulin-canvas snapping sound. It seemed far above me, as it then moved to my left and suddenly I heard a loud snap somewhere above and at some unknown distance behind me. Then once more there arrived the silence, complete and debilitating silence. Even though I strained with everything that I had, I was unable to hear anything. Then, as I attempted to turn around, my left foot slipped as I nearly lost my footing and screamed as only a dying man would. Within mere seconds, I found myself gasping for breath and began shaking like a leaf on a windy day. My nerves were completely shot by this point as warm tears ran down my cheeks to compete with the cooling mist. Five and then ten minutes past, as there was still nothing but the unnerving silence.

Then somewhere off to my right, in the distance and curiously, somewhere beneath me, it spoke once again. They were horrible and terrifying words. They were awful and morbid words. It seemed impossible that anyone or anything could possibly know enough facts to speak such words.

"I watched closely by his side as your little brother died. It truly was an awful and pitiful thing to observe as it happened. He kicked his legs and flailed his arms in the hot bathwater, but it was to no avail. Even though he was very small, he valiantly struggled for his life. It was such a sad thing to witness. How horrible it must have been for you to find him as you did. Although I don't possess the ability to read your mind, I clearly observed what was so obviously written upon your face." Then once again, there was a rush of wind as that same total and miserable silence returned.

How did it know that? There wasn't anyone else there in the house besides my father and my siblings. I certainly didn't recall anyone else there in the bathroom when I discovered my brother's lifeless body as it floated in the tub. But what about those words? How could that be? What did it mean when it said that he had struggled? In the years since that time, I had been told that he had climbed over the side of the bathtub, had hit his head, had become unconscious and had quietly drowned. My parents and everyone else said all along that it had simply been an unfortunate accident. So, what was meant by those words about a struggle and just who was it that my little brother had struggled with? Who had been in that bathroom with him before I discovered his body?

Then the voice spoke again as if it were somewhere nearby and was intently reading the emotions on my face. "He struggled as desperately as any little baby could. He fought for air, he fought for his life and the person responsible for his death is someone that you know very, very well." I stood there on my precarious post in complete shock and disbelief, wondering what would happen next. Then the voice added something that literally sucked the air out of my lungs. "Did you know that your mother, at one point in time, convinced your named father that you had something to do with your brother's death?" It then urged me to search my mind and replay all of the memories. Then it made the statement, "Just think about it. Remember that after all, he was your father's absolute favorite. Don't you remember the way that your father looked at you that day as he carried your brother through the house while wrapped in that towel? Didn't you ever notice that with every conversation that the two of you ever had, that it had to be? Think about the way that he looks at you. Think about it, just think about it." Then once again there was silence, total and complete silence. Nothing remained but the racing thoughts as they ripped scars of permanent pain throughout my mind.

After some meager time had passed, I detected more movement. From somewhere below it moved, as it then stopped somewhere in front of me if only for a moment. Then, just as that item registered within my brain, I detected that it moved rapidly upward while still making that same flapping canvas noise. What was it? I just couldn't figure it out. Then the thought raced to the forefront of my mind as I immediately attempted to discount it. Oh, no way, there was just no way! Was that thing actually flying? Then the other thought occurred to me nearly as quickly. What could it do to me? Images, both prehistoric and nightmarish rapidly sped throughout my mind. Then out loud I cried, "Where am I? Where am I? Let me out of here! I don't deserve any of this! I don't deserve to be tormented like this!"

Then the voice spoke once more. As it did, I nearly fell from my precarious stand. Although it was still unseen, I observed and believed that it was very close and nearby. To my senses, it appeared as if it were directly in front of me, possibly no more than twenty feet away as near as I could fathom. Upon hearing its voice, I violently shook from far more than the mist and the cold. I had never been that frightened of anything before, not in my entire life.

Then it continued to speak, "I was there on Euclid Avenue. I know the name of the man in your mother's bedroom. It was not your uncle. I saw it all. I have seen everything in your pitifully short life. I was there sitting on the branches of that oak tree on Harrison Avenue. I saw all of those girls. I know all of their names. I saw all of the drinking, the drugs and all of the other items of note and importance. I saw it all. I saw everything as it happened at that so-called church camp. I saw all of the manipulating little games that you played as you used the other children. I saw it all. I know who you are and exactly what you are. I was there as an eye witness for every evil and disgusting thing that you have ever done. I saw it all. I know everything." Then again there was silence, total silence that left me with nothing but questions racing through my tormented mind.

How could someone possibly know all of those things? How could someone see everything that I had done? Then there were the specific questions. Who was the man that was with my mother? Did I know him? But then I went on to other things as I wondered just how could someone sit on tree branches? Why would they watch someone like me, a mere boy? How could someone know about what had happened at church camp? But also, just what did the voice mean by the phrase that it used, the "so-called church camp"? What did all of it all mean to me? I just didn't understand, but then came the interruption followed by a few very unexpected and unanticipated words. They were words of unforeseen kindness.

"But I was there for you. Through it all, I protected you through every instance and every time and place. Remember all of the incidents in your life that could have gone so horribly wrong. They could have been far, far worse than what they were. It was I who watched over and kept you safe." Then there was a pause followed a slight change in the conversation. "We kept you safe and sound. We protected you as no one else could. We kept things from being much worse than what they could have been. We have always been there. We have always been with you and we have constantly been by your side. We are the ones that you have sought for guidance, direction, and help for so very long. Therefore your newfound friends have only been mistaken and it is not their fault, although they are indeed gravely mistaken. They have been completely misinformed and horribly misguided just as millions throughout time have been. They have been led horribly and completely astray. We alone have the facts and we have the real and proven truth. We alone have the answers that you seek. We are the true reality. No one else has ever presented themselves to you as we have. They worship a fable and a fraud. It is a misconception that has been passed down through the ages. We however, have been there through every step of human history. We are the truth. Ask yourself, has anyone else presented such facts as I have to you? Have you actually known any other reality? Haven't we shown you the way? We are the objects of your worship. We are what you have looked for all along. Your entire life has led you to this place and to this point in time. We are here to rescue you from the fable. We are here to provide you with the real truth. Believe and trust in us." Then without another word spoken, the silence then returned.

I just couldn't take it anymore! With everything that was pent up within me, I just blurted the questions out loud, "What is all of this? Is this just a joke? Have I gone completely delusional? Have I finally lost my mind?" Then I wondered if I were having a nervous breakdown. Was it all just my payment for all of the things that I had tried and done? Was it all just another bad trip? Was it just a bad dream? Then I stopped for a moment and gathered my thoughts together.

It really didn't matter. It didn't matter who or what I was. It really didn't even matter what I had become. None of that mattered at all anymore. Then I spoke into the darkness with all of the bravery that I could possibly muster within me. I had seen the evidence and had witnessed enough. I had made my decision.

I then spoke to whatever it was. "I'll tell you this, whoever and whatever you are. Just as soon as I wake up from whatever this is, I am going to do exactly what I need to do. I am going to do what my real friends have told me that I need to do. I am going to take that next step. I am going to believe in who I think is real, the one that you call a fable and a fraud. I am going to make that choice. I am going to take the path that I believe to be right. On this very day, just as soon as I can, I am going to meet *him*. *He* is the only one who can take all of my past away. *He* is the only one who can take all of my guilt away. *He* is the only one who can wipe my slate clean. *He* is the only one who can make me clean and new and whole. My life will be new and all that I have to do is to call upon *his* name. As a matter of fact, I don't think that I have to wait until I wake up. I think that I can and should do it right this minute. Why should I wait? I have waited long enough and it has been far too long. I will do it now. I will do it at this very minute. And *his* name is—"

It was absolutely the loudest noise I had ever heard. It was an unbelievable deafening roar of a noise. It was more than a voice; it was a noise that scoured its way through my ears and felt as if it would explode inside of my head. It was piercing, painful and physically deafening. It literally erupted within that place and seemed to shake every last bit of it. It literally knocked me off of my feet and left me sobbing hysterically as I clung for my life on that perch. I barely kept my grip, as bit by bit, I was able to pull myself up to a sitting position. There I sat where I had been standing and wrapped my legs around the post for support and out of unimaginable fear. The roar was intensely loud and lasted such a length of time that I had to cover my ears due to the pain that it caused. When it finally ceased, I quickly looked around in anticipation of its next unknown move. But then, as the silence returned, slowly, but very slowly, I sat upright. Then as

I kept my legs wrapped around the post, I cautiously removed my hands from my ears. Again there was silence, nothing but total and complete silence. Where was it? Where had it gone? Once again, I was unable to hear anything although I strained my ears with everything that I had.

Snap! A huge jaw filled with horribly large and discolored teeth violently snapped shut within a mere inch of my right ear. Out of the corner of my eye, but only for the briefest of seconds, as I was immobilized by the overwhelming fear, I saw the size and color of those teeth. In pure terror, I quickly closed my eyes, as I had no idea of just what would happen next. I then shuddered uncontrollably as it moved and literally felt it brush up against me and then move but a few inches away. When it exhaled, it was the smell of death, of dead things, the stench of which made me physically gag while shaking my entire body. Then it purposely waited for me to fully comprehend my perilous dilemma, while carefully pausing for effect and only then did it finally speak once again. When it did, it was with venomous hatred as if the words literally dripped from its mouth in vile anger. Each word was spoken slowly, with extreme calculation, but very loud and with defined hardness as every syllable was over pronounced for added effect. I was absolutely terrified beyond belief or human comprehension. I clung to my perch in unspeakable fear as the waves of terror continued to race throughout my body. However, it seemed overwhelmingly intent upon gaining my understanding.

"It is time for you to hear the purest of truth. No one can save you. No one else can protect you. Don't you understand? Why can't you understand? You must understand! Only I have been with you. You belong to us. It is the very purpose of your life. Everything that those so-called friends have told you is false. It is all a lie, a myth, and the worst sort of fable. None of it is true and none of it has ever been true. The only truth is right here with you. What is he really to you? What has He ever been for you? What has he ever actually done for you? Where is he now?

Is he here to rescue and comfort you? He doesn't exist. He never did. His story was the contrived work of foolish and ignorant men. What your alleged friends want you to initiate is merely an ancient, powerless and foolish magical formula. It will not work. I know. We know. We have seen it fail on countless occasions throughout the ages of time. We have seen it ruin human lives for centuries. Nothing about your life will change no matter what you do. You belong to us, and we are the masters."

My head felt as if it were going to explode. My mind raced forward and then bent back upon itself while creating a thoroughly tangled mess. Thankfully the voice had ceased to speak but the ragged breathing could still be heard and smelled. I was trapped on my precarious perch and honestly didn't know what was in store for me next. One fact was perfectly obvious. I was in the presence of a very great and incredible evil. I knew it in my heart. I heard it as the teeth snapped and ground together inches from my right ear as it spoke every cutting word. I shook so badly and my legs cramped to such an extent that I barely maintained my slippery position. My mind desperately raced while searching for answers, for some semblance of normalcy, as I just didn't know just what to do next. Fear and desperation then set in with an overwhelming severity as it continued its otherworldly speech. I wanted to panic, to scream out in unbridled terror, and then throw myself off into the unknown darkness. At one point, I nearly surrendered to it. But somewhere inside, something within me was quietly stirring. It was indescribable and previously quite unknown to me. Whatever it was, it was something deep inside, at this point undefined and unnamed. Something within me was beginning to awaken or possibly, and more accurately, had begun to awaken me. Although I was obviously in imminent and extreme danger and had no reason to feel otherwise, I was now being filled with a peaceful awe.

It was a still and quiet voice. It was an incredible voice, a voice such as I had never before known. It was unheard by my own ears and was inaudible to anyone else, but possessed greater clarity than anything that I had previously experienced. It was calming, soothing and unearthly peaceful. From deep within the words came forth, "Speak my name. Speak my name. Speak my name." It was so softly stated, but strongly and firmly spoken. It caressed and surrounded my heart with majestic peace and protection as it immediately drowned out the voice of the creature beside me. In complete ignorance of my newfound experience, the creature continued its self-centered repetitive ranting and boasting. In the midst of all of the roaring and proud words, within I only heard a still and quiet voice as it softly, but with undeniable encouragement pulled me forward. Speak my name. Speak my name. Speak my name. Then just at the instant when that unknown emotion became the utmost of full earthly understanding, I found that I could stand it no longer as I simply spoke with my mouth what my heart so supremely understood. Out loud the words burst forth from my lips in such as fashion that I couldn't have contained them had I tried. The greatest of all Truth was revealed within my heart, as I then knew that I only had to speak one precious and eternal name. I said the words loudly and then even louder yet, with a joy that no human being can possibly ever fully describe. Jesus, Jesus, Jesus—save me!

It was a bloodcurdling scream, but from a very curious source. It was a horrific noise that itself was brought about by great and unimaginable pain. It was ear-piercing in its intensity as it violently ripped through the very fabric of the air. However, the voice was not mine. It was the other voice, of that boastful creature, a voice that came from that mouth full of teeth, from that voice of evil and hatred. It appeared to be in outrageous pain. It writhed, flailed and threw itself about in the darkness in torment of the utmost of apparent agony. It was all at the sound of that Name. Just the sound of His name destroyed the abilities of that creature as the tables were amazingly turned as it suddenly and immediately become the object of torment. Then that dark and sorrowful place became filled with not only the creature's painful screams, but with many others as a chorus seemed to involuntarily join in the painful song.

In an awesome and outrageous instant everything before me changed. I then felt strong, loving and fatherly arms surrounding me with comfort and safety, such as I had never felt before. It was an immeasurable and infinitely indescribable love. To suddenly be so completely protected, so incredibly safe and so eternally secure. It was an infinitely pleasurable and loving feeling. It was as if I were, for the very first time, a small, wanted and needed little child. For the very first time in my life, I felt truly loved, needed and of extreme importance to someone. Everything literally also changed before my very eyes as the damp, dark, and evil domain instantly vanished before my eyes. It was then replaced by a living light, the most brilliant and glorious light. Everything was now different, so very different, and everything also seemed to be so revealed. It was as if I were seeing everything with brand new eyes. The very best and precious part of the entire transaction was the fact that I had received mankind's greatest and eternal gift. It was also an obvious fact that not only had I received it, but it had cost me nothing more than simple faith and a heartfelt decision. But most telling of all was the humbling awareness that I didn't deserve any of it. I had been hopelessly and eternally lost with absolutely nothing of any value to give. It was grace, purely grace, and I was the unworthy recipient.

Then with a blink or two, I opened my eyes. The only thing before me was a dusty, cluttered old shop desk in a very familiar office. However, it was one of the most beautiful things that I had ever seen. The clock on the wall revealed that a mere five minutes had passed since I had sat down in the chair. However, I knew full well that I had spent an unknown amount of time in that gloomy and terrifying place.

But then again, I also didn't feel at all like me. I didn't feel anything close to what I ever had before. Every measurable fact or item that I brought to my mind was now changed. As I stood up from the desk, I felt unbelievably lighter on my feet. With a burst of energy, I flung open the office door and stepped outside. I stood there in the parking lot with my head tilted backward and my arms outstretched. I probably looked like an idiot, but I couldn't have cared less. The sky was brighter, the air actually seemed cleaner and even my vision was detectably crisper. I possessed an unbelievable, unspeakable, difficult to define and totally unknown before, outrageous joy within my heart. It was simply freedom, sweet, and indescribable freedom. I had never previously experienced anything remotely similar in my entire life. I was new within it seemed; all new and it was an incredible feeling. But then, as I gave it my full consideration, it was actually more than just a feeling.

It was what an immigrant must have felt upon arriving on our shores as he experienced freedom for the first time, but my gift from Him was so much better. It was what a convicted man must have felt as he was finally released from prison only to discover that complete and everlasting forgiveness for his crimes was now his. But then he also found that his crimes had been thoroughly wiped away to be remembered no more and that he had been fully restored to society, but His perfect gift to me was far better.

It was what life as a slave from birth must have been, as that slave then suddenly found himself purchased by a new master. But then he experienced an awesome surprise as his chains and shackles were not only removed, but had been thrown away. But then better yet, he found himself treated as if he were a blood born member of the master's family, but even still His gift to me was far better. It was better beyond description, it was far better than mere human words could ever possibly describe. His gift was just so much better and then there was the greatest part of it all, I would never lose it because it was eternal. I had been gifted with the greatest freedom of all.

After lunch was over and everyone had returned to work, the news of my decision was announced and as a group, we celebrated for a few precious minutes. It was the best afternoon of my life. At five o'clock, the shift was over, and I couldn't wait to get home to share the great and wonderful news.

As I walked through the door of the apartment, I quickly realized that no one was there. But even so, it really didn't matter as I was obviously in far too good of a mood. The obligatory note taped to the television stated that she and the baby had gone off somewhere with her sister and her mother. Therefore I was stuck at home with time on my hands and so very much to say. Then the thought struck me. There were a number of illegal items in the house that given my very recent decision simply had to go. They didn't fit in with the person that I had become and the person that I needed to be. With a bit of amusement, I realized that none of it had a place in my home. It simply didn't belong there anymore and I wanted nothing to do with any of it. The desire for such things had just simply vanished and was completely gone.

Therefore, I spent the following hour or so as I cleaned the place in a real old-fashioned way. I began by pouring all of the alcohol down the kitchen sink drain. Then I located every possible stash of marijuana, pills, and all of the other nonsense in the house. I then flushed them down the toilet as after the day's prominent decision, it was exactly where that sort of stuff belonged. I even took a bit of inventory of contraband before I disposed of it. There was pot stashed in plastic bags, some hash wrapped in foil, and probably a hundred pills of various types and for different purposes. It was incredible and inspiring as none of it mattered to me; it was all worthless trash. I just flushed it all away. When I was finished, the house was completely cleansed of any and everything that could have easily gotten me arrested. It was, without a doubt, the second-best feeling of the day.

When she finally arrived home, the puzzled look on her face revealed to me that she recognized that something about me had changed. I informed her that something tremendous had occurred earlier and that she needed to hear about it. I seated her at the kitchen table, as then in detail, I told her nearly everything that had happened to me that day. I described to her my momentous decision and took pains to divulge to her just exactly what that decision had meant. I told her just how much different that it made me feel and that truthfully, it was far more than just a simple feeling or emotion. I then informed her that it meant that I was a brand-new person.

At that point she looked at me as if I had just arrived from another planet. As I attempted to describe the matter in its entirety, she became more than a little impatient with me. As she began with that sort of attitude, I decided at that point not to reveal to her or anyone else anything about the dream, the vision, or whatever that nightmarish ordeal had been. But as I wrapped up the discussion about my decision and what it had meant, I then informed her that I had flushed and dumped everything that had been in the house. Initially, she was horrified and stared at me in utter disbelief as the emotions raced across her face. Then I watched as the anger within her boiled and then rose to the place where she just simply exploded. She just went completely off.

She screamed, yelled, and cursed as if I had taken away her only reason for living. It was as if I had removed her sole and primary purpose in life. It was as if I had taken away her one true love. It was as if I had stolen away her very soul. It was at that moment that I fully realized that I had removed the one and solitary item that was of any importance to her. Once I had taken that action and had implemented it as well, the truly ruthless remainder of the five-year war was on in earnest. What semblance of restraint she had employed previously, at that moment simply vanished into the air as her anger shifted into full danger mode from that point forward. I was in for the fight of my very life.

The Five-Year War (Continued)

It's just after eight o'clock in the evening on that wonderfully warm and breezy July night. I was just twenty-four years old, and it had been only four years since my miraculous conversion to Christ. Although I was four years older, it certainly did not insure that I was any better off in my life or wiser in my Christian walk. However, it had indeed been an incredible four years. As I sat there in the quiet back yard of my little bungalow style home, I could only think about the four years that had passed by so quickly as so very much had happened that it nearly boggled my overwhelmed mind. But the visible end as well as the final result of those four years was now a very empty house.

As my walk with him began, having gained Christ provided me with a family. My experience could only have been compared to that of an adopted child, who had been lost and adrift in society. I was someone who felt alone, unwanted and then was suddenly found. However, it was that *someone* who had found me, as he came along side of me as a true Father. Then I experienced it more fully as He drew me into the fold of his family. Or perhaps, in another way of speaking, it was as if I were a long, lost relative, completely forgotten and then newly found. They were all vague comparisons to be certain, but there really was no proper way on this side of eternity to accurately describe the change made when *he* came marching with absolute power into my life. It was by far the very best thing that had ever happened to me.

But I also found that the Christian family was actually not very different than any other family. While there was love, assistance, assurance, support, and fellowship, there were also occasions of self-striving, postulating, power grabbing, and strange traditions that defied all reason and logic. Upon questioning those traditions, I found that they were also to be upheld at all costs, as if they were of the utmost importance. This created quite a roadblock for me. However, despite that and other singularly human issues, I learned much, grew to appreciate much, loved much within my new family, and had unfortunately began to despise more than just a few very curious things.

As I began my walk with Christ, I naturally made the decision to attend the church where my friends and my employers attended. It was on the very northern edge of town and was by any measure, the largest church in the city. It was quite a place to observe on Sundays with dozens of classrooms as well as a large auditorium that was packed every week to the tune of nearly fifteen hundred people. Although I greatly appreciated the sound instruction and guidance I received within the first six months, there were however, other difficulties. Sadly, those difficulties created quite a stumbling block within as I sought to live my new and respectable life. Interestingly enough, the majority of them actually had very little or nothing to do with the biblical church.

But a good portion of my troubles centered about the never-ending war within my own home. It was clearly obvious that she despised church, God, religion, Christ as well as any and everything remotely attached to it. Apparently, as far as she was concerned, such a lifestyle represented the sum total of a way of living that she sincerely wanted nothing to do with. It was, in fact, the absolute antithesis of the lifestyle that she decreed was hers to live. It was not only her stated desire, but it was also her steadfast ultimatum that everything within our household was to remain the way that it had been prior to my life-changing decision. It angered her beyond measure and instigated the strife and fighting between us that went to a new level and seemed to never end.

The hostilities all centered about the immovable fact that I steadfastly refused to permit drugs or alcohol of any sort inside my home. Other than the obvious reasons, why would I want such poison nearby and within reach of the baby? What would happen if my little daughter, as a toddler had gotten into anything that had been left lying within reach, as were *her* habits? Then what would we have done? Would she have felt any guilt about her selfishness over that? Wasn't my daughter's safety of any concern to her in the very least? In actuality, it was my belief that nothing mattered to her at all. She was only concerned about her own selfish needs and desires and certainly nothing more.

In the end, no amount of logic or common sense changed her opinion. Due to her refusal to change or adjust, even for the safety of my daughter, she repulsed me in every sense of the word. I had witnessed that same sort of self-centered and diabolical treachery throughout my life. I previously had experienced just those types of parental decisions which ignored a child's well-being and future. I watched it played out on a daily basis within the various houses that I grew up in. She no more cared for my daughter's safety and future than my own parents had cared for mine.

She also despised the fact that I went to church on Sunday mornings and took my daughter with me. As a practical point, I had no other choice as I couldn't leave the baby unattended, as she never got out of bed any time before noon. Perhaps another reason was due to the fact that I couldn't trust her to maintain control of any aspect of the household or what happened within it. Then again, perhaps it was an unknown something else or a dozen other reasons that I never found out until much later and after many years had passed. Therefore, we were set at odds with one another, we diametrically opposed and there were few options that could possibly draw the two of us back together. As with any opponents in war, the line was drawn and the battle was on.

It was an immovable barrier between us. I knew what I had experienced on that special and precious day which meant there was absolutely no going back. I sincerely made that decision and it was based upon the most steadfast reality that I had ever known. As far as I was concerned, I didn't care one bit if my change in lifestyle infuriated her to the point where she decided to permanently leave my home; it was final.

On one particular occasion, when someone from the church stopped by to visit, she proceeded to put on quite a show. There was a knock, I answered the door, and I invited the older couple inside. Upon learning their identity and purpose, she quickly left the living room and hid out in the bedroom. But no sooner had the couple seated themselves and our conversation had begun, then she made her grand and shocking entrance. I was never more embarrassed in my entire life, and they certainly were as well. She strolled theatrically into the room after dressing herself in next to nothing. She had a beer can in one hand, a cigarette in the other, and let loose with a string of profanities, which announced her arrival a minute before she physically entered the room. Naturally, they were visibly horrified and tried to compose themselves as I embarrassingly attempted to say and do anything that would have changed the subject. As she strutted about the apartment, she was obviously very proud of herself and appeared to be thrilled beyond measure at what she had accomplished. But it was nothing new as I had witnessed such impromptu drama before.

She conducted such performances whenever the opportunity presented itself. Perhaps she believed that if I were embarrassed enough, I would surrender, submit to the defeat and return to our previous way of living. But she had no idea just how sadly mistaken she was about that topic. I was simply not that same person and could no more go back to what I once was than I could change my species. I couldn't do it and simply had no desire for that former lifestyle. However, within my own household I also experienced no peace, no contentment, no stability, and certainly no measure of safety.

Every day was a constant, unending, angry, and nasty battle that coursed throughout my ever-waking hour. It ranged throughout the spectrum of daily habits and living. She used any and everything that she could find in her effort to anger, upset me, and even to possibly destroy me.

For example, in those four years I purchased over a dozen bibles. If I was careless, forgot about her habits for just one moment, and left one lying about, she would invariable take it and rip it to shreds. Upon returning home from work, I would find what was left of them in the garbage can or even thrown outside into the yard. On occasion, she went so far as to blame it on my daughter. It was all a very, very sad way of living one's life.

Each day as we shared our home, we grew farther apart as neither of us made any real attempt to put anything back together. But in to retrospection, I wondered if it had ever been together in the first place. Did we ever truly realize a life of togetherness and mutual appreciation? Did we ever join together as one on anything? Was our lives based upon anything that actually mattered and had any importance? Did we ever accomplish anything beyond simple existence? Therefore, the facts were incredibly clear. We were walking two very separate, distinct, and completely different paths.

But if that weren't enough to deal with, I experienced difficulties every Sunday at the church itself. They had traditions that I just couldn't seem to wrap my head around. What disturbed me the most of all were the unwritten and man-made rules that were set in place to govern the membership. They certainly weren't rules that were found in the Bible, as I diligently had looked for them without success. It would have been easier for me to believe and understand all of them.

The rules that were foisted upon the membership were previously unknown to me. They were simply rules that I couldn't comprehend. I supposed that it would have helped if they had been written down somewhere and actually had some merit. But then such rules usually are not governed by simple logic and common sense. Initially I believed that they were only intended to be understood by the informed and enlightened, but found them to be quite perplexing as one of the newly arrived.

I was keenly aware that the church had a disturbing reputation as the city's premier religious country club. It always possessed that sort of air about it, and I felt it the very moment that I walked through its doors. However, I attended there due to the urging of my employers and for the natural respect that I had for them. But with each additional Sunday, the more troubled and upset that I became.

If the goal of a church was following God's perfect will and purpose, then why did they persist with such an overbearing emphasis on appearance? Did it really matter what sort of clothes I wore on Sunday? Why was it appropriate to wear certain kinds of clothes to certain places and then at the same instant, declare them to be wrong if worn to others? Just what difference and just what meaning did a certain day in the week make? Why were such reasons and requirements so necessary? What were the actual differences between dress slacks and blue jeans? Didn't they serve the same purpose? Didn't they accomplish the same task? For men, what was the deal with dress shirts and neckties and for women, similar situations regarding dresses of an allegedly appropriate length? I didn't own a necktie and never bothered to learn how to tie one in the first place. Why did it matter what sort of clothes that I wore? Since when was what I placed on the outside of my body reflective in any conceivable fashion of just what went on within my soul? In my mind, it was quite bewildering and impossible to overcome.

But such were the rules and they were steadfastly enforced by self-appointed administrators and compliance officers. I heard about it every Sunday. It just didn't make any kind of sense to me. Why did women have to wear dresses and why did men have to wear suits and ties? Why were these things so incredibly important to everyone? When did God ever care about what I had tossed on my body before I walked out of my home and into a building called a church? Then there was that nonsensical idiocy they frequently spoke of that if we loved God, we would dress the part for him? However, if He truly looked upon only our hearts, then why did anyone care what it was that we wore? He certainly didn't look upon that, did he? After all, weren't clothes simply sewn bits of cloth and churches nothing more than buildings constructed as any other?

I also wondered what were the strange issues was about alleged proper haircuts and whatever that was supposed to mean. Then there was the obvious disgust that some of them had for motorcycles and how it was vocalized that only awful and evil people rode them. Then there were the extremely divisive issues over the subject of music. With that particular item I literally had no comprehension or understanding of their claims. For what intelligent reason did the majority of them believe that guitars and drums were intrinsically evil? As I had heard it from the pulpit, demons themselves actually lived within those guitar strings and drums skins. What thoroughly angered me the greatest was that it was argued to my face that such beliefs were not just opinions, but were presented as the cold hard facts that all church-attending people should follow. Conversely, what intensely angered some of them was the fact that I even dared to oppose them. I frequently challenged them to show me in the Bible just where they were so right and where I was so completely mistaken. Therefore, every Sunday morning began with a nasty argument at home immediately before I left, followed by condescending stares and barely polite discussions before and after the morning worship service. After a few months of enduring this spiritual punishment, I decided that it simply wasn't worth it anymore. It had gotten to the place where I spent my time at church in discussions where I learned nothing, beat my head against the wall and found myself spent and angry. I accomplished nothing worthwhile and in order to further my own spiritual walk, I simply had to leave.

Within a week I had found another church that was much smaller and was located within the downtown area. It had some interesting and somewhat confusing beliefs of its own that I didn't quite understand, but the members didn't require anything from anybody that attended. It didn't matter to them what I wore, who I was, or where I had come from. They believed that the Bible was the total truth from beginning to end and that nothing needed to be added to it. They didn't place any stock in man-made rules and had no need for them whatsoever in their worship. They naturally had rules necessary for organization and operation, but none of which that overrode the simplicity of anything that the Bible had to say on any given subject. Whenever a question arose about anything, they simply referred back to what the Book stated. According to their statements, those foolish men made rules and regulations were exactly what was *not* how life was supposed to be governed and directed. It was a very liberating feeling.

I was not judged by my outward appearance, but merely by my deeds, actions, my words, and more importantly, simply by my motives. I was always urged to look inside and ask more about why I chosen a particular answer rather than what I chose as a decision. As a group they were loyal to a fault and looked after each other extensively as any family should. Whenever someone was in need, they simply banded together, organized the effort, and accomplished the necessary task. It didn't matter if it were a need for groceries, utility bills, yards that required mowing or a house needing a coat of paint. They simply looked after and served one another. For the most part, they stayed by my side until the very end of the war and some, even afterward.

I considered everything in my life as I neared the end of the five-year war. Fighting about church obviously wasn't the only traumatic event that happened within my home. There were occasions that I honestly, but naively believed it would somehow make things better. However, it didn't improve anything within my household at all; it just caused them to be nothing more than just different. In many ways, the problems themselves simply worsened. But not everything within my life took a turn for the worse.

Within a few months after my conversion, an incredible opportunity arose regarding employment. Although everything at the shop was actually going well and I had never actively considered a change, new employment was presented to me. It was sudden and arose out of nowhere as far as I was concerned. It was an opportunity for a once-in-a-lifetime career at the automotive engine plant. There before me was the opportunity of a well-paid career working for a national automobile company. It didn't bother me in the least that I was on an assembly line tediously building one engine after another. It certainly couldn't be more boring than the work I performed in the mailroom. However, the process of getting hired historically had always proven to be difficult for the vast majority of applicants. It was the sort of employer that had quite a reputation as a difficult facility for anyone to be hired if you didn't have the proper connections. It was nearly mandatory that you had to be related to a current employee in order to obtain an application, much less to gain employment there. Additionally, I was informed by those in the hiring office that walking in their door was not enough. For even though I had gotten that far, it would have taken a small miracle for someone at the plant to even bother to look at my application. I wasn't related to anyone that worked there, and I didn't know the first person that worked in the factory. Therefore, it was quite a shock, as I not only received a phone call from the factory but was also granted an interview.

The interview itself was quick and decisive. The gentleman who spoke with me sized me up the moment that I walked in the door. He asked a number of questions about cars, mechanical knowledge and associated topics. Before I realized or expected it, he completely floored me as he stated that the job was mine. However, I was required to accept the new job instantly. I therefore could only give the shop four days of notice despite the belief that they deserved more. However, later in the day, when I presented the opportunity to them, they not only accepted it, but were also thrilled that I had gotten the job and wished me well. They truly had my best interests at heart.

That new job affected every aspect of my life. My weekly paycheck increased more than three times over what I made at the shop. There were the health benefits that were truly amazing and other raises that came about soon after I was hired. But curiously, all of those financial blessings only resulted in brand-new arguments at home.

We disputed the dispersal of every dime that came into the budget. It was her immoveable belief that I should weekly give her a blank check for clothes, hairdressers, or anything else that she wanted or deemed necessary. In my mind, I believed that money should be put into savings every week for the future, such as to finally buy a house. It was my inner understanding that money should be put into a savings account, not blown on whatever whim and for whatever useless or idiotic purpose.

It wasn't long before I caught her shaving money from the grocery budget. That coincided with the obvious telltale signs of pot smoking and even worse. I also discovered that she was successfully acquiring more unneeded drug prescriptions. When I confronted her with the issues, she simply blew if off as if my words had no real meaning, and she didn't want to be bothered.

It didn't matter how often I destroyed the contraband; she always found other ways to supply her needs.

If there was any possible item that could be argued or fought about within my household, then it certainly was. She was completely methodical as she left no stone unturned. We argued about my hours at work, the shift that I worked, the days that I worked and anything that could possibly be considered. She actually acted as if she hated that I had gotten the opportunity to work there. I thought and believed within my heart that it truly was a gift. But none of those accomplishments seemed to be worth it as we literally argued about any possible subject, particularly those concerning money.

We also argued unceasingly about how to take care of and how to raise my daughter. We argued about how and what as we bought items for the apartment. We argued about personal habits, preferences, and desires. We argued about everything. However, it wasn't only an increase in the frequency of the fighting turmoil, but the intensity of it as well. It was awful and it made for a thoroughly miserable way of living and she was relentless about it. There was absolutely no peace; there was no avenue for rest as she simply never stopped or even let up in the slightest. There truly cannot be anything in life much worse than having to share air or live in a house with someone who hates you.

Within my mind, there was certainly no doubt whatsoever that she truly hated me. However, it wasn't something that I had to leave to my imagination. She made certain that I was reminded of that belief, verbally, emotionally, and physically at least once a week and usually daily by dozens of different examples and means. When she wasn't involved in perpetually arguing, screaming, or yelling, then she played one of her seemingly endless and ridiculous games. They ranged anywhere from fixing only enough food for dinner for my daughter and herself, to only cleaning their laundry, to stacking mountains of things on my side of the bed and forcing me to sleep on the sofa nearly every night of the week. The missing money episodes were a major part of it as well as the secret and unauthorized loans to members of her family. There were instances where she arbitrarily loaned our car for days or a week at a time to a family member. What was I supposed to think about that? However, the real deal breakers were her endless contacts with other men in town. She always maintained that it was harmless talk and that it was only friendship. Just how stupid did she think that I was? But once again, as with everything else in life, time proved out everything perfectly and in truly condemning detail.

From that time in my life until my moments of introspection in the backyard, much spousal information came my way. Unfortunately or perhaps not, that information proved my every suspicion to be true. Each and every one of those suspicions revealed themselves as cold, hard, and angry facts, just as my entire life had been. Within any adult life there can be nothing more degrading, demeaning or even dehumanizing than to be the foolish victim of a purposeful and habitually adulterous spouse. I was embarrassed beyond words as I attempted to live the sort of life that was expected, to the best of my abilities only to discover that within my own home life I had been a total fool. But not only was I a total fool, but I was a fool before and in the eyes of everyone that I knew, as well as everyone that I would ever meet.

I saw the obvious and telltale signs that an unknown person had been in my house, in my car, in my garage, and most importantly, in my own bed. Was there any possibility that anything could induce more destructive anger than that? Even worst of all was to walk past other men, somewhere or anywhere in public and receive from them that all-knowing smirk. That look instantly informed me that they had been with her. It was that superior look upon their smug faces that proved that they had conquered my life at its very core and that I had been vanquished. It was the worldly fact that they had taken territory, if even momentarily and had gained the spoils of victory. But their decision had been made selfishly and with utter disregard for the lives that would be destroyed in the process. It was human selfishness and depravity at its very worst.

Finality was reached four years into the marriage war, sometime during the spring. My job at the engine factory took a very bad turn, as had the entire economy in our area. I received the dreaded layoff notice not long after purchasing my first home. Upon receiving that notification, I was laid off from the factory, was given no date of return, and was informed that there was no return date in sight. The new career that I believed was a gift and had so based my entire life upon was immediately and permanently gone.

That blessed event occurred in late February, and from that point forward I was home nearly every minute of the day thereafter. Most of my fellow former coworkers thought that it sounded like a vacation, but for me it certainly was not. There wasn't a single day of rest with her, and she certainly didn't allow for even a moment of peace. My life progressed from bad to worse to awful to downright intolerable. It quickly became human misery at its very finest. It was hell on earth, and I didn't think that it could possibly get any worse. However, I was wrong, just as I always seemed to be.

It was late April, and I spent the better part of the week day chasing down job leads both in the city as well as one that was out of town. At that point in time, the situation within my household had become extremely desperate. By my estimations, every bit of money as well as every program of unemployment and training would run out before the end of the year. With each passing week, my level of income decreased until there was barely enough money left for anything. Desperation and anxiety set in hard and fast despite everything that my newfound faith taught me. It was the most difficult thing that I experienced to date in my life. That internal struggle, that tug-of-war between my natural fears and doubts faced off against the new faith, which required that I must simply trust and believe. I attempted to believe that God was indeed in control of everything even though everything in my life was rapidly falling apart. It was the hardest thing in the world for me to do.

As I pulled into the driveway at three o'clock that afternoon, I knew that something was wrong. There was an aching within my chest and something just didn't seem to be right. I parked the car, turned off the key, and just sat there for a moment and wondered about it all. I looked at the house from one end to the other as everything appeared to be fine, but something just felt disturbing and out of place. Finally, after waiting for those feelings to vanish, I got out of the car and went inside the front door. Upon entering, I proved that my suspicions were correct, as she and my daughter were gone once again. On that occasion it was different than all of those others had been before, as she had taken her clothes as well as all of my daughter's things. She had also taken a fair number of other items in the house. A few useless telephone calls to her family and to a few of her friends gained me nothing for my trouble. Then, just before six o'clock, as I walked around outside of the house, I met one of my neighbors. He was a much older gentleman who had always been quite polite, but reserved. After a few pleasantries, he then related to me an unexpected story. I was sickened and angered at the same time. It was a real punch in the stomach.

He informed me that he had noticed a car had pulled into my driveway just before noon earlier that day. He then sheepishly admitted that he had observed that same car in my driveway on plenty of other occasions before. Previously, he had paid little attention to the matter as he and his wife generally minded their own business.

But on that particular day, he had gotten a good look at the driver. It was a man, and by the way the two of them acted, there was no possible way that he was related to her. He certainly wasn't a brother, a cousin, or anything close to it. That man had helped her carry everything out of the house, which he then put into his car. When I asked for a description, he reluctantly provided one. I knew precisely who he had described. I knew his name, where he worked, and even where his parents lived. I knew, without factually knowing, that her sort of nonsense with that individual had probably gone on for years. He was one of many who allegedly wanted to speak with her for advice. I had heard his name spoken within the walls of my home far too often. But I instantly wondered to myself, just what sort of man was I that I had allowed my life to be reduced to such status?

Weeks went by with nearly no news of my daughter or of her. Tiny bits of scattered information often came my way. But in using those facts in an effort to find them, my searching always turned out to be fruitless. There was a sighting in the supermarket or a few details of a brief conversation that someone had with her in passing. However, there was nothing substantial for me to use in order to locate my daughter. I could have cared less about her or what she was doing.

However, I also had to deal with the purposeful and blatant lies told by her family for the expressed purpose of throwing me completely off course. What in the world did they have against me? What had I ever done to any of them? I had always been good enough to have around whenever they wanted or needed something. I was always there when someone needed help moving. I was always there when one of her sisters had gotten kicked out of another apartment after yet another breakup in a long string of boyfriends and once again, needed a temporary place to stay. There were the groceries that I purchased, clothing purchased and given, the trips taken to doctors' appointments, and a hundred other things. They always managed to say nice things to my face, but when the money was exhausted and I implemented an extremely strict budget, their true natures were revealed. They were nothing but vultures and leeches, exactly as my own good for nothing family. There may have been a very few exceptions, but by and large, they were all the same.

It was the second week of July. I hadn't seen my daughter for nearly three months. On that particular afternoon, I had only been home from my new part-time job at a nearby carry out for about fifteen minutes when the telephone rang. It was the pastor from my church. He had something very important to talk to me about and wanted to know if he could stop by for a visit. When I asked what it was about, he only responded with words that it was a surprise and that I would be pleased. It was a good point that he only lived a few minutes away as my curiosity was practically at its limits. I waited on the front porch steps until he pulled into the driveway.

However, his face was a curious mixture of different signs. Since it was nice enough outside, we sat down in the grass in the front yard as he quickly began the conversation. Evidently she and my daughter had stopped by his office earlier that morning. He went on to relate that she behaved quite differently than the few times that he had spoken with her on previous occasions. She informed him that the reason she had left my home a few months previously was because she needed time to think about her life. She stated that she also needed time to clear her head and had also arrived upon a decision concerning church. She decided that it was exactly what she and our family needed most of all. He then told me that he was quite convinced that her decisions were indeed genuine. Having said all of that, he then looked me directly eye to eye and stated that he did have a few very personal questions for me.

Was it true that I had struck her, had physically hurt her, and had done so repeatedly over the course of our married years? Did I always hide money from her and never let her have anything to do with the budget? Did I force her to do without because of the restrictions that I had placed on the budget? Did I actually spend money on motorcycle items and not allowed her buy clothes for my daughter? There were a dozen other questions, but they were all basically cut from the same cloth. She had told a convincing story, which portrayed me as an evil, controlling, and demanding husband who was impossible to live with.

I sternly but politely informed him that each and every one of the accusations were completely false. Declaring my integrity to be firmly intact, I flatly denied them all. I went on to relate my entire side of the whole story as I then let him in on everything that I knew about her. I told him about the infamous wager at the newspaper, the intrusion of other men in her life, her outrageous family, the laundry issue, and everything else that had ever happened between the two of us. But once I finished, there was still something in his eyes that revealed that he was yet unconvinced. He didn't have to say what was so obviously written upon his face. I knew then just where I stood with those that I had trusted with all of my heart. Instantly I was depressed, humiliated and was quite angry. He believed her lying story. But in my mind, I wondered just how she had pulled it off, and why had he believed her?

However, none of that really mattered all that much. As a Christian, I initially believed that I was forbidden to divorce her and send her on her way, despite her infidelities. Then there was the most important factor of all, my little daughter. I missed her terribly and I believed that I was willing to put up with nearly anything for the opportunity to live with and to raise her. Weren't children supposed to be that important to parents?

Part of me wanted to believe, as there did not appear to be another path before me to even hope against hope that God would someday and somehow become important to the unfaithful spouse. That would have gone a long way toward straightening out the mess of a life that we were living. But then my cynical nature stepped in and asked the very real question at hand. Was he real to her or was it all just a part of yet another sorry and well played little game? What if I let my guard down and then discovered her to yet be a fraud once more? Then I would have allowed myself to be slammed face first into the dirt once again. I hated the taste of it all and wanted no further part of her and the drama that always followed. But, more than anything else in the world, I just wanted to see my daughter again.

My pastor went on to state that he had spent quite a bit of time talking with her about relationships, responsibilities, and just where those very important items fit into the lives of people. She allegedly had also revealed to him her history and the reasons as to why she experienced and caused so much trouble. He then also revealed that she wanted to come home.

But she also confided to him that she was very much afraid to do so. Therefore he had arranged for the three of us to meet early the following morning at his office. We would be his first and if it were necessary, the only appointment for the day. He then warned me (?) that there would be guidelines to the meeting and that those guidelines be followed to the letter. There would be no screaming, shouting, cursing, or name-calling. Then he practically demanded my agreement to all of those arrangements. Nearly everything about the entire matter seemed out of place.

I wondered just what had she told him as it obviously was not the truth in its entirety. Why was he so harsh and demanding with me? I had never done any of the things that he described and certainly wouldn't have done them in his sight. But in the end, despite my misgivings, I agreed to the meeting. But I also informed him to watch her closely, to keep his eyes and ears open, and to observe everything. I informed him that nothing was as it seemed, as I was not the one who needed to be warned about their behavior. Then I let him know that not only was I blameless in the entire matter, but that I knew that my heart was exactly where it should be. I also stated that I had verifiable witnesses to every incidence that we had discussed. Then I added that I would be willing to do almost anything to get my daughter back. It was then that he informed me that as a Christian, I was duty bound to the marriage no matter what, no matter what had happened and no matter how bad that it would ever get. That didn't serve to give me any hope for the future.

_____

I arrived at his office half an hour prior to the appointed time. He and I spent a few moments discussing the scarcity of the local job market and other non-relevant items as the two of them walked into his office. My little daughter yelled my name as I dropped to my knees and hugged her until the tears freely flowed. It had to be the best moment in a long string of very bad days, weeks, and months. But for the remainder of our appointment, however, everything went exactly as I anticipated.

She told a very good story about a woman trapped in a situation that she was unable to do anything about. She was a helpless victim, she had always been a victim, and she had been caught up in circumstances that were well beyond her capability to control. I found it interesting as I listened, in that not once did she say anything even remotely derogatory about me. But all of her answers to the pastor's questions were usually one worded. She also seemed to be in quite a hurry to have the whole ordeal over and done with. She had called for the meeting, and then it appeared as if she wanted little or no part of it. Or perhaps, having accomplished what she was after, she then wanted to move on to whatever step was next.

She was always quite skilled at guiding whatever situation she chose to take part in. I personally witnessed how she manipulated people and was quite adept at fully playing her audiences well. Due to that history, deep down within me, the alarms of warning went off as she spoke. None of it was good and something about her words and actions just simply didn't feel right. It didn't feel right at all. Something about everything that went on in that office was sincerely wrong. But I just couldn't quite decipher what it was at that moment. However, I knew that soon enough, whatever it may be, it would certainly make itself known. It did on every previous occasion and therefore I wanted to prepare myself. I wanted to see it coming, whatever it was.

So later that afternoon, I moved the two of them back into my home. Despite all of my doubts and fears, as well as my feelings, all that I could do at that moment was to smile. My daughter was so thrilled to be home that she ran all over the house. She spent most of the afternoon in her bedroom with her toys. But most of all she was home, she was excited, and she was happy. She now had everything that any three-year-old could need or want.

Everything else seemed to be acceptable; however, it appeared to only be all on the surface. Outside of my daughter's return, there was no real joy, happiness, or tenderness. Therefore, it certainly wasn't any kind of a reunion. From the moment we left the pastor's office, she immediately replaced the unfamiliar face she wore in the meeting with an instantly recognizable one. But throughout the ride home, she didn't say much of anything and appeared to be deep in thought as much could be read on her face. It was as if she were planning something or following a curious script of some kind. Obviously within her mind, something very mysterious was going on. Obviously something was yet to come.

From deep inside of me, I was fully aware of it and knew that, whatever it was, I wasn't going to like it. However, there was nothing that I could do about it as I was completely and firmly trapped. By the vows that I had made and also by the faith that I possessed, I was bound to that woman for better or for worse. I had rarely seen moments of anything better with her and in fact, I didn't recall a single experience. But as for the worse, there was certainly more than enough of that to go around. The emotional prison doors were closing tightly shut with each passing moment as I was duty bound to attempt to make the best out of the mess that my life had become. I sincerely hoped, for my daughter's sake and for mine, that there wouldn't be any new disruptions in my life to deal with.

Later that evening, just after I had put my daughter to sleep in her room, a most confusing thing occurred. For no sooner did I confirm that my daughter was asleep, when she responded with an instantaneous physical forcefulness in my own bedroom that was both unexpected and decidedly uncharacteristic. However, once the act was over, it was over with a finality that was more than a little harsh. With all of the emotion of a task accomplished, she called it a night, turned the lights out, and immediately went to sleep. It appeared that she had gotten whatever it was that she wanted. The physical event had lasted only for a few moments as if it were the only thing that was necessary. I was bewildered by the entire ordeal.

The very next morning I awoke to a strange new world. Apart from my daughter, everything in my home was clothed in polite coldness. It could be felt in the very air as I moved through each room. Throughout the remainder of the day she didn't fight or argue about anything and barely spoke a word. One-word answers were the only given response to my many questions as I received nothing more. I awakened to discover that although she was no longer argumentative or violent, she had become an ice queen. I pondered her motivation for the little act the previous evening as well as those for everyone else the day before. As I considered it all, I thought about just what part of the game was the new scenario supposed to be. Was that fitting into her scheme and just what part would I be forced to play? I knew that she wouldn't say it out loud, but even without any words, I instinctively knew that the game was indeed in full force. But just what kind of game would it turn out to be? I really didn't know for certain, but I knew that the answer would arrive soon enough.

Throughout the following days, the ice queen reigned supreme. She simply wouldn't talk and when forced to answer a question only stated that she didn't feel like talking. On more than one occasion, I noticed her staring intensely out of the window and looking at what seemed to be nowhere or nothing.

She was obviously very deep in thought about something. Each and every inquiry from me brought about the same answer. Nothing, nothing at all, was her only response.

However, just barely two weeks after she had returned home, I walked in the front door late one afternoon to find her completely changed. She was smiling, half-singing, and was very busy in the kitchen cooking a huge meal for supper that evening. She was almost ecstatically happy, it was all very, very strange, and I was instantly on my guard. Once again, as they had done so many times before, the alarms began going off loudly within my mind. I could only wonder just what would happen next. Strangely enough, it seemed that all that she could do was smile as she appeared near to bursting as if she were barely able to contain herself.

Once in the house, she quickly sat me in a chair in the living room, instructed me to get comfortable, and patiently wait while she worked in the kitchen. Then as she went back and forth through the house, she repeated the same curious phrase over and over again. Great news, she had great news! It was weird, strange, and ominously reminiscent of my mother's antics. With each repetition I became more and more uncomfortable. It was almost a crazy person's chant. What in the world was she babbling about? First, I endured nearly three weeks of icy silence, tolerance, gloom, and soberness, and then all of a sudden, it was if a switch had been flipped and now she was hysterically happy. What had gone on there in my home during that day? Something was up, and whatever it happened to be, I didn't like it already. Deep within, I was aware that something absolutely wasn't right. Then, as I was deep in thought, she returned to the living room, took me by the hand, and walked me into the kitchen. There she sat me down to a very well-prepared meal and promised me that greatly hyped "good news" would be delivered, but only after I had finished my supper.

Once I had finished the meal, she sat in the chair at the table next to me, grabbed for my hand, missed, looked me in the eye, and then informed me that she had just received great news from the doctor's office earlier that morning. The words barely left her lips as my suspicious instantly grew. My mind raced down rabbit trails at breakneck speed taking me to all sorts of strange places. I just couldn't help it, as it just came to me while filling me with all of the dread in the world. The more she danced around the issue and ignored my requests for answers, the sicker to my stomach that I became. Whatever it was, I knew that it was very bad news despite her smiles and antics. Then all at once and as if on cue, she simply blurted it out, just as she had presented the identical news four years earlier. She was pregnant and was so thrilled about the news that it disgusting me. The scene and the announcement were obviously so contrived, so planned, so well thought out, but also so very poorly acted. But as I steeled myself against it, the very worst of it was yet to come. I could feel it even as it approached. But my mind foolishly tried to convince me that it just wasn't so. Nothing about the announcement fit together very well with the obvious and apparent facts.

Just how could she possibly be pregnant, why at this particular time considering the severity of our circumstances? My unemployment income from the factory was scheduled to expire soon, and I was already on the verge of instituting a number of very unpopular financial decisions. In my mind, the confusion set in hard and fast as I wondered just how could this be while realizing the instant that it raced through my mind that it was indeed a stupid question. The deed had only happened once, the evening that she had returned, and I knew full well that once was enough. But something about the entire matter just didn't feel right. I had absolutely no peace about it as my ingrained suspicions about the entire matter simply wouldn't go away. Actually, I made very little attempt to shove them away and was also well aware that my face openly betrayed my emotions, as it always seemed to do. She understood it as well, and she wasn't pleased; she simply wasn't pleased at all. She also didn't care too much for any of my very demanding questions either.

Just what exactly did the doctor say? When could I speak with him? Why didn't she want me to talk to him? Just what was the actual due date, and where was the paperwork from the doctor's office? As I continued with my interrogation I quickly calculated the numbers in my head. However, the more questions that I asked, the quicker her mood changed into something that I was much more familiar with. It was obvious that she didn't appreciate any of my questions. But then again, I certainly didn't care for, nor did I appreciate any of her obvious dodges to any question that I posed to her. I instantly felt trapped, more so than I had ever felt before. I felt forcefully shoved into a corner by a huge, immoveable, and unseen opponent. At that moment, my life instantly became nothing, as if it were far removed from anything I wanted or intended it to be. Once again, I felt as if I were a man condemned to prison. But there was no apparent way out of my dilemma as I was again firmly stuck within the intolerable situation. I wanted with everything within me at that moment to just get up from that kitchen chair, grab my car keys, and run for my life. However, I couldn't abandon my daughter and my faith wouldn't allow me to leave no matter how much I wanted to. Therefore I was completely and involuntarily forced into an emotional straight jacket and confined there without trial or jury. Having received the news of her pregnancy, my new life sentence was confirmed. She once again had won the battle, if not the war our never-ending marital strife. I determined in my heart that I would tolerate whatever I was forced to but would derive no enjoyment from it. Two overwhelming facts were of a certainty, the numbers simply didn't add up, and the war between us would most certainly continue.

It was now February, and I had clearly experienced the longest seven months of my life. I daily wondered if my life could ever become more difficult than what it happened to be at that moment. Could anything emotionally drain someone to a greater extent than living with a person who fought every day and about everything? The daily battle began from the moment that I woke up until the time that she finally decided to cease complaining, arguing, and screaming well into the night. She simply never shut up.

I arose early with my daughter every morning and saw to it that she was dressed and fed. I then straightened the house and read for a short while as she played nearby with her toys. Heaven forbid if either of us made any noise before eleven o'clock that might have disturbed her precious ten or twelve hours of sleep. On occasion, something of that sort did happen as we then paid dearly and immediately for it. In those instances, she came out of the bedroom screaming and yelling while knocking things over and breaking whatever she got her hands on. I desperately attempted to control the situation as best as I could as my daughter hid beside her toy box in fear and with many tears. I found it to be an intolerable daily issue that stressed both my daughter and I to the point where we were physically hurting. She treated both of us cruelly and she clearly knew it.

As each passing day brought my household closer to the alleged due date, she became more and more difficult to live with. Then, while waiting in the doctor's office one day, I was called inside as he announced that the baby was due to arrive at any moment. Therefore, the alleged due date and subsequent facts became clearly obvious. Some lies told in this life simply cannot be hid from sight or ignored. She was full term, and it was happening quickly.

At the hospital the following day, it was an all-too-familiar sight. Although it was basically the same process as before, it was also quite a bit different. It was the same in that a birth is a birth, and the people in the hospital follow the same structure that they did a thousand times before. It was also the same in that as I looked through the glass as the nurse held that newborn little girl, my emotions softened immediately. I was amazed at just how something so small and fragile could change a person's hard, immense and overwhelming attitude. It became an incredible surrender. But there were other difficulties that I had to work through.

They were the words. These were words that came to me within my mind. However, they were actually very good questions. Did it really matter under what circumstances a child was brought into the world? Wasn't the most important fact of all was that she had indeed been born? Didn't she have the right to live and to exist? Wasn't she one of the innocent ones? Was she guilty in any way of the actions that brought her to my household? Wasn't she still desperately in need of someone to care for and to protect her? Did I actually believe that I was any better than chosen servants of old? Through such examples, I had read of men in biblical history who had tolerated turmoil such as I was experiencing and far more. As depressing as it sounded, I then fully realized that as a father and as a parent, I was purposely called to that particular station and for a specific reason. It was simply as the words had stated—"for such a time as this."

But it was just so blasted difficult! All that I had before me was the all-too-familiar phrase—"just do the math!" I repeated those words to myself over and over again as my memory searched my brain for recollection. As those cryptic words from my teenage youth flashed through my mind, my brain froze in mid-thought before another word could be formed. Then just that quickly, clarity of memory threw the phrase back into my face almost as if it were a fist. I had stated those exact words previously, at another time and in another place. It was a time of great drama and turbulent confrontation that had resulted in an outrageous aftermath. I had foolishly thought far too highly of myself.

I had looked down upon my parents with judging scorn over just such an occasion as the one that I now found myself within.

I had derided them and had been thoroughly disgusted with the both of them over a nearly identical incident just as the one that I was now forced into. I had looked upon my mother as if she had been the filth of the earth for her actions and for all of her manipulations. At that very moment, in stunned realization, I recognized that I had married someone who was, in nearly every conceivable way, just as my mother had been in her personality, traits, and actions. I had also looked in disgust upon my father as if he were the greatest fool on earth. Although it was truthful that he indeed was such, at that very moment, I realized that I was now, in many ways, just like him. It was at that precise and revealing moment that the second item hit me.

As I stood there at the glass wall gazing in awe at the new lives before me, including my new daughter, an overwhelming fact struck at me with an incredible forcefulness. The emotions behind it were so powerful that they nearly took my breath away while grasping the newly formed thought. The magnitude and the enormity of where I stood at that very moment grabbed me by the heart, causing me to be lightheaded. Once again, the heart-searching questions began.

Was it possible that I was standing on the very spot that my own father had stood when he had first seen me? Did his mind battle through the same turmoil as mine was at that moment? It certainly could have been. Did he also pass through the same whirlwind of emotions that was involuntarily tearing my heart and soul to shreds? Did he feel just as trapped and hopeless as I now did? Did he also feel as if he were thrown in and then swept along in a raging river of water while pretending all along the way that is was a normal life? Did he also believe that he had no control over his life and that there was nothing left to do but simply give up and allow it all to happen? Therefore, was he just like me and was I just like him? But a far greater question pushed itself to the forefront of my mind. How could I, from that moment onward, ever live day by day, knowing that it was all a carefully concocted scheme? I had certainly done the math on this particular subject and therefore had found the spouse guilty of a host of nefarious crimes. But most importantly of all, I truly hated playing the part of a spineless and willing fool.

Everyone had been home for two weeks and outwardly all seemed to be going well. It had gone so well that it made me very nervous. In the back of my mind I reminded myself that perhaps the reason for it was that we had visitors at the house nearly every day. Perhaps she was just putting on an extravagant act for the audiences. Whatever the cause or her motivation, I figured that it was all due to end soon.

But other curious items of note also entered into the picture. All of my options at my factory dream job had unfortunately expired. There were no more unemployment payments, no additional benefits, and certainly nothing financially to look forward to. The future outlook for the engine plant was bleak at best. Men who had ten years of seniority had been laid off, which gave me zero chance of ever returning there. I only had the sad little job at the carry out which only paid the minimum wage. But I had also secured an on-call laborer's job, which paid substantially better, but only resulted in a few days of work on a very irregular basis. Therefore, I had to institute very drastic measures to maintain the household budget.

I sold my car and paid off the balance of the loan, which allowed for the purchase a very nice but older car. I also listed the house with a realtor in the hope of gaining a sale price sufficient enough to pay off the mortgage. When I brought the recently purchased car home and informed her of the housing news, she was outraged and furious beyond belief. How dare I take that car away? Why did I sell it and purchase another one without her knowledge and permission? How dare I put our house up for sale? Even though I had previously given her the cold, hard facts pertaining to the budget, that payments couldn't be made and that my financial back was against the wall, it simply made no difference to her at all.

Then her tirade continued unabated. If I were any kind of husband at all, I would make certain that she kept everything that she had worked so hard for. Just what sort of nonsense was this kind of talk? She had never worked a single day throughout the course of our marriage. In fact, she hadn't worked since the day she walked away from her job at the little sandwich shop next to the newspaper. I alone brought into the household the only money that we ever saw and worked every ounce of overtime available at the engine factory.

She made only one attempt to gain employment during those few years, and I shot that one down in flames. At one point her stepmother attempted to have her hired as a stripper at one of the bars where she worked. Although it had held the alluring promise of very good money, I shut down that nonsense even though my budget was in dire straits. Amazingly enough, it brought about an outrageous argument within that portion of her family over my perceived ignorance, stupidity, and falsely placed morals. It was just another addition to the list of items to fight over.

Therefore, as disruptive and nearly unlivable as my household had become, the situation soon worsened. One horrific episode seemed to follow another as life quickly deteriorated far beyond what it had ever been before. While I believed that my life previously had been unbearable, it became apparent that it was nothing compared to what was waiting for me just around the corner. We literally fought over everything imaginable issue or topic, as pettiness certainly never got in her way. We fought about the newspaper, how it was read, in what order and even how it was disposed. We fought about how to run the sweeper over the carpet and that my daughter wasn't allowed to disturb the marks that it had made. We fought about how many lights were permitted to have on in the house and over her insistence that all of the curtains were to be kept pulled tightly shut during the day. It was far beyond stupid or ridiculous as it then became ugly beyond belief.

It was then that the accusations began. They were the type of accusations that accused me of various and sordid marital violations. She was very bold and quite detailed about every one of them. I had no idea of just where she gained her information, as I didn't even possess the imagination for some of them. If I left for work two minutes early, then according to her, I was stopping off somewhere to have sex with someone. It didn't matter that she always called the carry out five minutes after I left the house. It also didn't matter that someone or anyone could have verified my whereabouts throughout every single minute of every day. It didn't matter at all. According to her, everyone was in on the conspiracy to deprive her of everything.

It also didn't matter whether the person was a pastor, a good friend, a police officer, or even a member of her own family. Actually, when a family member did stand up for me, it only made the situation worse as the competition between those sisters never ceased to continue. Any attempts by anyone to help and to intervene with the truth only served to further her dramatic hysteria. Then the stupidity became almost beyond belief. As the unbelief mounted against her from all sides, her accusations then stepped into the realm of paranoia.

Soon she began telling stories that had me slipping out of the house to go carrying on with one of the neighbors. It didn't matter that such a neighbor never said anything more than a casual greeting to me. No matter what the circumstances or occasion, any woman became the enemy as she threw all logic out the proverbial window. It didn't matter if all that I did was to say a simple "excuse me" as I passed someone in the supermarket, that woman became the enemy, was added to the list of suspects, and then became the evening's argument topic. It didn't matter if the women were twenty or eighty; she was still a woman, and to her it always meant that any contact that I had with them ensured that I was up to no good.

However, I was not complacent about the subject as I was instantly angered and became quite furious as well. When no evidence of any kind could be brought to light to confirm such fables, instead of giving into common sense and reason, she simply stepped up the attacks. It was then that she began accusing me of bringing those very same women into our home. She ranted, raved and threw outrageous temper tantrums as she tore the house apart looking for any kind of evidence. When she could find no proof to back any of the fairy tales, in my unlearned mind, she then proved just how unstable that she had become. It was then that she really crossed the line as she posed the most outrageous accusation to that date. For she then decided that not only had I brought these women into our home, but had also engaged in sexual acts with them in our bed *while she was sleeping in it!*

Shortly thereafter, she then methodically went through all of the towels in the house. She literally spent hours picking them apart looking for any type of evidence to prove her bizarre case. She sorted through the dirty towels from the hamper, the clean and fresh towels from the closet which she herself had recently washed and nearly anything else in between. When that fruitless investigation naturally failed to produce anything, the next thing happened. I knew that I really should have seen it coming, but somehow, in my never-ending confusion, I simply didn't see it coming.

I went into my closet for something to wear to church on Sunday morning and was instantly horrified at what I saw. Every dress shirt and every pair of dress slacks had been ripped to shreds by a large knife. It was, in fact, a huge butcher knife as she had left it lying there on the closet floor. That produced a full-body chill right there on the spot, as I instantly perceived that both my daughters and I were now in real and imminent danger. Additionally, the clothes weren't thrown on the floor, but were arranged on the hangers as if I were yet in them. I quickly searched the house for my daughters to ensure that they were safe.

When I discovered her in the kitchen and asked her about my closet findings, she acted as if nothing had happened. It was as if she didn't hear any of my words as she then walked away with a smile on her face while humming a strange little tune. I honestly didn't know what to think or what to do. I began to be afraid to go to sleep at night.

I called and discussed the entire matter with my pastor and described the entire ordeal in detail. Shortly after our conversation, he and his wife stopped by the house for a visit. They both talked with her privately while I attended to my daughters. Their visit lasted for over an hour as I overheard the telltale sounds of crying, of tissues pulling from the box, and that sort of thing. When it was over, I met with the three of them in the living room. Then, at the pastor's urging, I turned the youngest daughter, who I had been holding, over to the ladies and followed him outside.

There outside in the yard, he shook his finger at me while using a number of harsh and very stern words. There he berated me for my carrying on with women in the neighborhood, women in her family, women at the grocery store, women at the hospital, and women in general everywhere. I was completely shocked. I was in total unbelief and bewildered by his actions as well. I gathered my thoughts and then forcefully reminded him that it was I who had called him to my home for assistance, guidance, and direction. Why was she the one that he always believed? Just what sort of hold did she seem to always have on people? Why couldn't anyone, especially a pastor, seem to understand when he had been conned and manipulated? Why after speaking to her didn't he simply believe in me? Was I that foolish? Unfortunately, it was also at that time when I then lost my temper.

I informed him he would be far better off if he checked the facts before attempting to scold me like a child ever again. Then I questioned him as to just when I had ever exhibited anything that even approached that sort of behavior. When had I ever acted in such a disgusting manner? It was then that I openly dared him to find anyone, anywhere in the city that could or would testify that I was committing such atrocities. As he was now in shock, he gave me a thoroughly blank look. I then demanded that he do it. With that, I then gave him one week, asked him to leave my home, and requested that he not come back until he had all of his facts straight. I then waited a moment, calmed down a bit, and from my pocket handed him a long list of names. They were people that he needed to talk to if he had any intentions of discovering the truth. I informed him that each person listed would give confirmation as to the actual facts. Then we simply stood there face-to-face as I stared him down with all of the anger that was within me. With that we shook hands as he and his wife then left. However, it didn't even take a week, as justice naturally prevailed, and he returned to the house to fully apologize. However, it didn't matter one bit as to who was right or wrong as she certainly still had her own agenda.

As I walked back into the house on the day of the confrontation, I was met with an awful and otherworldly strangeness that filled the house. It was downright creepy, almost chilling, causing my hair to nearly stand on end. I immediately checked on both of the girls, found them in their bedroom with the door closed, just as the oldest one had been told to do while I was outside. I instructed her to remain there, play with her toys, and that I would return in a minute. After I had closed their door, I then called out for her. But there was no answer.

As I looked about the house, I couldn't find her anywhere and wondered if perhaps she wasn't even in the house. She obviously wasn't out in the front yard as I had walked into the house from there. I then wondered if she might have gone into the backyard. But once again, it was very strange as the alarms were sounding loudly within my head. Something was certainly wrong, but I couldn't seem to pinpoint the danger.

I walked through the living room, and then just before I entered the doorway to the kitchen, those same words marched through my mind once more. Be ready, be careful. But as I stopped for only the briefest moment, they flashed through my head again, but I shrugged them off and then walked through the doorway anyway. I really should have known.

Pain! Pain! Pain! It was white-hot, vision-blurring, mind-collapsing pain. She had been hiding by the kitchen cabinet just inside of the doorway and had angrily driven a small paring knife deep into my forearm. As I gripped that arm in pain, she stood there holding the knife while smiling the most evil smile that I had ever seen in my life. Then with a sneer on her face, she asked if I wanted more. I said nothing intelligible as I fought to regain control over the pain in my arm as the blood from my arm dripped through my fingers and onto the floor.

Then she began half-shouting, taunting me and then informing me that I was nothing but a foolish little boy. I instantly became enraged and lost all logical control right at that moment. I felt my eyes fill with anger as I grabbed for her and the knife. As I did so, her eyes snapped opened in understanding as she suddenly dropped the knife, turned, and ran from the kitchen and into the garage. I followed close behind as she jumped into the car and locked the doors. She then fired the engine and backed out of the building at full throttle with the engine roaring. I didn't know what she would have done if the garage door hadn't been up. In reverse she flung the car sideways into the street as I sprinted after her.

As I ran out into the street, I observed that she had stopped the car at an angle with the back bumper shoved into the neighbor's bushes at the street. The front end of the car pointed toward the other neighbor's yard across the street. I foolishly believed that she had the vehicle stuck in the yard. As I walked past the right front corner of the car, the engine roared once again as she floored the accelerator. The front bumper struck me in the leg, knocked me onto the hood as I careened through the air. I was then tossed further airborne while clearing the left fender and landed on my side sliding on the pavement and bouncing into the gravel. I looked up just in time to watch her blow through the stop sign at the end of the street. I heard the tires scream in protest as she made a hard right hand turn. As I lay there in the gravel at the side of the street, I heard the car fade off into the distance.

Struggling to my feet, with my right hand gripped my left arm, that I limped back into the house. Once inside, I told my oldest daughter through the still closed bedroom door to just stay there for a minute while I went into the bathroom. She didn't need to see how I looked as it wasn't a very pretty sight. There was blood everywhere. There were small markings of it across the kitchen cabinets, on the wall and even a few spots had found their way onto the ceiling. It had run down my arm and was now inside of my shirt. As I stood over the kitchen sink, I wrapped my arm with torn towels and gently cleaned my stinging face. Then I turned my attention to the other arm to deal with the scrapes that I received and checked on the massive bruises on my leg from the car bumper. I was a mess and should have gone to the hospital. However, my insurance had lapsed, and the budget simply had no allowance for it, so I made do with what I had in the house.

I changed into fresh clothes, put on a long-sleeve shirt to cover everything, and then checked on my daughters. Once they were settled in for the night, I called my pastor once again. He and his wife then stopped at my home for the second time that day. They were horrified by the events of the day, a bit ashamed of themselves as well, and offered any assistance possible. On that night they heard the entire story from beginning to end, every bit of it and every last detail.

She finally returned home two days later. As she walked in the front door, she carried on with showers of tears, emotions, and other assorted bits of drama. She hadn't been in the house any more than two minutes when she asked me to call the pastor. Without any hesitation, he and his wife stopped by shortly afterward that evening. The two of them talked to her for a considerable length of time. As the pastor related to me later, they covered nearly every possible subject. Over coffee, the two of them stayed at the house for nearly four hours. That just happened to be Thursday evening.

The following two days seemed to go well enough. There was no fighting, yelling, or screaming of any kind. She even played with my oldest daughter at her toy box, which was most unusual. I went to work without any kind of drama, questions, or accusations. We actually ate meals together at the dinner table just as normal families do. For just the briefest of moments I actually believed that perhaps a corner may have been turned. However, in actuality that corner had indeed been turned, as I would soon discover that it was exactly the opposite of anything I could have expected. After all that I previously experienced with her, her schemes and devices, I really should have known better.

That particular Sunday morning she even went to church. Upon returning home, we had lunch, and I took care of a few normal household chores. At suppertime, however, my oldest daughter and I spent a few moments alone at the dinner table. As we sat there talking, she came along, interrupted, and informed me that the youngest had a bit of a temperature, which required her attention for the remainder of the evening. After making that decision, I then went to Sunday-night church alone.

It was a typical Sunday evening service, and afterward I went directly home. I pulled onto my little street just after eight o'clock that evening. No sooner had I done so than the words appeared within my mind once again, "for such a time as this." Then the statement repeated six more times before fading away into silence. Once more I gave in to confusion and befuddlement rather than asking for leadership and guidance. Something was about to happen, but I truly had no clue as to what to expect.

As I turned left into the driveway, I could tell that something was wrong, very wrong. The house itself was dark, completely dark as not a single light shone in any of the windows. I thought to myself that certainly she hadn't put the girls down for bed that early in the evening. As I got out of the car and walked onto the concrete stoop, a very bad feeling instantly gripped my heart as if it were held in a vise. I hadn't any idea just exactly what it was. I only knew that it wasn't good.

As I reached for the doorknob, it opened with just the slightest touch, as it wasn't even latched, much less locked. With a mind now full of questions, I put the keys back into my pocket and slowly walked onto the sun porch. The door just beyond to the living room was also wide open and the room was dark within. I called out everyone's name, but received no response. As I walked into the darkened living room, I instinctively reached for the light switch. I flipped it a half a dozen times in aggravation, which produced nothing, no results at all. As I stood there for a moment and allowed my eyes to become acclimated to the lack of light, the awful truth of my situation became clear. It was completely amazing and unbelievable all at the same time.

For not only was my home empty, but it was also completely empty. There was absolutely nothing left in the house but cold and barren walls. Every last piece of furniture was gone. All of the appliances had been taken as well. Every last picture, as well as every item of decoration that had been on the walls, were also gone. As I moved from room to room, it simply became one astonishing and depressing discovery after another.

The kitchen cupboards had been completely cleaned out, as she hadn't left behind a single plate, dish, or pan. Further investigation revealed that there wasn't even a scrap of food left behind. There wasn't a container, a bread wrapper, or even a lone potato chip left in a bag. There wasn't anything left to eat in the house. It had all been taken.

Everything in the bathroom was also taken. There was no shampoo, deodorant, toothpaste, a toothbrush as not even a sliver of soap remained. The room had been swept clean, as there was nothing left but the cobwebs under the sink. As I walked into the bedroom, the situation there was nearly the same. All of the furniture had been taken from that room as well. As I checked the bedroom closet I discovered that every item of clothing was gone and even the hangers as well. In a corner I found a small pile of clothes lying in a heap. Closer inspection revealed that they were mine, although the majority of them had been ripped to shreds. But then there was the other most obvious matter. I was instantly filled with raging anger, but despite that, I laughed out loud all at the same time.

She had taken everything of value that I had accumulated over the course of our five years of marriage. She had taken living room furniture, bedroom collections, the kitchen table and chairs, dishes, pots, and pans. She had made off with silverware, dish and bathroom towels, and every other imaginable item in the house. But it simply wasn't hers to take. She had never held down a job of any sort and therefore had never contributed one dime to the household budget. I had worked nearly every day, I had brought home the paychecks, and therefore, I believed, that all of the missing property was mine. But it wasn't that she had taken everything; it was that she had taken it all with a vindictiveness that even I had never before known.

Every lightbulb in every fixture in the house was gone. She had taken every last one of them. She had taken them all. It was no small wonder that the house was so dark. But even more amazing was the fact that she managed to empty an entire house of all of its contents within the space of less than two hours. She obviously didn't accomplish that feat alone. She had solicited and had obtained a great deal of help. That much was certain.

But the reality of the matter was the fact that my house was thoroughly cleaned out. Everything that I had worked so hard for and for so many years had now disappeared. It quickly became more than obvious as to why she was gone for those two days. Although there were probably a number of reasons, but clearly during that time she arranged for her departure, orchestrated everything possible and merely waited for just the right moment to make that move.

But even so, there was a strange and oddly comforting peace to be found in the now-empty house. It was a quiet stillness that pervaded the place as I sat there alone, prayed, and waited. It was then that the words came to my inner understanding as only God himself can send. As I sat there in my outward emptiness, I contemplated much as I heard that still voice within my heart. It was only on such occasions, as I quieted my heart and surrendered my situation, that I heard his voice within and then felt His peace.

For the most part there was only one word. *Hope*. It resonated so deeply inside of me that I instinctively knew just exactly what that word meant. I knew it so well and so fully that it was as if an entire speech or sermon were contained within that single word. *Hope*. However, as I heard those unspoken words, it wasn't false hope for a contrived and doomed from the very start marriage. It wasn't hope for any sort of a man and woman adult relationship. However, it was a clearly understood hope for at least three people. It was hope for my two daughters and it was hope for me. It was only hope that could give me strength deep within. Strangely and for no apparent reason, as I sat there in my now empty home, hope beyond all hope was showing itself to me. As I sat there and surrendered myself to a great and future unknown, an actual glimmer of hope rose within my heart for whatever that unseen future may be. In that precise moment and in that darkened and empty shell of a house, one singular thing was certain. I had finally found hope.

The Next Step

The legal paperwork arrived in a relatively short period of time. According to the official notification, within a few short days I was to appear in divorce court. Once she had obviously gotten any and everything she possibly could from me, she then took the next step and didn't waste any time about it. She had taken everything that she possibly could. Characteristically, she waited until all the incoming funds had ceased, my savings had evaporated, and all visible hope for a future had vanished. However, it was the entire pretense of the matter that was laughable at best. When the paperwork arrived via certified mail, I read the documents over and over again in appalling disbelief and natural anger.

The documents listed two primary causes for the divorce proceedings, which naturally placed me in the title role as defendant. The entire matter was both inconceivable and outrageous. The court documents stated that I was charged with neglect of duty and extreme mental cruelty. As I read further into the documents, the primary listed cause of neglect of duty was specifically due to the loss of my job at the engine factory and that I was no longer providing her with the standard of living to which she was accustomed. However, two thousand people and more had been involuntarily and permanently laid off within months of my own departure date. It wasn't as if any of us had a choice. The other listed charge was for extreme mental cruelty.

I hadn't the slightest idea as to what that had meant. I believed I did everything there was possible to do as I provided for my family. Although I wasn't sorry she was gone or I missed her in any conceivable way, I was fiercely opposed the slander on my name as it was the only thing that I had left. If she wanted to be set free, then so be it, but everyone would soon hear the truth from me.

Although it was apparent that no one had any difficulty finding me, I had no practical idea whatsoever as to just where she had gone my children. However, that in and of itself was not without its merit. Many important pieces of information were revealed as I began the search for my daughters. She and her family had constructed quite a scheme in order to ensure my failure. I then embarked on a never-ending series of dead ends in my search for their whereabouts. It became especially painful as messages left for me at the house then led me to believe that I would see my daughters. When the scheduled time came and I arrived to pick them up for visits, the results were always the same. No one ever answered the door. It was the same sorry and pathetic little game every week. But even so, I willingly took the bait and always remained hopeful for a break in the stupidity.

As a group and with few exceptions, they also created quite a nasty smear campaign as well. They made certain that everyone they met and everyone I ever knew understood just exactly what sort of a horrible and awful person that I was. Together they purposefully put forth every effort possible to inform every one of just what sort of human trash that I not only had become, but always had been.

The primary accusations that made their way back to me through the proverbial grapevine were of the all too familiar variety. They were the very accusations that had already related to me by my pastor on that fateful evening in late June. Therefore, it really wasn't of any big surprise as they certainly weren't original. The fascinating item was that every accusation laid against me happened to be the very charges that I held against her with clearly based facts throughout our marriage.

But I honestly had never expected any better from any of member of her family. After all, I personally witnessed the very same thing as they sought to destroy every former boyfriend and husband of every sister over the course of five years. They were a truly ruthless and diabolical group to observe. Therefore, why would I ever expect any better treatment once it became my turn on their proverbial dartboard? However, they weren't the sole suppliers of my distress and torment.

It was the church that I attended. It was the place that I believed to be my safe harbor and refuge. But more specifically and accurately, it was the people in the church who caused my dismay. Once the terrible news hit the congregation that a divorce within my household was imminent, the attitude of the majority of the people changed overnight. People ceased to ask about my day, my life, and how I was getting along. After the announcement, there were no more invitations to a meal and no further meaningful discussions over a cup of coffee. When my life's drama became apparent, all pleasantries instantly ceased.

It even rose to the place where I received no further requests of help when someone needed a hand moving, painting a house or anything else of the sort. Mothers pulled their children close as I walked near, while their husbands placed themselves between us. I did nothing more dangerous than convey a brief greeting of good morning and hello prior to the worship service. I involuntarily became a pariah, a leper, and an unwanted human being within the church body. I was rejected, abandoned, unneeded, and cruelly despised. The saddest part of it all was that it felt far too familiar.

I had contracted a most dreaded, incurable, and awful disease, at least in the eyes of most church people, that of divorce. It instantly, completely and for all time, set me apart from the remainder of the church family. It was as if the disease could be contracted by touch or that someone could be infected, just by being in my company. Suddenly there within the church body, there was no compassion, no understanding, as very few of them even made the attempt. There evidently wasn't even a dose of pity to be given as there was now only judgment. Whatever the cause, the reason or even the excuse, as far as they were concerned, it was final. However, more than anything, I was more perplexed and hurt than angry.

But what happened to his grace? What happened to the basis for our Christianity and specifically that core issue of forgiveness? What became of the bearing of one another's burdens? But also and more importantly, what about the victims of the acts of sin and sinful decisions? Didn't it matter that there were three of us who this had happened to? Why didn't anyone bother to think about the three of us? My daughters deserved at least that much consideration.

But it wasn't as if I were the one who had fallen so badly, so openly and so convincingly. It wasn't as if I were the one who committed some horrible atrocity. It wasn't as if I had even committed a small misdemeanor. Although I certainly wasn't perfect, I endeavored to live life to the best of my abilities. I daily attempted to be the sort of person I should be since the day of my conversion. I was fully aware that everything between God and I was just as it should have been. Therefore, why did I ever care what people said or thought? But in my mind, there was one very special thing that was beyond reproach, my integrity was perfectly intact.

But I knew that I possessed intense anger within me and also had a ferocious temper to daily deal with. However, I never deserted my family, never abandoned anyone and never ever would. To be certain, I had been distant to her a majority of the marriage. But then again, the majority our time was spent in arguments, fighting, or dodging flying objects. There were also many occasions when she just simply wasn't there.

Many were the occasions as I arrived home from work only to discover the girls had been shut up in their bedroom alone. They were left alone countless times and had gone hungry on more occasions than I ever actually knew. It broke my heart into countless pieces as I discovered well after the fact that they had been so mistreated. I myself had cared for them every single day and knew that, given the opportunity, I would do so until they were raised to be adults. I knew with everything within me that it was something I was called to do. It didn't matter what kind of parent that she obviously hadn't been. The only item of any importance was just what kind of parent that I determined to be. I vowed to be the very best parent that I possibly could be. I owed that much to my two little girls and certainly at least that much to *him*.

It was nearly the last day of September as the weather suddenly turned quite a bit cooler. That proved to be a debilitating issue as the gas for heating the house had been turned off due to a lack of funds just the previous week and the electricity was shut off just that morning. The house which I was so proud of owning would be sold in less than a month. Therefore I knew that I had a roof over my head until then, despite the lack of lights and heating. However, I had no idea of just what would happen once that date arrived. Perhaps the situation would prove so desperate that I would be forced to live in my car. My life had deteriorated to that extent.

At that time, I worked just one week out of the month. That provided me with only enough money for the barest amount of gasoline to get to the job. The remainder of the money I spent buying the necessary items to live on. It was so incredibly difficult to take one week's pay and attempt to stretch it out for thirty days. I always bought the very cheapest items that could be found and then used as little of them as possible. However, even with strictest of self-rationing, there were many occasions as I was forced to skip meals for the day. Once I even made it through two days without a meal until the next paycheck arrived. Realistically, all of those stringent policies were unnecessarily self-imposed.

I fully understood that I could easily drive to the other side of the city to my mother's house. There a meal could be mine every single day, a hot shower, and a warm place to stay during the cold nights. I knew she would gladly provide all of those things for me. But there were two major issues at the forefront that comprised a very heated argument. In the end, however, it simply became just another personal decision while easily recognizing her true motivation.

The first item pertained to the reality that she and the remainder of the family anxiously awaited the opportunity to observe my life as it crashed and burned. They were the epitome of human vultures in every conceivable way. They had all been there, on one occasion or another, as they knocked on my front door. They arrived soon after I had gotten the job at the engine factory as each one came looking for a quick loan that none of them had any intention of repaying. Each one became more than a little upset as they quickly and personally discovered my refusal to share my new blessing with them. They all gave the same speech and received mine in return as I declared that I was not a bank and never would be, especially for any of them. Therefore, in the year since I had been laid off from the factory, they had all waited for the opportunity to "help me out."

But one item was of a certainty as I was not about to grovel before them. It was far too high a price to pay. I would be forced to listen to their questions, their stupid comments, and especially their insolent remarks. I chose the opportunity of starving rather than stooping to those repulsive depths. But there were other pressing and historical issues which drove my decision as well. Humans are creatures of habit and unfortunately those habits rarely ever change.

It was the reality that her method of housekeeping had only worsened after my moving from her house. I had stopped by there on only one occasion, some months before as she made noises about being deathly sick, leaving this world and other hypochondria sort of melodrama. I saw it all before and had unfortunately experienced it on far too many occasions. No one living was ever sicker than she was and no one could ever be worse off. But even I couldn't tolerate the constant badgering by means of the telephone, so therefore I went to see her.

Her house was every bit as disgusting as I had remembered it and was actually even worse. As I pulled into the driveway, I clearly observed that everything was just as I figured it would be. Broken down cars were situated on concrete blocks, knee-high weeds made up most of the yard as loose trash just blew around everywhere. I wondered just what her neighbors thought of living next door to such nonsense. As I got out of my car and closed the door, I could smell the stench of the place while still outdoors. It was horrible.

Walking inside the house, it was as if I came face-to-face with a disgusting wall. The open sewer stench offended my nostrils so badly that it nearly caused me to physically gag. The situation within that house was so deteriorated that the roaches were everywhere as they boldly roamed the walls of the house. They were on the kitchen counter tops and on every other surface unbothered by people and in broad daylight. Turning to the left, I saw family members sitting on broken down and cast off furniture, while smoking and watching the blaring television. Every disgusting detail within that house nearly forced me to vomit.

I stayed for less than ten minutes until I simply couldn't stand it any longer. Even though it was just a momentary visit, it seemed to last for hours. Afterward, I drove all the way home with every window in the car open. Once at home, I stripped off every piece of clothing while walking in the door and threw them into the washer. Therefore, despite the hungry pains, I actually believe that it would be healthier digging through a dumpster behind the nearby supermarket than going to her house. But I did possess some common sense and dignity despite the groaning in my belly. Some would consider my decision as complete foolishness but, I simply felt as if I had no choice. Therefore I decided that doing without and maintaining my distance was far wiser and more prudent than a full belly and family companionship.

As I sat there alone in my cold and vacant house, I only marveled at the wonderful and almost indescribable peace that came over me. I had no cause whatsoever to be at such peace as there were no visible reasons for it. The woman that I had been unhappily married to had successfully divorced me and secretly, I was so incredibly thankful for it. But I knew full well that I couldn't share those feelings with my Christian brothers. I was fully convinced that they couldn't understand the decision that I had made. However, I couldn't fault them as none of them had ever walked in my shoes. Therefore none of them could comprehend the upbringing that I had endured and very few of them had experimented with those illegal things that I had converted into habits. It wasn't that I held to any pride over my past sinful accomplishments, it was that they simply couldn't feel my pain.

I didn't know if they truly understood the loneliness that had worked its debilitating poison throughout my miserable life. Although my children had been taken, I had to trust him to keep them safe and protected. I had to hold fast to this despite the despicable nonsense inflicted upon me by the ex and her anger laden family. However, despite the obvious and overwhelming obstacles, I believed I would see them soon as it became my last hope. But I also had to recognize the overwhelming fact that I had nothing to give to my children.

I was, at that particular moment, flat broke without sufficient income to rent an apartment of any sort. I didn't even enough money in my wallet to purchase groceries for myself on a regular basis. I had nothing and not much more than the clothes upon my back as I was now destitute and clinically homeless. I had nothing to look forward to and nothing that showed even a glimmer of promise. But despite all that mortal eyes can see, I still had something. It was the strangest and oddest reason that I ever gave to myself. Despite whatever my own eyes surveyed, I felt as if I had everything that I possibly needed even though there was no sensible reason for it. I had no logic or definable facts to back up my decision and my emotions. But I had something that was very nearly indescribable. I had hope.

In those four years, I learned, each day as I lived it, that the Christian walk was longer, deeper, and harder than anything that I could ever possibly imagine. *He* had taken me to places in my life and revealed truth to me that I absolutely would never have discovered on my own. I learned in real and practical ways that nothing in life was usually as it seemed. I wisely learned that I could not rely upon my flawed human feelings as they would and did get me into trouble every time. I learned to seek after him through his Word and when those paths crossed mine, I would gain answers to my many questions. I learned to either have patience or the lessons of patience would be inflicted upon me. I learned that he always has my very best interests at heart, that I can trust him fully and that he has my life completely planned. If only I am faithful to his call. However, as I soon was to discover, none of it would be easy as I would find out just how ill prepared I actually was.

But despite it all, one fact remained. Through Christianity I had at last found a family. However, as in every family, there are found both the genuine as well as the phony, which was revealed in fascinating fashion as the divorce was finalized. There were people in my life whose motives were good, just as well as those who were entirely self-centered in their beliefs and actions. I was either treated badly or was treated as a son or a brother. Close friends with whom I had shared everything turned and walked away. People who I barely knew previous to the announcement attempted to give me a place to stay. However, as I didn't want to leave my house, they then provided oil lamps and candles to read by, a winter coat for the cold and even a sleeping bag in order to stay warm at night. But it was difficult for my foolish human pride to accept such gifts. Even harder still, given my budgetary constraints, was to accept an offer of lunch after church. That was a personal difficulty nearly beyond words. It was however, not as difficult as trying to eat slowly while not letting anyone realize it was the first meal eaten since late on Friday. But the hardest part of all was realizing that someone cared enough to do those things. It was equally intriguing that the very most they ever expected in return was a simple thank you. This was true compassion, honest, understanding, and for the very first time in my life, perhaps an inkling of what love actually is. But even so, I continued to grow more apprehensive about my future. As each unsuccessful day passed into another, the fears became harder to deny as worry and imminent defeat battled with my faith.

There were a mere eight days remaining before I had to be out of my house as the new owners were ready to move in. I was unable to formulate any plans and had no real ideas of where I was to live afterward. However, I reminded myself that a substantial blessing had been received in that the house sold for just enough to pay off the mortgage. After the fees and other associated items were taken care of, there wasn't any profit remaining. However, it was just as well as I was required to split any profit on the sale of the home with the ex.

From my point of view, she had already taken enough and would probably spend any influx of money on something detrimental. I knew without fully knowing that she wouldn't spend it on my daughters. Rumors passed to me by specific individuals throughout the city indicated that she had returned to her habitual drug and alcohol use. Therefore, the house sale was, as far as I was concerned, not a defeat, but was in fact a victory. I endeavored to treat the matter as a lesson to be learned and resolved to daily review my life, even hour by hour, or occasionally even minute by minute. But even so, I found it extremely difficult to surrender to not only an unseen guiding hand, but an unseen and dismal looking future.

It was a warm early-October evening as I sat in the back yard on a large log while leaning against an old mulberry tree. Watching the sunset fade into darkened sky, I had nothing to do that evening but sit, think and consider everything in my life. However, the more I gave into such thoughts, the more fiercely the emotions within me churned. The more they did so, the more His incredible words spoke within me, knowing full well they were not heard with my natural ears. I knew the source and understood the necessary words of comfort to my soul. Sitting there alone in the back yard, while pondering that comfort as well as my impatience and immaturity, I came, to a profound decision. I simply believed that it was a time where *he* and I just had it out, so to speak as I let Him know precisely how I felt and what I wanted from *him*. I knew it was foolishness spoken through anger, just as a child would address his father with profound immaturity. It wasn't as if *he* wasn't already aware of every last detail. Therefore, not only was I acting as a child, I was *his* child.

Three Prayers

Sitting there in the backyard on my final day of home ownership, an incredible change took place that I did not anticipate. I fully intended to have an argument with God about my decrepit situation. I was going to tell *him* just how upset I was about everything and just how unfair I believed *his* decisions to be. I read the verses, committed a few of them to memory, counseled with wise people, and somehow believed that I had certain rights. I believed that I had kept my part of the spiritual bargain and that *he* had an obligation to keep *his*. I fully believed that I had lived the sort of life that *he* expected of me, but had not received the blessings that I believed I deserved.

I believed that I deserved answers to a number of questions. Why did *he* take my children from me? Why had *he* saddled me with an adulterous and violent spouse? Why didn't *he* simply take her out of this life which would have certainly left me better off? Why did *he* give me a great job with a great company and then allow it to be taken away? Why did *he* permit me to become a homeowner only to have the property sold and taken from me? If *he* was in such complete and total control as I believed *he* was, then why was my life such a total wreck?

But I no sooner began my little tirade as I heard that quiet and still voice stating a simple and solitary word within my mind. "Understood," was all the voice said. With each complaint I uttered, as I took a breath, once again I heard that one quietly spoken word. However, each time I heard it I foolishly went on to the next complaint, but continued to weaken as I spoke. When at last I came to the end of my mental list and could go no further, a softly spoken sentence came to my mind. "Now you must understand." As those words echoed inside of my head, I found I could do nothing but sit there on the log in amazed silence and awe. As my mind attempted to grips with understanding, another solitary word came and my silence followed closely behind it. Job.

The word was not spoken as it appeared in print, as the vowel was a long one, not a short one. However, I knew full well what the name meant. I had read and reread the entire story of that Old Testament man, the book that bore his name and felt a tremendous closeness to him and his situation. But it had only been a story, albeit a very good one, but certainly nothing more, until that very moment in my life.

Although I was unaware, it had been decided years far in the past that I was to endure that very sort of test. I had no idea why I was chosen for it as I knew for certain that I was not of the same caliber as that esteemed man of old had been. I had no lineage, no standing and certainly possessed no favor of any sort in the city where I lived. I asked the question over and over again why I was chosen to travel such a path. Although I knew his story, quite frankly I wanted no part of it or any further sorrow as I had already tolerated enough.

Naturally, I wanted relief from my pain and misery while feeling that I somehow deserved it. At twenty-four years of age, I had lived a multitude of miserable, degrading and detrimental lifestyles. I had found my brother's dead body and endured years of turmoil over those visages. I had been entrapped within my parent's lies and subterfuge as they forced me, through treachery, into servitude, and had stolen thousands in dollars in cash and property from me. I had, by my own decisions, become ensnared in immoral physical relationships and illegal contraband that only led to drug and alcohol addiction as well as the wager that resulted in a thorough fraud of a marriage. Therefore, my life was an out of control disaster and I certainly didn't want it to become any worse. I was nearly out of hope.

"For such a time as this," the voice stated. Once again, the words softly came to my mind as I failed to fully understand them. Then as I quietly grasped them for the very first time, I literally felt the Father's arms about me, embracing me in infinite tenderness and care. It was something remotely familiar, but only as a very young child from my grandparents. But this was far grander, fully complete, and it reached through my body and into the innermost depths of my very heart and soul. *He* knew me, *he* understood me, *he* had plans for me, and *he* felt every ounce of my pain. But most important of all, *he* loved me in ways and to such an extent that I could never fully comprehend.

It was only then that I began to access the beginnings of understanding. *He* allowed everything to be taken from me for a number of specific reasons. *He* not only had my best interests at heart, but also everyone whose life that I touched. But it was only in order that *his* name would be found with glory before all men. As people looked at my life, they would readily discover that only *he* was capable of bringing me to the place where I now stood. Once again, I heard the phrase "for such a time as this."

Just as with Job, I lived a life that I dreamt of only to have everything forcefully taken from me. I realized then that it had to be done in such a manner, as I certainly did not possess the maturity, the wisdom or the wherewithal to set it aside. As with Job, I also sought relief, compassion and understanding from friends and others close to me. I also experienced the same drama as similar friends believed they knew the reasons for my turmoil. Just as with Job, my friends had perceived that I had some hidden sin that God was choosing to address. My friends then offered their particular brand of advice along with pointed declarations and categories.

As also with Job, not only had I lost my children, but had deeply ensconced enemies within my own household and extended family as well. Just as he was, I too was informed that my beliefs were foolishness and would be better off if only I renounced them. As with Job's human relationships, I also found myself quickly abandoned as my outward life had deteriorated into assumed self-destruction.

But I found the truth as it was presented. As I sincerely considered not only his story, but the very real fact that *God himself* had chosen to include it in the most important book the world had ever known, I simply surrendered and believed. I considered the fact that Job had been covered with physical afflictions from without and the dust that he had heaped upon himself spoke specifically to me as well. I too, had been afflicted from without and had heaped trouble upon myself in remorse and anger. But, as with Job, I decided that I would not allow those physical attributes to define me. I decided to choose the one and only viable option left to me as I surrendered to whatever *he* had in store for me and surrendered to someone that I could not see.

I submitted to the fact that as a true *father*, *he* had my best interests within *his* eternal heart. I knew, without knowing the intimate details that *he* had already prepared my path for the remainder of my life. I also understood, that as I was faithful, *he* would then grant the desires of my heart. At that point in my life, those desires were simple and few. As a number, they were actually only three.

Number one. I asked that *he* would do whatever was necessary in order to protect my little children from harm. I then told *him* what *he* already knew, but as a loving and understanding *Father*, *he* allowed me to ramble anyway. I reminded *him* that they were in the hands of an untrustworthy and very unstable person. It was my belief that there was just no conceivable way for anyone to know just what she was capable of. I pleaded with *him* to keep them safe, to hedge them about with the host of heaven and to allow no harm of any kind to come to them. I asked *him* to do whatever was necessary to accomplish such things. Then I asked that once their safety had been secured, that *he* would make a way so that I could see them. Then I further asked if *he* would grant me the honor of raising them. I knew that fathers usually weren't permitted to do that and that society generally didn't approve of such decisions. But I believed it to be not only my right, but that it also was certainly my responsibility.

Number two. I needed a job, and I needed it desperately. At that point in time, I couldn't even support myself. How could I possibly take care of two little girls if I didn't have the means of taking care of myself? I knew it would be great if I could be recalled to my factory job. But, in actuality even that really didn't matter, as I had decided that I would take a job doing whatever or wherever. At that point I didn't care if it was in a factory or at a farm-shoveling stuff; it really didn't matter to me. I simply knew that it was my daily bread and that *he* instructed me to ask for it.

Number three. This was the most embarrassing request of them all. It was about the overwhelming task of being a single adult in society. I knew full well there were verses in the Bible that covered just this sort of thing. But the matter was of great concern to me. Therefore, I discussed the situation with no one other than *him* as only *he* knew just how much it actually concerned me.

Therefore, if it was *his* perfect will for me to remain single for the remainder of my life and raise my girls alone, then I would accept that (but I really didn't want to). However, that was to be as I now needed *him* far more than ever before. Given my sordid history and knowing myself all too well (as only *he* knew just how disobedient I could be), then *he* absolutely had to choose her. Then I rattled off my seemingly impossible wish list for just such a perfect person.

She had to be kind, sweet, and someone who believed in *him*. She needed to be from a good family, one with real parents. She needed to be intelligent, self-motivated, and someone who thoroughly enjoyed being her own person and was comfortable with who she was. I also asked if she could be funny and possess a great sense of humor. I asked if she could possibly be someone who had a laugh that would brighten the very worst of my days. I then added, could she be endearing, charming, and would *he* help me to be all of those things and more for her? Would *he* help me to overcome all of the scars which had so hindered my life to that point?

I promised *him* that I would treat her as the very gift from *him* I knew that she would be. But then there was that one last item. I knew it wasn't remotely biblical and that some would think it silly or petty. I really didn't know for certain why I asked for it, as I had never seen it outside of a dream. But I asked if she could have green eyes? Within my mind and through those dreams, I had been captivated by just one certain pair of sparkling green eyes. I knew without specifically knowing them that they were eyes that sang and danced. I knew they would look like jewels, as *he* and I both know that eyes always say the very things that mouths either cannot or will not say. Then I added, if all such things were not too much to ask of him.

All I asked for that moment was that *he* answered those three simple prayers. To be certain, there would be many other dreams and requests, but at that particular moment, just those three would do. However, there were just three more things to remember. The first was that although I had suffered greatly, I was not a victim. The second was that despite all that I had been through, I was completely responsible for all of my decisions. The third was that despite all of my fears, doubts, and unbelief, the God of all creation, the God of all eternity was in complete and total control. I had to believe that.

But over and above all of that, it was the fact that these three lessons so deeply burned within me. As I stood to my feet there in my backyard, with my future unknown and my faith now secure, I walked around the house to face whatever was to come my way.

CPSIA information can be obtained
at www.ICGtesting.com
Printed in the USA
LVOW04s2057120816
500060LV00016B/290/P